My Way

My Way

PAUL ANKA

WITH DAVID DALTON

ST. MARTIN'S GRIFFIN

NEW YORK

MY WAY. Copyright © 2013 by Paul Anka with David Dalton. All rights reserved. Printed in the United States of America. For information, address St. Martin's Press, 175 Fifth Avenue, New York, N.Y. 10010.

www.stmartins.com

Designed by Kathryn Parise

The Library of Congress has cataloged the hardcover edition as follows:

Anka, Paul.
    My way : an autobiography / by Paul Anka with David Dalton. —
First US edition.
        pp. cm.
    Includes index.
    ISBN 978-0-312-38104-2 (hardcover)
    ISBN 978-1-250-03520-2 (e-book)
    1. Anka, Paul.   2. Singers—United States—Biography.   3. Canadian
Americans—Biography.   I. Dalton, David, 1945–   II. Title.
    ML420.A7307A3 2013
    782.42164092–dc23
    [B]

2013000635

ISBN 978-1-250-04449-5 (trade paperback)

St. Martin's Griffin books may be purchased for educational, business, or promotional use. For information on bulk purchases, please contact Macmillan Corporate and Premium Sales Department at 1-800-221-7945, extension 5442, or write specialmarkets@macmillan.com.

First St. Martin's Griffin Edition: April 2014

10   9   8   7   6   5   4   3   2   1

*First and foremost, to my mother and father,
for the foundation that they gave me on
which I have built this life and profession.*

*And to Anne, Alexandra, Amanda, Alicia, Anthea, Amelia,
Lisa, and Ethan*

Contents

Acknowledgments

I have many people to thank for their encouragement and guidance in the writing of this book:

My entire family, daughters, their wonderful mother Anne, my son Ethan, my beautiful and wonderful girlfriend, Lisa, and my sister Mariam.

Stuart Silfen, my friend and attorney for many years, for introducing me to Steve Cohen, our illustrious leader at St. Martin's, who got this ball rolling. And to Elizabeth Beier, whose energy, professionalism, smarts, and enthusiasm spurred me on and kept me focused. Also, the amazing Michelle Richter, John Karle, Laura Clark, Sally Richardson, Matthew Shear, Steve Snider, Lauren Harms, Kathryn Parise, and Eric C. Meyer.

David Dalton, for all the hours and patience. And my friend Tony Lofaro, of the newspaper *Ottawa Citizen,* for his support and contribution.

My staff for their day-to-day involvement and perseverance: Julie Zhu, Nancy Callihan, and Craig Woods.

Skip Bronson and especially Howard Stern—because of one of the greatest moments I had being interviewed by one of the best interviewers—and his fans and his listeners who called in to encourage me to write a book. Thank you Howard!

Annie Leibovitz, the great one, for her talent, her generosity, and her sharing. Thank you for that beautiful photograph.

And last but not least, to my fans, who for years have been requesting what you are about to read.

My Way

Introduction

As far back as I can remember, I always wanted to be a gangster. To me, being a gangster was better than being president of the United States. . . . To me, it meant being somebody in a neighborhood that was full of nobodies. They weren't like anybody else. . . . I was the luckiest kid in the world. I could go anywhere. I could do anything. I knew everybody and everybody knew me . . . I was part of something. And I belonged. I was treated like a grown up. I was living a fantasy.

That's Henry Hill's rap at the beginning of *Goodfellas*, but it might as well have been me—not that I ever wanted to be a gangster, I just wanted to be part of a cool scene. My own fantasy was hanging out with Frank Sinatra, Dean Martin, and Sammy Davis Jr. I wanted to be those guys. I wanted to live that life.

Vegas was a kind of adult Magic Kingdom, where everybody goes by the code, there's lots of money and girls and champagne and great performers, and everybody is impeccably dressed. We were America's contribution to civilization. Outside of politics and megacorporations, we're a hedonistic culture that, let's be serious, is the way we represent ourselves to the world. That was Vegas in the sixties; pure high-gangster style.

It was another world, a dream world, the Sh-Boom Sh-Boom Room where everything is mellow and cool, where life could be a dream, sweetheart. The soft pink glow from the little lamp on your table, hot chicks, champagne on ice. Torch-song paradise. It's my version of the American Dream: the gold-plated pink Cadillac, the sharkskin suit handmade in Hong Kong, the $300 Italian shoes.

Frank Sinatra, Dean Martin, Sammy Davis Jr.—they were little gods in black tie and patent leather shoes. They didn't talk like other people, they didn't behave like other people, they didn't have to play by the rules the way other people had to, the normal day-to-day regulations didn't apply to them. As Henry Hill says, "I mean, they did whatever they wanted. They double-parked in front of a hydrant, and nobody ever gave them a ticket. In summer, when they played cards all night, nobody ever called the cops."

Vegas was the Rat Pack's Camelot, and Vegas, let's face it, was a hell of a lot more fun than Camelot. That's why JFK hung out with Sinatra at the Sands. To a lot of us teen idols Sinatra was a god—he was revered and respected. Then this new revolution started happening—"funny music" he called it—in other words, rock 'n' roll. But Sinatra was such a legend, he'd been a big star since the '40s—so it didn't really affect him the way it did other crooners. In a way, rock 'n' roll enshrined him. We all looked up to this Sinatra Rat Pack because in the beginning that's all there was—that and us.

Eventually Frank and the rest of the Rat Pack adopted me. I got little jewels of wisdom about performing and behavior from them. From watching the rehearsals in the Copa Room in the Sands Hotel I learned about style, and an insider's insights about how to present yourself on stage. It was like going to the college of cool. Frank was a perfectionist in everything he did and I guess that I'm that way, too.

There were the spectacular showgirl acts called production shows at the Stardust, the Lido, and the Copa Room. The showgirls would often open the show at the Copa sands. Shirley Ornstein (who later came to play a small part in my life) was an eighteen-year-old Copa showgirl until she caught the eye of Burt Bacharach. Barbara Sinatra, Frank's last wife, started out as a showgirl at the Riviera. These shows were big-production numbers with lots of elaborate sets and costumes, the show-girls with their big feathers like erotically plumed birds in skimpy g-strings and long sequin-studded gloves. The orchestra striking up, the curtain is pulled back to reveal a secret world. Then backstage, a little tawdry, cramped, and sweaty with showgirls and performers putting on their makeup, getting their hair done, pressing their clothes, and the support groups hovering: the makeup girl with the powder puff, the costumier with clothes on a hanger, the hairdresser, the agents, the stage manager, the MC. All the stars, all of us had to play for two to four weeks, two shows a night. If you didn't like it, you didn't get the job. It was very tough on the voice but nobody cared—anyway you had no choice.

Vegas in those days was the kind of place you never wanted to leave. You wanted to live there forever. That's the way I felt when I first walked into the Copa Room at the Sands Hotel in 1959. Vegas in the old days was very theatrical. Every night was a spectacle. You'd go from the showroom—packed with out-of-towners there to see the big stars, comedians, and showgirls—into the casino. When the showroom emptied, all the people poured out into the casinos. It was not uncommon to see Dean, Sinatra, and Sammy taking over from the dealers and handing out cards to the guests, visiting stars from L.A., high rollers, and so on. There weren't tourists in Vegas in those days the way there are today—it was an exclusive, elite group of people and the gaming areas were small.

You'd see some movie star look at his cards and say, "Hit me," but Frank or Dean would tell them, "Aw, in your position? You don't wanna hit." There was that kind of playfulness going on. We'd deal a table, give them winners—there was a lot of frolicking about it. It was loose and had its own cinematic kind of touch to it. It was the place to be. The people were elegant, and there were real movie stars there, European royalty, and then Kennedy and other politicians would secretly come in. You knew you were on this happening roll. It was the only place in the country with something like that going on. It's not like today with the boy bands and the generic yeah-yeah rock groups. It was cool, so it was cool to be around it. And elegant—very different from what you see today in Vegas, with the mobs of tourists in madras shorts and trainers.

And then there were "the boys"—or whatever you want to call them. They came in all shapes and sizes. In most cases they talked very low key, they were nattily dressed, always wore tailored shirts, expensive suits, and they walked with that kind of authority you would if you owned Las Vegas. The mob had run Vegas since the beginning. The mob-type guys that were running the casinos were everywhere then, but they didn't look like the gangsters you see in the movies. They were businessmen and behaved like gentlemen—unless you were skimming, pocketing markers, or committing other no-nos. Those were the kind of no-nos that could get your legs broken or your head cracked open—outside the city limits, that is. Who knew how many bodies were buried out there in the desert. Even when Howard Hughes took over he still needed the mob and their guys to operate the casinos.

When the guests had gone to bed a whole unseen underworld emerged. The connected guys would relax, get casual, but be out of the sight of the public. When the showroom emptied the owners would clear, say, twenty tables, create a space, and they'd all sit down and play gin. They'd take off their jackets, loosen their ties, sit there under a little work light playing gin at some ridiculous level, like a dollar a point. You'd play cards all night with the boys, then you'd walk across the street, hang out with another crowd at breakfast. You have to remember there were only five hotels there back then—and beyond the strip just desert and sagebrush.

By and large the mob understood the perception the public had of them, but they were businessmen. You've got to remember that once you establish a place like Vegas, you're not operating out of back rooms in New Jersey or a grungy office in the meat district in New York, dealing with backdoor deliveries of merchandise.

Vegas was a classy place, and these guys believed in dressing up. Everybody dressed. Frank and the boys dressed to the nines. When you ran into connected guys they weren't these scary characters. They were very gracious; women were magnetically attracted to them. There wasn't anything they wouldn't do for you. Comp your room, give you complimentary markers . . . It was a much looser situation. Whereas today you pay for everything—unless you're a high roller, then you do get comped and are given all kinds of extravagant gifts like white fur coats and other stuff.

Early in the '60s, you'd see a classic mob guy like Johnny Roselli in the lounge. I'd sit with him at the bar after my show and he'd say things to me like, "Keep your nose clean, Paul, be a gentlemen, blah blah, blah," giving me advice you'd expect to hear from an uncle of yours at Thanksgiving. Funny, because "Handsome Johnny" Roselli was a mobster, connected with the Chicago outfit involved in the CIA plot to assassinate Fidel Castro.

But socially he was a dapper kind of a guy, an essential character on account of his knowledge about what went on at every level. Because of his looks he moved easily in the Hollywood scene in California, and because of his links with the mob they eventually moved him out to Vegas.

Roselli hit Vegas in 1957. He was a very charming and well-dressed guy. We all knew he was monitoring everything for Meyer Lansky and Frank Costello. He helped with the loans with the teamsters—the Riviera Hotel was constructed with their cash. By the mid-1960s Roselli & Co. had already figured out what to do before Howard Hughes arrived and started to buy all the mob casinos—and in most cases he overpaid for them. They were trying to clean up the town, trying to lose the mob image, but Roselli stayed on.

Roselli was a major presence in Vegas until around 1966 when word had it he was extorting from the key casinos and Ralph Lamb the sheriff started looking at him. That led to the confrontation between Lamb and Roselli at a coffee shop. Lamb put Roselli in handcuffs and shoved him into the backseat of a squad car. His decline started at that point. In 1969, he was convicted for rigging a card game in Los Angeles. The rest of the story is public knowledge. In 1976, a fisherman found his body floating in Dumfoundling Bay, Florida, in a 55-gallon steel drum with his legs cut off and a pink washcloth stuffed in his mouth. That is when the mob shipped out their new enforcer from Chicago: Anthony Spilotro—and things started to get really wild, about which more to come later.

I'd be sitting around the Sands, hanging out with all those guys or lounging in the steam room with a whole other pocket of people— Sinatra, Gregory Peck, Don Rickles. Today it's hard for people to get an idea of how incredible Vegas was in those days, the kind of intensity that existed there. The sense of fashion, the sense of klieg-light visibility the casinos stimulated. You walked in, you were already on stage. You were ready for your close-up every time you went through those doors.

I don't think there's ever been anything quite like Vegas in its golden era. Today, Vegas is this huge Disneyland for grown-ups where you get all of this stuff thrown at you: spectacles (with no real heart and soul, none of the real magic of what Vegas was back then), a few square blocks of glitter and glamour like a glitzy oasis in the desert with sand everywhere, and no high-rises. The type of people that run the casinos today are a different kind of animal altogether. Today it's all corporate, which means lawyers and contracts and fine print.

And eventually, I made it into the innest in crowd there ever was: the Rat Pack. I got to hang around with singers who hung around with gangsters, politicians, movie stars, a who's-who of people. I got to live the life. It was a high wild life—something I'd only dreamed of back in Ottawa.

One

OTTAWA

Upstairs in our house in Ottawa we had huge storm windows with wooden flaps. Underneath the flaps there were three small holes the size of a silver dollar. You couldn't just prop open the window or you'd freeze to death, it was so damn cold. I'd jam a pencil through these little holes to hold open the flaps so I could look outside. I used to sit there at my window and the snow would be falling, snowflakes swirling outside in the wind, the windows all frosted—it was so beautiful, with all that magic snow and the whole smell of winter and I was snug and warm in my room. And then, I don't know why, an unexpected thought would pass through me: "I can't stay here, one day I have to get out of here."

The odd thing was I had a great life—my sister Mariam, my brother Andy, my father Andrew and mother Camy, my relatives, everybody in my family were all close and loving. We weren't rich, but we were a tight, comfortable, and happy family. But for some reason I felt like an outsider. Everyone I knew was going about their lives and they were happy, focusing on school, on sports, on their friends, on their hobbies. They were content with their lives. On the surface I did all the things other kids did at school. But I loved hockey the most. I *loved* hockey. I drew, made model airplanes, had a stamp collection. I was very athletic and I was always very busy; I would go out as much as I could. But at some point it became claustrophobic. Something was missing and I didn't know what it was.

Everybody loves the idea of small town life, happy families, people sitting on their porches in the evening, neighbors strolling past and chatting—like in the movie, *It's a Wonderful Life*. But then there are the exceptions, and I was one of the exceptions.

There was no media blitz like there is today, no twenty-four-hour news cycle or hundreds of channels. In 1954, for instance, there was maybe six hours of television a day. This was before the version of *American Bandstand* that featured Dick Clark. He didn't come on the scene until 1956. And we're not even in the USA, we're in Canada! The only word to describe that was "provincial." Ottawa was the epitome of provincial. All I knew was I had this thing inside me— there really wasn't any model for me to follow like today with talent shows and *American Idol*. However you'd describe what motivated me, I felt like the first kid in the world to try and do it.

People in show business come from all kinds of backgrounds; quite a few come out of poverty-stricken or dysfunctional families. If you're from an abusive family where your parents are always fighting and they beat you and there's no money or your parents are drug addicts, of course you want to get away from that. But that wasn't the case with me. When I had these thoughts about leaving, I'd ask myself, "Why are you doing this? What is your problem?" I didn't know.

When I was twelve, I had all the energy and desire in the world but I had no idea what I was doing. I didn't know if I wanted to be a lawyer, join the circus, discover a miracle vaccine, or be in show business. I don't know where my drive came from, but from an early age I felt I had something inside of me that needed to be expressed. Many people grow up believing they're talented at something, that they have a gift—but it's not just being good at something that makes the difference, it's the urge to be the best at it. I could never pinpoint where that came from, but I know I always had it. It was just so far out of most people's range of thinking that it was scary, this desire to embark on some out-of-control journey.

For me it was never the unknown that was scary—it was the predictable. That's what I found oppressive. Ottawa was a small town—relatively speaking—and in any case it had the same conventional, old-fashioned values as any little town would have, and like all small towns it had small expectations. You were expected to grow up and take over the family business. It was assumed, for instance, that I'd go on to run my dad's restaurant—that's what people thought was a good thing back then. Today anything is possible. There are so many alternatives that kids can dream about—you want to be a sportscaster, you want to be a Web designer, a venture capitalist. Ambitions of that sort didn't exist back then except in rare instances. Expectations were limited; there were fewer things to aspire to. The big difference today is that kids walk around saying, "I want to be famous." As a kid in those days you might daydream about being a famous baseball player or a movie star, but nobody took these fantasies too seriously. My ambition was particularly odd given the time and place I came from. Now everybody wants to be famous, but they don't necessarily know what they want to be famous for.

They did a survey of kids in England about what they expected to do in life. They were asked, "What do you want to be when you grow up? Many just said, "I want to be famous." Fame has become an end in itself, unattached to any achievement. It was different back when I was growing up. One kid wanted to play hockey, another wanted to be a football player; my friend from school wanted to be a ski champion. As soon as I figured it out, I knew what I wanted to be: a writer. That's what I aspired to. I wanted to write—I had no idea what that might lead to, but somehow I knew I had an aptitude for it. Whatever being a writer entailed or how you became one were still a complete mystery but that didn't faze me one bit.

Throughout my childhood, I ran into the occasional racial taunt from my classmates. Because of my swarthy Middle-Eastern complexion, they called me "the black Syrian." While this was painful and humiliating, in one way it did me a favor: at a young age I became aware of the stupidity of prejudice. I remember one night when my uncle was throwing a drunk out of my father's restaurant, the guy said, "You lousy Jew. I hope the Arabs beat the hell out of all the Jews in Palestine!" When my uncle pointed out that he was an Arab not a Jew, the drunk bellowed, "You lousy Arab. I hope the Jews beat the hell out of all the Arabs in Palestine!"

They tried to categorize us as part of the black race, as they did the Jews, which is why many of my friends were Jews. We were all lumped together in one package, when in fact we were Lebanese Christians.

Despite problems out there, life in the neighborhood felt safe: we lived in modest homes, life was family-driven, there were always lots of friends around, lots of relatives. It was a friendly, sheltered, suburban neighborhood. My cousins and our families were very close. I'd go over to Aunt Jessie's or Uncle Mike's, and all the children that went with it: eleven on my father's side and five on my mother's, so there was a constant rotation every weekend. Merriment, food, partying—just very close-knit families.

I was a wildly lively child. I was all over the place.

My father was the first of the brothers to own his own home and so all the brothers and sisters from all the families would congregate there on the weekends. Altogether it was a huge family with his sisters, some fourteen kids—two of the babies tragically died falling into a tub of boiling water so then there were twelve, but still the house was absolutely teeming with relatives. With me on the dining room table singing away. My father's youngest brothers loved me. One would stand at the top of the staircase and the other at the bottom and they'd throw me up and down the stairs with great hilarity and to my mother's horror. And I've stayed close to people in my family. To this day I've stayed close to my cousins Donny Abraham and Bob Anka. They've all been in and out of my life throughout my career. In fact I took my first trip to Paris on December 3, 1958, with Bob Anka, and that was a pretty interesting experience to say the least. My cousin Bob Skaff was one of my dearest friends all the way from the 1960s to the '90s, in my earlier years traveling with me and doing promotional work. He was so helpful to me through his support and loyalty and in promoting my records over many, many years, until his death in 2012.

Ottawa was a small government town, somewhat conservative, but beautiful, even idyllic, from the fairy-tale tower of the House of Commons building to the dappled, leafy streets with the whir of kids on bikes and the ice-cream truck. It was a wonderful place to grow up. Life was pleasant, uneventful, and predictable, which is why I eventually left.

Ottawa for me was pure innocence. We would run water onto the lawn and freeze the backyard, and I'd play hockey on it. I had my chickens and my dogs. There were strawberry bushes all around the yard, which I tended. I would get as many apples off the trees in the neighborhood as I could being chased by dogs down the laneway that separated the yards. To this day I love apples.

I was born Paul Albert Anka in Ottawa on July 30, 1941. My parents were of Lebanese Christian descent and the name Anka itself had an almost folkloric history attached to it. It means "noose" in Arabic, and it came about in this way: In a small town in Syria called Bab Touma—where my ancestors came from—a man raped a young girl of thirteen. The parents of the girl were distraught to the point of madness, but the man had powerful friends and no one would bring him to justice. My grandfather and his brother took the matter into their own hands. They caught the rapist, made a noose from a length of rope, and hung him from a tree. Eventually my grandparents immigrated to Canada to escape revenge from the man's clan. The immigration officer asked them what their name was. Not understanding the question they began to tell the story and during their explanation the story of the noose came up. The official heard the word "anka" and that became our surname.

When I came into my parents' lives, they ran the Victoria Coffee Shop near the House of Commons building. That's how I got my middle name, Albert, from Prince Albert who was Queen Victoria's consort. We lived above the coffee shop until I was three or four. Then we moved to Bayswater Avenue, which was a much higher-end area.

As a child I sang in the St. Elijah Syrian Antiochian Orthodox Church choir where I got to know the choirmaster Frederick Karam, with whom I would study music theory later on.

I've always been an irrepressible ham. I remember going up to my grandmother's and just acting stuff out. If I'd seen a Gene Kelly movie, I'd go and act out the whole thing for her, running around the living room, jumping on the chairs and singing. She was a sweet old gal, a very good-hearted woman, and later on somehow always knew when I needed money to buy records. She'd give me a couple of bucks after every living room performance. Maybe my businesslike approach to music started there because I was so comfortable with her, she was so indulgent of me—and I always got rewarded for my antics. She had to suffer through all my early amateur-hour performances—but she always made me feel as if I were giving her a great gift. Although sometimes I went too far, like banging out rhythms with a fork on her best china. She'd yell, "Paul, will you stop that! I don't wanna hear that racket!"

I was a big music fan from a very young age. I loved music—every type of music. As a kid, I remember listening to a lot of different kinds of stuff, but I guess the first song that really hit me big was the Five Satins' 1956 doo-wop hit "In the Still of the Night." I used to play it constantly and get all my friends to sing along with me.

But my career as a shameless ham began long before that. At age ten I discovered I could make people laugh by singing and sobbing like Johnnie Ray. I was always performing: after we'd seen a show, after dinner, on vacation, in the backseat of the car. I'd serenade the neighbors from my back-porch stage, singing for housewives hanging out the wash in their backyards.

It was probably around the age of twelve that I got seriously smitten with the idea that I myself might get involved in the music business. Music soon became an obsession with me; I was drawn to it like a bug to a bright light.

When I found out that I had a voice, that I could carry a tune, I started out in the great American tradition of impersonating contemporary stars, crooning idols like Perry Como, Frankie Laine, Sinatra, and Elvis Presley in his ballad mode.

I remember in 1956 the big kick was color television—Pat Boone was all over the place as well as Elvis Presley. "Don't Be Cruel," "Hound Dog," and "Love Me Tender" were the songs I was singing. Guy Mitchell doing "Singing the Blues," Frankie Lymon's "Why Do Fools Fall in Love"—that is the stuff that I was listening to, along with Chuck Berry, Fats Domino, and that crowd.

Different people, singing different styles, from Presley to country to rhythm and blues to doo-wop groups—it all fed into my brain. After doing that for a couple of years, I absorbed these styles and either subliminally or consciously incorporated them into my own. Once I started finding my way around the piano, what came out was not so much a copy of any one of them as a blend of all of them—which eventually turned into my own style. I think I acquired my vocal chops first, and then once my writing developed I could say, "Okay, here's my stamp. Here's the best I can do with that." It was a case of constantly evolving, week by week, picking up whatever was happening, listening to the radio and generally being the prototypical fan, studying songs and imitating performers whenever I could.

When early rock 'n' roll came along I could do that easy. I was very influenced and a big fan of all the music that was happening. Bill Haley and His Comets with "Rock Around the Clock"—at fourteen I could imitate them, no problem. I sang the songs of Fats Domino, Bo Diddley, Pat Boone, and Perry Como. When rhythm and blues groups were the rage I could do them, too. Then along came the white R&B emulators like The Crew-Cuts and The Four Aces and The Rover Boys.

Pat Boone would copy Little Richard, and there were other groups copying Little Willie John, The Moonglows, and so on.

I began to think, "Wow, what if I could perform covers of these songs; that would be cool! Next thought: "I should start a group!" I ran into a couple of kids from Fisher Park High School who sang—Gerry Barbeau and Ray Carriere—and we'd sit in my basement, learn the latest songs, and harmonize together. At that point we formed a vocal group called the Bobby Soxers. We'd hitchhike back and forth to colleges in twenty-below weather for twenty or thirty bucks. Then we got a gig in a traveling fair in the summer. Every city in Canada had one, with Ferris wheels and hot-dog stands. There was a big fair that summer of 1956, George Hamid's World of Mirth Fair, with rides, shoot-the-balloons, corn on the cob, and cotton candy.

The fair traveled with a woman named Dixie Allen, who was partners with Hamid, the guy who owned the outfit, and she ran a cabaret as part of the fair called Club 18. It was in the midway, right next to the sideshow with all the freaks. Perfect! Club 18 was an attraction where they had "exotic dancers"—in other words, scantily dressed girls with pasties on their nipples wiggling suggestively, but in between, while the girls changed, they'd either have a musical act or a comedian. I talked Dixie Allen into hiring us. I told her we had this group the Bobby Soxers. "Why don't you let us do all the current hits between the dancers? We'll be great!" They gave us the job 'cause we were local kids. We did songs like "Happy Baby" by Bill Haley and His Comets, which was on the B-side of "Dim, Dim the Lights (I Want Some Atmosphere)," "Down by the Riverside" by The Four Lads, and "Young Love" by Sonny James. I used to do some Hank Williams stuff, too, like "Your Cheatin' Heart" and "Jambalaya." I've always liked country music. I think it's the purest form of American music: great stories, very honest and basic. And when we weren't performing I'd go sit on a crate and peel potatoes and onions to make a little extra pocket money.

That's where I got my first chops: going on between exotic dancers.

We were all too young to go into the main part of the club itself so I couldn't flirt with the dancers. I used to hang out in the dressing room and dig holes in the walls with the pocket knife I carried around with me so I could ogle the girls getting undressed in their changing room. That was my cheap thrills at the amusement park.

We were pulling down $35 for the week's work—which seemed like a fortune to us in those days. Then George Hamid forgot about me until I was proposed as the headline attraction at Hamid's Steel Pier in Atlantic City a few years later in 1960. The price my manager Irvin Feld quoted to him was $3,500. Hamid exploded. "What do you mean $3,500? I had this guy for $35 with two other kids thrown in."

Other than my wild dreams of fame, I was a fairly average Ottawa kid. As a teenager I was smaller than my classmates and overweight. I went to Fisher Park High School, and even though I played on the local hockey team, I knew by age fourteen that I wasn't going to go any further. Unlike my uncles, Louie and Johnny, who continued to play hockey, I became a cheerleader. I was an avid hockey fan—still am. Later on, after I'd had a few hits I'd get to go out on the ice with all the hockey players in Detroit to do the warm-ups—Gordie Howe, Sid Abel, and those guys. Gordie Howe was with the Detroit Red Wings; he was Wayne Gretzky's idol. Up in Montreal I hung out with Wayne and his girlfriend before it all hit for him. I've got the pictures! I saw him go through his whole transition from local hero to international idol. I still see him from time to time. I love hockey, it's a far more interesting game than football. With football, there's basically only twelve minutes of action when you clock it, out of the whole game. With hockey, these guys are on the move every minute—they have to be, they're on skates! Hockey became such a passion for me that ultimately I got involved in buying the Ottawa Senators. But I obviously wasn't cut out to be a hockey player.

Hockey players from the East Coast used to go to Lake Tahoe to practice, and one time in the '70s while I was working at Harrah's—Bill

Harrah's place, big gaming mogul, up in Lake Tahoe—I got a call from the bellman saying, "I have members of a hockey team in the lobby, and they want to talk to you."

"How many?"

"Forty people."

"Who?"

Turned out to be the Montreal Canadiens. They did all their practicing up in Lake Tahoe, while on the West Coast run of games. I got them all tickets and brought them to the show.

Initially I thought I'd pursue a career in journalism and from ages thirteen thru fifteen, took typing and studied English literature. I ran around and did odd errands at the *Ottawa Citizen,* wrote some short stories, and won some awards for my poems and stories in school. My next plan was to lift lines from Shakespeare and make them into song lyrics. All this sounds industrious and precocious but I wasn't exactly a model citizen, not at all. I had my share of run-ins; you know, tearing down lilac trees, running away from home. My dad was the disciplinarian of the family—not that it did him that much good. I was headstrong and hell-bent on following my own crazy schemes. But I could always count on Mom—she was always there to make excuses for me when I'd do something wild.

Dad worked long hours at his restaurant, the Locanda, until midnight or one o'clock in the morning—that's life in the restaurant business—so Mom was the core of the family. She spent endless hours with me and encouraged even my wildest daydreams. If my dad was the practical, sensible one—"Paul, you're going to need to get a real job, you need to start thinking about creating a foundation for your career"—my mom was the one who believed in my fantasies, however far-fetched they seemed. She understood that the more unlikely your dreams are the more fiercely you have to pursue them. The idea of becoming a pop singer back in the mid-fifties was a truly fantastic thing to aspire to—it was literally like building a castle on air. A singer was a voice on the radio, on a record. Who knew how it even got there—and singers in clubs, where did they come from? What did they tell their parents?

My mom was the one who knew how much I loved music and understood that my dreams were my most valuable asset. My dad was far more cautious. He mostly heard my stories secondhand, and naturally was skeptical about my outlandish ambitions. You have to remember the era we're talking about. In the mid-fifties, even the thought of making a career in pop music was a very long shot. Today every other kid wants to be a rock star; back then it was pure fantasy. There was no precedent for it. Today with hugely popular shows like *American Idol* and *The Voice*, parents start grooming their kids at three to be performers. There are courses in producing, engineering records—you can even take a course in how to be a road manager. Who even knew these things existed? Now parents see the money, the celebrity involved, and even if becoming a pop star is as remote a possibility as winning the lottery, parents take the possibility seriously. The thought that their kid might get the chance to become famous, get a record contract, be a star, and be rich and famous is worth all the risk. As it was, pop music barely existed back then and as a career it was a pure cloud cuckooland. My dad's attitude was pretty typical, more like "You've gotta be kidding!"

My dad came around eventually. What else could he do? He saw nothing could stop me—not reason, not common sense, not fear of the poorhouse. He started letting me go to see shows, even letting me bring performers back from the clubs or he'd cook a meal for them at his restaurant. Even then I'm sure he was still very dubious; he probably thought it was a phase I was going through and that I'd grow out of it. But whatever they thought, both my parents could see I had the personality of a performer. And then they saw me starting to write songs, although they didn't quite know what all that meant, either. As time went on, they felt, "We gotta get him to somebody who knows about this stuff. We have to find out what to do with him 'cause he's driving us nuts."

Out in the world, Dad was a very even-keeled kind of guy. He would always take the high road, always very diplomatic, to the point where people in Ottawa wanted him to run for mayor. Everybody loved Andy, everyone went to him for advice about business, social issues. He was just very methodical and stable; maybe I got a little of that from him. Just a little—but enough to save me from going crazy when fame and money could easily have gone to my head in my early days. His level-headedness was just the right ballast to offset my wild impetuous side.

My mother worked at Sears Roebuck, so she had her own money and out of that paid for my piano lessons and gave me money to buy my records. My father, of course, was taking care of the restaurant 'til all hours. We were a modest family, but as we prospered we moved from downtown above a coffee shop that my dad owned when I was a baby to a house on Bayswater Avenue, then ultimately out to Clearview Avenue, where I had a piano in the basement.

As a kid I had a bunch of different jobs. I was a caddy, I worked at my dad's restaurant in the kitchen, peeled potatoes, carrots, stuff like that, and I had a paper route. I was keeping about four, five, six bucks a week. I'd spend a couple of dollars on a movie and popcorn, I'd buy my comic books. You could do a lot with a buck or two in those days. I always was taught that you had to get a job and I realized early in life that work was important.

By thirteen, I'd become a regular at nightclubs in the Gatineau region across the Ottawa River in Quebec. You could buy booze there. There was nothing like that on the Ontario side. Montreal was the cultural capital of Quebec—it was a sophisticated town compared to Ottawa or Toronto. Montreal was the closest thing to an urbane European city on the North American continent. It was the Paris of North America.

I was underage and wasn't allowed in the main part of the Gatineau club, so I'd go up and hide in the light booth. From there I could look down and catch the different acts. I even entered talent contests, anything to further my career. One of the more outrageous things I did was to take my mother's car without her knowing to a club across the river from Ottawa. I was about fourteen at the time and desperately wanted to get across the Champlain Bridge to the French side. Over in Quebec there was liquor, the clubs were a bit racier and what have you—which was always more fun, but this particular night I had a very specific reason for going there. I wanted like hell to take part in this contest I knew was going on at the Glenlea Club. I just had to get to that contest; I really needed the prize money: forty or fifty bucks and all you could eat. My mother had an Austin Healey, and knowing this was the key to my making it to the contest. I practiced driving it in the little lane by the house, not letting my mother know what I was up to. I was an odd combination of being reckless and calculating. Even then I was premeditated in my recklessness. I knew she always went to bed early . . . after she did her crossword puzzle. So I bided my time, and after she drifted off, I snuck into the Austin Healey.

I backed the car out, which wasn't that easy. This was the first time I'd taken it farther than the driveway. The Champlain Bridge was about two, three miles from our house. The first time I crossed it with ease. But as soon as I got a few more miles from home, I was hit by a blinding snowstorm. By this time I was so far away I didn't even consider going back. I made it to the club okay and won—that was the easy part. When I started back a couple of hours later, the storm was a lot more intense. By now the roads were icy and slippery and the little sports car was sliding all over the road. Worse, visibility was almost nil. I could hardly see a few feet in front of me and of course I could barely drive the Austin Healey. Man, was I gonna catch it! Did I mention it was a stick shift? The car had gears and just when you'd think you had the knack, *crunch*! The storm wasn't helping; I couldn't get the car into second or third, so . . . I had to go all the way home in first. Well, as close to home as I got, anyway. There I am, right in the middle of the

Champlain Bridge and the car starts to shake like an old washing machine. I was so scared of my parents by that point that I forgot to be scared for my life.

Suddenly the piston rod goes right through the roof—*wham!*—and pieces of the car were falling all over the highway. There was an exit off the bridge right there and I managed to pull off onto it. Luckily, right near where the car had self-destructed, was a place called Café Champlain, a French restaurant on a little island under the bridge—its parking lot was a well-known lovers' lane. I rolled the car off the highway, down the exit. It went down below the bridge, so I could just coast down there. It ended up on this little island in the middle of the bridge. And I just slid into a slot in lover's lane—the car by now was smoking like a chimney. I'm sitting there going, "Goddamn, now what?" when suddenly I see the flashing red beacon in the rearview mirror. The cops! The RCMP, the Royal Canadian Mounted Police, big guys. They piled me in their squad car. You'd think I'd be somewhat relieved, but all I could think about was what was going to happen when I got home. I knew that's exactly where they were going to take me and what was waiting for me there. The police knocked on the front door of my house. Down the stairs came my poor mother, still thinking I'm asleep in my bed. She was standing there with me squeezed between two humongous cops, staring at me like she'd seen a ghost. She doesn't even want to hear the story.

Dad beat the living Jesus out of me on my ass with a belt. They sent me to juvenile court; I stood there trembling in front of the judge, wondering why my dad had subjected me to this. Little did I know that Dad had cooked up a plan with my uncle Mike who was a lawyer and eventually became a Queen's Counsel. Uncle Mike knew the judge and set the whole situation up to teach me a lesson. The sentence was going to be a serious one. I was to be sent to reform school. It scared the shit out of me.

After that my mom decided it was no use trying to make me stay home and go to bed early, so when I went to the clubs she'd go with me to make sure I kept out of trouble. She would go out with me on school nights and my dad would never know about it. But soon people began drifting into my dad's restaurant late in the evening and telling him they had seen his son Paul singing at some club. "You what?" At first he got mad and gave Mom hell for letting me out on a school night. But that didn't do any good, either.

I just kept going over to the Quebec side of the Ottawa River to perform at Glenlea Golf and Country Club. I'd cross over the bridge to Quebec and make $20, $30, $40 a night. I'd imitate Elvis doing "All Shook Up" with a guitar and the wiggle. I gained a lot of experience that way and got my wings as a performer. I was very much the ham doing impressions and all that. So you could say when it came time to go out on the road and promote my first record I didn't exactly have to come out of any shell. I look at Elton John, The Beatles, people who have made it through the years. And they all put in about two to three thousand hours of experience before they made it. They really worked their asses off at little clubs, halls, gymnasiums. Those are the places where you find out what you are made of. You don't make it right out of the box—nobody ever does. You really need all that experience before you become something—you've got to put in that mileage. The Beatles in Hamburg, doing six shows a day.

As a kid, I saw Frankie Laine and Johnnie Ray at the clubs a lot. I loved to imitate Frankie Laine—that's how I started out, impersonating these guys. Johnnie Ray and Frankie Laine both had very distinctive voices which made them easy to do. My specialty was mimicking singers and actors. That's why I was such a huge fan of Sammy Davis Jr.—a lot of his early work was impersonation. He'd do Tony Bennett, a lot of different singers and actors. He did uncanny imitations of Frankie Laine singing "Jezebel" or Billy Eckstine crooning, "It Isn't Fair," and so on and after I caught his act I started doing them, too. I wanted to be able to do it all.

Johnnie Ray was one of the first people I wanted to see when I went to the clubs—he was all the rage back then. I saw him first at the Desert

Inn and Copacabana in New York City. You have to understand, this guy was like Sinatra in terms of his intensity. His presence on stage was magnetic. From the Copacabana to Vegas people queued up around the block to see him. His teenage following was huge. Screaming girls. He had a hearing aid, so he'd developed this very appealing style of singing with one hand up to his ear—it was very effective, people went nuts. I was a big fan of this guy; I had all his records, I used to do all of his songs.

His real name was Francesco Paolo LoVecchio, and he had been a huge star since the thirties with a big dance band, a big guy with a really long career—seventy-five years. But a performer's life is an illusion and when the mask slips you get disenchanted. I went to see Frankie Laine one night at the Dunes Hotel in Vegas and the night I was there, he did some great songs: "Jezebel," "That Lucky Old Sun (Just Rolls Around Heaven All Day)," "Georgia on My Mind," and "That's My Desire." He had a riveting act and got a standing ovation. At the end of his show he leaned over, ringside, and this woman put her hand in his hair and his toupee came off in her hand. And I was going, "Wow! This is major, man. I just saw Frankie Laine lose his hair!"

Johnnie Ray was very close to a woman named Dorothy Kilgallen, a huge columnist, the biggest there was. She was on the TV show, *What's My Line?* She and Ray had some kind of an affair. There was something going on between them—what nobody quite knew because he was gay. So that was odd, too. Sometimes I'd meet these guys at my father's restaurant and sometimes they'd come to my home, and that's where I really dug information out of them.

The Platters, The Four Aces, The Four Lads, The Rover Boys, and Tony Bennett were a few of the performers I met at my dad's restaurant or later in the Gatineau Club or the Chaudière Rose Room. I would always wrangle my way backstage, using some outrageous story. I'd ask them a hundred questions about show business. I was fearless. I'd buttonhole stars like Tony Bennett or Buddy Greco, who had a bunch of swing albums out, and ask them for advice on how to make the big time. They'd always give me something, like "Your first talent isn't going to be singing, kid, it's going to be taking rejection—just don't let it get you down." Or they'd say something witty ("It's just vaudeville, kid, unless you get lucky and offend someone, and then it's art."). So I'd go away with a glow, thinking I'd just made contact with the guys who made the magic and learned one or two of their tricks.

The summer I was fourteen I went on a vacation with my parents down to Gloucester, Massachusetts, where we visited a friend of my dad's. He was a fisherman with lobster traps, but the important thing about him—from my point of view—was he knew a guy who had a nightclub: Johnny's Club it was called, a little local place where they held amateur contests where you could go and sing. Anyone could perform there—once. When the guy saw me do my act, he flipped. He took me right into the hotel dining room and had me put on my routine. I sang with the band and the guests started to throw money on the stage. By the time we left, I had about $38 in my pockets from tips. People threw everything from pennies to five-dollar bills on the stage. After that episode, even my dad was starting to get sold on my crazy ideas.

Meanwhile, back home, our gigs with the Bobby Soxers got few and far between. We did a couple of songs on the radio, and then it just started to get tough, what with schooling and so on and eventually I decided to go out on my own.

I sang in church, I did some choir singing at Fisher Park High School, anything I could do to keep me ambitious about singing. That was my passion. School was okay, I got good grades when I wanted to, but there was this burning and yearning in me to perform—whatever that thing is that drives you on. Wherever I could sing in any fashion, or get my arms around a little more experience I would do it.

I continued to make appearances at local clubs and the occasional local TV program. I'd pick up $10 or $15 a night for doing impressions of Elvis, Frankie Laine, or Johnnie Ray. Later that year I won an amateur contest, which brought me a week's engagement and a chance to mingle with more seasoned entertainers.

I'm still in school, meanwhile, doing odd jobs at the *Ottawa Citizen*. A reporter, Joe Finn, told me I should study shorthand at school so I could take detailed notes fast when I went out on an assignment. The class consisted of me, forty girls, and a friend of mine, Fred Tommy, who came from a big skiing family—they'd won Olympic medals. But my mind was obviously elsewhere because I couldn't concentrate and after a couple of weeks I got thrown out of shorthand class. I was upset at first, but then I realized I wasn't ever going to have a chance to use shorthand.

Actually, getting thrown out of shorthand class was one of the best things that happened to me. I started taking music lessons in school—I studied drums, trumpet, and music theory, but I wanted more music instruction and so I asked my mother if she could find someone I could take music lessons with. As it happened a Mrs. Winnifred Rees lived right around the corner. She had amazingly curly hair and was very, very English and terribly proper. We'd have tea and I'd sit and practice my scales, and then, when I saw her attention drift, I'd slip into playing a modified boogie-woogie on the piano, a sort of *oom-boom-boom boom bamalam,* swinging into rock 'n' roll beat. That would wake her right up. She'd say, "No, no, no, no, no, Paul, we'll have none of that." With Mrs. Rees it was strictly classical music: Beethoven, Chopin, and Brahms.

I spent a lot of time with Mrs. Rees, starting with the scales and the classical music and all that stuff, which I actually found to be okay, although it was pretty boring at times, especially after I got seriously into the pop music I was hearing on the radio. As someone once said, sending a child to piano lessons to become a better pianist is like sending a kid to the Colosseum to become a better Christian. I'm impatient in general, so naturally I wanted to get cooking once I found my chops and soon I started just banging away, trying out different rhythms and tunes. I learned to pick out melodies on the piano and the guitar. Many of the melodies I began tinkering with on the piano I adapted from old Middle Eastern music my parents put me in contact with. I'd hear these melodies in church, at festivals, and on records around the house. I'd just got into that minor key mode, and once I realized I could actually write songs myself, I began by applying minor key melodies to rhyming schemes I'd found in the works of Shakespeare. That's when it got really exciting: I started doing my own stuff.

Mrs. Rees would say, "Come back next week" and I'd think, "Ohhhh, God, how many weeks do I have to do this?" At one point I thought of going to Juilliard, but it probably wouldn't have worked out—I couldn't even get through Mrs. Rees's lessons! Anyway, soon enough my hit record mania got in the way. It was "Roll over Beethoven, tell Tchaikovsky the news . . ." and that was the end of my music lessons. I wish I'd gone on, though, so that I could have played better, had a better grasp of it all. But I've noticed a curious thing. Most singers today are stylists and, aside from the guitar wizards, not many of them are that accomplished as musicians. Conversely, virtuoso musicians and most great arrangers do not make good songwriters. They're too complicated, they don't write for the masses. The secret to song writing is simplicity. You should be able to play the melody using only one finger; that's a hit, you just bang it out with one finger.

My basement was the place: piano up against the north wall and me banging away and writing and writing and writing and making notes and memorizing and more memorizing. I sang all my early songs to my mother first. After work she'd hear me banging on the piano and come down every now and then and sit next to me and ask me, "What are you writing?" I'd sing her "You Are My Destiny" and "Don't Gamble with Love" and tell her, "Mom, this is for you, I wrote these for you." She would be incredibly touched, a glow would come over her face and tears would stream down her face out of happiness. She was so thrilled with my writing, that all her faith in me—like protecting me from my dad and buying me records—had come to fruition.

When she heard those songs she was so moved, she could see it was all worth it, she could see my dreams were coming true, and she was overcome with joy and pride in me.

While taking piano lessons and getting the sense that I wanted to write songs, I was still going to high school, of course, and taking a lot of compulsory general education classes. This meant I was reading books, lots of books. I had a report due on a book I read that summer called *Prester John,* written by John Buchan, who had been the ex-governor general of Canada and was a famous novelist (he wrote *The Thirty-Nine Steps,* among a lot of other books). The town in which the book's story took place was called Blaauwildebeestefontein—it's a place in Africa that really exists. I was fascinated with the name. I guess I'd been building up to gradually writing a song, playing piano, setting my poems to music, and suddenly I found myself writing "Blau Wilde De Veest Fontaine," which was really my first legitimate song, a lead sheet, my first here-I-come-world song.

The important thing for me at that time, coming from a small town, was that I felt very frustrated, and I knew that I would go on being that way until I could get things in focus. My daydream goal was to have a glamorous lifestyle, and to realize everything that was not affordable to me in Ottawa. Canada was in the shadow of the United States, where everything was happening—and what was happening in music was R&B. What you have to understand was that the '50s was the preface to rock 'n' roll music. I was listening to Chuck Berry, Fats Domino. Country music had not really come out of Nashville yet and R&B remained the foundation of pop music until it was "white-ified" by those of us who took from it and gave it to the masses. What we were all listening to was R&B. The sanitized rock 'n' roll I and the other white singers were creating was far more acceptable, because there'd been a lot of controversy about rock 'n' roll and its so-called crude rhythms. We listened to Elvis Presley in high school, and his music had its roots in R&B, and country music. I remember being impressed by Elvis, but when you're as young as I was, with my background, I just didn't have the means or opportunity to do what Elvis did, which was go record your own songs in a little studio in Memphis. On the other hand, curiosity was something I had plenty of, along with a burning desire to get to New York whatever it took. I guess I did have a huge dose of crazy optimism, too, because most people don't actually think they're going to win a contest and go see New York City from collecting soup-can labels! And yet, that's what happened to me.

What happened was that a contest was announced in the local newspaper, sponsored by IGA food stores. You could win a trip to New York if you were the one to collect the most Campbell's soup labels. Well, I had what I considered a great in: I was bagging groceries at our local IGA supermarket. So I made a plan (I tend to do that): I wrote down the names of the women who bought three or four Campbell's soup cans. Like many small towns, Ottawa has its neighborhoods where everybody knows everybody else, and from delivering newspapers I knew where most people lived. Whenever I got a chance I'd sneak out and go to the houses of the women who'd bought the cans of soup, ring the doorbell, tell the lady that there's a contest, so please don't throw your cans away. The plan was actually pretty intricate because of course I often had to go back more than once—people usually wanted to eat the soup before giving me the label! I also had to convince them to let me go through their garbage.

Needless to say, I collected a lot more labels than the kids who were just getting their labels from the soup cans that they ate at home. I won the contest for my district. Along with forty other winners from all over Canada, I left Ottawa on a train for New York. We all stayed at the Sloane House YMCA. I went to the Brooklyn Paramount Theatre, walked down Broadway, got a feel for the town. Just getting out in that environment and seeing something like New York, coming from where I came, well, that was the beginning for me. New York was a total cultural shock. I sniffed it out, I said to myself, "This is what I want—this and music." I knew I belonged. And I'd yet to write a song and get it recorded!

At the hotel I remember sitting way the hell up on the thirty-fifth floor. I'd never seen that before. Looking at Manhattan down below, looking at the traffic, the streets, the buildings. I was blown away from the impact. In the '50s it's hard to describe what New York was to me. All our high spirits spilled out into pranks—waste-paper baskets trashed and thrown out the window, doing what kids did.

———■———

I never thought anything would come of the first song I'd written, "Blau Wilde De Veest Fontaine," but that summer fate intervened with a visit to my uncle in California. Uncle Morris was an opera singer, and it was principally because of him that the music I heard around the house was classical. By the time I figured out how to get out to California, I knew quite a bit about the music scene, demos, and that kind of thing.

Right after my fifteenth birthday, I used my summer job savings to buy an airline ticket to L.A. I wanted to go to California to get away somewhere else in the States. I had the lead sheets for the song, but I didn't have a plan in mind for pitching it; I just went out to be with my uncle. I got to L.A., and looked for a summer job. My uncle was also an actor and he was working in a play called *Bullfight* at the Pacific Playhouse on La Cienega and Santa Monica. I got a job there selling candy bars, and even parked cars.

A popular R & B hit in the country that summer was "Stranded in the Jungle" by The Cadets. A mile or two from where my uncle lived, if you went straight down Sunset, to Sunset and Vine, was Wallach's Music City. They had all those booths where you could listen to the records about four-by-four feet and eight feet high. I took "Stranded in the Jungle" into the booth and looked at the sleeve and it said, "Modern Records, Culver City, California."

So Modern Records was in Culver City—and was therefore only fifteen minutes away by car. I hitched a ride out there to some place on Washington Boulevard, carrying the lead sheet to my song. Modern

Records had a little garage front-office setup—like early Motown or what Sun Records, where Elvis started out, must have been like. I walked in and there were two guys, Jules and Joe Bihari, and their sister. It was this mom-and-pop record business that produced the hit record "Stranded in the Jungle."

I didn't have an appointment, I just walked in off the street. It wasn't exactly a busy, bustling establishment. There wasn't anything urgent happening every two minutes like there is at a modern-day record company. Everyone was just hanging around. It was in the infancy stage of the business. They were just living off this one hit they had, probably almost by accident. They were waiting for the next call. They had plenty of time to listen to me.

They first looked at me and were somewhat taken aback, as well you can imagine they would be, presented with a fifteen-year-old in jeans and a white T-shirt off the street representing himself as a singer-songwriter. To them I was this curiosity they were looking over with fascination.

"Whadda ya want, kid? Who are you?"

"Well, I got this song, gonna be a hit," I said.

"Okay, sing it to us." And I did. It just spilled out, whatever it was emanated from me to them and right away they said, "We'd like to record it." I was surprised, but not all that surprised—like any teenager I believed everything I did was magic and certain to be a surefire hit.

Later on they said, "Well, how'd ya like to do it with The Cadets?" How would I like The Cadets to be on it? Are you kidding? I'd do anything to record with the folks who had a hit record in the country. "Hell," I said, "I'll take anything. You guys could sing it—but The Cadets . . . wow! Okay!" I freaked out—the hit group of the summer was going to sing on my record. How could it fail?

I met with Ernie Freeman, who was the A&R director (artists and repertoire), who was just starting his own successful career. He went on to produce all the Bobby Vee records, and later worked as an arranger on Sinatra's "Strangers in the Night." He became huge, but this was right at the beginning of his career. We arranged a session and in two weeks, there I was in the back room doing "Blau Wilde De Veest Fontaine" with The Cadets. We did another song I'd wanted to cover, an R&B number called, "I Confess," on the flip side.

You could do things like that back then. It wasn't like the media-driven society that we have today. There was a kind of innocence in those days, when pop music was in its infancy stage.

That was the first song that I ever wrote and it actually came out! "Blau Wilde De Veest Fontaine" doesn't sound like too promising a title, I know, but when you're just feeling your oats, and when the business wasn't really that big a business, it was enough. There was melody to it, without which it would have been just a novelty song. The business wasn't as precise as it is today, it wasn't as competitive. It was an environment where everybody had a shot; it was this new business— nobody knew what was going on. That was the difference.

As unusual as the title was, that's what I thought we had going for us. I thought it would attract attention; I thought people would say, "Wow, 'Blau Wilde De Veest Fontaine'! What is that?"

Well, not surprisingly, the record was never a hit—it only sold about three thousand copies. So I went back to Canada, a failure at fifteen! Okay, it did get me on a CBC-TV show called *Pick the Stars,* but the only guy who played the song was George Lorenz, who called himself "the Hound Dog," out of Buffalo.

The song got me a little notoriety, but not for long. My career had started . . . and ended just as fast.

After the record went nowhere in the fall of 1956, I re-enrolled in tenth grade at Fisher Park High School and went back to school in Canada. At that age I was sort of a cross between *The Apprenticeship of Duddy Kravitz* and *What Makes Sammy Run?* The former was a film with Richard Dreyfuss and the latter a popular novel by Budd Schulberg about the driving ambition of the story's central figure: Sammy Glick. I was a blend of these two characters and anyone else who had the burning desire and dream to get involved in some improbable schemes. I eventually did play Sammy Glick on Broadway a few years later.

That fall semester I took a course in music and as my involvement grew, I began to get excited again.

I'd been very aware early on that rock 'n' roll was the new wave in music. That was the future and I wanted in on it. Once I made that decision, I realized that if I wanted to record any new songs, I'd have to write them myself. All the established songwriters of the day—Cole Porter, Sammy Cahn, and Irving Berlin, among others—were busy writing songs for crooners like Frank Sinatra, Bing Crosby, and Perry Como. They weren't about to start writing songs for me, that's for sure. Anyway, these guys hated rock 'n' roll, thought it was the death knell for most crooners and the guys who wrote songs for them. Overnight it was a brash new world that the older writers found cheap and corny. They figured it was just a novelty sensation that would go away. Rock 'n' roll had made serious inroads into the charts but it wouldn't be until The Beatles and the British Invasion in the early sixties that the big band singer became obsolete—except in Vegas, but then Vegas is another country (as we'll soon see). Presley didn't make it in Vegas the first time he went out there—they were in a time warp for a long time as far as youth culture was concerned. Crooners flourished for years in clubs— they're still out there, that's never going to go away. The Beatles spelled the end for the Jimmy Durantes and those type of singers but it took almost ten years for rock to take over the charts—up till then there was a mix of different genres on the radio, in the Top Ten.

Even if you were famous like Elvis or Pat Boone, there just weren't many writers out there writing songs for rock 'n' roll singers. The singers who pioneered the rock 'n' roll revolution—Little Richard, Chuck Berry, Jerry Lee Lewis, and Fats Domino—had mainly written their own songs. The only guys writing pop and rock 'n' roll songs for other people in the fifties were the Jerry Leiber and Mike Stoller duo, and the inimitable Doc Pomus.

Meanwhile, by the late 1950s rock 'n' roll had become the overwhelming force in American pop music, and in that blitzkrieg nothing was more culturally important than The Biggest Show of Stars. It was this giant rock 'n' roll show that traveled by bus throughout the United States and Canada, hitting the major cities at least twice a year. It was basically R&B driven. It featured some of the biggest names in rock 'n' roll including Fats Domino, The Platters, Chuck Berry, The Everly Brothers, Eddie Cochran, The Drifters, The Crickets, and Clyde McPhatter. These acts had some of the hottest hit records at the time and were adored by teenage fans. I was a huge fan of these guys—they were my absolute idols.

When I heard the tour was coming to Ottawa I wasn't going to miss out on that. Other than Elvis Presley coming to town, the rock 'n' roll tour was the music event of the year. The tour bus rolled into town for a show April 18, 1957, at the Ottawa Auditorium, an old downtown hockey arena. My goal was to get backstage and meet the performers. I had a plan and I was going to succeed come hell or high water. I had been to hockey games, so I knew how to get backstage. After the concert, when no one was looking, I snuck into the backstage area and went looking for my musical heroes.

You had the stage, the seating, and a decrepit, crumbling backstage area. Security was tight. There were a lot of young female and male fans running around, wanting to meet the stars, and one of them was me. The others didn't get very far; I was the only one who managed to sneak backstage.

The dressing rooms were built with cinder-block bricks that were loose enough so you could move them. I'd bought a new black jacket with white sleeves, and I wanted all the stars to sign the sleeves. I pushed one of the cinder blocks in and through the opening, I yelled to Fats Domino, "Can I have your autograph?" And that's when Allen Bloom, one of the show's producers, came out and reprimanded me.

"Get out of here! What are you doing backstage? You're not supposed to be here!"

"But, I'm a singer," I said indignantly. "My name is Paul Anka. I have a record out here in Canada called 'Baluuwildebeestefontein.'"

"Blau-what?! I don't care who you are, you can't be back here, you have to leave!" he said, before calling for security to lead me away.

They threw me out one door and I went back in through another. Nobody was going to stop me. So I get backstage again and I was just hanging around, determined to talk to Fats Domino and Chuck Berry. I see Berry, but he is more interested in chatting with a pretty eighteen-year-old girl who had an autograph book.

Chuck Berry was one of the first people to hear "Diana." He just hated it! "You're too young and she's too old?" he recited sneeringly. "That's horrible," he went on. "What is this stuff? That's not a song, man, that's a conversation you have at the Dairy Queen." The story's in his autobiography, actually.

To put it mildly he wasn't too interested in me or my songwriting. "Diana" must have seemed very corny and simple-minded to him, one of the greatest songwriters in all rock 'n' roll. I played it to him and he as much as threw me out of the room. "Listen, kid, let me give you a bit of advice, quit what you're doing and get a real job." Which I totally understood 'cause you know that's what was so great about him, the stories in his songs are great Southern tales all painted with broody landscapes, neon, and fast cars. Here I was, this kid, with this dream and a fire in the gut, and just blurting out this very basic emotion. It was like telling the rock 'n' roll Shakespeare you just wrote a sonnet and it goes like this . . .

Undaunted I went over to see Fats Domino, who was in his dressing room, hoping for some better luck. I said, "Mr. Domino, I've got a song for you." Domino listens to "Diana." He looked at me quizzically and then beamed in that way Fats did, flashing his big teeth. "Now that's sincere," he said, and laughed. "Not my kinda thing, son, not a song I could sing, understand? I'm old." Big laugh. "You want people to hear that song you best record it yourself." By this point, Bloom showed up and sees me. He's furious that I broke through security a second time and he's ready to throw me out himself.

"I told you to get out of here, kid!"

Just then, Irvin Feld shows up and I call out to him, hoping to get his attention.

"You're Mr. Feld!" I said to him.

"Yes?" he said, like why would that be of any interest to me.

I quickly take out a piece of paper, write down my name, address, and telephone number, and hand it to him. I said to him, "You've never heard of me, but you will!" Then I told him my name was Paul Anka, that I was a songwriter and I'd written this song called "Diana."

"Okay, kid, see you later," he said, brushing me off as quickly as he could. The wild thing is that he would eventually become my manager.

—■—

When I came to Ottawa in 2005 for a reception, John Topelko, my former Fisher Park High School teacher, remembered me as a young kid coming to him for advice in the fall of 1956. I was in turmoil back then and I told him, "I've written up a song, and I'd like to launch this thing, but I can't see how I could possibly do it without taking a little time off from school." Mr. Topelko had said, "If you really have a lot of confidence in getting this thing done, by all means go for it." The song I was in such an all-fired hurry to get recorded was "Diana."

I've always been attracted to mature women. I found that out at an early age. When I was fifteen, I developed a crush on a nineteen-year-old girl who worked as a secretary in the offices of the Royal Canadian Mounted Police in Ottawa: Diana Ayoub. It's been said that she was our babysitter—and she may have been a babysitter for my brother, Andy Junior or my sister Mariam, but my relationship with her wasn't as titillating as "babysitter" sounds. I saw her in church and at community events—and I was smitten.

Diana was my first infatuation, I had such a serious crush on her. I made my advances as a youngster and failed dismally. She wanted nothing to do with me. Diana was my inspiration, the fantasy girlfriend—

and imagined problem ("I'm so young and you're so old, this my darling, I've been told"). In truth it never got anywhere near that. I think she just thought it was funny someone so much younger than her—three years!—wanted to date her. That's where songs come from: out of stories you tell yourself in your mind.

I started to pester my father for permission to go to New York City again but he was against it. He didn't want me taking time off from school, didn't want me traveling alone. That's when I really turned up the pressure.

The following spring my hopes about a singing career revived when an Ottawa disc jockey called my father with startling news—to my dad anyway. "Andrew," he told my father, "your boy's too big for Canada." Harold Pounds, an executive from Quality Records, and Gerry Myers, an Ottawa disc jockey, had independently been sending reports on me to Am-Par headquarters in New York. They urged Paramount to grab me and sign me up. They wrote back telling the Canadian talent scouts to hold off.

I also found out that some friends of mine, a Canadian group called The Rover Boys that I'd met over at the clubs across the river, were going down there in April. They were a little older and already had a recording contract with ABC, but I talked to them and we came up with the idea that I could go down there with them. Who would've known what it would all come to? I wanted to cross that bridge into the future. For me it was always just *Go! go! get! do! Make that fifteen bucks! Sing! sing! sing!* Until it got me to New York, from which everything emanated. I borrowed money to go back to New York a second time with The Rover Boys. That's when I got the ABC contract. I went down to smell the town.

Just before I left for New York to try and sell my songs, I auditioned for a recording contract at the local record company (Canadian Broadcasting Company). The audition led to an offer of a ten-year contract at $150 a week. In 1957, $150 was a lot of money. For a sixteen-year-old boy, it was astronomical. My family was prepared to accept the offer until friends began dropping hints that there was no provision in the contract for advancement or hit records. Ten years later, I would still have been drawing $150 a week from the CBC. Hah!

I decided to go to New York on my own and see if I could interest someone in my songs. I had already written a few songs including "Diana," and I wanted to leave home and try to get it on as a songwriter. Before the trip, everything I had been listening to came from New York. The industry operated from there, so I knew that's where I had to go to make it. I was a very precocious, adventurous kid. I guess I had that mixture of curiosity and ambition and everything else grows out of that. Of course some basic aptitude for what you do plays a big part in success in the music business, but without the rest—ambition, drive, relentless pursuit of your goal—you got nothing.

I wasn't all that promising as a matinee idol: I had problems with my height and weight, I was swarthy, and like all teenagers I was preoccupied with my hair. What was I going to do with it? I was forever combing it back, pulling it down in the front. But I had the performing bug like crazy. The writing began to develop, and at that point it all started to come together. Then it just became a question of singing my own material, which was so custom-made for me that nobody else would want to do it. Everyone sensed I had it, this energy and crazy drive in me, but where is he going to go with this? Timing is everything in this world, especially the music business. To want a career in rock 'n' roll you had to have the guts to pursue it beyond reason because back then the singers you heard on the radio were almost entirely older, established performers and vocal groups. I was the first kid of that kind out of Canada, so it was understandable that not many others even tried to get into it. I didn't even know what it meant.

Later on, much later, Leonard Cohen, Neil Young, Celine Dion, they all left. Celine Dion went to Berlitz to learn English; she was French Canadian and hadn't had a chance to learn English as a kid.

In April 1957, with $500 from my dad I went to New York with my songs—it was do or die. The songs I took to New York with me were

"Diana," "Tell Me That You Love Me," "Don't Gamble with Love," and "I Love You, Baby." All were written somewhere around '56, into '57. I would have been fifteen or sixteen, I'd say, when the writing bug really took hold, when the ideas started to come, and now I was ready. I wanted to do the most impossible thing imaginable: take my songs to New York City and see if anybody else would buy my dreams.

Two

TEEN IDOL

Two weeks later, I'm in New York City sharing a small hotel room with The Rover Boys, trying to figure out where I'm going to sleep 'cause there aren't enough beds! I didn't care: I knew my life was going to change in a big way. So I put a mattress down in the bathtub and charted my course.

We stayed at the President Hotel, a small place in the West Forties where musicians and theater people stayed. I was having a great time, hanging out, meeting people. I'd go down to the coffee shop to eat or get a doughnut. Every little thing was just magic for a kid from Ottawa. New York wasn't dangerous then. You could walk down Eighth Avenue, Broadway, go to the movies in the middle of the night on Forty-second Street!

I checked out the jazz clubs that you could still find on Broadway. I wanted to get a feel of the city and everything I'd read about the music scene in New York.

While eating in the hotel coffee shop one day I ran into this guy from Cuba, a real charming guy, a fantastic bongo and conga player named Chino Pozo, cousin of the great Afro-Cuban percussionist Chano

Pozo who virtually invented Latin Jazz. Chano was a tough, rowdy guy who got killed in a bar in Harlem over a bag of marijuana at age thirty-three. His cousin Chino was a sweet mild-mannered guy, very different from his hot-tempered cousin. I used to see Chino play with Peggy Lee in a little jazz club, Basin Street East. It was a very tight stage and I'd be ringside so we'd notice each other. Later I'd see him back at the hotel and say, "Chino, you're going to work for me one day." This obviously amused him—"Who is this loco kid?"—but he was always nice about it. Soon after I had my first hit I ran into him again and I said, "Chino, I'm ready! Are you coming to work for me?" He worked with me for years, right up until he died. I ultimately moved him to Vegas and bought him a car—he was amazed, he'd never even driven a car before. He used to cook up a big pot of paella and bring it backstage. You always wanted this guy around—very loyal, and I was loyal to him, too. That's how it was back then. Somebody's with you from the beginning, you don't ever let them go. All my life, he was my bongo player/percussionist. One day in 1980, we were on our way to the airport to go on tour in Canada and we stopped by his condo to pick him up. We knock on the door. No response. Eventually we open a window and climb inside and find he had died in the night.

The Brill Building at 1619 Broadway was the action spot of the music biz, along with the other hive of publishing and songwriting, 1650 Broadway. The Brill Building was a big office building with a restaurant in the basement. We used to go and grab a huge bowl of shrimp for a buck. It was where W. C. Handy and Irving Berlin had hung their hats so that was like walking into the tower of song. Meanwhile, 1650 Broadway was maybe a little hipper since the younger songwriters hung out there.

When you walked down any given hall in those buildings, you would hear piano playing coming out of the doorway. You'd hear Hal David working with Burt Bacharach, who was tinkling a melody in one room, and Jerry Leiber and Mike Stoller harmonizing in another.

It was like a music factory, piano plunking and *oo-pah-pahing* on every floor. Doors open, people hanging out in the hallways, smoking, talking, schmoozing, joking, paying off bookies, trying out riffs on each other. In the offices, guys would be playing cards, some of the older guys there praying that rock 'n' roll would go away. It was the kind of building where you could hang out in just about any office. Everybody knew each other; going from office to office was like a musical guided tour. If I wanted to hang out with Artie Ripp and a bunch of the doo-wop guys, I went up to the fourth floor and stood around the piano, everybody doo-wopping. All the music and talent came out of that building. Hard to imagine today, that we could walk from office to office and see the guys actually writing the hits.

Creativity and thievery flourished side by side in the early days of rock 'n' roll. There was the notorious Morris Levy, who was part of the Genovese crime family, a handsome, slick, ruthless character like Bugsy Siegel. He took co-writing credit on Frankie Lymon's "Why Do Fools Fall in Love" and sole credit for "I'm Not a Juvenile Delinquent." And that was nothing unusual. There was a famous saying of Morris Levy's, "Write a word, get a third," meaning if you came up with a word or a phrase in a song, you got one third of the writer's and publishing proceeds. And Levy made sure he put his contribution into as many songs as possible. He'd say stuff like, "No, no, not 'sun' it should be 'fun.'" If anyone asked him about royalties, he'd say, "Royalties? If you want royalties, go to England."

That year, "Party Doll" by Buddy Knox was my favorite record. I loved anything by The Everly Brothers. The Rover Boys had a big hit, "Graduation Day," and they brought me in to see Don Costa, who was a producer at ABC-Paramount Records. With that I got my foot in the door and launched into my sales pitch. "Aw, let the kid in, see what he's got." They thought it was funny, me being so young and enthusiastic and green about how you do things in the music biz. I guess I was pretty good at promoting myself, because the guy was sold enough to convince the company president, Sam Clark, and the suits to come in and hear me. I'd basically just walked in off the street and plunked out four tunes on the piano—and here were big shots at a major record company taking me seriously.

Imagine the scene: in walks a fifteen-year-old who's very positive and who has a song ("Diana") that says something—even though the song is pretty basic—and the whole picture adds up. I mean, I was hardly a pretty boy and barely tall enough to see over the lower half of this Dutch door they had leading to their office stockroom!

Costa had his own funny description of my arrival on the scene: "There we were, jammed into my office listening to little Mr. Five-by-Five pounding out the songs. It was like the movie *Words and Music,* about Rodgers and Hart. Paul was Mickey Rooney playing Larry Hart. Everything frantic, hammed up, overplayed; but he had something."

I had a tape with my entire catalog on it at that time . . . four songs: "Diana," "Tell Me That You Love Me," "Don't Gamble with Love," and "I Love You, Baby." I played everything I had on the piano for the record company executives. After Costa and Sam Clark heard them all—the room was still vibrating with the last notes—they said, "Paul, you should call your parents and tell them we need to talk about signing you to the label." I had only been in New York for two weeks and they're offering me a contract! Right there in the office I called my parents and told them that ABC wanted to sign me. That fateful meeting with Don Costa changed everything: my life as a teenager ended at fifteen.

My parents were taken by surprise but they did have a bit of prior conditioning from my "Blau Wilde De Veest Fontaine" adventure. I'd done local TV in Canada and they'd heard certain industry people say often enough, "Geez, he's got something. I'd keep an eye on him." I was hungry, always fighting my parents' common sense because I knew what I wanted. Knowing how bull-headed I was, they probably figured I was going to stay with it no matter what anybody said.

But New York City, that was a different matter. It's the Big Apple, the scene, and they're obviously overwhelmed, very openly humble about it. They sure weren't show business parents, but still my father wasn't stupid—he was a very astute businessman. Even after I hit, my dad kept me centered. That's how Canadians are—anchored. We keep the lower 48 from floating off into the blue.

My parents signed. Don Costa signed along with the president Sam Clark, a great guy, and Larry Newton and Irwin Garr signed, too—these were the top executives at ABC. They wined and dined my parents and came up with a formula. They'd give me a hundred bucks a month to write for their publishing company. The contracts got signed and the folks were sent home. I stayed, and my life began.

Costa started working with me right away, suggesting arrangements, finding the musicians, and generally getting me ready for the recording date. Don's first assignment for me was to complete the last couple of lines in the bridge for "Diana." I had to get ready to cut the record in the studio in a couple weeks. I wrote the song real fast—it was a poem first—but I didn't know how to finish it. The morning of the recording I overslept—I'd been up late the night before enjoying being in New York. So I was late for the date, which was for two o'clock. Uh-oh! I think I got up at ten to two and ran like a son of a bitch down Broadway. I got to the Capitol studio but I still didn't have what I wanted. I said to myself, "I'm not gonna blow this. Just go in and wing it!" My problem was I didn't have any words for certain notes, that's why I used those "uh-ohs" at the end of the bridge in "Diana" that every other rock group would soon be using in their songs. I just threw the "uh-ohs" in, but because of the urgency of the song, they seemed to be expressing inarticulate teen yearning. What began as a filler line was seen as a deliberate stylistic move. And that became one of the song's hooks. You have to be open to chance—mistakes can often turn into innovations if you can find a way of flipping them.

We recorded "Diana" over at Capitol's studios. It all happened so fast it kind of blew the top off my fifteen-year-old head. This was the big time and I had very little preparation except for my experience in clubs in Ottawa and my one failed recording. I came out of an environment of fan magazines where all these people were on a pedestal. When it happened to me, it was so unreal—I felt like I was dreaming.

I had good ideas, but musically a lot of them weren't right. They needed fixing and Don was the doctor. He was a guitar player, but he was also a well-rounded musician and like a lot of the other A&R directors he could pretty much do everything. Writing, arranging, figuring out the chords and the voicings. The voicings, you know, come about when you're thinking of an arrangement—it's the way you put a song across. Every professional knows instinctively where to take the basic track they've heard played on a piano with just a rough vocal sung by the songwriter on a demo.

That's when you start laying it out, figuring out at what moment the strings could come in. The horns, are there going to be backup singers? That's an art, to come in and know how to arrange a song, to reinforce the emotional tilt but still stay out of the singer's way. They don't write like that today, believe me. Don had a lot of heart and soul, along with good commercial sense. When we sat down and did "Diana," it was as if the song I heard in my head came leaping to life out of that simple calypso melody I'd played on the piano. Costa and Nelson Riddle, and many like them are the unsung heroes of the music business.

Michael Jackson was a classic example of a songwriter who began with very basic ideas. He was not a great musician, not particularly talented at playing an instrument—piano, guitar, whatever—but he had this great way of singing out the parts so that the arranger could hear the latent potential. Costa was a genius at catching that. He had a fantastic command of creating arrangements. I would get together with him, lay down a feel; I would scat, I'd go *eah-eh-eh da-da-dada,* just to get me to the next verse. That way it all came out so honest, and that direct current was intrinsic to the songs I was writing at the time. Don would take my basic black-and-white scripts and turn them into Technicolor, widescreen little movies. That's where one and one makes three,

Costa was the most instrumental, creative person in my life. I would come to him, we'd sit down at the piano, I'd play my songs to him and try to tell him the sort of sound I heard in my head. I never physically wrote the notes down; I just tried to articulate to him what I felt as best as I could. He was able to pick up on those little hints, capture them, and turn them into orchestrations. By the second year of recording I was writing down notes, coming up with chords.

When Costa heard where I wanted to go stylistically, he'd take the lick and put in a sax and lock it to the guitar line to give it that signature sound. We were all hip as to the necessity of the hook—the hook is the money in the song, the refrain that grabs you and sells it. These are the things that bind a song together, the underlying elements that the listener is only subliminally aware of—but if they aren't there the song doesn't work. In most of these early songs it was either the hook or the intro that grabbed you right off the bat. My whole thing has always been to get the idea out immediately, so every title primarily came off the first line—"Puppy Love," "Put Your Head on My Shoulder," "You Are My Destiny," "Lonely Boy," "My Home Town," etc. That became a bit of a pattern with me because I wanted them to get what the song was about right away.

And I was a kid. When you're unsophisticated, your expression is raw, raw but pure. I wasn't afraid to sing "This is not a puppy love" or "I'm just a lonely boy." Those were natural things that most guys felt at that age, but I could put them into words. And that was really the backbone of my early songs and that has been my approach to songwriting through the years . . . continuing to just say what I felt, how I felt about it, and the dilemma of being out of place, not getting the girl—the pain and ecstasy of love.

Don would sit down with me and say, "What are we hearing here, Paul, what do you think we should do in the bridge? He was always thinking ahead. The innovations he developed out of my homemade songs were kind of revolutionary. To do what he did on "You Are My Destiny," make a pop song into a swelling operatic number with strings, girl backup singers, and a big band sound behind it, was out there. He made this little pop song sound like an aria from Verdi or Puccini.

Don always knew where we were going and with what instruments, but he never overwhelmed me; he would create pockets, comfort zones for me to lay in my vocal. I would have ideas, suggestions, licks, but basically it was all him.

Like "Lonely Boy" and it's *a-a-a-a*: Don took it and really framed it ingeniously. "Lonely Boy" was a bit doubtful in the beginning. We had to strip it down piece by piece and rebuild it, mainly by the arranger and the musicians, ingenious mechanics who tinker with a song and make it run. Those are the guys! Look at Sinatra, at Presley, all of them—there's always that brilliant arranger involved, finessing, amplifying. I was very fortunate to have somebody like that in my corner. The managers, the agents are different, they're like those little fish sucking off the big sharks; and they come in later. Very few of them start out with the artist and really put their balls on the line. Costa was the guy who made it happen, who brought everybody else to the table. And that was such an important spoke in the wheel. It doesn't matter how great a songwriter you are, your songs are not going to work without the framework of a great arranger. Those are the guys who know the notes, the voicings, the orchestration. It's a hell of a feat: to sit down with a melody and a sketch of a lyric, and know which note goes where and how to voice it and what triad you want to use where. It takes talent and long, long hours and when it's brilliantly done nobody knows you did it—the artist gets all the credit. But without that critical group of musicians improvising with head arrangements it would never have come off as spectacularly as it does.

Don Costa was about five-foot-seven, balding, always heavier than he should have been, very much a Francis Ford Coppola–type Italian. He carried himself in a very natural way, instead of the pseudo way of so many other producers. My great, gray Don. At the end he grew a beard, and the gray beard and the goatee were his thing—"the look."

Not very contemporary, but timeless. Which is funny, 'cause that man did have an incredible sense of time—and a sense of humor.

What a guy! Incredibly talented, genius arranger, a man with great A&R ears, and one of the warmest individuals ever. It's all about making hit records and Costa was one of those guys who could spot talent, even a talent as crude and unshaped as mine when we first met. Right from the first to the end, we were very, very tight. He had everything to do with my making it—there's no way I could ever repay him . . . although I did introduce him to Sinatra! And that led to him producing one of my favorite albums, *Sinatra and Strings.*

Not that we always agreed on everything: Don thought "Don't Gamble with Love" was a surefire single. He thought that "Diana" was just a bit too crude, but I insisted we make "Diana" the A-side. I knew it was gonna be a hit *because* it was so direct and unsophisticated. I even wrote Diana Ayoub and told her so in a letter!

Well, in twenty hours I'll be releasing my new record. I helped pick out the instruments and the feel and all the arrangements are great! You want me to tell you what it's called? "Diana"! It's favored as the hit record by everyone, they said it is a different sound and it'll be the one. Now listen, don't say a word or I'll . . . I'll just kiss you if it sells, because you started it.

Well, it didn't happen quite as overnight as I'd written to her. It took a few weeks before they were ready to record it. "Diana" with "Don't Gamble with Love" on the B-side, was recorded in May 1957 with four musicians: Bucky Pizzarelli on guitar, Irving Wexler on piano, Panama Francis on drums, Jerry Bruno on bass. Plus six backup singers, three women and three men.

When Don Costa figured out how to orchestrate arrangements for my songs he began to apply the same method to other singers. Carole King had a contract with ABC-Paramount records. She worked with Costa, and some of her early stuff sounded a little like my records—

that was the sound that Don Costa knew how to create. He also produced Lloyd Price and Steve and Eydie—Steve Lawrence and Eydie Gormé (aka Sidney Leibowitz and Edith Gormezano).

"Diana," with "Don't Gamble with Love" on the B-side was released in July 1957. Both songs got play, but eventually it went right over to "Diana." It was on its way to selling a million copies by mid-summer, the week after my sixteenth birthday! I was on my way down to Philly to do *American Bandstand* with Dick Clark when I heard it on the radio. There's nothing in this world like hearing your first hit on three different radio stations as you're driving down the highway.

Dick Clark's *American Bandstand* was the show that broke everything. He was the key back then; the kids all watched him. He was it: the all-American boy-next-door, very friendly, very different from the other disc jockeys. Not that old razzmatazz approach. He felt like part of your family, rather than a deejay. Always looked that young, which was a spooky thing. It was like he had a painting in the attic. . . . He wasn't gruff, wasn't like a lot of the other people in the industry, just a very straight-ahead business kind of guy, always a gentleman—that's why I continued to work with him.

Dick was close to that whole Philadelphia group—Fabian, Frankie Avalon, Bobby Rydell, and James Darren. Those kids from Philly. The guy behind the Philadelphia sound was Bob Marcucci along with his partner, arranger and songwriter Pete DeAngelis. After I broke out, it allowed a whole different kind of crowd to come in. Marcucci was the subject of the movie *The Idolmaker,* starring Ray Sharkey. I was a consultant on that film and spent a lot of time with Ray (who played Marcucci). We became friends, I continued to see him from time to time. In the early '90s he was diagnosed with AIDS and died in 1993.

When a single came out in those days the record companies sent advance copies out to all the radio stations. Then you made the rounds: you'd go stop by the local deejays around the country, do their hops, and if it caught on you'd have a hit record within two weeks. You'd literally leave the studio, take this tape, get a piece of vinyl made with the song on it, a rough test pressing, and they'd ship it out to disc jockeys and you'd follow up with personal appearances at the radio stations. Your whole life, your whole career depended on a piece of wax you made in ten, fifteen minutes. Cheap acetate demos became essential when you were trying to sell a demo because often the producers, record company guys, and especially the artists, couldn't read music. People still don't comprehend all the acts or new artists I work with, they just can't understand that we had to walk into a room and stand there and get that performance all in that moment—that's a tough thing to do.

In the beginning people would sometimes confuse me with Neil Sedaka partly because we both came from Middle Eastern backgrounds. But Sedaka was a completely different animal. I'm an autobiographical songwriter—even when I'm writing songs for other people. Sedaka's a craftsman, a Brill Building–type songwriter. Part of Sedaka's magpie talent was that he could rewrite songs sideways, and change the chords of the song even as he was listening to it. They say "Stupid Cupid" was partly based on Jerry Lee Lewis's "Great Balls of Fire"—though I can't see it. Sedaka was so quick and adept, he once wrote a song based on pages from Connie Francis's diary! And he worked with a brilliant lyricist Howie Greenfield.

At that time, the writer/performer had not really emerged within the pop scene—it wasn't until the 1960s when The Beatles came along that that all changed. Until then there were only a handful of singers writing and performing our own material. Presley, like many other pop singers, was using other people's material. Leiber and Stoller and Doc Pomus were among the few writers who were creating hip pop songs at the time. The record industry was focused on the USA; everything came out of the States. It hadn't yet spread internationally. England didn't have its own scene until the 1960s—up until then British singers were using American music. The big stars in England at the time were Tommy Steele (a kind of Brit Elvis), who became famous covering the American hit, "Singing the Blues," and Cliff Richard who covered Lionel Bart's "Living Doll."

"Diana" was number one in England before it reached the top in the USA. It became a worldwide hit by September 6. I always felt "Diana" had such a big international appeal because of its Semitic melody line. The way I sang and wrote those early songs got an instantaneous worldwide reception—from Mexico to the Middle East to Japan— because they were in a minor key and people around the world could relate to that. Everyone recognizes the minor key; it's the way all cultures moan out their troubles from the blues to Inca flute melodies.

That was the secret ingredient in Cole Porter, you know—most of his songs are in minor key and that's what makes them so attractive. But Cole Porter was a very sophisticated songwriter—maybe the most sophisticated writer of lyrics ever with songs like "Night and Day," "I Get a Kick Out of You," and "I've Got You Under My Skin." But what I did in my form of singing was to fuse a minor key melody to gut, honest emotions—which I spelled out in romantic semaphore.

I had this talent for stupid little teenage songs at a moment in time when teenagers wanted to hear simple little teenage songs. I was a lonely boy and I knew there were plenty of us out there—I'd see other lonely boys at the hops I'd play. Put your head on my shoulder—that was your objective that weekend . . . plus maybe getting a kiss and your hand in her blouse. All that I understood only too literally by the mere fact that I *was* a teenager. I was going through all these emotions myself. I didn't second-guess, I didn't try to be clever. What I was writing and performing was just an unabashed teenage lament. All of that early stuff was intensely personal, drawing from what I knew, which was pretty basic.

As soon as "Diana" became a hit, stories began to circulate about how it came to be written. They printed endlessly that my teen crush Diana Ayoub had been my babysitter. I just got tired of stomping out that fire so I let it live. It was a cute little story. That was the fifties. If you were a sixteen-year-old boy, you only dated a girl younger than you. The opposite situation was just taboo in those days. And Diana wasn't just older than me, she was much more sophisticated. You know how girls are—even back then teenage girls were a lot more grown-up, more grounded. Guys are still immature at that age. And that was me. The three-year difference in our ages made romance impossible. The only way to declare myself was through that song.

My limitations were my greatest asset. Out of necessity or ignorance, nothing I did came out contrived or manufactured. All my songs back then were a composite of things I really felt myself and I decanted them directly into primitive adolescent songwriting. What else would kids my age want to hear?

I was a teenager writing for other teenagers—and however simplistic that was, it was new, appealing, and kind of sexy in a teenage way. "You and I will be as free, as the birds up in the tree, o please stay by me, Diana."

The pop music business was just beginning to grow; there were a limited amount of record studios, record labels. People were wondering what the next decade would bring and here was this kid who almost by default was hitting all the right buttons and kids are relating to him. Not long after I hit, the Avalons, the Fabians came along— groomed by the Marcucci-DeAngelis Chancellor Records stable. We really were a clergyman's answer to rock 'n' roll: we "white-ified" it. But back then, just to get an idea for a song was a major achievement; to get it recorded and on the radio was out of this world. We were part of that second wave of rock 'n' roll that was about to hit. As the first white kid singer-songwriter, I became the unlikely model for a type that soon became extremely popular: the teen idol. Being short, Semitic, not exactly in the mold of the current matinee idol, I was a most improbable candidate for this role. But I made it in spite of all that— maybe even because of it.

The Frankie Avalons and the Fabians of course had people writing for them, but because I was actually going through the stuff I was writing about there was no guesswork about how teenagers would react to my songs. I *was* one. Every generation is going to have its own needs, its own flock of screaming teenagers. A lot of people in the business are going to scratch their heads and not be able to get what's going on. But this was my time. I may not have been the best at any one thing, but somehow the package came together: writer, performer, the right age, the look and that was it.

When "Diana" went to number one in the USA in September, a month after my sixteenth birthday, I found myself all of a sudden booked on *The Ed Sullivan Show*! Aside from *American Bandstand* all we watched back then was *The Ed Sullivan Show*. Sure, there were other shows—*Milton Berle, I Love Lucy, Howdy Doody*—but *The Ed Sullivan Show* was the thing. One minute I was sitting there as a fan and then, all of a sudden, I was going to be on it. I was scared to death.

I had to fly into New York from wherever we were on tour, Pittsburgh I think it was. Originally, *The Ed Sullivan Show* had been filmed in this little studio where David Letterman is now, but for some reason they moved it to Madison Square Garden and I didn't find that out until I got there. So there I was, rehearsing in this *huge* space. The band is *way* the hell over on one side and I'm *way* the hell over on the other side—not intimate at all. This was only my second time on national television in the U.S. and I'm, like, "Shit!"

Also I'm singing live, unlike *American Bandstand* and shows today where they play the tracks and you're lip-synching to the band. It was a very weird situation: you'd have a hit record that you'd cut in mono in a studio with simpatico musicians and then you'd have to sing it with a band that not only *hated* the music, but were simulating the instruments on the record—a sax and a trumpet, a guitar—with an orchestra. The sound had nothing to do with what was on the record. You're standing there live and you *know* it's live so you can't stop and go back and start over again. I remember walking in there and going, "Shit, I've got to just stay focused as I can, 'cause I don't know how I'm gonna get through this!"

And Ed Sullivan? Stiff, unusual-looking guy, big jaw, but stylish, always a custom-made shirt and tie, sharkskin suit, which kind of hung weirdly on his shoulders. You never felt relaxed when you talked to him. He remained a columnist at heart; they put him in the position of being an emcee but he was never at ease with it. It was a tough gig for him. He was very uptight, an odd, almost Frankenstein-like character—big, with this funny pronunciation. Head too big for his body. A truly strange guy to be an emcee. Emcees usually are, "Al*right,* and here . . . they . . . are!" As if you're about to hear the greatest band on earth. Ed often sounded almost embarrassed and he never got all the names right. That was Ed. It was like one of those movies where the wrong guy gets shoved on stage and has to ad lib. But he was always a gentleman.

"Diana" entered the charts in July and stayed there for eighteen weeks, replacing Debbie Reynolds's "Tammy," which was number one at the time. I think "Diana" was initially a bigger R&B record than it was a pop record. That's how my future manager Irv Feld, who produced the The Biggest Show of Stars, knew it was going to be huge—because he sold R&B records at his drugstores in Washington. He had the superstores right in the middle of Rhythm & Blues Alley, you know, and they would come in and whatever they were buying, whoever the hits were to the largest amount of audience, then he would know who to book for his tours—all on account of his drugstores!

He'd put speakers in the windows and play the new records as they came out to attract customers. Soon the music part of the business became bigger than the drugstore or the soda fountain, so over time he converted it to a music store. Eventually he had three record stores in Washington—the first record-store chain in the U.S.

At that time there were only a few record companies—a little like today with the three or four multinational conglomerates—but back then everything was still simple and not very sophisticated.

The record companies would send Irv demos, "white copies" they were called, 45s with the big hole in the middle. At home Irv would play them and ask his son Kenny and his friends and, eventually, me, too. "So what do you think about this one?" It was a kind of kitchen-table market research. Irv would say, "Okay, this one's going to be a hit—let's buy it cheap now." Then he plunged right into show business.

Started these Show of Shows tours around the country. When he found a record he liked or it became a hit he would book that act—at first the artists were mainly black R&B performers—on his Biggest Show of Stars tours. And that was the case with me. Irv received a copy of "Diana," played it in the office for his brother Izzy and his partner Allen Bloom. He'd thrown me out of the Biggest Show of Stars for 1956 spring show at the Ottawa Auditorium, the big hockey arena, the year before when I had snuck backstage.

Irv was a little guy, about five-seven, very slight, thin, with curly sparse hair and thick glasses. Very brainy, very smart, always cooking something up. To this day he's seen as one of the smartest guys in the industry and revered by people in the business as an innovator and far-sighted thinker. He met a lot of people, what have you, and they'd give him their numbers and he'd keep all these pieces of paper in his pocket. When he'd get back to Washington, he'd take them out and review where he'd been and who he'd met.

On the other hand, Al Bloom was a big, husky guy with a Roman-esque nose, piercing eyes, who looked like a bouncer and tried to pull off the tough-guy act, but wasn't. More of a businessman type.

Anyway, Feld and his brother Izzy and Al Bloom would sit around and listen to stuff. Irv had a hunch about "Diana." He had a great ear for talent, and he was real good at that, which was surprising because you wouldn't have pegged him as a pop music fan. But he must have heard something he liked because he signed me to go on one of his tours, much to the objection of Al and his brother Izzy. They were looking for a new act for their *Show of Shows*. Al and Izzy wanted this guy named Teddy Randazzo, who composed a bunch of classic pop songs such as "Goin' Out of My Head," "It's Gonna Take a Miracle," and "Hurt So Bad." Remember Teddy? He had some kind of a record out at the time that was doing well. But Irv was the boss and he stuck with his decision to take me on the tour.

With Irv, it was all about business, but he was not the tough kind of guy you'd expect to find in the rough-and-ready rock 'n' roll scene. It's just that his ability to pick talent was uncanny, he had great timing, and he was a lot more honest than most of the managers around today. Irv knew "Diana" had the sizzle. He was the packager for the rock 'n' roll shows, he was *the guy*. He had an alliance with Buddy Howe at my agency, the General Artists Corporation.

Irv used to pick the show's stars. I honestly think Dick Clark learned a lot from him. All Irv ever did was see what the blacks were buying in his stores and those were the acts he'd pick for his rock 'n' roll tours. He'd invite around fifteen acts to go on the road, whoever was hot. He told me he'd kept my number from that show in Ottawa, but he probably didn't know who the hell I was until I walked into his office.

He calls my house that July and says he wants to speak to my father, Andy, about getting permission for me to go on the Biggest Show of Stars tour that fall.

I handed the phone to my dad, who was reluctant at first. He reminded Feld that I was very young and still in high school. He was worried about sending me out on the road alone; he didn't want his son running all over creation with strangers. But he didn't want to stand in my way, either—he knew how desperately I wanted to be a part of it. It was a tough sell for Irv—it took a few phone calls—but in the end he convinced my father to let me join the tour. This was what I had been waiting for all my life.

The tour started the first week of September in New York at the Paramount Theatre and continued into late November, a three-month tour that ended up at the Mosque in Richmond, Virginia, on November 24. Before I knew it, I was rehearsing with The Drifters, Clyde McPhatter, The Everly Brothers, Frankie Lymon and The Teenagers, LaVern Baker, Buddy Holly and The Crickets, and Chuck Berry. A year before I'd been in Berry's dressing room, pitching "Diana," and he'd almost thrown me out, telling me not to quit my day job. Now "Diana" was number one in the country.

I was scared to death about being in the company of these stars. I tried to fit in as best I could with the other performers who were all older than me. I was trying to stay cool and confident, but, of course, many of the singers misunderstood and thought I was an arrogant little twit.

My dad negotiated with Irv how I would be treated on these tours. He was very nervous about the kind of situation I was being thrown into. I was very young; the other acts on the tour were much older and seasoned performers. I had no idea what I was getting into. Irv assured my dad that I would travel with him by plane. But occasionally I wanted to hang out with the other performers—most of them, after all were my idols—so I'd ask to get on the bus with all the other acts. I was the youngest member of the group, traveling with all these guys who were already living legends: Chuck Berry, Fats Domino, The Drifters, Buddy Holly, The Everly Brothers. As the tour began, the first people I got close to were The Everly Brothers, Fats Domino, and LaVern Baker.

The tickets were $2.50 a piece for something like twenty acts, plus a movie. But, aside from Irv's tours there were no other venues that had any validity. It was Irv Feld's concept—he started it, he invented it. And that was it, aside from the occasional high school auditorium or a DJ record hop. When we played at the Paramount Theatre in New York I'd start singing at 9 in the morning, then there would be a movie. Then I would perform five or six more times a day with the movie in between. We would go out for eighty to ninety days. The other acts on the tours became your extended family. Cramer was this cute little guy with a bum leg, who brought you on stage and brought you off. There was a band leader, Paul Williams, and Harold the stage manager, and that was it, aside from Irv and Al Bloom.

What was it like being on the road and away from my family for long periods of time? There was the excitement of being with the other stars, the thrill of performing, of course, but there was also the other side to it, the pain of being separated from my family. Many of the performers were young but except for Frankie Lymon, few were actual teenagers like myself. It's as a teenager that you first begin to figure out who you are—and you need your parents for that, even if it involves rebelling against them as most teenagers do.

Later on, when Fabian, Bobby Rydell, Frankie Avalon, and all those guys came on the tours, they were very competitive with me, always battling for who was the greatest, who was going to end up on top. Clyde McPhatter, who had been the lead singer of The Drifters, was also managed by Irv and he was *insanely* jealous of me and my success. He was a bitter, angry guy for someone who sang such sweet songs. The turnover of records on the Top Ten was incredible. A new record from a major star would come out every four weeks, unlike today when rock stars will take a year—three years—to make a record.

I guess I was precocious and bratty enough to get people's hackles up. I used to stick it to everybody on the bus, telling them "*Nyah, nyah, be seein' ya! I'm going on the plane tomorrow, suckers!*"

It wasn't so much shoving it in their faces—though that had its own sweet reward for me—it was more that sense of feeling different. I was younger than everyone else. My white middle-class background was different from that of the older black performers; I was even different from the Southern guitar-slinging white boys, Buddy Holly and Eddie Cochran. And I guess I did have a cockiness about me, I was pretty damn sure of myself—had to be, to survive in that atmosphere. I've also always gotten a kick out of practical jokes. Not everybody, however, shared my enthusiasm for pranks.

Because I was so precocious and cheeky, the tables were soon turned on me. They were itching to give it to me because I was an irritant, just by being who I was, by being younger, writing my own songs, not being part of that wild, drinking, Southern group. And I had a big hit no one my age had a right to have. I think we were in Moscow, Idaho, at a university when all the performers on that tour came to Al Bloom and said they wanted to take me downstairs to the basement after the show and tar and feather me. As an initiation thing, right? They weren't going to use real tar—it was just cold cream and all that. It was all spearheaded by LaVern Baker—she was a real loud character: outgoing, sexy, experienced, a jokester, and the ringleader of everything. Like Big Mama, you know? They all knew of my closeness to her, and that I'd go along with anything she said, but first they went to Allen and Irv and told him they were going to do it. Irv apparently flipped out. "What are you, crazy? What if the kid has a heart condition?" So they talked me through it, and I think Allen came to me before the initiation and said, "Something's gonna happen tonight. Don't worry, it's an age-old tradition in show business, after the show, your last number, I'm gonna take you downstairs and they're gonna . . . tar and feather you." "They're going to do *what*?" "Well, Paul, you see they were planning to surprise you, but I just wanted you to be aware of it, so that you don't panic when it happens, blah blah blah." So after the show some of the kids dragged me down to the basement, stripped off my clothes right down to my underwear, and then they started lathering me all over with this dark cold cream and sticking feathers on it. Everyone was laughing at the miserable, pitiable expression on my face. They had a real good time socking it to me.

After I'd gotten what was coming to me, the tour settled down to a normal routine and everybody got along great. And after that I wasn't so aloof or stuck up, thinking I was better or different than them. But can you imagine that nobody took a goddamn picture of it?

I remember opening night at a show at the Syria Mosque in Pittsburgh, where some of the performers showed up completely unprepared. All they brought with them was their record to play to. The band had to scribble some notes down on their lead sheets and improvise as best they could with these singers. Not me. I came in with all my music and charts. It was all copied, very neat, organized, and professional-looking. I came with my music for my three songs, "Down by the Riverside," "Diana," and "Don't Gamble with Love."

Even though I was sixteen years old and the youngest on the tour, I was totally prepared for each performance. I have a strong work ethic, always have. I'm very fastidious—all my music has to be laid out beforehand, the arrangements neat and clean. If there were any mistakes,

I had them copied over. Something was always driving me to stay on top of things. I would walk in to a session and say, "Take it from the top." You know the band would look up and say to themselves, "Who *is* this kid? Is he an alien?"

You can see a bit of the Anka alien in the film *Lonely Boy,* the 1962 documentary about me directed by Roman Kroitor and Wolf Koenig, especially in that scene in the station wagon where I'm sitting there, totally cool, calm, and collected, affectless with people yapping away all around me. It's an odd scene for somebody all of twenty-one, even I have to admit—but if I hadn't had that kind of self-control I'd never have made it.

As brash and sure of myself as I was offstage, with my audience I was always humble and sincere—with them I could unabashedly express my most heartfelt emotions. I identified with them. They were me, in a sense, magnified through music. That was the difference between Bobby Darin and me. I had an abundance of feelings for my audience . . . and treated them like a lover wooing his main squeeze. Darin didn't care to project that kind of warmth. He came off as aloof and arrogant—he was trying to do the Sinatra thing—which was his way of interpreting Rat Pack cool. We were different in that way on stage, but offstage we were both very cocky and self-confident.

On tour I was pretty much by myself on stage and off. I would couple up with The Crickets and Buddy Holly, but when I performed by myself, it would be just me, a band leader, a drummer, the piano player, plus my pick of the in-house orchestra. In the beginning, my group consisted of Irv, a couple of musicians, and my cousin Bob Skaff, one of the biggest guys in the promotion business and my close friend up until he died in 2012. And that was the whole group. It evolved into a bigger unit in '58 and '59 when I put my own band together. I was never much for excess people, the glam brigade and all that stuff. I had just what I needed around me and that was it. I never wanted a bunch of people buzzing about, confusing me or kissing my ass. I just stuck with the necessities, people I needed to do certain things, and that's the way it was for a while.

Touring was tough. Real tough. Not like it is today. It was literally an era when you could get into the Top 20 on the *Billboard* chart, and next day you'd be on a bus traveling eight, nine, ten, twelve hours to your next gig. Star treatment for pop singers was nonexistent. And once you get into this trip, you have no friends outside of show biz. These guys were your friends, and you weren't going to get any special treatment from them. The first thing you learned was to fail onstage. You learned a lot more from your failure than from your success. In an industry that was just starting out you could fall flat on your face in Frozen Sneakers, Ohio, and there wouldn't be any critics there to record it.

While on tour I stayed in touch, but leaving my family behind was painful. I was constantly worrying about my mother's diabetes. I would always be checking with my brother and sister and my dad to see how her health was at this point or that, frequently calling home to see how she was doing, how she was feeling. The realization that I could lose her was devastating. This was the woman who sat with me so many afternoons as I tried out my songs on her, who had encouraged me from the start when there was only the first glimmer that I might have some talent in this department. She gave me unqualified support, urging me on. "Paul, you can really do this, you are that talented, you are going to go places." My mother always deflecting my father's doubts about my pursuing this stuff. My dad was a wonderful person but like any parent—or any sensible adult, actually—he was concerned I was getting carried away by my fantasy world. It was my mom who saw my vision and believed in it. She gave me her unqualified love. This is the woman whom I lived for, for her approval and encouragement. As my mother's diabetes got worse, she would have accidents, at one point blacking out and crashing her car into a tree. I remember one devastating time calling home and my dad telling me that medical conditions arising from my mother's diabetes were getting worse and worse, that her eyesight was deteriorating. My mother was the glue for me until the day she died, when I was eighteen and out of town touring.

—■—

No pop or rock stars today would stand for what we put up with on those buses. The condition of those buses was *horrible*. There were two of them: one of the buses was for the band and the other for the tech people. These buses today, with the bathrooms, DVD players, and beds, didn't exist. I can remember clearly the time when we broke down in the cold in some godforsaken spot. I'm freezing my ass off up in the luggage rack with a blanket. It was the pits.

Then, after you'd sit there on the bus for hours on end, looking at cornfields, you'd get to a broken-down theater where you'd line up next to each other in the crummy dressing rooms with your pomade and your hair dryer to get the hair just right, hang your suits in the shower to steam them out. It was hard work, but we had nothing to compare it to. It was a pleasure just to be there because we were earning a little money, everyone was friendly and there weren't a lot of ego clashes, which is odd considering half of us were teenage hot shots. We knew we were a part of this special little group that was just starting to break out. In the beginning only a bunch of teenagers embraced us. I went straight from delivering papers for three dollars a week to getting on the bus with guys whose music I loved and being paid $300 a week with the number one record in the country. And loving it! What did I know back then? The conditions on the tours were the absolute worst, but you learned to live with it, you had to be philosophical about it, or it would drive you crazy.

The key guys on those early tours were Fats Domino and Chuck Berry. They were kings. They didn't travel on the bus, they followed us in their Cadillacs.

Fats was a humorous guy, who'd been doing this stuff since 1949. Nothing fazed him, he made a joke out of everything—and he liked his liquor and pigs trotters. He and Chuck were the "Big Daddys," the guys you went to for advice. They were colorful, legendary guys.

When we would leave a town, we'd get on the buses and Fats and Chuck would pile into their Cadillacs. To this day, Chuck wants a Cadillac waiting for him at the airport and demands to be paid in cash. He hires a pickup band when he gets there and when the show's over he is gone. That's his whole thing. He used to carry his own guitar into whatever gig he was playing. Didn't bring a band with him, he'd just hire one in the town he was playing. Chuck was a funny, moody guy. You would go backstage and talk with him and it was like he was your best friend and then the next day, he would be sullen and uncommunicative.

These rock 'n' roll tours would run as long as eighty days, we'd do as many as seventy cities—nobody got any sleep. We were kids, everybody was grateful for the fact that we were getting three or four hundred bucks a week. In a sense we were in that unspoiled period before stars began making ludicrous sets of demands. Today you can't get some of these people to go to work for two million dollars. Back then you were running on fumes and excitement—not that you weren't tired, not that you weren't pissed off, but it was a lot of money for us and then when the camaraderie of being together as a family sunk in, you felt you were part of a team. In most cases, whatever the conditions were, we were just happy to be out of our neighborhoods, our environments. Instead of griping we looked at the big picture: we were having a lot of fun together, traveling to cities we'd never been to before, making music, getting all that adulation from the fans.

To our own core group we were *it,* we were getting written about, photographed everywhere we went, called heartthrobs, screamed at by hordes of young girls. What could be bad about that? Radio played our stuff all the time. We were the Top 20. Sure we complained when the buses broke down, bitched about the lousy food, the flea-bag hotels, but mostly we just accepted it as part of the deal and knew that if we made too much of a fuss we wouldn't be asked to be on the next tour.

We'd even get bilked on the bus. There'd be Otis Redding in the back or James Brown selling chocolate bars, candy, and Coke for three, four, and five dollars, stuff you could buy in stores for twenty cents?! I remember later on being in Paris on tour. Otis was singing at the Olympia Theatre and he wanted to buy some diamonds, so Bruno Coquatrix, the owner of the Olympia, says, "Why, yes, of course, Monsieur Redding, we take you over to Harry Winston and you pick something very fine, yes?" Bruno is this big guy with a little pencil-thin moustache, impeccably dressed, a connoisseur of wine, women, food—Mr. France. So Bruno, Otis, and I went over to Harry Winston's. "What is it that we might interest you with this afternoon, Monsieur Redding?" To which Otis, with great panache, says, "Aw, just show me your *latest* diamonds!"

"It was a golden age of camaraderie," as Phil Everly would say. "Everybody was so young, so thrilled to be part of it all. It was like being in a fraternity. It only lasted about three years before everybody got too big to work together. But many of us who are still around keep in touch, and it's so great to know someone a whole lifetime."

The tours were long and tiresome. The average sleep you got was fifteen to twenty hours a week. We played all-night poker games to pass the time. At first I didn't participate, but then as time went on, boredom set in. It was better than looking at your reflection in the bus window. You'd try and sleep, you'd take the instruments out and have jam sessions—not much more to do than that. Other than that, we were just resting up, anxious to get to the next gig, and in most cases if it wasn't the hotel, you'd go straight to the arena and set up. We only did two songs each. The stars of the show would do maybe three or four.

It was as if a curtain went up and suddenly there I was with all my idols, these larger-than-life characters. I'm on the tour with Fats Domino. Fats was exactly like you would imagine. To be hanging out with Fats Domino was a dream come true. I just loved his music and he was a real lovable guy. I couldn't believe him (and he couldn't believe me, either). He remembers when he first saw this cheeky little kid sneaking into his dressing room to get an autograph, and when he saw me again, he said, "Hey, little Paulie, I'm so proud of you, little Paulie." Once I was in, I was finally behind the scenes, in the trenches, seeing how everything works (or *doesn't* work). The one indelible picture I have of Fats was before he'd go on. Because of his deviated septum, two of his aides would pick him up by his ankles and hold him upside down, then another one would come along and put Neo-Synephrine in each of his nostrils to open up his airways. Then they'd prop him back up again. When I saw that, I said to myself, "Man, I've really made it. I'm on the inside of the in-crowd. Look at this: my idol, upside-down!" As he's standing there, seriously, going "Oh, thank you so much," I'm looking at him, he's looking at me, 'cause I don't want to make fun of the guy, this is my hero, one of *them*. So that was the first thing I learned after getting on the road: open that nose up every night. Funny. Fats's eyes were big and glossy, everything about him was supersize. These guys already had a big body of work by the time I got there—and they virtually invented rock 'n' roll. You're sitting there in the wings, watching it, getting off on it, still pinching yourself that this is all really happening to you. I'm one song deep with "Diana" and I don't even know what I'm going to do next—I think we were still doing shit that I did with the Bobby Soxers for the first year. You watch Fats, Chuck . . . These guys had an arm's length of a head start by the time I came on the scene. I'm still checking out how it's done because nobody choreographed moves like the black acts.

The black acts always had great names: The Royals, The Drifters, The Miracles, The Majestics. The Anglos had all these demeaning names like The Crickets, The Spiders, The Beatles, The Animals, The Zombies. None of them had a name that would generate any respect. What were they thinking? Reverse pride, I guess.

Cool clothes—on and off stage—were an absolute necessity: your shiny, sleek body armor, your second skin. The first buck you got went to get that custom-made shirt, the suits, and the perfect tie. We wanted to dress elegantly—you had that one suit that you protected with your life. Your focus in the beginning was to buy clothes you couldn't afford. You had to have the high collar, so you'd go down to Sy Devore's, the suit and shirtmaker in Los Angeles. Slowly my fashion sense evolved. I became very alert; dressing in cool threads was an absolute necessity. When I was a kid I went to a guy in New York, Lew Magram, or to Nat Wise on the West Coast. I'm small enough that even as an adult I would go to the Saks kids' department to get clothes. I needed the custom-made look, because the other stuff didn't look good on me. We all became very aware of carrying ourselves that way. French shirts, Italian suits, gold cufflinks.

Bobby Darin and I, we used to all talk about clothes all the time. What it came down to was emulation of the Rat Pack. As kids we looked at them and said, "We wanna be like those guys." They were always immaculately well dressed, coiffed out to the max and done up. We knew they were the coolest, suavest cats on the planet and that was the look we had to get. Bobby Darin idolized Sinatra, although his first song, "Splish Splash," was one song that Sinatra would never have been caught dead singing—especially in a bath tub the way Bobby did it on TV.

People tend to forget that when I started out, hard rock hadn't hit yet. The Beatles hadn't hit, so it was up to me and Darin to find a way to reinvent ourselves. What we came up with was, "We gotta be like those guys—Sinatra, Sammy Davis—put on that tux, do those cool Rat Pack songs. We gotta gotta gotta." That's what we kept telling each other. That was our whole motivation back then: "We've got to Sinatra-size ourselves—or we're dead."

I was always in a suit, a shirt, and a tie. You look at all of my older photos, the historical stuff, and I'm pretty much in the same Rat Pack junior outfit, always kind of the same thing—dressed to the nines as I stepped out the door. Lights, camera, action and I'd be ready. Every now and then I'd get a white suit or a casual outfit. Then there was the "at home" look. Back then, for all of us, the teen idols, Frankie Avalon,

Fabian, it was sweaters for the relaxed photo shoot. Then shirts and ties for most of the group shots, everybody on the rock 'n' roll package dolled up like we're going to a wedding. Chuck Berry had his own look, even Fats: tuxedo, bow tie, maybe a blue sequin jacket. They were all up for the colors and the other flashy stuff. It was really something when they piled off that bus, climbed out of their Cadillacs, and into those backstage areas. The locals at most places we played had never seen anything like us—it was like the circus coming to town.

Backstage, it was a riot to see us all lined up, working on our hairdos. Hair was the next big priority—it had to be flattened, straightened, and sculpted. I don't know how we didn't blow the electricity with all those hair dryers going at the same time and the pomade—it was unbelievable. Everybody with the goddamn pomade and hair dryers! *Wooowoooo.* The comb doing the do. Ducktails, flips, pompadours.

On stage James Brown seemed like a wild man, but everything had to be perfect, offstage and on. Shoes shined, suits pressed, hairdos duded up to the copacetic nth degree. He'd fine the band if they played a wrong note. He'd fine them if they forgot shirts, shoes unlaced, if they swore. And I feel the same way! When one of Brown's bands started to complain he just got rid of them in the middle of a tour and had another one sent out from Cincinnati. It was like boot camp. He was tough on his guys. We always had the Sam Taylor band on those tours, an all-black orchestra—Sam Taylor and Paul Williams were the two band leaders.

Little Richard, on the other hand, was a hoot on these trips—a real crazy. Full-on crazy shuck 'n' jive talk, dirtiest jokes you ever heard. "Oh my, honey, didn't recognize you with your clothes on! Now, my sound, the Angeltown sound, make the knees freeze, the liver quiver, oweeee!" And then he'd lurch off into one of his possessed raps.

Little Richard, now there's a case in point: He wrote some great songs, but he essentially wrote the same songs four or five times. They were a little repetitious, but no one cared because that was the crazy x-factor of rock 'n' roll. When Richard saw that white singers were trying to cover everything he did he just made his songs faster and faster. His songs got so fast, that Pat Boone couldn't cover them anymore. "Let that Pat Boone in his saddle shoes try to do this one—he'll get his tongue in a twist like it don't exist." It wasn't all that easy whiteifying Little Richard's roller-coaster raps or Fats's gumbo-mumbo, but there was a huge market out there for deracinated rock 'n' roll—and we were there to give it to them.

In the beginning most of the rock 'n' roll artists were black: The Platters, Frankie Lymon, Chuck Berry, The Drifters. Then along came The Everly Brothers, The Crickets, and Frankie Avalon. It kind of fluctuated. For the most part, the white acts were the younger element on these tours. The black acts were mostly older, more experienced, more polished, and professional. They were the older statesmen of rock-and-roll. Then there were the Southern boys: the Everlys, who would merge with Buddy and the Crickets, and Jimmy Bowen, and all that group. And then there was Buddy Knox, another Southern guy, with "Party Doll." It was quite a mix of people.

Eddie Cochran was a typical rock 'n' roll kid from California, but had the same aspects as the Southern guys. He was a quasi-cowboy, a cool cat. He had that swagger about him, the James Dean look. There was a definite attitude to that whole Southern contingent. Not rednecky: it was more that Southern-drawl-hang-out-drinking-beer thing—almost had their own language. They came from their own world, but we still all communicated. Eddie Cochran had his first hit "Sittin' in the Balcony" and then had been in the movie, *The Girl Can't Help It*. He kind of mumbled like Marlon Brando and Dean, and was a hard drinker. Eddie Cochran was fun to be around, a delight. He was a ladies' man, a good-time party guy. You'd think that he was going to be late when his cue came out to go on stage and play; you thought he wouldn't get there on time. Then the door would pop open and there he was. He wore his overcoat in the European style over his shoulders like they do in foreign movies. He'd walk straight through the stage door, drop his coat, and in one full swoop pick up his guitar and walk on stage, never missing a step and being right on time. Buddy was tight with Eddie Cochran. They had a lot in common, except the drinking.

Then there was the Northeastern contingent: Avalon, Bobby Rydell, the Fabian crowd from Philly. All those guys were in the same bag. Very Italian-family-type stuff. The difference between us was that with those guys, the teen idol types, there was always the manager hovering, telling them how to dress, what to say, how to act. The Bob Marcucci–type manager. They were well behaved because they'd had a good upbringing, close-knit families. They had a definite focus on behavior and the look and the Italian upbringing, which was totally the opposite of the Southern boys, where there were no hovering managers and the skies were not cloudy all day. I loved hanging out with them— they were all really warm people, especially Fabian and Frankie Avalon. We've all remained in touch, close friends to this day.

There we were all these different cultures mixing and melding: the older black cats, the groomed Italian *ragazzi*, and the Southern rebel boys—it was our own United States blend. On the bus you could hear people swapping different stories of their backgrounds in the Bronx, or from West Texas.

The conflicts when they erupted would happen between the Southern rock 'n' roll boys, from Buddy Holly to Jimmy Bowen to Jerry Lee Lewis. With these guys, there was a real difference in terms of attitudes and upbringing. A lot more drinking, more volatile, and more opinionated would be a polite way of putting it. Jerry Lee Lewis himself was off the charts. I can't even explain how abusively unpredictable this guy could be. His whole lingo and attitude were redneck obnoxious—it was just nothing like I'd ever seen before. Now we're hip to bad behavior; it's almost a requirement in the movies and the music business these days. But back then it was just off the wall: white trashy spew, that's what it was.

Jerry Lee eventually got raked over the coals by the English press for marrying his thirteen-year-old cousin, but Chuck Berry was the biggest offender in that respect. He wound up in jail at the end of one tour. Buddy Holly was the only one who knew how to deal with Jerry Lee. Buddy was utterly unshockable—the worst that Jerry Lee Lewis could throw at him, Buddy had already heard in gutbucket Texas bars his whole life. Jerry Lee's behavior didn't faze him one bit. He'd fish Jerry Lee, totally soused, out of bars, drag him back to the hotel, put him under the shower, and get him to the theater on time.

But the rest of us didn't frequent bars or hang out or get into that, because we were these clean little white boys who were watched day and night, told what to do and what not to do. We weren't masters of our own destinies—we were just going along with the program.

The Philadelphia pop singers were all of Italian descent—they referred to themselves as "meatballs." Fabian was discovered on a stoop, supposedly. Or anyway that was part of the mythology. Unfortunately, he had no control over his pitch. He just had a basic punkish grunt, but even with his failings as a singer, teens identified with him. Most of his early songs were written by Doc Pomus and Mort Shuman. Then there was Dion DiMucci from the doo-wop streets of New York. He had been in the notorious Fordham Baldies gang and had started using heroin at age fourteen.

Marcucci would look after the Philadelphia boys and Irvin Feld was looking after me. We were given a menu of behavior. For one thing we couldn't take girls up to our rooms. As a seventeen-year-old, you couldn't just invite a girl up from the lobby. Impossible. You'd have to sneak them in, meet them somewhere else. I only started to get adventurous when I got to the continent, in France, parts of South America, and even that was tough (let alone the fact that there were two thousand kids outside your hotel room every day).

One of my first romantic ventures was with an Iberian Airlines stewardess I met going to Chile—a beautiful girl, Jenny, I think her name was. Every time she'd fly in or I'd fly Iberian, we'd hook up. That's usually the way it happened.

Then there was June Wilkinson in Great Britain. She is usually described as a model and actress, but her main claim to fame was her boobs—she had the biggest tits in the world—which is how she got the nickname of "The Bosom" after her first "pictorial" in *Playboy* in September 1958. She was a big, healthy girl with a great sense of humor and huge tits. She was taller than me so I loved to dance with her, her boobs bouncing in my face. They sort of had a life of their own. Later on she was in a bunch of silly films and in the early '70s married NFL quarterback Dan Pastorini. I got introduced to her by Lew and Leslie Grade, British impresarios who began as music hall performers, became superagents and the producers of shows on ITV and on movies like *The Exorcist* and *Sophie's Choice* and the early Muppets movies—with his jowly face and big cigar, Lew was a kind of Muppetish character himself. When I knew them they worked out of a tiny one-room office, straight out of a vaudeville routine. I was the one who brought June Wilkinson to the States—and they were just as crazy about her impressive endowments over here as they were in the UK.

But, hard as it is to believe, it was generally really tough to meet girls, and bring them into the hotels. We'd go to Scandinavia, thousands of kids—they'd sneak in, you'd find them in your closet or under the bed. You never knew how they got in there. They were very adept at watching the doors and hiding in broom closets. One of these Swedish girls who hid under my bed ended up in Vegas as a showgirl.

Fabian was a nice kid, a wonderful guy to hang with, but his career had pretty much been manufactured by Bob Marcucci. We all knew he was an invention because we were with the same label. The guy just didn't have the vocal chops. He wasn't a singer in the true sense, he was a pretty boy. That's what was selling at the time. Being with the same label you knew who had the talent and who didn't. We understood what was happening. We all recorded at the same studios, Bell Sound, and once I saw what seemed like a hundred pieces of tape they'd spliced together to get one good take for him. It was all monaural in those days so it was done with razor blades and tape. To his credit, Fabian admitted he wasn't really a singer—he was very honest about it. We all knew it, but the public didn't and that was the difference.

Frankie Avalon was another sweet guy I really got along with; of all the Philly group we stay in touch. Frankie worked hard on his singing to get through the tapes, but there was no way Fabian could stand there and just sing it straight through. He listened to the management, Bob Marcucci, and the little girls loved him. Was there a future in it? Obviously not.

Now, Bobby Rydell, he was talented, he had a good voice, he could really sing—maybe the most vocally gifted of the Philly lot. He also played the drums, different things. Frankie Avalon played trumpet, too, but Bobby Rydell had the best shot, from my point of view, of really evolving into something. His big problem was he didn't write his own songs. All of those guys—their material was written by others.

Neil Sedaka wasn't part of the Philly crowd. He was strictly a New York cat, a Brill Building kind of guy, who wrote his own stuff, mostly melodies. Howard Greenfield supplied the lyrics. That was the difference between him and me.

People called Bobby Darin obnoxious and arrogant, brash and cocky. Darin's real name was Walden Robert Cassotto. He wasn't exactly a pretty boy. He had the rugged good looks of a bulbous-nosed, crooked-mouthed hood, but still attractive—a John Garfield type. Like me, Bobby sprang from obscurity in 1958 and became famous with a recording of one of his own compositions, a rock 'n' roll ditty called "Splish Splash." Later on he made a hip transition into the adult field with "Mack the Knife," from Kurt Weill's *Threepenny Opera*. Louis Armstrong had made a successful recording of it a few years earlier.

Darin's dad was a hoodlum, but he'd died several months before Bobby was born, so he never knew him. Darin used to say, "I have a chip on my shoulder. Who wouldn't? The only person I loved until I met my wife Sandra Dee last year was my mother, and she died, too." He talked this tough-guy dialogue straight out of the movies. He'd been brought up by his grandmother, a vaudeville singer, and one of the odd things about his childhood was that he only learned years later, at age thirty-two, that Giovannina Cassotto, who he thought was his elder sister, was actually his mother.

Bobby was kind of an acrobat, very agile, and would try anything. I think if the microphone cord had been long enough, he would have climbed the curtains! He was the king of the finger snappers. He picked up the old Sinatra trick of snapping his fingers with sexy innuendo to the beat of the music.

Buddy Holly was an entirely different story. He had a soft shyness about him. Very straightforward kind of guy. I was impressed with his guitar-driven sound and he respected what I did as a songwriter and business-wise. Buddy was aware of me even before his record, "That'll Be the Day," climbed the charts. In the beginning I was Buddy Holly's nemesis. Buddy and I were neck-and-neck all the way with "That'll Be the Day" and "Diana." He'd look at my picture in record-shop windows and say, "Who is this kid Anka, anyway? And who does he think he is, pushing me off the charts?"

Buddy's closest friends on the tours were The Everly Brothers, especially Phil. Phil was very high-strung and fastidious—meticulous, very organized but with a sense of humor. They were all from the South, the Everlys and Buddy, and had both started out in country music. Like me, Buddy wrote his own songs so he wasn't dependent on outside writers like Boudleaux and Felice Bryant, who wrote the Everlys' songs. He also had his own group, The Crickets; he didn't play with pickup bands like the Everlys. We were all buddies, but those guys had that country-western, Southern clique thing going, and at the end of the day were in a bag all of their own.

The difference between me and the Southern boys was that I wasn't a guitar player, I had no idea where all of that was going, that guitar-driven rock sound. But in 1957, who could have guessed what the next wave of rock would be: the group sound with wailing electric guitars. The incredible sound that Buddy got on his guitar was the secret ingredient he passed on to The Beatles and The Rolling Stones—all the

British bands. They were all ultimately disciples of Buddy Holly and Chuck Berry. They were very influential with everybody in the next generation that way. You found that out as time went by and you talked with English musicians that the guitar was the key to the new sound. When we would go to Great Britain, you could see his influence right away, how his guitar-playing style was adopted by the bands over there along with Bo Diddley's and Chuck Berry's.

Buddy was not a sophisticated person at all. He was very raw, simple, modest, and sensitive, a country boy, guided by Norman Petty, his manager, and not unlike a lot of us on tour with our managers. Whether it was Irv Feld or Norman Petty, we were always told to keep it clean. No smoking or drinking or drugs. Buddy was a beer drinker, all the Southern boys were, but it was not something you would see very often out in the open.

In the beginning we all used to tease Buddy about the dopey glasses he wore when we first went on tour together. We talked him into wearing the big black glasses that became his trademark. Buddy liked the way the Everlys dressed—they always looked very natty in their Brooks Brothers suits, that three-button British look. As soon as Buddy hit New York he went straight to Brooks Brothers.

Buddy's influence was in the simplicity of his approach—he was hip in the sense that he was quick to pick up on things. The influence of his Fender Stratocaster sound was where all his genius lay. In Britain they'd never seen anything like it. They thought it was an outer-space guitar. English kids found his guitar sound sexy, and the glasses only added to his appeal among British teenagers. And then there was that great hiccupy way he sang, "Love like yours will surely come my way, *A-hey, A-hey-hey.*" His '55 Stratocaster got stolen on that tour and he had to finish it with a blond Gibson.

In comparison, Elvis was a different animal altogether—sexy and dangerous. The look couldn't have been more different. There was no overt sexuality with Buddy like there was with Elvis. Buddy was also a singer-songwriter and that was the big difference between Elvis the entertainer and Buddy the confessional storyteller of his own life. That was the key change for The Beatles, The Stones, etc., so Buddy's influence in the end was more far-reaching than Elvis's. Elvis was a larger-than-life CinemaScope American image. Buddy provided the scaled-down guitar-band blueprint for most of the '60s bands, especially in Great Britain.

I was the kid—and a singer to boot. Like kids in bands are today, the Southern boys were guitar mechanics. I barely knew one guitar from another. They'd tease me with questions like, "Hey kid, what's the difference between a Stratocaster and a Les Paul?" Who knew? Buddy gave me an old acoustic guitar and that's what I wrote "It Doesn't Matter Anymore" on.

Eddie Cochran was the other guitar slinger who had a huge influence on the next generation of rockers. Eddie Cochran became a rock hero in the sixties on the basis of "Nervous Breakdown" and "Summertime Blues." In terms of attitude he was way ahead of his time.

On these big tours with as many as twenty different acts on the bill, I always had to combat the fact that I was a young unsophisticated kid, a little different from anyone else in the show and a little too successful for my own health. Kids can be cruel and they are even crueler in their teens. I'm not black, I'm not a Southern boy, and I was doing Canada and my own thing and was very outspoken, so the other acts started out with a real attitude toward me. They had no intention of becoming buddy-buddy with me, but despite that we ultimately became friends. As you can imagine it was a constant battle of egos, and I was their prime target. I was always thinking differently and I looked different. My ambitions were alien to them. Vegas and that whole Sinatra Rat Pack thing is what I aspired to, and they couldn't identify with that at all.

—•—

After playing in Pittsburgh, we headed into the southern United States to places that I had never been to or knew much about. In the late

1950s, the civil rights protests were happening and I saw horrendous scenes of racism firsthand in those cities that I'll never forget. It was a depressing spectacle. On the tours we had white and black performers traveling together and this caused problems when we stopped at places in the Deep South.

On the way from Atlanta to New Orleans, police stopped the bus and segregated us, putting all the white performers on one bus and all the blacks on the other.

In Canada I hadn't been exposed to any of that. I was disgusted by it. The magic of rock 'n' roll may have brought black and white kids together, but it didn't keep people from getting their heads cracked. Police dogs attacking defenseless blacks on the street, police spraying crowds with water hoses and swinging their clubs at protesters. We performed in cities where both audiences and performers were segregated, the black acts invariably treated like second-class citizens. The black performers could sing on stage, but offstage they encountered prejudice whenever they tried to enter segregated public places.

When black acts couldn't get into hotels and restaurants we'd all eat and sleep on the bus. We couldn't go to restaurants together, either. I had to go in and get food for my black friends. There were separate bathrooms for the black performers, who could only get to use them by going in through the back door, so what we'd do was slow the bus down, open the door, and piss outside.

I was the only white kid on the bus in some cases. The only redeeming thing about it was being thrown into that experience. Going down South and seeing how they treated black artists was eye-opening. Outside the realm of show business it was a racist world—North or South. For a young Canadian kid it was a scary time.

The black acts—Chuck Berry, Fats Domino, the guys who had a string of hits and had the most exciting acts—closed the shows. You wouldn't want to follow these guys anyway. Black experience is what's driven every decade of American music. Back then I didn't have the experience. I had the hits, but the older black acts like Fats Domino had the chops. Anyway Irv would be the one to decide who closed the show—there was no argument about it.

By rights Chuck should have closed the shows, but mid-tour he bizarrely insisted he *open* the show. This puzzled everyone until we realized that if he went on early he could cruise the audience for girls while the other acts were playing. Chuck Berry was the guy, but touring got kind of funky for him because of the racial laws on the road. When we were in North Carolina, Chuck stopped the bus at a roadside café, and everybody piled out. The owner, backed up by some scary-looking patrons, shouted out, "We don't serve niggers!"

"That's all right, I don't eat 'em," Berry replied and everybody laughed. Nobody ate and the bus moved on. Buddy Holly always joined the protest; he was very vocal, as we all were. We would tell these bigoted restaurant owners, "If you won't feed these guys, we're not going to eat here, either." Not that they cared.

At another show the son of the white mayor bought a ticket to the show and then found himself sitting among black kids. He went to the box office and said there must be a mistake and wanted to get another seat. But they told him, "Sorry, son, the show is sold out." He asked for his money back.

Since the tours of the late '50s always featured black performers, we tried to figure out ways to get around the absurd rules in the South.

When we performed in certain areas one side of the audience would be divided into two sections: blacks on the left, whites to the right, with a curtain dividing them down the center!

Even backstage the restrictions didn't break down: the black performers had their section and we had ours. When we got to Birmingham, the chief of police came to check out all the performers because of The Crests. They had a hit with "Sixteen Candles." It was a truly interracial group. The lead singer, Johnny Maestro, was Italian-American, and there were three blacks (including one female) and a Puerto Rican. As you can imagine Southern cops had a serious problem with that. When they came backstage, they were horrified to see whites, blacks, and Puerto Ricans all mingling together. The police chief was apoplectic. "There's a nigger on stage with white musicians!" he yelled. "We don't abide that kinda behavior down here." "What kind of behavior would that be?" Irv asked. The police chief just stomped out of the theater. Allen and Irv tried to protect the black kids from the worst excesses of racist cops, but it wasn't easy.

It was right on the cusp of integration so everyone was pushing the boundaries from both sides. If you didn't provoke the racist bullshit by defying their stupid rules, you weren't really pushing the envelope—you were just acquiescing. The situation down South seriously aggravated the black performers, they'd do things to deliberately piss people off, like bringing white girls up to the room. That was either asking for trouble or the beginning of integration, depending on the way you looked at it.

The racist element only added fuel to the fire: rock 'n' roll was the new plague and the press, even the so-called respectable press, exploited the situation ruthlessly. One of the worst incidents I remember was in Hershey, Pennsylvania. It was a phony alarm—but when has that ever stopped the press? Most of the stuff you read about was instigated by the press. At that show *Life* magazine was trying to get kids to take off their shirts—they were actually *paying* kids to act up, so they'd have good photographs of a rock 'n' roll riot. And once *Life* had started this nonsense, all the other magazines started trying to get kids to do the same thing and up the ante. They'd give them money and say, "Tear up the seat!" "Throw trash!" "Start a fight!" "Take your shirts off." They wanted to stage it. To show that rock-and-roll was running wild.

Back then we were getting criticized like crazy, they were all over us, saying, "This music's abominable, it's a menace, it turns kids into juvenile delinquents!" Allen and Irv got tipped off what they were up to and kept a close eye on the concerts to make sure that didn't happen.

The white Southern boys and the blacks all smoked weed in those days, but it was never out in the open. Pot smoking was pretty much hidden behind closed doors—the window open, the wet towel under the door—because the managers strictly forbade it on the tours. They were all sneaking, hiding it. Everybody had to be very cool about it or you got thrown off the tour, but we all knew who was getting high and who wasn't, for sure. Even as far back as Ray Charles, pot, cocaine, heroin, and all that stuff was around.

Frankie Lymon, he'd be shooting up in the stall in the bathroom, you know, before the show, or late at night when nobody's looking on the bus. He'd tie up, get high. We all knew what he was doing, it was so out there. Nobody said anything but you'd see it through the crack in the door of the stall. When they needed it, they needed it, that's all there was to it. Nobody wanted to go cold turkey on tour. We all knew who in the cast was doing what. And it wasn't just the black performers. Dion DiMucci, polite little Italian boy from New York, I remember him doing heroin, too. There's so many times Irv or Allen Bloom had to go down to the local jail, bail him out.

Frankie Lymon died of a heroin overdose in the end. I saw that coming. It was stupid and self-destructive, but these guys were desperate characters. Frankie Lymon wasn't the innocent-looking teenager you saw at the shows and on television. Which is why him singing, "I'm Not a Juvenile Delinquent" was such an irony. Try running a clip of him OD'ing, slumped over in a bathroom stall, with that lyric in your head. Great little performer, but real edgy—he was an arrogant little guy with a big overblown personality and a chip on his shoulder. He was going with Zola Taylor, one of the original Platters who were on tour with us—and she was just one of his girls. A junkie, a bit of a con man, but no matter—the girls loved him. Quite a few of the musicians that traveled with us were just whacked most of the time, too. He wasn't the only one. Another of The Teenagers died of an OD in prison.

I don't know what Chuck was doing because whatever he did, he did in his limo, but there was always something going on with him. We'd be driving from New York through Pennsylvania, on our way to

Ohio, but we had to let him take off 'cause he was wanted in Ohio for something or other. Transporting minors across state lines or just to harass him for dating white chicks. He'd show up again in Phoenix. He'd picked up this sixteen-year-old girl, we'd drive up the West Coast, across Canada, the girl's still with him. They arrested him in St. Louis, put him in jail. I mean this stuff—minors, blacks with white girls—that went on a lot, but Chuck was permanently on the prowl.

Buddy Holly loved "You Are My Destiny" with its big Don Costa production. He'd taken his own song style as far as it would go and he was looking for something different. "I need to change my arrangements and try what you're doing with your songs." He wanted to leave The Crickets and move on. He asked me to write a song for him—and I did. That's how I came to write "It Doesn't Matter Anymore." The direction he wanted to go in was to add string arrangements to his songs, develop a lusher, sweeter sound behind his vocals. The whole focus of "It Doesn't Matter Anymore" was to do it with a big band, with violins and horns, a big, plush orchestral sound that would frame his voice, impart a more romantic aura to his songs—like a movie soundtrack. That's what that was about, which, in retrospect is pretty funny because it was Buddy's rougher, guitar-band sound that would inspire the next generation—certainly not lush orchestrations!

By the time of that first tour, which ended just before Thanksgiving of '57, we'd all gotten comfortable with each other. I'd seen Irv in action and I was impressed. If I were going to continue in this business I needed serious representation. "Destiny" had just taken off and I told him, "I'm not going to work for you again 'til you become my manager."

"Let's talk in a few weeks," he said in his I-gotta-think-this-through-and-so-do-you manner. "We'll see what we can do," he said. Now he only had me under contract for one tour; there was no other deal signed beyond that. I went home and within the next week or so my dad called him and said, "Look if you're comfortable working with Paul, and I know you are, he wants you to manage him."

My father and Irv met at a restaurant in New York. We all sat down and went over everything. He wanted, first of all, to make sure that was what I wanted to do with *my* life, that the one hit I had wasn't just a whim. I, for my part, wanted nothing else. I wanted to dive in headfirst and not even come up for air.

Irv was very smart. He said, "He's going to make mistakes. Everybody does. Let's have him make them far from home. When he gets back, he'll be a giant."

Irv had his own inimitable vibe. Always dressed in silk suits, a cigarette dangling from his mouth—he loved his cigarettes—he never needed any sleep. He was up day and night, worked very hard, and sold what he believed in. He was a salesman in the sense that he could persuade you to see things through his eyes. A true believer. Smart, shrewd, and aggressive, but also very trusting. Irv was the first guy to take me to a tailor and get me a suit before I started out on tour. He took me to a famous Italian tailor, where they created some sharp suits.

Between tours I lived with Irv and his family. His home life was not all that pleasant. His wife was a schizophrenic. They knew that she was very sick but in those days they didn't have the antipsychotic drugs they have today. She would rage at Irv almost daily. She resented the amount of time Irv spent at work, seven days a week. His idea of quality time with his son was to take him to the store with him when he went to work. Irv's wife didn't resent me, she resented the time he spent on my career.

Because I was away from home a lot and was a minor, Irv became my legal guardian on the tours. When I was in the States during time off between tours I'd stay at Irv's. I spent a huge amount of time at his house and at his apartment in Washington. I shared a room with Irv's son Kenny. I was seven years older than he was so I became the big brother Kenny never had and was probably as annoying as any biological sibling.

I was so full of electricity coming off the road, I would be bouncing off the walls. I'd be up all night, and given my natural proclivity for pranks I'd get into a lot of mischief. While Kenny was sleeping I'd put gel in his hair, paint his face. He'd wake up in the morning, look in the mirror and he'd have spiked hair; there'd be blue dots all over his face. Remember that well into my twenties I was still a kid because I'd missed my childhood by going into show business so young. But at Irv's house I knew I could get away with almost anything so I could always be a kid there.

Because I was a kid I felt I had to prove myself, and Irv was the ideal person to help me do it. I was perfectly in synch with Irv—and he got me fame and money beyond my wildest dreams. I remember the time Irv booked me into Freedomland, a theme park in the Bronx built by the master developer William Zeckendorf—who built half of New York—where top acts would perform in the summer. It was Zeckendorf's idea to hire me and Irv got me the fantastic sum of $100,000 for one weekend's work, an unheard amount of money—it was the highest amount an artist was ever paid in history up to that time. It was so huge, in fact, that when Irv called GAC (General Artists Corporation), my talent agency, to write up the contract, the agent thought it was a mistake and wrote it for $10,000. Irv went berserk, but it got fixed, of course. Part of the documentary *Lonely Boy* was shot at Freedomland, where you can get the essence, the feel of the time, the frenzy of the girls, crying, going crazy—pre-Beatle, pre-Beatlemania.

Before Irv became my manager, my agent Buddy Howe at GAC had been my mentor. Buddy was a great guy and helped me immensely in the early part of my career, but Irv was something else again. He was an original, everything he did was an innovation—there were no templates for pop music yet. Irv was the first manager of pop acts to think globally. He planned my first European and Japanese tours. He was always someone who wanted to break open new frontiers. And because of Irv, I was the first American pop artist to tour behind the Iron Curtain.

The music scene began to take off overseas when "Diana" became a hit in Europe and a lot of other places around the world. Then "You

Are My Destiny" became a smash in July 1958. My next few records all took off internationally, too. Between the ages of seventeen and twenty, I toured Chile, Paris, London, Belgium, Japan. That became my lifestyle; I was a travelin' man.

I went on my first European tour, opening the Trocadero Theatre in London on December 7, 1958.

In England, I met the singer Helen Shapiro, who was then fourteen. I wrote and produced a song for her, but given her age that's as far as the romance went. There was no swapping spit. It was the reverse of the situation with Diana.

"Teen idol" was the new word. With rock 'n' roll came a new set of clichés—and problems. I got mobbed in Paris. There's a photo of me trying to get out of a car, but can't because of the crush of fans. It was just a sea of people pushing *toward* me, mostly screaming girls. You might say, well, what's so bad about that? But a crowd is a crowd—it's a mindless crush of bodies and is a very scary thing to be in the middle of.

The minute I got back to the States in January, I was out on the road again with Buddy Holly and The Crickets, Eddie Cochran, The Rays, Royal Teens, Danny and The Juniors, Hollywood Flames, Mello-Kings, The Shepherd Sisters, Margie Rayburn, and The Tune Weavers on an Everly Brothers tour.

The Everlys didn't have their own band. They would pick up musicians in the towns we played, unlike The Crickets—Buddy's band traveled with him. I didn't have my own regular band, either. When I performed I was just trying to transpose the sound of my records to a performance situation. I would pick up a band, we'd rehearse together, and they would go on tour with me. Very unlike the concept of what was to come in which the band became a fixed entity in rock 'n' roll and you got to know who played drums, who played bass, who played lead. I didn't get my own permanent band until I got a little older and started playing the clubs.

After the Everly tour I headed out with Jerry Lee Lewis and Jodie

Sands with Buddy and The Crickets on Buddy's Hawaiian tour and after that his ten-day Australian tour before returning to Hawaii for another performance.

It was crazy how much touring we all did, but who knew if it was going to last? The critics were saying that rock 'n' roll was a novelty and would quickly fade away. Believe it or not, it could have easily happened that way, too. Phonographs weren't exactly a household item—especially for teenagers. Also, there were very few places where rock 'n' rollers could perform.

It was this little seed that got planted and turned into a monster industry. I just happened to be at the right place at the right time. I got in on the ground floor and it has just kept going up and up—well, until recently, anyway. I watched that whole evolution as young people began to dominate the music industry. By the mid-sixties I found myself surrounded by young people, but in the beginning we were few and far between.

Buddy Holly and The Crickets, me, and Jerry Lee Lewis going to Australia . . . oh man, that was some trip! Those wild, drinking Southern boys were one thing, but Jerry Lee Lewis was just a nightmare. I didn't like him and he *hated* me. We fought constantly. He was a mean redneck, a real nasty guy spewing venom at me at 25,000 feet crossing the Pacific Ocean.

We were fighting and yelling and throwing things at each other. Admittedly I was this annoying young brat, very aggressive, very brash, and it was especially grating to him that I had all these hit records. That really got his goat. He loved to pick on me, saying I looked like a squashed-down Danny Thomas. I wasn't too shy about shoving it in his face that I was higher in the charts than he was. Mean white trash aboard Pan Am first-class luxury modern, in those days, prop planes. Pop heartthrob vs. the Killer, round one.

When we got to Hawaii and later in Australia, Jerry Lee was always cooking it up because his name wasn't as big as mine on the billboard. This really bothered him. I, the little shrimp, was stealing the show from the Killer; in Hawaii and Sydney, there was my name towering above his. I was the one getting mobbed at the airport by reporters, fans, and *girls*. This did not sit well with Jerry Lee—the Killer playing second fiddle to this little squirt. Jerry was the Killer, and I was the boy millionaire.

There were pillow fights on the plane to Australia. The Southern boys at one point tried to force me to drink some beer or whiskey—I wasn't a drinker at that point and they wanted to initiate me. I staggered about the plane singing Calypso songs and kissing the stewardess.

Jerry Lee Lewis's second single was "Great Balls of Fire." Although Buddy and The Crickets had three hits in Australia ("That'll Be the Day," "Oh, Boy!," and "Peggy Sue"), Jerry Lee demanded his name be bigger than anyone else's on the bill. Buddy said that was okay with him, as long as they got extra money, but in the end my name got top billing, which *really* rankled Jerry Lee.

It all came to a head on January 27, 1958, in Australia. The promoter, an ex-patriot named Lee Gordon, had brought us down under and in the end he was the one who got things resolved. The solution was that Buddy would get more money and Jerry Lee would get his name bigger.

Buddy started to steal the show in Australia. He was emerging as the forefront of a new generation of fans, and was slowly starting to be picked up by people we would soon hear a lot about—The Beatles. That's why they gave themselves that name—after Buddy's group, The Crickets.

I remember once—accidentally—pulling out the power plug from Buddy Holly's amp, blacking out the entire stage. I already had this reputation of being a snotty kid so security assumed I was just being a brat and chased me around the theater. On another occasion I took a tube out of Jimmie Rodgers's amp, blowing his set mid-song. This wasn't Jimmie Rodgers, the father of country music, this was the pop singer who had huge hits with "Kisses Sweeter than Wine," "Oh-Oh, I'm Falling in Love Again," "Secretly," and a bunch of others.

In November 1957, we were on tour playing in a small Canadian town. During your time off everybody on these tours is trying to kill time one way or another: walking around the city, going to a movie, shopping. This particular day we had nothing to do so Phil and Don Everly and I went into a department store, which had black motorcycle jackets on display like the one Marlon Brando wore in *The Wild One*. It also had some of those biker caps that gang members wore. So we all bought these brand-new shiny motorcycle jackets and caps. There were three of us so now we looked like we were a gang. Why we did it I still don't know. We're going down the escalator and as we're going down there are three real mean biker guys in motorcycle jackets coming up on the other escalator. Here we were in our brand-new shiny motorcycle jackets and there they were in their real broken-in scuffed-up knife-slashed jackets, like guys would wear in a genuine biker gang. In comparison to them, we resembled the ice cream man. This didn't look good and from the glares they shot at us, it did not bode well.

Phil was about eighteen at the time and I was all of sixteen. We started walking a little faster as we got off the escalator because by now we could see these guys had turned around and were coming down the escalator in our direction. We started high-stepping it down the street. It was a small town, and once we made it to the corner we pretty much thought we had gotten away with it. So we went into a movie theater. We were still in our motorcycle jackets when we hear them come into the theater and sit right behind us. The theater was mostly empty but you could hear a horde of people muttering and mumbling in the row behind us. Phil turned around, and glanced sideways from the side of his eye without moving his head. "Aw, don't worry about it," he said, "it's just a bunch of kids." So we continued watching the movie.

Suddenly we start hearing this tough-guy talk behind us. "That was one hell of a fight on Saturday, was it not?" one of them says. "But nothing like it's gonna be here," says the other goon. And they started laughing in this brutish way. Suddenly this is starting to smell like trouble. Phil, still thinking it was just a bunch of obnoxious kids, turned around and asked, "What did you say?" And right then a guy with the head of the gorilla in a biker jacket with the sleeves cut off so he could show his muscles has his face right next to his. "Why?" he said in a threatening voice. Now Phil was concerned. He turned back around to us and said, "We've got to get out of here."

They turned out to be the same bunch of louts that we encountered in the department store. We waited a few more minutes and very quickly exited the theater and as we were leaving we could hear that whole row getting up. There were some fourteen people back there. They looked like juvenile delinquents—the genuine article. As we came out of the theater we knew we were in trouble. They were gonna start some kind of a rumble. Just at that moment the whole orchestra came walking down the street, some twenty black guys. We traveled on these tours with a big black R&B band, the Paul Williams Band. They played in the background behind everybody. They could sense something odd was going on so they said, "What's happening, guys?" "Well, see, these guys are after us. . . ." "Hey, you mean *those* guys?" they said with disdain. The goon with the jacket with the cut-off sleeves saw this group of big black guys coming toward them and all of a sudden these gang members who'd been after us came to a screeching halt. They went into shock. This was in Canada where they weren't used to seeing that many black people. The big guy with the cut-off sleeves had on a Mickey Mouse watch. He looks at it and goes, "Oh, Jeez, looks like I might be late for work," and dashes off. And that was the end of that close shave.

After that Phil put that jacket in his suitcase and shipped it home. I continued to wear it on the airplane but not on the streets of strange cities ever again.

To this day I still see Phil—I love being in his company. Don I don't see at all. It's well known that Don and Phil Everly had a contentious relationship—they fought all the time. The two brothers were opposites in so many ways. It was insane! Phil was warm and ingratiating; Don was very quiet and shy. They fought so much some nights you wondered if they could ever go on stage together, and yet they sounded so angelic with those incredible high Appalachian harmonies. They were great-looking guys—James Dean-ish. Phil went on to marry the stepdaughter of Archie Bleyer, who owned Cadence, their record company. It was through them I first met Wesley Rose of Acuff-Rose Music, the big Nashville publishing house. They had the finest catalog of country-western music, including all the great Hank Williams songs. Wesley was very much the Southern gentleman with the *Gone with the Wind* moustache and cowboy hat, courtly, polite, but very shrewd.

Unlike today, these guys were true song-pluggers, publishers who went out and worked their catalog and had a sensitivity to the material and placed songs with other artists. That's how you got records made and made money for your artists. Now the publishing business is more like the banking business.

When we got back from our big Australian tour Irv Feld signed us up to do Alan Freed's Big Beat Show at the Brooklyn Paramount Theatre from March 28 through May 1958. No Jerry Lee, but me, Buddy Holly and The Crickets, and The Everly Brothers joining up again with Chuck Berry, Clyde McPhatter and The Drifters, and Frankie Lymon and The Teenagers.

After we did that show, Alan Freed, the disc jockey, wanted to manage me. He was chasing me around, calling the record company. In those days, you could be a disc jockey *and* manage someone. Different set of rules back then. There's a definite conflict of interest there, but the business was looser.

I was wearing fancy suits, trying to act like an adult but basically I was still just a kid. I'm pretty sure I was still watching *The Mickey Mouse Club* and stuff like that. It got confusing. I remember doing this interview with May Okon of the *Daily News* in March 1958 when I was doing the Big Beat Show and telling her how I'd watch the other kids going to school from my hotel window and a smile would come over my face because I didn't have to go to school but that I felt two contradictory emotions: on the one hand I seemed to be so beyond kids of my own age but I'd buy toys and claim they were gifts for my kid brother back in Canada when they were really for me. The contradictions in my life were piling up. It was a poignant moment for me as I realized that in one way I'd leap-frogged over my schoolmates into fame, money, and mock adulthood, but at the same time realizing I'd forfeited my childhood—something that you are never going to be able to get back. I think that irony was one of the things I felt I had in common with Michael Jackson when I began to work with him.

Freed was a kind of forceful, tall, imposing-type guy, who had an ego and a half. All attitude, because he knew he was the guy. He had the power and he really worked it. He was a true innovator in radio programming, but he ended up a kind of a tragic figure, getting caught up in the payola scandal. Payola was a common industry practice whereby record companies would make under-the-table payments to deejays to get their records played on the radio. Everybody did it—you could barely walk into a men's room in the Brill Building without seeing someone handing a deejay a big envelope of bills. But Freed got nailed as the fall guy for the practice—which didn't stop, by the way.

September 1958 was my first tour of Japan. I played the Shinjuku Koma Theater and the Asakusa Kokusai Theater. When I got to Japan that's where I really got into that girl action. We were introduced to some hot young Japanese girls and I was inviting them left and right onto the train. The mothers would be following me to the next city. I was feeding my sexual appetite; I've never been that accessible with girls at home. You couldn't get any action. But in Japan the girls were throwing themselves at me. I wasn't even looking for them; they were just coming to me. In Germany there were the Kessler twins. When I got to Paris I wanted to meet Brigitte Bardot. And I did. Let's leave it at that.

Buddy was getting even more dissatisfied with The Crickets: he wanted to go out on his own, he was outgrowing them. There was some dissention going on in the ranks. I saw that Buddy had an amazing future ahead of him.

We became close, tight friends. We got to the point where we were talking about writing songs together and combining our different strengths as songwriters and producers, creating a situation where we could work together. We planned to start a publishing company together. By the end of the all-star tours we were separating ourselves out from the rest of the pack.

During much of the time I knew him, Buddy was involved in some form of litigation with his manager (over money issues), and disputes with The Crickets (over the direction the band was going).

Sometime that fall, after I got back, Buddy called Irv and me. He was sounding a bit desperate. He'd broken up with The Crickets and was having problems with his manager. He told us he was out of money, and was going through problems with his management—his manager, Norm Petty, had apparently stolen money from him and his band. While he was away and before he could explain what he was doing, The Crickets had sided with his manager and he felt betrayed. He married this woman he'd met in New York, Maria Elena—she was the secretary at his record company—and wanted to move there. Buddy said he needed money fast, and could we bring him out on a tour?

So we created a sister tour, a parallel tour to the one we were on, just for Buddy. The tour was called the Winter Dance Party, just some name to make it sound lively and fun because it was in the middle of the winter and it was way out in these remote ballrooms and arenas in the Midwest. It was Buddy, the Big Bopper, and Ritchie Valens. Waylon Jennings was Buddy's guitar player at that point—Buddy I think was paying him 75 bucks a week, and incidentally, he never got paid for that tour.

In 1958, Buddy went into the studio to record what turned out to be his final hit, "It Doesn't Matter Anymore." I really loved the way it came out. Right before Buddy went in to record it, he told Dick Jacobs, the A&R guy at Brunswick Records, that he had this new song I'd written for him. Jacobs got his copyist to quickly write the lead sheets from Buddy's guitar version. They wrote the arrangement very quickly that afternoon, for strings and rhythm.

When I got to the studio there was this eighteen-piece orchestra, including eight violins, two violas, two cellos, and a harp, as well as string players recruited from the New York Symphony Orchestra. These were top session players, like Al Caiola and Abraham "Boomie" Richman from the Benny Goodman Band on tenor sax. Buddy sang it in his classic up-tempo Texas voice. His characteristic "buy-bees," "golly-gees," and hiccuppy vocals were so infectious and worked so well against the lush orchestration that when he finished he got a round of applause from those initially dubious studio musicians.

He talked about his new wife, Maria Elena, endlessly. Maria Elena had wanted to come on the tour, but she was pregnant and throwing up, and Buddy wouldn't let her. Bizarrely, before going on the tour, Buddy had had a dream that he was flying with his brother and they landed on top of a building. They had to leave Maria Elena and he said, "Wait right here, I'll be back to pick you up." Buddy would tape songs for her on his Ampex tape recording machine at his apartment. He'd written the song "Maria Elena" for her, recorded a few years later by Los Indios Tabajaras.

Buddy Holly's story was that of love. He sang about what he knew and the pureness and the simplicity of his voice reinforced that sincerity. Elvis, on the other hand, *performed* his songs; he personalized them with his own theatrical delivery, but by the sixties this type of song interpreter had become less convincing than groups and singers like Buddy writing their own material.

Chuck Berry wrote some great teenage anthems—"Hail! Hail! Rock 'n' Roll," "Roll Over Beethoven," "Sweet Little Sixteen"—but Chuck was in his thirties when he was writing these songs. I was writing about teenage problems from inside. Chuck *described* teenage problems— they were great Kodachrome slides of teenage life—while I was living it and expressing it as a teenager. What we both had in common, along with Buddy Holly and Eddie Cochran, was that kids believed these were musical autobiographies, our own personal stories, that they weren't songs made up by writers in the Brill Building. It was Buddy Holly's story in the same way that it would be John Lennon or Paul McCartney's story.

My style was the result of studying the dynamics of everyone who came before me. I have that Semitic, Middle Eastern cry in my voice. Buddy's approach and the sound of his voice were very different. He wrote in major keys: A, E, and D. That was Buddy's magic. Buddy's vibe was always very upbeat, optimistic—The Beatles picked up on that, that major key, very true and very simple, and all about love.

He was happy to be working with Tommy Allsup and Waylon Jennings (on the brand-new Fender bass guitar Buddy had bought him). He was very up; he wasn't as preoccupied and defensive as he had been on the Summer Dance Party tour. He was happy he'd finally gotten rid of Norman Petty. He wasn't the only one with problems with his manager. Don and Phil Everly were fighting their ex-manager over money, too.

When Buddy talked about all the plans he had for a new studio and his European tour, he was just bursting with energy and optimism. He was planning to create a songwriting partnership with me and Niki Sullivan, guitarist with The Crickets.

One of the reasons he did the Winter Dance Party deal was that it was a General Artists Corporation production and he knew they were planning a British tour and wanted to be on that. He had really loved England—and they loved him there like crazy.

By now Buddy was getting to be a real spiffy dresser: polka-dotted ascots, leather shortie overcoats, the whole deal. He had grown up in poverty, wearing Levis and T-shirts, but as soon as he got the opportunity he became a serious clothes hound. Stage tuxedos, cummerbunds, a blue blazer. He also went and got his hair done, taking his dark curls and putting them in a permanent wave.

I don't know if a lot of people know this, but in the interim period—between splitting up with The Crickets and getting his own thing together—Buddy was taking flying lessons in New Jersey. He was fascinated with planes. Loved flying. He was about to qualify for his pilot's license to fly light aircraft.

And since he was a pilot himself he believed he knew as much about flying and weather conditions as the pilot and that's what emboldened him to make the pilot take off that fateful day, February 3, 1959. Before takeoff there was a big discussion as to who was going to go. It shook down—disastrously—to those three guys: Buddy, Ritchie Valens, the Big Bopper.

They all went round and round as to who was getting on that plane, you know. Six or seven people were earmarked because they were all chipping in to buy a share in the cost of the flight. They all wanted to get to the next city, to the hotel, get their laundry done, and get a good night's sleep. It was back and forth as to who was going to fly. Dion decided he didn't want to pay the thirty-six dollars it was going to cost. Waylon Jennings also took a pass that night.

Irv had two tours going on at the same time that winter. I was on one tour, Buddy was on the other one. One of the reasons Buddy took the plane on that fateful night was because of the way General Artists Corporation had planned the tour, without any logic to the geography involved. Also the buses were breaking down more often *and* it was February and the heaters barely worked.

That area where the plane crashed has become something of a Bermuda Triangle. Otis Redding died somewhere near there in another plane crash. And then Stevie Ray Vaughan crashed and died in that same area. But in Buddy's case there was nothing mysterious about it—it was all winter-weather related. Whether it's wind, snowstorms, or ice on the wings, you can't mess with the weather.

Outside of weather conditions, most airplane accidents are manmade. If it involves machinery that's often a question of maintenance—in other words, human error. When I started out, my dream was one day to fly in a private plane. I bought my first Learjet in the seventies, but I don't fly it myself.

Have I ever been superstitious about flying? I always think about it when I fly. I don't take unnecessary risks and I don't fly in bad weather. I'm just very cautious. To this day, whenever I get on a plane I think about the possibility of it crashing. With fate you never know. We're all just a blink away in this world.

Dion was on that tour. His drummer had frostbite that last night they played, so Buddy sat in for him on drums. Dion introduced him as Dion & The Belmonts' new drummer. When they left the stage Buddy performed a *"Gotta Move On"* solo.

He would have been one guy who lasted, Buddy. He and Bobby Darin. The only time things started to thin out for Buddy was when the Frankie Avalons and the Fabians—that manufactured pretty-boy look—came in. That was when things got kind of iffy for him. But his influence as a musician was really deep. He was basically just a country boy, very methodical about his music and the direction of his band, but not sophisticated in any other sense. He and Presley are all about that "yes sir, yes sir," and "yes ma'am" country courtesy that always sounds a bit put-on to Northern ears. You could get a toothache listening to these guys!

The crash that killed Buddy Holly, Ritchie Valens, and the Big Bopper left an unfillable gap in rock 'n' roll. It was such a monumental disaster it may even have triggered the next wave—the following year The Beatles started playing in Hamburg.

I had spent so much time with Buddy, touring, touring, touring—and then suddenly he was just gone. The Winter Dance Party tour ran to its scheduled end with other performers filling in. Bobby Vee and his group with Bob Dylan on piano joined the tour the next day as did others until it concluded its run on February 15. You just went on. In shock.

Three

LONELY BOY

When I wrote "Lonely Boy," that wasn't some clever notion I'd come up with—that was *me*. I'd left my family and friends behind in Canada and suddenly I was out on the road, performing in front of thousands of people. I was envious of the camaraderie, the pranks, the dirty jokes, and the silly games of my contemporaries back home. As corny as it sounds, deep down I really was a lonely teenager— because, invariably, I *was* alone. I was out there singing, and I'd see teenagers together at those dances. It looked like another world, a movie, almost. That kind of romance wasn't possible, living on the road. Sex, however, was another matter.

I'd always thought if only I could make it in the music business, everything would be perfect, but ever since "Diana" hit, my life was just more working and touring and writing. The tour bus was my home. You knew everyone and they became your family. Especially at my age, you take family wherever you find it. But, even as sibling rivalries go, it was a pretty competitive family. You'd wonder who was going to have the next hit and who wasn't. In 1958, five of my songs became hit singles: "You Are My Destiny," "Crazy Love," "Let the Bells Keep

Ringing," "Midnight," and "(All of a Sudden) My Heart Sings." It was all happening so fast. When I came down from Ottawa, Canada, here I was sharing charts with The Everly Brothers and started touring. I remember the hula hoop being huge that year.

In 1959, I met Bobby Darin for the first time. I thought to myself, "Gee, I'm really touring big-time now!" "Mack the Knife" came out in August and I tried to bump it off with "Put Your Head on My Shoulder," which hit in September; in November, "It's Time to Cry" came out. Frankie Avalon had one of his biggest hits, "Venus," in 1959. I had four hits that year—and "Lonely Boy" got featured in the movie *Girls Town* with Mamie Van Doren. Big year—four songs in the Top 100. I got friendly with Lloyd Price who had a hit with "Stagger Lee," produced by Don Costa on ABC-Paramount where I was recording. Originally a morbid tale of a murderer by that name, Dick Clark thought the lyrics were too dark and made him change them. It was at ABC where I first met Carole King—you could see right away she was going places, that's how talented she was.

Things *were* good, but then things changed. They always do. After the plane crash in February 1959 that killed Buddy Holly, Ritchie Valens, and the Big Bopper, the road just wasn't the same anymore. When you're very young and something like that happens, everything seems to come to a standstill. It was strange, very strange. Time really seemed to just stop, Buddy's death left a big hole in my life, an enormous silence.

That was when I started touring less and doing more television—Ed Sullivan's *Toast of the Town, The Perry Como Show*. I pretty much became a regular on *The Dick Clark Show* and *Dick Clark's Saturday Night,* and, of course, *American Bandstand,* which was just getting off the ground. It was based out of Philadelphia, and was all the rage on weekday afternoons, not only because of the music, but also the personalities, the romances, who was dancing with whom. A cross between a reality show and a soap opera, kids felt they had to keep up on a daily basis. I wasn't that much older than they were.

The whole key to doing those shows was faking it. The first thing you had to learn was how to lip-synch. They emphasized—and overemphasize—that you needed to get it down flawlessly or you'd end up looking like a dope. We were all very conscious of the fact that if you messed up you looked like a badly dubbed foreign movie—your lips are moving but no sound comes out. There was no live band so you had to rehearse—with yourself. You'd practice in the mirror, see if you could pull it off, catch yourself fluffing the line.

Of course, there were the inevitable "technical hitches." One time when I was on *American Bandstand*, we were live, and I was singing "Diana" when, in the middle of the chorus, the record stuck. I was left standing there just repeating the words "Oh my darlin', oh my darlin', oh my darlin', oh my darlin'," until finally, I just started fucking laughing and that was that. They just shut the record off. Kids watching probably had no idea what had just happened. And it certainly didn't become a scandal, like it did for poor Ashlee Simpson on *Saturday Night Live*.

We all dreaded going on these shows. You did it one way in a studio and then you had to mimic it syllable for syllable on the pop music circuit. You'd do it over and over again—*exactly the same* as on your record—at all these record hops, so it seemed like you'd been doing it forever. I don't remember how good any of us were at it, but lip-synching was the key. Getting on any of these local bandstand shows—that would make or break you.

A little later Dick Clark developed his local clique, Frankie Avalon and Fabian and that whole Philadelphia gang. But, of course, eventually Mr. Squeaky Clean was brought up on payola charges.

That was like a big shock for all of us because, you know, everything was supposedly so honest and innocent back then—most of all Dick Clark himself, who projected this wholesome image, and suddenly his name comes up in connection with this squalid "pay-for-play" business.

I remember Congress announcing their intention to hold hearings over payola in November 1959. It hit us like a bolt of lightning.

But why should I be surprised? When I joined ABC and began to have hits, they were making so much dough—most of it from my hit records—that they used to take bags of money out on an airplane to L.A. just to keep the television branch of ABC going. It was just getting started and they needed money to to keep it operating. Everything was so casual, nothing was computerized, money was flying out of teenagers' pockets and into the coffers of the record companies and radio stations—and into the hands of the mob, too, since they controlled the jukeboxes and the clubs we performed in.

In those early years—we're talking 1959 and 1960—I was making mad money, more than a million dollars a year, which some reporter figured out was equal to the combined salaries of the president and vice president of the United States and half the U.S. Senate—and I wasn't even old enough to vote yet.

When *American Bandstand* first took off there was a lot of hanky-panky going on between the deejays and the guys promoting the records, lots of money changing hands to get air time for their records. That's what payola was—paying to get your record played. We were just clueless young artists—what did we know? Our songs were becoming hits and then we started hearing the word "payola," and all the rumors about who was paying who to plug your record.

In the beginning music publishers and songwriters used to walk around with music sheets; they'd sit at a piano and plug a song—that's years and years ago—but this eventually gave way in the late '50s to the new wave of promotion guys. They were called "promo men," guys who would be hired by the record companies to go around and pay off disc jockeys.

It was a common business practice but eventually people started questioning it because these disc jockeys also happened to be in the publishing business themselves. They frequently got writing credit on records they had nothing to do with, and they often had a piece of a record company, too. There was definitely a conflict of interest there, but everybody would turn a blind eye and say, "Hey, what can you do, y'know? That's just the way it is." Still, it was a dirty business. No respectable businessman would run his company like that. But for the record companies payola was a very useful tool—you could just buy yourself a hot record. What a racket!

It really got out of hand by the late '50s. By then, there were squads of these promo men, like the guy The Stones make fun of on "The Under Assistant West Coast Promotion Man." These were slick guys who plugged records, which at that time simply meant paying off these disc jockeys. You'd go into the men's room and right out in the open there'd be promo guys handing over huge envelopes stuffed with cash. I don't know how deep Dick Clark was into all this—he went on denying it, but the evidence kept piling up and so did the rumors.

Dick Clark used all kinds of rationales to justify his participation in it. One day Leonard Goldenson, the head of ABC, brought him into the office and, you know, really grilled him and what they found out was that he'd been given the publishing—I think all or part of it—to my record, "Don't Gamble with Love" as a payoff for getting me on *American Bandstand.*

I was just a kid, so what did I care? They gave me three hundred bucks a week—I was in heaven, you know? I was just writing away on a record contract and when Congress started asking questions of all these people, it all came out in public that they'd given Dick Clark a piece of my publishing.

But Dick Clark was never indicted because the stuff that went on wasn't, strictly speaking, illegal, but still it was definitely frowned upon. So even though they tried to nail him on it and there was a lot of bad publicity, they really couldn't do anything. Nevertheless, for Mr. Clean-Cut Dick Clark, it was a really big, big deal, and it went on for some time. I know they dragged his producer, Tony Mammarella, down to Washington for sessions with the subcommittee. They brought him down to D.C., and he started naming names and telling about the money that had changed hands—he admitted to it all. And they brought in other people, too. Dave Maynard and a guy named Norm Prescott— these were all disc jockeys—and they started spilling the beans. They'd say stuff like, "If you played a new song, you'd get a thousand bucks right there on the spot, and then if you got it into the charts they'd give you another ten thousand bucks." Those were huge amounts of money back then and people were outraged. It just boggled the mind to think that these hit songs were *fixed*. So right away you knew they had to find a fall guy.

That's where Alan Freed comes in. Freed was a revolutionary deejay and rock impresario who did more than anyone to promote rock 'n' roll. He plugged all the R&B artists and really changed the scene; nevertheless, he was the guy who got crucified in all of this. He was indicted in 1962 on two counts of what they called "commercial bribery" and was fined $300, which wasn't much of a punishment money-wise, but it was all they could do. It was the resulting public disgrace that exacted the real price, though, and led to his downfall. He was blackballed by the industry, and lost everything—his livelihood, his self-respect. He was made the scapegoat for the whole thing. Everybody had a hand in the pot, but Alan was the one who was made to pay. He was a nice guy and a true rock visionary, but for some reason they just had it in for him. Within a year or two of those hearings he was ruined, and a year after that, on Lyndon Johnson's inauguration day, January 20, 1965, he was dead.

Okay, what now? Here I was, a bona fide teen idol, but I knew that wasn't going to be enough. A lot of us had a good run as teen singers in the fifties, but we weren't going to be teenagers forever. Those of us who wanted to survive knew we had to do something else to prove ourselves. It's the law of pop music: every three years you have to reinvent yourself. After you've done that a few times, you get to stick around.

Irv, thank God, was just such an astute, resourceful manager. After I'd had a few hit records he knew I was going places, but he also knew I was going to make mistakes, right? So he figured, let Paul Anka fail out of town. It was a way to test the waters for my new songs. If they hit there, bring them back to the big city. It was a brilliant formula.

I'd always had this attraction to the Rat Pack, Sinatra and those guys. I wanted to wind up like them. So when I told him what I wanted to do, he came up with an ingenious plan to take this teen idol kid, smooth out the rough spots, put me in a tux, and transform me into a performer who could become an attraction for adult audiences— get me headlining at night clubs like the Copacabana in New York. His first move was to get me to record an album called *My Heart Sings,* which featured old standards like "Autumn Leaves" and "I Love Paris," and included only one of my so-called teen songs. I also did a big band album, *Paul Anka Swings for Young Lovers* and later on a live LP, *Anka at the Copa.*

In 1958, Irv Feld made a deal for me to open for Sophie Tucker at the Sahara. At that time I was riding the crest of all my teenage success. There I was in Vegas, long before The Beatles set foot in the States. So when they did come, I already knew where I was going. I wasn't going to get blown out of the water like all my other soft-pop contemporaries.

So I opened for Sophie Tucker at the Sahara Hotel in Las Vegas. I had finally made it to the fabled land of the Rat Pack. When I showed up in Vegas I was way ahead of myself. I was the youngest headliner ever. Wayne Newton came out much later doing his 1963 hit, "Danke Schoen," becoming a Vegas fixture. I was different, not only in that I wrote my own songs, but I'd taken the time to become a polished cabaret act. Because I was underage and I wasn't allowed in the casino, they would bring me into the hotel through the back door.

I did about twenty-five minutes opening for Sophie Tucker. There were a lot of families in Vegas, their kids listened to the radio and watched *American Bandstand,* so they knew me, and, all of a sudden, they've got five hundred kids in a showroom at a Sophie Tucker concert going nuts. I wasn't even on stage yet when this huge hooting-screaming-whistling barrage of noise came on. Then you've got Sophie Tucker coming on and going "Some of these days, mama can I have another, uh, banana split, mama" or whatever the words were. The kids started screaming as soon as she came on. She was a trouper, nothing fazed Sophie, she was like a great old battleship, but in the end it was too unsettling for her, they were driving her *nuts*. She was a grande old dame, and after opening night she asked me to close the show for her. She just said, "My boy, I hope that you could come on after me so that I don't get pelted with spitballs." Funny lady.

She was this very big imposing aunt of a woman—Paul McCartney once referred to her as "Our favorite American group, Sophie Tucker." She was like the lady next door yet had a good strong sense of who she was. She had her game down. She was a legend who had so many years of being a success, she was like a singing Statue of Liberty.

She was great to work with. I used to hang with her after the show. She'd sit in her big robe and sign autographs and meet people backstage. I held the cigar box she put the money in. But she wasn't anybody to hang out with really. She was like ninety-two—born in tsarist Russia in another century. We didn't have all that much in common. The girls I was going to bed with were just a bit younger and a lot skinnier.

My bringing soft, preachified rock 'n' roll to Vegas helped business and I started getting invited back. Rock 'n' roll, even preachified rock 'n' roll, was not the kind of music Vegas favored but, after all, money was money, numbers were numbers.

At first I was so young I wasn't allowed into the casinos other than to walk the halls, stay in the room, etc. I loved entertaining, I loved meeting people, but, initially I didn't—wasn't allowed to—socialize. Basically I hid in my room. The irony being that I was headlining, filling a show room, and yet not allowed to go near a casino because I was underage. So I would look through the outside window, go back to my suite, and watch television, or I'd stay in my room and write songs. Lonely boy in Sin City.

That was really the beginning of my other career. Meanwhile, the whole teen idol thing, once thought to be a passing phase, was getting a lot of mainstream attention. The music business had gotten behind it and suddenly there was this huge "teen market" that hadn't existed before. But there was I, just trying my damndest to get away from it. For a while I had a foot in both worlds, but I knew which one I wanted to follow.

Then Irv Feld carefully arranged the perfect setting for my nightclub debut—the first time I would appear in a show not designed specifically for teenagers. It was a big step. New Year's Day, 1959. On that day, Paul Anka's second incarnation began.

There was a lot riding on this move, so Irv next cleverly booked me at the Lotus Club in Washington, D.C. It was his hometown and as he put it, "I could paper the joint with friends and celebrities who came free and made a lot of noise." On February 15, the day after Valentine's Day, I began a weeklong engagement there.

Just a genius move on his part. And true to his prediction, there was a virtual who's who of music-biz people, deejays, press, and publicists on hand my opening night. And because my nightclub debut was a success there, I got booked into top clubs in Las Vegas, Boston, Philadelphia, and Buffalo.

Irv Feld and I always felt: hit the clubs, break into Vegas. He wanted me in those places and I wanted to get in there. When I first went out, I saw Johnnie Ray, an old idol for me and all these older guys who took the business in their stride. Eddie Fisher and Nat King Cole were the best-selling artists at the time, playing Vegas and New York. They were all very supportive of me, considering I was just a snot-nosed kid.

———■———

Annette Funicello, the princess of afternoon TV. What can I say? She was not exactly model beautiful, but just so cute with her dark curly hair and big personality. We all loved Annette. See, back then, 1958–59 we're talking, with the limited programming on television, you couldn't cherry-pick through tons of shows, you just took what was there, and that was one of the big ones, obviously. Everyone watched *The Mickey Mouse Club*. And she was one of the Mouseketeers. I was kind of a fan of the show and had a serious crush on her even before I met her.

Disney wanted Annette to get all the exposure she could—they had a huge investment in her. Coming out of the Mouseketeers and that Disney stable, the only other available performing venue for her was to be out there singing. It was on Dick Clark's Caravan of Stars tour in October 1959 that she met me and Fabian and Frankie Avalon, that whole gang—young guys with their tongues hanging out. You could say we hit it off with her, but you'd have to see it like a Disney cartoon—the Seven Goofy Dwarfs and the Disney Princess.

I think there were three or four of us who were looking to get on base there. I didn't feel I was the obvious one. I was intimidated and a little afraid to the point where I was overly humble, overly polite. We were a new phenomenon on the scene and people were looking at us differently—we were a novelty, not unlike hula hoops. We were told what we could and couldn't do—and that would definitely include: *not* date Annette Funicello. Funny thing is, I later found out (in her book) that one of the reasons I eventually got to date her was "his attitude toward life in general was more intense, more serious, than that of most young men." Well, I guess being the shy one helped out for once.

Annette and I kind of gravitated to each other and it didn't hurt that her mother liked me. I must have looked like the most promising out of the bunch of mutts because I was the songwriter. Anyway, Annette and I hit it off, but the mother and the chaperone were all over her like white on rice. No one could really get near that. At first. Later on we'd learn to get around her. Like the time we made out in the bathroom of the hotel while her mother read a book in the other room. She once even let us fool around in the backseat of the car with her right back there with us, pretending to doze.

I think the real glue between us came about when I started writing an album for her—*Annette Sings Anka*—and getting involved in that part of her life.

She had a big hit previous to that with her song "Tall Paul"—not written by me—which played off of our romance. Big irony there, huh? The paradoxes of life, of which I am all too aware!

So, she'd already had that one hit under her belt—I think the Sherman Brothers wrote it—but her management wanted her to do a full album, and that's when I got involved. She did about twelve tunes of mine—"Train of Love" was the single—and I oversaw the production with Tutti Camarata, her A&R guy.

So, you know, we *dated*. Of course, I was constantly traveling, so it was mainly a lot of long-distance phone calls. We were always on the phone. Still, it was probably her first real serious relationship. According to Annette, "We sort of fell in love over the phone, during several of the hundreds of three-hour-long late-night conversations we shared over the next few years."

Of course, from a woman's point of view and coming from her background, I think what she really wanted was to get married. She and her mother looked at every potential suitor with an eye as to maybe this could grow into something where he'd be the husband. Or maybe it's me who saw it that way (typical guy's point of view).

And the fan magazines were all over it. It was "Paul and Annette" this, "Paul and Annette" that. It generated a lot of publicity and teen-romance nonsense. Annette was doing her movies (not the beach movies, that was a little bit later, but the ones for Disney) and I had just broken into film myself, so we were all over the place, running around doing television shows, acting in dopey movies, performing—and generally stirring up lurid, sugar-coated dreams in a million teenage brains.

Let me tell you about my so-called life as a teenage movie star. I got my start in movies when I was hired to write the music for a movie called *Girls Town*. Teen movies had to have songs in them—that's the way you appeal to the teenage audience. And once you were there on the set they'd go, "You want to be in movies?" No prior experience—in life or in the movies—required. You certainly weren't required to act, you barely had to know your lines. This wasn't Shakespeare.

I mean, who the hell doesn't want to be in movies? When you're seventeen and look the way I did—I wasn't exactly Tab Hunter—you figure, hey, somebody's making a big mistake here, but, what the hell, you're gonna go for it, 'cause you may never get the chance again.

I found acting fascinating and boring at the same time. I didn't want a full diet of it. What I really loved was performing in front of an audience—you're on stage, the MC comes up to the mike and says, "Ladies and gentlemen, Paul Anka!" You go on, do your thing, get your check, and go home. With movies, you start at eight in the morning and by the time you leave at nine at night, you've done all of thirty seconds of work. I did not want to do that for the rest of my life. But I enjoyed it, and it gave me some ideas. If you could put songs into movies, you could also put mini movies into songs—which is what "My Way" is. You see someone at the end of their career defiantly watching a home movie of their life.

I was in three . . . what? I guess you'd call them teen movies. The same guy, Albert Zugsmith, was the producer of the first one, *Girls Town,* which came out in 1959, and also the director of the second one, *The Private Lives of Adam and Eve,* which was released the next year. Then came *Look in Any Window* in '61, so it was boom-boom-boom, three in a row.

They were all really just vehicles to exploit this whole new teen market that hadn't even existed before—and, improbable as it seems, that's how I ended up in a movie with Mamie Van Doren!

What was she like? *Hot!* Sexy, blond bombshell type, real luscious, everything that you would imagine. I don't want to spoil your image of her as a bad-girl vamp, but off camera she was a very sweet person.

No one even cared that a woman over thirty was playing the part of a high school bad girl or Eve in the Garden of Eden! There was a huge Mamie Van Doren crowd. She had a fanatical following—here was a big, healthy *va-va-voom* broad you could have wet dreams about without too much trouble.

She was very sexy and all of that—and *knew* it—and here I was, a kid, virtually speechless in the presence of this sex goddess, and she's trying to be as nice as possible. I would sit there with my ukulele, teaching her to sing, and by the time I had, I'd sweated half my body onto the ukulele.

Did I have an affair with Mamie Van Doren? Can you call two and a half minutes an affair? I think I came before I walked in the door. I walked in with the ukulele to teach her a song. The next thing I know my pants are down, the ukulele is in my left hand.

Girls Town was a real soap opera. Mamie played the proverbial bad girl with a past, named Silver Morgan who becomes the number one suspect in the death of this kid named Chip, who at the beginning of the movie accidentally gets thrown off a cliff trying to rape a girl. Not a very subliminal message to teenage boys: forcing yourself on a girl is a bad idea! My character is a singer she has a crush on. What I'm really there for is to sing, and that's what I do.

These movies were so unbelievably corny and unrealistic, they're now considered classics—camp classics! One scene involves the "people" in Mel Tormé's car, who are so obviously dummies that even teenagers laughed out loud in the movie theater. But then, that was Albert Zugsmith's MO. He was known for trying to throw in a little bit of everything, especially the outlandish. Reality never got a chance in his films. *Girls Town* is in everyone's Top Twenty episodes of *Mystery Science Theater 3000*. (By the way, they have quite a bit of fun at my expense!)

The second movie I was in, *The Private Lives of Adam and Eve,* was even crazier than the first. It opens with my character, a singer named Pinkie Parker (by now I'm sure you're wondering who comes up with these goofy names, but that was a name that really fit the era), singing while steering his $400 hot rod with his feet on a highway outside Las Vegas. Then a really bad thunderstorm hits as only those desert storms can, driving me and a lot of other people to seek refuge in an abandoned church. Moral of the story: don't drive with your feet!

Anyway, they all fall asleep in church and dream they are in the

Garden of Eden. At that point everything in the film, which was in black and white up until then, goes Technicolor.

Tuesday Weld was a real cutie. She was the first person I saw who would drink a lot of hot water with lemons in it to shrink her stomach and stay thin. She didn't appear in the dream sequence, but really sparkled for the time that she was onscreen.

Teen movies like these are a vanished genre, but back then there was a big audience for them. They were poor movies, very formulaic, but not trashy. Some of them even had decent storylines and involved such a diverse group of people that the cast was like a Hollywood police lineup. Mel Tormé, Mickey Rooney, Martin Milner, Tuesday Weld— eight or nine stars in *The Private Lives of Adam and Eve* alone.

It wasn't *Gone with the Wind,* of course, or *Citizen Kane,* but the movies sold and we made money. Movies gave me a chance to expose some of my songs and hit my target audience for records. I would show up for one or two weeks' work and then I was gone. The acting was no big deal and it was cool to be able to tell people about them—just so long as they didn't go see them.

Even though I was playing these different characters, I was just being Paul Anka and singing my songs, which was great for me because my audience could see me as well. That's all they wanted.

There were a bunch of my old songs in each of them. Plus, I always wrote the title songs. "Lonely Boy," which was used in *Girls Town,* became a big money-maker.

I'm sure these directors knew how to make better films, but they were following a formula, trying to establish some kind of career. Same thing with the actors. You look at all of these guys, guys like Jack Nicholson. They all started out doing B movies with Roger Corman. That was good thinking, like working in a repertory company. These films definitely didn't age well, but they're true to the time, little 1950s time capsules.

The Private Lives of Adam and Eve caused kind of an uproar when it came out, which surprised everyone involved, because it wasn't a big theme movie, just a light sort of '50s morality tale, cloaked in a send-up of the book of Genesis. From the outcry I guess there were a lot of people who weren't ready for that kind of satire. Considering the prudish morality of the time, a lot of people were probably offended by the fact that Mamie Van Doren and Martin Milner appeared to be naked in the dream sequence, and being in color somehow made it worse: naked people in Technicolor making a mockery of the Bible!

After that I didn't really pursue movies. I wasn't going to take any part that came along, I was so busy with my music and performing. I was offered plenty more parts in similar type productions, but by then I'd had it.

Bobby Darin and I, as we were making our little pop records, started thinking, "Okay, what's next? Where is this going from here? Could we be doing something cooler than this?" Those of us who wanted to survive knew we had to move on from the teen idol thing to prove ourselves.

At some point I said to Irv, "Let's bring in a big band and just—with my young little squeaky voice!—do some swing."

I loved that stuff. So that was how I made my first big band album, *Paul Anka Swings for Young Lovers,* which was released in January 1960.

I loved making that album. Swing was with a big band, as opposed to going in the studio with five or six pieces and making a little pop record. And it gave me a taste of what was to come. It seemed so hip and cool to have a big band behind you.

The album came out at the start of 1960, and shortly before that I'd moved my family down to New Jersey. I bought a house in Tenafly so we all could be living together again under one roof, including my mother, because I wanted to spend as much time as possible with her, and my dad because he couldn't run the restaurant and deal with my business at the same time. I especially needed his help because I was still a minor and couldn't legally sign contracts on my own. And, of course, my brother Andy and my sister Mariam—who are both younger than me, came with us, too. It took a while to get the house together so initially we stayed at the St. Moritz Hotel until the house was ready. That would have been toward the end of 1959.

My mother was not doing well, she was suffering badly from the diabetes and that was a big worry to me, so it was good to have her nearby, closer to New York. She'd been diagnosed with diabetes when still a young girl, and after Mariam and I were born, the doctor had told her she wasn't supposed to have any more children but she did anyway.

My sister Mariam is two years younger than me and then there is Andy, who is the youngest. Andy is very sweet and gentle and quiet. He'd be happy plunking away at his guitar while I'd be showing off singing from the top of the dining room table or something crazy like that. Mariam and I are more alike in that way, more outgoing and outspoken. My mom, who had always been a force of nature, was now weakening just at the point when I was achieving my great success, and because of my success it meant that I was away from her more and more on tour. So my achievement as a pop star had a bittersweet quality for me. That summer, on June 23, 1960 I was finally set to headline at the Copacabana in New York, the one spot I'd been shooting for.

I can't tell you what the allure of the Copacabana was in those days. It was the ultimate place to play in New York, the fanciest, swankiest club there was, which is why I wanted my parents—my mother especially—to see me there. Sinatra and Sammy Davis Jr. had made it the most famous nightclub in the world. It was like inviting them to the prince's ball where I would be the star attraction. It was the culmination of all my mother could ever have wished for. My dad took her to get a new dress and her hair done for the occasion. We got her dressed up and made up, and I took her out for a night on the town, including a front row seat to my show at the Copa. I wanted her to be part of my success. It was the moment when I could express my love to my mother and thank her for all she'd done for me and show her that all these dreams we'd hatched in the basement of our house had come true.

I didn't know it at the time, but Irv had to bargain to get me top billing at the Copacabana. My regular salary in the clubs by this time was $7,500 a week, but Irv told the Copa they could have me for $3,500 if I was billed as the star of the show. It was a big gamble, but it worked.

The night before I opened, the manager of the Copa, Jules Podell, called Irv and said, "You gotta help me out. We're oversold six hundred seats. Could the kid do three shows instead of two on opening night?" I said okay and then nearly collapsed. Not even Sinatra ever had to do three shows on an opening night. That's when I knew we were going to make it.

Because of the layout of the club, all the performers had to go into the Copa through the hotel next door, the Hotel Fourteen. The club was basically a basement. There was only one entrance with a door to the left of it that went up to the Hotel Fourteen.

There were no dressing rooms, per se; it was, literally, a hook with a drape down the stairs. Before you went on, you had your tea, and then upstairs you had a room in the hotel. We were all supposed to go in that way, already dressed, and pretty much straight onto the stage.

There was nothing casual about the Copa. In the clubs, you had to dress up. Every night was New Year's Eve. The Copa had showgirls, sexy girls, and they'd come on before the main act; sometimes they'd have a comedian. You didn't have a tux, you didn't go on, period. It wasn't optional, it was mandatory. The comedian Jackie Mason opened for me on my first night at the Copa, and as he was walking into rehearsal, someone told him he had to wear a tuxedo for the show. He panicked, so I lent him one of mine. Could he fit into it? Yeah, back then he was kind of my size.

The truth is, so much stuff was happening I didn't have time for stage fright. You have to maintain your cool whatever happens—otherwise you're *dead*. And that's definitely a place you don't want to go. You have to learn quickly, know how to handle every crazy situation smoothly—because if you show anxiety they'll eat you alive. You have to have that confidence even if you're quaking in your patent leather shoes. I studied, looked at how everyone else handled it, saw how they maintained their cool, and applied my own take on it. I may have been terrified out of my mind that first night at the Copa—but I was cool!

Gene Knight in the *New York Journal-American* headlined his report: "Anka Sizzles in Copa Debut."

When he appeared, the seething Copa audience applauded, whistled, cheered. Immediately he and they were en rapport. . . . The ovation at the finale of his act was the greatest I have heard at the Copa in years. I call Paul Anka electrifying.

Lee Mortimer in the *New York Mirror,* comparing me to Bobby Darin, said:

And now comes even younger Paul Anka, who is no objectionable child prodigy. . . . His humility is infectious. His voice is beautiful. His material is entertaining. His showmanship comes naturally. At 18 . . . he is one [of the Copa's] all time greats.

I was the youngest act ever to play the Copa and after that I performed there a few more times and became very good friends with Jules Podell, the club's owner and manager—he ran it for Frank Costello, the head of the Genovese crime family. He was something: very tough-looking guy, heavy-set, bulldoggish face with greased-back hair and a big cigar. Smoking like a chimney, drinking—drinking *all* the time. He was the epitome of that whole Mafia thing. Everyone was scared shitless of him. In *Lonely Boy,* the filmmakers asked him to repeat the incident where he kisses me—they hadn't caught it on camera— and I thought he was going to kill them! That's the way he was—you crossed him at your peril.

That place was something, what a scene. You didn't fool around at the Copa. And he was something, that man. Jules Podell. Uncle Julie.

He was notorious for the tight ship he ran. If somebody was out of line, he would rap his big diamond ring on the table. It would echo all over the place and people would just be terrified. He would look at someone and just say, "Beat it," and they'd be tripping over each other to get out that door. Nevertheless, he was a gentleman and when he liked you, he was there for you. He was something. All of those mob guys were.

Opening night was a huge hit, these prom kids—Guys in white dinner jackets, girls in their crinoline dresses—from all over began showing up and the place was sold out in twenty minutes. The next night, the lines went all the way around the block.

And Mr. Podell, every night would have his position right there inside the front door, sitting at a little round table where he could watch everything with his drink in front of him and his big ring. He was kind of a diamond-in-the-rough himself and as hard as cut glass.

And there was Jackie Mason, who has always been an aggressive, arrogant-type guy and funny as hell. Because of the crowds and the big hullabaloo going on his chest was pumping—wearing the success of the night before—and he decides he's going to walk in through the front door of the Copa instead of from the Hotel Fourteen.

So he walks in past the kids and into the club and past Podell and he goes, "Good evening, Mr. Podell!" Jules looks up and says, "Get back in line, kid!!" and throws him back out the front door before he can say anything. Someone who could make Jackie Mason speechless, that's the kind guy Podell was.

One night the actress Gene Tierney was there (God, she was beautiful!) and Podell went over to her table to greet her. She was there with some people and when he came over she was very snobby to him—she was offended by the ballsy manner of this hoodlum, so Podell says to her, "Well, you ain't such a hot contender in the ring yourself, babe!" Podell was making a pun on the famous Gene Tunney–Jack Dempsey boxing matches in 1926 and '27.

The stuff that went on there! On Friday night, it was all these mob guys with their girlfriends. Then Saturday night, the same guys would turn up with their wives. It was always a tense vibe in there with the mob.

Uncle Julie checked every dish as it came out of the kitchen, lifting each cover to check the size of the portions, the appearance of the plate overall, making sure it was as near to perfection as possible, sending a waiter back to change his jacket if there was a pinhead-sized spot on the lapel or the sleeve or, God forbid, his shirt wasn't crisply starched.

There was a Chinese chef, Lum On. Under him there were actually about twenty other chefs, mostly French, but he was head chef. And the Copa—even though it had an art deco décor with a tropical Brazilian vibe and was run by Jews and Italians—was known for having some of the best Chinese cuisine in town. So the place was a real melting pot, just like New York. Aside from the main showroom there was a lounge at the Copacabana, Wayne Newton and his brother were playing the lounge when I did my show there. That's what they were in those days, a lounge act.

Every night after the last show, I would meet Podell in the bar. I liked to just schmooze, have a steak sandwich, or sometimes I would sit in on drums with the trio in the Copa's house band.

There was a guy at the Copa named Doug Coudy—he did just about everything to do with the show: lights, sound, the whole thing. He was a nice-looking guy, tall, thin, gray-haired, but boy, did he stutter. It would take him forever to say all the things he was going to do for your show in the way of lights. "Paul, you know when you go into the bridge, I could f-f-f-f-fade out the bl-bl-bl-bl-blue sp-p-p-p-p-pot. . . ." You'd tend to say, "That's great, Doug, why don't you try that" before he'd even got to the end of the sentence.

One night I overheard Podell talking with Doug about new songs for the fall show, so the next night, I come in with a ukulele and say, "Hey, boss, I got a couple of songs you could maybe use in your show." I played them and that was it. He says to Doug, "What a kid. In two years he'll be bigger than Sinatra." Who can resist over-the-top stuff like that? I loved the guy for that.

I wound up writing a lot of the songs for the big productions there. I did that for a couple of years, actually. I wrote all the music for the shows that came on before the main acts—the Copa girls, who were just about as famous as the Rockettes, would come out and do all these racy numbers. They were some beautiful showgirls.

The Copacabana was the ultimate status symbol, and this was its heyday. If you could headline the Copacabana in New York you had it made in the shade. There would be Carmine at the door, huge guy, behind the velvet rope. My life really changed when I started to do the Copa, that was the way I got into that Rat Pack world, because after that, all of a sudden, you felt legit, you'd separated yourself from the rest of the teen pack. As a performer—and in life in many cases, too—everything's been done, so you always want to learn from someone who does it better. That was my new playground. There comes a time when you realize you don't want to be the smartest person in the room.

Jules Podell was an impulsive guy, but I liked him and he could see where I was going. I performed at the Copa a few more times. After I headlined there on June 1, 1961, I got the kind of reaction from the press I'd been looking for—in other words that I was no longer a just a pop star who appealed to teenyboppers.

In the *New York Mirror,* Lee Mortimer's headline read: "Adults Love Teen."

There's no teenage audience at the Copacabana these nights, where Paul Anka the teenage phenom is playing to turn away audiences of adult sophisticates. For Anka, though only 19, is no callow rock 'n' roller, but a consummate artist whose talents are far beyond his years. Of all the juves making show business history this year I have a feeling that Paul is the only one who will outlast the craze. . . . Engaging, personable and no smart aleck kid trying to seem mature. Anka's showmanship is excellent.

Variety saw me as the first of a new wave invasion: "The young pop singers are now taking over the citadels of adult sophisticate as well. . . . Across-the-board appeal to the oldsters as well." The *New York World-Telegram* quoted my main ambition: "Paul Anka the almost twenty-year-old pop singer from Canada, frankly admits 'trying to break through and reach the adult audience.' If the reaction to his opening night audience at Jules Podell's Copacabana is any criterion, the colorful young balladeer has achieved his goal." Milton Esterow at *The New York Times* called me a "personable baby-faced, dimpled phenomenon of our time. He is a polished performer, confident but not brash. There is a charm and a voice that easily handles sentimental and swing songs. Mr. Anka could give lessons in showmanship." And Gene Knight at the *New York Journal-American* ("Anka's Aweigh at the Copa") said that I did it again as the "do-it-yourself type song man. . . . Secret of his sensational success is his high-speed method of presentation—a method you can't equal, Paul is possessed of unlimited showmanship."

Jules Podell was pleased. He sent the word out that he wanted to see me. I guess I'd brought a lot of business in to the club, so he told me, "Go to Tiffany, kid, and buy yourself a nice watch." I went to Tiffany and picked out a cool-looking watch. It was silver and elegant, and being unsophisticated I had no idea what it was—anyway it was getting charged to Julie Podell. The next day Podell calls Irv. "What the hell, Irving! I told Paul to pick something out—and what does he do? He selects a $10,000 watch. A fucking platinum watch!" What did I know? It was bright and shiny and I wasn't paying for it. It wasn't exactly what Jules expected me to choose, but he bought it for me anyway.

—■—

Annette and I were still an item and the interest level in us and what we were doing was high. From what the fan magazines said, you'd think we were always together, had lots of time alone, et cetera, but it was all strictly Hollywood hokum. Her mother was always there, or the Disney people, "handlers" as they're now called.

Annette was all about family, and what she was looking for was exactly the perfect kind of people who would fit that family mold. I was educated, well-mannered, and as sophisticated as any nineteen-year-old can be, but I wasn't ready to fit into anyone else's mold, even Annette's sweet, delectable mold. Her mother was the classic stage mother, but she cared madly about her daughter. The father was a hard-working guy, and her brothers were great.

And Annette herself was just this sweet, conscientious little starlet, who behaved just like the person you saw on TV. She was always respectful of what Disney—it was always "Mr. Disney"—wanted her to do. There wasn't one Annette on TV and then some other personality in her private life, like many young actresses today who in their personal lives are drinkers or druggies or what have you—fun as that stuff is to read about. She was always committed to her work, doing the best job that she could. She was a very warm, very passionate girl. She wasn't at all inward or reserved, just very open and expressive. On TV she was magnetic. Everybody loved Annette. She really deserved the stardom. She realized what kind of commitment that adulation involved and respected that. She was very conscientious in that way, a professional, trying to meet a heavy schedule, with no back drama.

Not that Walt Disney was hanging around her, exactly—he had his infrastructure of people who would account to him. Still, he was very hands-on and she'd see him whenever she had to at the studio. The executives and what-have-yous were always very much in evidence. She was a hot commodity and they wanted to protect her. They didn't want a pregnant Mouseketeer, or have her eloping to Tijuana with a used-car salesman.

So dating Annette was a frustrating situation. You had these two young kids who were hot to trot trying to deal with all the Victorian restrictions imposed on them, the chaperones and the teachers, and all of that. We'd say, "We need more privacy!" And that of course involved getting rid of the mother! But sexual frustration is a great stimulus to ingenuity and I came up with a plan. I went to one of the guys who were always around and got him to divert the mother by playing cards with her, so that Annette and I could lock lips and get in a room together alone. The chemistry was definitely there and we were getting more and more curious about each other.

Things got so bad with me and Annette and all the restrictions, that I was banging into walls or walking into doors. Sexuality, of course, back in the '50s was a lot different than it is today; everything was just so religiously hypocritical and morally protected, but humans will be human and teenagers will get horny. And all I wanted to do was to get her alone, maybe in her room at night, with no supervision.

The funny thing is when I did get into her bedroom there must have been thirty stuffed animals on the bed—big bears, bigger tigers, giant monkeys. It was unbelievable! Some of them were bigger than I was. Annette was very passionate and intense. Having an affair with Annette was an absolute fantasy come true, but I realized it wasn't going to go anywhere. She was always direct about where she wanted romance to go—wedding bells—and she ultimately married my booking agent Jack Gilardi, whom she'd met through all of us pop singers.

—■—

Anyway, around the time Annette and I broke up, I got this offer, toward the end of 1960, to play the lead in a film called *Look in Any Window*. I got to write and sing the title song, too.

It wasn't as silly as the other two teen movies I'd done, so I signed on, playing the role of Craig Fowler, who was kind of a troubled teen, a common theme in these movies. They were always directing a message at the kids. You might call it an anti-teenage-delinquency film. The movie's tagline was, "The shades are open and their morals are showing!" It was a Peeping Tom–type thing and I played the lead. Basically, it was just another teen movie with higher aspirations. Sure, I was spying on people, but it was because my parents didn't understand me. . . . You know, I'm just doing it to see how normal people live. Unfortunately, the neighborhood is full of alcoholics and perverts!

Paul Anka, age 2.

My sister, brother, and me (1950).

I was the team mascot (in front in the white hat) for the hockey team, the Connaught, in 1954.

(left to right) Akihiro Hirao, me, Chie Me Erie, and Rei Ko Dang on my first trip to Japan in 1958.

Jerry Lee Lewis and me in 1958, on board a Pan Am flight to Australia.

Mamie Van Doren and me in the movie *Girls Town (1959)*.

Me and Dick Clark, 1960.

Getting smuggled out in a box after a mobbed appearance at a Woolworth's, San Juan, Puerto Rico, 1961.

Receiving my first gold record from Sam Clark (l) and Don Costa.

With my proud family in the 1960s.

The famous Diana *(left)* with me and her cousin.

With Sophie Tucker; this was my
very first appearance in Vegas.

My birthday party (I think it was my twenty-first) at the Sands with (clockwise from front left) Eddie Fisher, Pat Boone, unidentified, Peggy Lee, and me.

My movie debut in *Look in Any Window* (1960), with actress Ruth Roman.

On *Hullabaloo* in the 1960s.

With Annette, on tour with The Coasters.

Paul Anka at the Copa.

Backstage at the bar at the Copa with *(from left)* Irvin Feld and Jules Podell.

Me and Ed Sullivan on *The Ed Sullivan Show*, December 17, 1961.

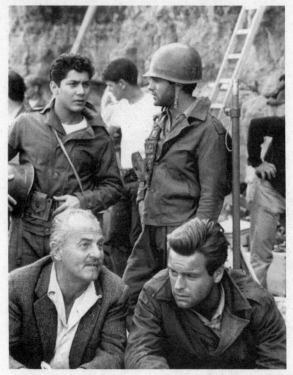

On the set of *The Longest Day, (clockwise from left rear)* Paul Anka, Tommy Sands, Robert Wagner, and Darryl Zanuck.

Scene in *The Longest Day.*

Frankie Avalon, Annette Funicello, me, and a dance instructor at a studio for a TV show.

Me and Annette Funicello.

Connie Francis and me. I wrote her song "Teddy."

At L'Hotel George in Paris with fans. This girl really went all out to show her appreciation.

(from left) Me, Bobby Darin, Frankie Avalon, and Pat Boone.

Me and The Beatles backstage at the Olympia in Paris before anyone in America knew who they were.

Anne and me in France, right after we were married in 1963.

Our first apartment.

Celebrating my Paris opening with
Anne at Maxim's (early 1960s).

Me, Anne, and Elvis.

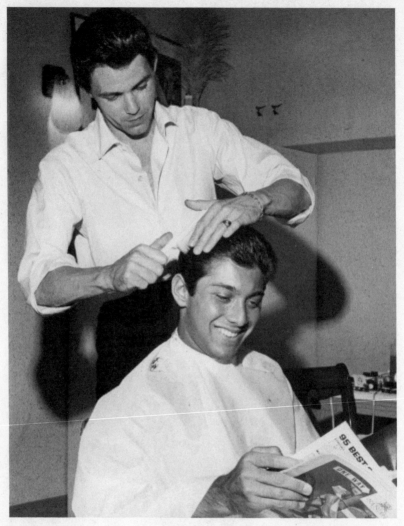

Jay Sebring giving me a haircut in the health club at the Sands hotel at 4:00 A.M .

Four

GLOBETROTTER

People think I went to Vegas, toured around the world, and made records in Europe because The Beatles came along and wiped us all out. Not true. I was playing in Vegas five years before anyone in this country had even heard of The Beatles. I was performing in London, Paris, and Tokyo while The Beatles were still playing in Hamburg.

It was all due to Irv's smarts. In the documentary *Lonely Boy,* at one point Irv says, "God gave you something that he has not given to anyone in the last five hundred years." That was a little over-the-top . . . maybe. Michelangelo, Leonardo da Vinci, and . . . Paul Anka? But just about everything else he did was genius. Irv was the first promoter/manager to foresee pitfalls for a pop singer in the rapid turnover in pop music. Performers came and performers went. After the bus tours Irvin began rethinking my career. He came up with two concepts: clubs and the world. These became the basis of my survival act. My style and my songs were smooth enough to work in the clubs, especially with a little tweaking of the arrangements. I was essentially a crooner anyway—my idols, after all, had been Frank Sinatra, Frankie Laine, and Johnnie Ray, not Chuck Berry and Little Richard. You couldn't put hard rockers like Eddie Cochran or Gene Vincent in a nightclub in those days.

As for his idea of going global, my new record company, RCA Victor, was an international corporation. They not only made washing machines and TV sets, they made records in Europe and Japan. With the arrival of transistor radios and TV broadcasts, Irv saw a new era was dawning. He thought that eventually everyone would know what was going on anywhere in the world. He believed that's why the Berlin Wall came down. It was the beginning of instant communication that would lead to e-mail, texting, Facebook—the tweeting age we're in today.

———◼———

It's 1960. No Beatles, no Stones, no Herman's Hermits even on the horizon, but my nonstop career life careened on as it had done for the previous three years and would continue for at least another four. After I opened up the Copacabana on June 23rd, I appear on *Coke Time* on TV. While touring I'm breaking in my nightclub act. From the Holiday Inn in Pittsburgh, I head to Reno. In August, I'm on the Italian Riviera. I'd become friends with Domenico Modugno, the songwriter/singer of "Volare," and started making records in Italy in 1960 with an Italian version of "Tu Dove Sei," which got to number four on the Italian charts.

In September, I'm performing in Rio de Janeiro, São Paolo, and Buenos Aires. Although I don't get back there that often "My Home Town" is my current single and although I'm not yet nineteen years old, I have an album out called *Paul Anka Sings His Big 15* like I've been recording for dozens of years. My life was so hectic it was beginning to feel like I had been around for several decades.

January 1961, I went to Puerto Rico. I was working at the Caribe Hilton Hotel, a big hang for visiting Americans. Halfway through an afternoon of signing autographs in the F. W. Woolworth store on Ponce de Leon Avenue, a mob backed me to the wall in a handshaking and autograph-seeking frenzy. They wrecked the place, and the situation was becoming life-threatening. After nixing a scheme to spirit me away in a coffin, the authorities summoned a naval helicopter. They broke through a wall, put me in a box (that looked like a coffin), took me out of the store, ran up a set of stairs where there was a helicopter waiting to lift me off the roof. *The San Juan Star* blamed it on my psychic powers: "He does things that foul up the feminine endocrinic mechanism in an age range from lower teens to the middle 60s." In February, I do *The Ed Sullivan Show,* and in April, Danny Thomas's Show, *Make Room for Daddy.* Then I'm back at the Fontainebleau. And on to Boston, Pittsburgh, and then the Copacabana again.

Look in Any Window, the Peeping Tom movie I'd made the year before, was released at the beginning of 1961 and was still playing in theaters that spring when I appeared on *The Perry Como Show* the night of May 10. The next day, my mother, Camy, died at the age of thirty-seven. So young, really, it's hard to imagine, but she'd been having a tough time with the diabetes for years. She died from uremic poisoning, which affects the kidneys; it's a degenerative development from diabetes. In those days they didn't have the technology we have today to deal with these things. If my family was my core, my mother was the source of my strength—I got it all from her until the day I buried her.

There were hundreds of people in the church. I walked up to the open coffin. She looked beautiful in the same elegant dress she'd worn when she came to see me perform at the Copa. I was so overwhelmed with emotion at that moment I don't know how I managed not to cry. I just knew I had to be strong. She used to show me her wedding ring, and say, "Your father gave me this. It will always be on my finger." And there it stayed until the day I saw her lying in her coffin. That ring was from another time and place when bonds between husbands and wives were forever. It was symbolic of the ancient cycle of life of birth, love, death, and rebirth that went back hundreds of generations. I, too, wanted to find someone with whom I would share that eternal bond.

Secretly I slipped the ring off her finger as a keepsake and to this day I still have it.

My mother's death was devastating, utterly devastating. I had lost my biggest supporter from when I was just a boy, the one who always believed in me. It was also very traumatic for my father. After she died, he just sat in a darkened room for days on end. They were very much in love and it was very tough for him. He was a good man. He didn't get involved with anyone for years and it was a long time before he got married again.

I later wrote a song dedicated to my father called, "Papa." When I looked back after a few years, I saw that it was very much about that time.

> When she died
> My papa broke down and cried
> All he said was, "God, why her? Take me!"
> Every night he sat there sleeping
> In his rocking chair
> He never went upstairs
> All because she wasn't there.

From my mother's death I learned about what we get and what we lose in this life. It had unexpected consequences for me. It gave me independence and propelled my unstoppable drive. For a whole year I had lived with that knowledge I was going to lose her. And then suddenly, a few months before she passed, I realized, "She's going to die!" I knew she was going and there was nothing I could do about it. From that loss I learned that part of life was losing, and that knowledge changed my music. By the time she passed I'd had a lot of hits, but thank God I'd played every single one of them to my mother in our basement.

After my mother died we eventually moved into the city to an apartment in the Carnegie House on Sixth Avenue and Fifty-seventh

Street, right off Central Park, it was the top corner apartment. My dad, being a widower, was having a hard time taking care of my brother and sister and dealing with my business as well. It all became too much for him. My mother had always wanted to send Mariam to a finishing school in Europe. So, after she died, I put my sister and brother through school. I sent Mariam to Le Grand Verger in Lutry, Switzerland; well-to-do kids from all over the world went there; King Farouk's daughters were students. My brother went to the Brummana High School near Beirut, Lebanon, a world-famous school run by the Quakers. The year before, they had all gone on a visit to the Middle East with my father and I think that's where the idea of sending Andy to the school in Lebanon must have come from.

I'd written "You Are My Destiny" for my mother—because she *was* my destiny. It was her faith in me that had driven me throughout my life. And, by sheer happenstance, I fulfilled one of her fondest wishes: she wanted me to marry a nice Lebanese girl . . . and I did.

I went to the Sands Hotel, then the Coconut Grove Club at the Ambassador Hotel in L.A., Eden Roc, and back to the Fontainebleau again. Right after that I'm booked at the Copacabana, then the Steel Pier in July—in the same month, the Frolics, the Concord, the Glen Park Casino in Buffalo, and in August the Wildwood at the Manor Hotel.

When I performed at the Copacabana in June of '61, the crowds that formed around the block out onto Fifth Avenue began to seem a bit alarming. Then it was, tomorrow the world! Later in August I left for Spain and performed in Barcelona. On these tours the enormity of the change in my lifestyle was boggling. In Japan, two thousand fans had waited in line in a typhoon to see me. In Sweden, twenty thousand fans waited to hear me in the rain. In Algiers, they'd called out paratroopers to control the mob trying to get into my show. And, to think, only a few years ago I'd been this short, geeky, not-exactly-popular kid in Ottawa, wondering who I was and what I had to do to get out of my little provincial town—and now I needed police protection from my fans!

On August 27, I was in London doing a Granada TV special—and that's where I first meet Johnny Carson, which led to me writing the theme for *The Tonight Show*. At the Sands Hotel that September I started to develop my relationship with the Rat Pack: Sinatra, Dean Martin, Sammy Davis Jr. Next, I'm booked to perform for ten days at the Araneta Coliseum in the Philippines, breaking all existing records, playing to more than 226 thousand Filipino fans. Irv was thrilled at the time to get me out of New York and away from Shirley Ornstein because of his concern about me being with an older woman who was separated from her husband. The fan repercussion was on his mind. Shirley had an earlier relationship with Burt Bacharach from before she was married and he continued to see her as her marriage was coming to an end. In fact it was Shirley who, in a sense, introduced me to Burt. While I was seeing her, Burt was still in her life, which was cool to both of us. Every time I would see her a week later she would be filling me in on what Burt was up to and what songs he was excited about writing. That was my introduction to Burt Bacharach and Hal David.

In December, I went to perform at the Caribe Hilton in Puerto Rico—this was to become a major turning point in my life because, thanks to Shirley Ornstein, that's where I was to meet my future wife, Anne.

Anyway, it was Shirley who first saw Anne on the beach one day and came back to me and said, "There's this beautiful model down there, from France, doing some commercial on the beach, blah-blah-blah."

That night I picked her out myself. Puerto Rico being the hang place that it was at the time, everybody always wound up in the same scenes. And there she was, at a party given by Tony Beacon, a socialite columnist. I saw her at the end of a long table with maybe twenty people, and I said, "Wow! Who the hell is that?"

"That's the girl on the beach," said Shirley.

"My God, you're right," I said. "Shirley, guess what, you're going home tomorrow!" She took it like the true friend she was, and the next day I started looking. I had to find that girl. The search went on for three days. I called around to all the hotels—no luck. I had my cousin Bob Skaff looking, everybody. Finally, she surfaced at a tiny hotel. I called her up and invited her to the show.

She was with a guy named Bernard Lanvin, whose family owned Lanvin, the big French clothing company. They came to the show together but I wasn't discouraged. I tracked her down again and said, "Please have coffee with me."

I finally wrangled some time with her and we did have coffee, talking until six in the morning. She told me about her upbringing. She told me she hadn't heard that much pop music because she'd been to a strict convent school where the nuns forbade her to play certain kinds of music—for example, her favorite, Elvis Presley. Turns out they did allow someone called Paul Anka. Lucky for me!

When she told me she was Anne de Zogheb, I asked her what kind of name that was and you should have seen my face when she said Lebanese! She was one of the top models at the Ford Agency. She was actually living under Eileen Ford's roof, that's how young she was. Otherwise, her parents never would have allowed her to leave Paris. Eileen was supposed to be protecting her from men like me and until I showed up, was doing a pretty good job of it.

I love Paris. I adore it aesthetically, culturally, intellectually—plus I speak French. I'm bilingual, I'm from Canada. When I was courting Anne like crazy—and she happened to be in Paris, which was whenever she wasn't working—my whole motivation was to get to Paris! Get to Paris! We dated for almost a year before I even got to meet her parents who lived there. They seemed to have landed from a whole other world. I was in Paris shooting some interiors for *The Longest Day* in which I play a kid from the Bronx who fights alongside the American Rangers on D-Day. Well, I went directly from the set to meet the parents—dressed in army fatigues!

They were very aristocratic, actual aristocrats. Her father was titled, her grandfather a count. They just started grilling me: "What do you want with our daughter?" and "Do you have enough money to take care of her?" Believe me, *that* was the longest day—and may I add the longest night.

In *The Longest Day,* I scaled the cliffs of Normandy under simulated battle conditions and all I got was a mashed finger. But working on that movie was an amazing as well as exasperating experience. First, you're waiting all day in a tent, waiting and waiting, the way one does on movies. And in walks John Wayne! He's *huge.* He's CinemaScope size. He's a wall. He walks in and he has full power, you know? He just sits down and without saying a word plays chess with me. And there's Richard Burton! Hungover and muttering something dire from Shakespeare's *Henry V*: "And gentlemen in England now-a-bed shall think themselves accurs'd they were not here, and hold their manhoods cheap whiles any speaks that fought with us upon Saint Crispin's Day." Robert Mitchum was already three sheets to the wind. He didn't have to act—he was already a classic noir character. So much charisma in one room, it was a little intimidating. You grew up seeing these people twenty feet high on the screen and then when you meet them they really do seem larger than life.

I'll never forget that first scene, running up the beach, and then onto the hill and up those ladders. All the singers were there: Tommy Sands, me, Fabian. We all kind of looked alike! If we'd all been wearing helmets, nobody would have known who was who, but as I was going up the ladder, I lost my helmet. I was trying to get my foot up as high as I could, put my head down, and my helmet hit the ladder and fell off! I thought they'd reshoot the scene but apparently they don't reshoot entire battle scenes because one soldier has lost his helmet. When the next scene comes up, the assistant director says, "You have to keep your helmet off to match the previous shot."

Well, little did I know that, for continuity purposes, the mistake had to be carried through the whole film. I wound up being the only guy in all those battle scenes without a helmet! Kinda good for me because all my friends could pick me out whenever I appeared. Everyone else had helmets!

We literally re-created the war there. All the airplanes and helicopters and boats came over from our armed forces in Germany. The magnitude of it was boggling! Not to mention the umpteen stars (everyone in the world was in it).

I started to get friendly with Darryl F. Zanuck, the producer, and one day eating lunch the natural thing to ask was, "Who's doing the music?"

"No music, *nooooo* love story," he said. He had his theories and he loved saying it—it wasn't the last time I'd hear it.

Okay, no love story was something I could wrap my brain around. Sticking to the book and all that, keeping it authentic. What do we need a love story for? But no music? No way.

So we would hang and drink beer together, and I would ask him again, "No music, Mr. Zanuck? Really?" I mean, I can't believe it.

"No music, no love story, no distraction of any kind!" he said.

Meanwhile, Zanuck's mistress was just about the only woman in it. So the only love story going on was *outside* the film. Irina Demick was her name. He was a hell of a guy, that Zanuck, just this really feisty character. I identified with him. He was my height, had the cigar—a straight-ahead, no-bullshit kind of guy. You shook his hand, you had a deal. I loved the guy. The son was great, too, but Mr. Zanuck, I loved.

Anyway, they liked what I did, extended my part, and invited me back to do more. That second time around was my big chance.

"Mr. Zanuck," I said. "I've got this melody in my head." And I sang it for him.

"Well, that's wonderful," he said, so I'm feeling really psyched. But then he added, "but no music." He was on a loop.

So there I was, in the road company, so to speak, part of this film, and very inspired by it all. I go home and I'm sitting at the piano and I just start banging it out, *da da da da, da da dee da,* you know? Like I say with songwriting it's all in the finger—that's where the hits are. It's one finger, right? That's what it was. Simple. You start to brainstorm. Okay, *The Longest Day.* I see many men, tired, weary, scared, inspired. And I was, too. My writing chops were there, I'd been doing this stuff since '57, since I was a kid. So you go *da-da daaa, da-da dee dah,* and then you go to your arrangers, your band, and you start putting it together and it comes alive. But it all starts with that piano, and finding the basic tune that captures the mood.

When I left the second time, I told Zanuck, "I'm going to go home and make a demo. You can throw it away, but I'm going to send it you, 'cause this whole experience has really inspired me. Just listen to it and do what you want."

I came home, spent a couple thousand dollars putting everything down on the demo, and I sent it to him. And he sends me back a telegram: THERE WILL BE MUSIC STOP LOVE IT STOP. That's how telegrams read back then. I couldn't believe it.

Happy as I was, I was still me, so I answered, "Thank you very much, and you don't owe me a thing. All I want is the publishing." And he said, "You got it."

When the head of Twentieth Century Fox caught wind that the music was in, they wanted to take the publishing, but Zanuck said, "You don't touch the kid's stuff. . . . He gets what I promised him." And then I got Maurice Jarre to score it—what could be better than that? I'd been to France, I love France, and I loved his work—he's just brilliant.

Then it was on to Japan again, where I had five of the ten top records in the charts. And you know the Japanese, they have great ideas, can produce and reproduce anything. So the first thing that happens to me is this guy comes up and says, "Mista Anka, look! I give you a lighter, one cent, you give it for presents." And he shows me the side of it, and, in a very oblique form of calligraphy—red lettering on silver—it says, STOLEN FROM PAUL ANKA. In other words it was written calligraphically in such a way it wasn't that easy to read.

"That's cute," I said. "It's a cute gimmick."

I loved that and of course I had to order a bunch of them. I must have bought three boxes of these lighters from him. And I start giving them out—to stagehands, to anyone who does anything for me. Back then it was a big deal for me to give out a gift, a lighter. One cent, they cost! Jeeze.

So I go back to France to shoot more scenes of the film. I give them out to all the key camera guys, the director, people who helped me, but naturally I've also got quite a few left over. Meanwhile, we begin to notice that every time we go down to Normandy beach to film—it took us a couple of hours to get to the location—we get robbed. And every time we'd leave these rooms in tiny hotels in tiny towns, we'd get robbed again. The whole world knew where and when we were shooting, and they'd go in and take clothing, jewelry, whatever.

———■———

By 1962, I began to feel my record company, ABC-Paramount, was losing interest in me. They were no longer doing as much as they had done previously as far as promotion and distribution of my records. Also I kept seeing all these RCA products in stores. Washing machines, refrigerators, radios. There was RCA this and RCA that—all over the world. They were an international company and I wanted to be associated with a global corporation who could distribute my records around the world. Secretly I began talking to Robert York at RCA Victor Records, and we had discussions that went on over a period of six months. At the end of 1961, I asked ABC if I could buy my masters back. No one had done that before. Then some time toward the end of '62, we got the deal pounded out. It took almost all of the savings I had, $250,000, but it was one of the wisest decisions I ever made. I knew the whole thing was going to come around again and I just had to sit on those masters until my songs had legs again. Before I left ABC, Ray Charles joined the label, and has a number one hit while I am there: "I Can't Stop Loving You." I met Quincy Jones for the first time and he introduces me to new artist Lesley Gore. I wrote "Danny," the other side of her big hit, "It's My Party."

By 1962, I am in my new offices on Fifty-seventh Street in New

York. My dad was there working with me, and I can remember watching TV when the Cuban missile crisis occurred. In February, Elvis's "Good Luck Charm" comes out and makes it into the chart's Top 20. Hey, I was now on the same label as Elvis! It's early 1962 and I'm kicking in with my new label, RCA Victor! We are getting ready for "Love Me Warm and Tender," my first chart record for RCA. In May, I released "A Steel Guitar and a Glass of Wine" (Top 30 record) on RCA and in November I followed it with "Eso Beso" ("That Kiss"), my interpretation of the bossa nova, a musical craze that people were starting to pick up on. I formed my own production company, Camy Productions (for my late mother), to manufacture and package the albums I was going to produce under the auspices of my new label. Then I started Spanka, my own music publishing company, and got my dad to help me run the company. By August, I was hitting the road again, playing to capacity crowds in Spain. Then back to the Sands Hotel in Vegas, and, of course, the summer circuit: the Steel Pier, Freedomland, and so on.

Then Zanuck arrives in New York. He comes to hear me at the Copa where I'm premiering the theme song for *The Longest Day* because the movie is opening the following week, on October 4, 1962.

We're sitting upstairs, bullshitting in the Copa lounge and he's telling me how he loves the show and suddenly he says, "Do you remember how people were coming into our rooms and robbing us all the time?"

I go, "Yes, of course."

"Well," says Zanuck, "I want to thank you, because we caught the guys."

Turns out that they brought in detectives from Paris and began eliminating hotel staff, *ba-da bing,* and after months of investigating they go to this one-room service waiter's house, and up in his bedroom *on the dresser* in clear view is the little lighter I gave everybody on the set, with the inscription in curlicue English script. But the thief didn't know English—it wasn't that easy to read as it was—so for all he knew it could have said MARSHMALLOWS IN HEAT.

The detective picks up his lighter and it says, STOLEN FROM PAUL ANKA. Aha! So they go into the guy's basement and they find all the missing shit, thanks to that one-cent lighter! And I didn't even smoke. Still don't!

———■———

In 1962 my song "Ogni Giorno" ("Every Day") got to number one in Italy and I made my first Italian video of the song "Estate Senza Te" ("Summer Without You") written by Carlo Rossi and Roby Ferrante and produced by Ennio Morricone. It was a pretty basic scenario featuring me on a pebbly beach climbing up and down on fishermen's boats. I learned to sing songs in Italian phonetically the same way I learned to sing them in German and Japanese.

———■———

I still had to deal with my relationship with Anne. Anne's parents were getting impatient, and gave us an ultimatum: "Either you get married or that's it. You guys aren't dating anymore!"

So we got married at the airport in Paris on February 16, 1963. First we had the civil ceremony at the local government office in the Sixteenth District, with six or eight people and a priest, and then we moved on to the airport, Orly. We had the big ceremony in a chapel there so we could get on our flight without any paparazzi hounding us. There was too much craziness, with photographers and all that stuff. After we said our "I do's" we stepped onto the plane and flew to Switzerland for our honeymoon.

Here we were, two young kids on our honeymoon at the St. Moritz Palace Hotel in St. Moritz, Switzerland, one of the greatest ski resorts in the world, lying in bed in a suite overlooking the mountains—the view was so beautiful and awe-inspiring, it was like looking at a widescreen movie through your bedroom window. Next door to us in the hotel was the distributor for Coca-Cola, a guy from Denmark. He had ten kids and they'd come pouring out of his suite every morning making an infernal racket, so there wasn't much sleeping late. We both loved children so we didn't mind. Anne was a lot more sophisticated than I was in the wine department—and the ways of the sophisticated French. Anne liked to have a bottle of red wine in the evening. I wasn't used to drinking at all and every night I would get drunk on a couple of glasses of classic French wine and fall under the table. I just couldn't handle it. We were two kids having a great time running around, skiing, skating, and riding in sleighs pulled by horses.

I didn't care about anything else in the world but being with Anne. At that moment, a Martian invasion could have been decimating Planet Earth and as long as they respected the DO NOT DISTURB sign on our door and know they could do what they wanted; we were in heaven.

Anne not only changed my life, she changed my whole image—I was now a married guy. I'd read an article in a magazine that many pop stars concealed the fact they'd got married because it might alienate their female fans. This was even true of The Beatles for a while. For a teen idol to marry a world-famous model was unheard of in those days. Now it's the norm. But Irv said, "Don't worry about it, it's not going to affect you that way."

However, the change in me was immense, and totally for the better, in the ways she helped to shape me, the things she introduced me to— her effect on my life was incalculable. She opened me up to art, fashion, wine, culture. Just the way I dress I owe to her. She was in the fashion business and she knew about style. Later on when I first went to France with Anne to work on *The Longest Day,* she took me to Cifonelli to get a suit made. She also introduced me to the incomparable John Lobb (a great shoemaker bought out by Hermès) and those essential Charvet shirts.

By September 1963, I was getting taken seriously in France, too. *Le Monde* called me "the Mozart of rock 'n' roll." *Le Figaro* said my interest now was in singing well, "far from the whimpering of his first successes. . . . He demonstrated that one can sing rhythmically without having convulsions on the floor." The *New York Times* correspondent,

Peter Grose, said, "The young man who brought American rock 'n' roll to France five years ago is back in Paris. It was a gentler and more mature Paul Anka who reopened the renovated Olympia Music Hall last week." The *New York Herald Tribune* was even more effusive:

> There are few performers in active practice these days who have anything approaching his stage presence. He walks on and the audience is his at once. His brash assurance works as magic for he never seems to doubt his ability to control. He is a show in himself.

I got mobbed by teenagers at a PX in Frankfurt am Main when German versions of my songs were released there. I was still popular in parts of the world I know practically nothing about: Sweden, Holland, Finland, Turkey, Portugal, Greece, Poland, Belgium, Denmark, Spain. By 1963, I was considered an international institution, at least according to my manager Irv Feld. He put an ad in *Variety* showing a globe of the world with pennants stuck in it with the names of the countries that I'd performed in on them, under the heading, "WORLD FAMOUS!" above my picture.

Then, in 1963 I headed down to the Caribbean and Latin America: Nassau Bahamas, Jamaica, San Juan, Puerto Rico, Port of Spain Trinidad, Curacao, Caracas, Venezuela, Panama, and Mexico City. That year I was back in Italy again where I released my first Italian LP, *Italiano*.

Back in Paris, again at the Olympia, there's a riot, and six busloads of cops arrive to quell a crazed mob, while overly enthusiastic fans demolish a chimney as they try to break into the theater. And that was just the beginning. On went the tour through Sweden, Holland, Turkey, Portugal, Greece, Finland, Spain, and France.

I met the Polish president on an airplane in Switzerland and he invited me to Poland. The State Department then arranged for me to go. I did the whole tour for $15,000, paid for by the Bank of America. While there I see postcards with my picture on them, an indication that people in Eastern Europe were buying my records, while in Cuba they're bootlegging them. In Poland I am playing to 10,000 to 20,000 people in stadiums. On November 22, I go to Warsaw but just before I go on stage I hear that President John Kennedy has been assassinated. I was unable to perform; I apologized to the audience and promised them I would come back, a promise I kept almost fifty years later, on November 16, 2011. Just to point out that things other than me were happening in the world, 1963 was also the year Frank Sinatra Jr. was kidnapped.

———■———

One of my favorite places to perform and to see other acts is the Olympia, a grand French theater from the Belle Epoque. Built in 1888, it had been the mecca of the great French chanseurs. I saw Édith Piaf there, and Jacques Brel, and Bacharach conducting Marlene Dietrich. I remember going to see Charles Aznavour there with Anne. In 1995, they were going to tear it down to make a parking lot, and there was a huge outcry. Finally Jack Lang, the minister of culture, declared it a national treasure and it was saved. The Olympia was run by the classic, Gauloises-smoking, wine-imbibing, *femme fatale*–attracting Bruno Coquatrix. He was like an old Gaul out of the French comic *Asterix* in a Pierre Cardin suit. He was my Parisian godfather, my French uncle.

One evening I walked into the Olympia—it must have been around 1962—and I saw a shocking sight I'll never forget. A British rock 'n' roll group was on stage, they were the opening act but they were phenomenal. They had a whole look: the guitars, the songs, *the hair*. I was stunned. Today we're all conditioned, but just to hear this new sound, you sat there and went "Holy shit! What *is* this?"

I had just come off of these tours on which you were used to hearing that recognizable, characteristic American sound, the R&B sound, augmented by these huge brass orchestras, and all of a sudden—this! They had been introduced by the MC as "Mesdames et messieurs, it is my pleasure to present, direct from England, les Beatles!" The *what*?

Pre-Beatles was a fun time to be around. It was a smaller scene, unlike today where eighteen dozen bands come out at a time and you don't know who the hell they are. It was more an underground scene back then: everyone knew everything that was going on, radio was limited.

Until then it had been a potpourri of sounds: Bing Crosby, Frank Sinatra, The Everly Brothers, Chuck Berry, then all of a sudden you're in this hall with these screaming Frenchmen—and they weren't even totally into it the way the kids at Shea Stadium would be. At first they sat there mesmerized and then the next thing you know they were whispering and analyzing it, as only the French can do. *Wait a minute, something is happening here*—that was the feeling, and what an absolutely boggling impact it turned out to be. Later that night I got to go backstage—I happened to be working there, too—and had my picture taken with them.

Before long, I got to hang out with The Beatles in London. I'd gone there with Anne, to the Colony Club, where the old Hollywood actor George Raft served as casino director. The first thing that became apparent about The Beatles was that they absolutely loved American music: Chuck Berry, Little Richard, The Everly Brothers—and especially Buddy Holly.

Paul and John were the curious ones; the other guys were quiet. Paul was the most forthcoming of them all—he was interested in everything, besieging me with all kinds of questions. We were backstage, talking about music, sounds, sound effects, audiences, girls. . . . Everything was small and cozy then, everybody was glad to seek each other out and you knew who you were every minute.

It was amazing being a firsthand witness to such a huge change in the making. They hadn't been to the U.S. yet, so it was kind of cool knowing about them before anyone else. The Beatles are coming! The Beatles are coming! They wouldn't know what hit them.

I had discovered them just as they were discovering us, but the thing is, Americans hadn't really caught up. We weren't living in the glare of the media, like we do today. I'd come home with these records and they'd say, "Vat, Beatles? Who are these guys? Whaddaya, crazy? Oy!

Nobody's interested!" But that was just part and parcel of American insularity. I'd come home and tell them about this fantastic French pastry that melted in your mouth, the croissant; I'd tell them about discothèques, bidets, about escargots. "They eat *what*? You mean they actually eat *snails*?" they said incredulously. I remember Sam Clark, the president of my company, staying at the Hotel George Cinq the first time he went to Paris with me on a promotional tour. He shit in the bidet. He didn't know what it was, thought it was the toilet. Turns the taps on, and the shit splatters all over the walls and the ceiling. It was a different era back then—only 2 percent of Americans had passports. Think about that. We were a provincial society, and there was, of course, no Internet, no cells phones, no Twitter, no around-the-clock news coverage. I always say, if there'd have been CNN in 1939 Hitler would never have made it out of Germany.

I started telling everybody I knew about this great group over there called The Beatles and how I felt they were going to cause a major change in the music business. And change the business they did. And here I was, promoting these guys that almost put me out of the business!

I'd come back and talk to Norman Weiss (my agent who later became my manger) and Sid Bernstein, one of the other agents that worked at GAC, and say, "You gotta listen to this!" And eventually it seeped in. That's how they eventually wound up on a little label: Vee-Jay Records out of Chicago.

Finally Norman listened to me, went over there, met with Brian Epstein, the Beatles' manager, and brought The Beatles back and put them on *The Ed Sullivan Show* in '64.

Oh, they were slow on the uptake—everything traveled at a snail's pace back then. They didn't get it. "Love Me Do" probably sounded very primitive to them. It was so new sounding that they couldn't wrap their ears around it. The business in those days was very basic. It was more like one guy phoning the next guy about an act, and if they got a bite, they'd *mail* you a picture. There were no fax machines, everything was slower, more cautious, you couldn't maneuver the world then the way you can today.

It took time for people to really grasp what you were talking about. You didn't just jump on a plane (or online) and go "Look! Something amazing's happening over here." It cost money and there wasn't a lot of that around. Guys weren't flying to Great Britain at the drop of a hat. Still, things were about to change. Everybody had been so confident that we were it, but, as it turned out, we weren't.

Changes were happening in the music business in part because of changes in technology, the advent of the stereo sound system, FM radio, three- and four-track tape machines, the electric guitar, transistors—all developments that made rock 'n' roll possible.

I remember in 1958 when Boeing and Douglas introduced their commercial jetliners, the 707 and the DC-8. I was very green when I first began traveling, and when they first took me to the airport to get on a jet I was scared shitless. I didn't know what a jet plane was. No, I'm not getting on *that*! I want a plane with those things that go round and round! What do you mean *jet* plane? What are you, crazy? I looked at the engine: You mean air goes in there?

The Everly Brothers, Buddy Holly, all those guys, were electronically driven, particularly in terms of guitars, making a personal statement through the way they played their instruments. I could never have used my piano the way a guitar player could use his guitar. Unless you're a flamboyant showman like Little Richard or Jerry Lee Lewis, you're not going to set fire to the keyboard or play it behind your back.

What The Beatles were laying down was a road map of vibe and attitude with guitars. The Everlys' harmonies were a huge influence on The Beatles and The Hollies, as they were on Simon and Garfunkel. I always felt that although I had supposedly "made it," I was quite a different entity than this bunch and always had to keep my eye on the ball. I needed to think of novel strategies just to stay ahead of the curve.

When I think of the difference between the way the fans saw me and the way they saw Buddy Holly, I feel it was because his approach was so personal and "in house," if you will. He played the guitar and The Crickets were his band, not like the kind of pickup bands I was using on the road. It was his bass player and his drummer playing both on record and on stage. My approach was to envision a big orchestra and creating an enveloping atmosphere around it. The Brit Invasion bands wouldn't have been intimidated by that kind of sound; it wasn't the kind of thing a Brit garage band could attempt, anyway—or even *wanted* to. They may have been in awe of the Don Costa arrangements but that was irrelevant to them because they could never orchestrate a song like that—and had no wish to. Theirs was strictly a customized sound. Like me, Chuck Berry had pickup bands but it was always him on guitar. The guitar became the predominant means of getting a song across and the concept of the group created a sense of camaraderie with their audiences.

Buddy laid down a vibe that was unique to him. No technology. One microphone for him, one in front of the band. Nothing like today.

The British were taken with the concept of the group, of three or four instruments—a riff-driven, wailing guitar assault. That's where I separated from the pack, because I wasn't ever going to be that guy in any shape or form. I wasn't a guitar player and I wasn't in a group. I wasn't going to be initiating any next wave.

Is there life after The Beatles? I felt a great frustration, as did other performers. Americans as a whole hadn't really embraced pop music in the '50s. The media as we know it was virtually nonexistent; fashion hadn't kicked in with the sound. Elvis was being shown from the waist up. No one really believed pop music would become such a big part of the culture. It was just a fad. Then came the British Invasion, and that turned it around. Suddenly, rock became part of the fashion industry. It keyed into advertising, lifestyle, everything. There was a whole fashion change going on, and I was getting with it, wearing bell-bottom trousers. The whole rock scene as I knew it had changed and I needed to get a new wardrobe.

The Beatles dominated everything right from the beginning. Hit after hit after hit. It was at that point that American artists just started to get wiped out. Something new and strange was happening—it was like a sonic comet had hit the earth and evaporated a huge segment of the American musical industry.

It didn't really bust out until The Beatles. Until then, the pop music business just wasn't accepted by the mainstream, and Madison Avenue hadn't embraced it. We were just looked upon as a novelty. Once it *was* accepted by Madison Avenue, pop music instantly became part of the culture. Once The Beatles hit, the media was all over us, whereas prior to that they wouldn't even *look* at us. All you ever heard was, "Oh, it'll never last" and "Burn those records" and "Elvis Presley is disgusting and vulgar."

So, after I recovered from the initial shock, I loved what The Beatles had wrought. As a businessman, I looked at it and said, "Okay, I'm off the radio now, because all you hear is British Invasion music, but I've had a good five-year run and now I have to figure out a new direction. On the other hand, the Brit Invasion had now gotten the whole world listening to music. I figured there's gotta be a place for me in there somewhere. I said, "Wow, there's a bigger window, greater things can happen, and everybody's got their time. I'm still writing and I'm still touring Europe and I'm even selling records in Italy." So I embraced it. No choice, anyway. That's where the hook-up with RCA records really worked for me. RCA had studios, and distribution in Europe and around the world. You get a much better quality record commercially if it's produced and manufactured in the country where it's going to be sold and played on the radio. The arrangers in these different countries all have different conceptions of how a record should sound in the area it's intended for.

How I made the transition from my moment of fame in the fifties to my new situation in the mid-sixties was that I knew a tidal wave was coming. The Beatles began having hits in England in October 1962 on their English label, EMI. By 1963, they were huge in England, but

EMI's USA subsidiary, Capitol Records, at first refused to distribute their singles, delaying The Beatles' success here by over a year. Their first American releases came out on the small American labels, Vee-Jay and Swan Records, but by December 1963 the demand for Beatles records had become so huge that Capitol began releasing their singles. "I Want to Hold Your Hand" came out on December 26 of 1963 and by January 10th, of the following year it had sold over a million copies. When they arrived at Idlewild Airport (subsequently renamed JFK) on February 7, Beatlemania had begun.

Most of my contemporaries couldn't compete with the new sound. There's only so much space on the radio. I was fortunate in that I continued to have songs on the charts for the next couple of years.

The group sound that came with the British Invasion was so prominent that nine out of ten records on the charts were by bands, and most were guitar driven. Something I dearly loved—having a streak of hits—had stopped happening. All of a sudden it wasn't working and I had some heavy thinking to do. I was still performing, but I was living on my past, and the past was receding down the railway lines. The Beatles had derailed us.

It was an especially bitter pill for me to swallow because I'd always been the youngest on the bus, the youngest in Vegas, the youngest this, the youngest that. I'd always been the kid. There was no precedent for what I was doing in terms of the industry. The R&B musicians (Little Richard, Chuck Berry) and the country rockers (Elvis, Jerry Lee Lewis) and even the guitar slinging Southern boys all come out of a tradition. I came out of nowhere, out of my own tormented teen head. It had always been uphill. I was always having to prove myself, always had to be better than anyone else, because the public weren't that accepting of young kids who sang teen heartbreak songs. They'd never heard one before me—and hoped they'd never have to again!

And then, after all you think you've achieved, you suddenly realize you're being left behind, the Cadillac you're driving is last year's model. You can be hot as hell and everything comes to you clean as a whistle, and then you cool off and your career goes into a long winter's nap that you pray to wake up from. Knowing the inevitability of change, you need to be ahead of it. I've always tried to anticipate what's coming next, and that's when I began to realize: Okay, this thing of mine could end, and will, so what do I need to build that's going to help me last where others in my crowd didn't?

——■——

Bobby Darin's dilemma was similar to my own but he dealt with it very differently. Basically his predicament was typical of the problems American pop singers had to deal with in the face of the British Invasion. In many ways he was a classic casualty of that shift as well as the impact of Bob Dylan and hard rock. He was a great artist, one of the most talented from that whole '50s, early '60s group of singers. So it's pretty painful when you've seen people like Darin hugely successful all of a sudden get shut down and are no longer working. Doubt is debilitating for a performer, and once it enters your life, it's hard to recover from it. Once the media abandoned certain performers, they lost their nerve. And once that spirit disappears in your mind, you're gone. I saw that so many times with friends. You don't know what to say.

When the changes happened, Darin tried to get on the new bandwagon but it just didn't take. He went totally into left field: he wore jeans, he played guitar, he took off his toupee, he did Dylan songs, which I didn't think he could pull off. You have to stay within the context of your musical personality, but Bobby changed his whole image drastically. And more than once. He tried to fit in, and ultimately it destroyed him—his career never recovered, never mind what it did to his health.

I said, "Bobby, you can't change everything about yourself every five years. You're Bobby Darin; they'll get over it, like they did with Presley."

He did manage to pull it off a couple of times, with "Simple Song of Freedom" and those things. He got more politically aware, hung around with Bobby Kennedy—but overall, I think he lost his way, lost his identity. When you forget who you are, when you change too much, you end up losing yourself in the shuffle.

When the British Invasion came along I remember Darin saying, "I don't know how we're going to survive this." I was never tempted to adapt to all the hard rock or guitar-driven stuff. I couldn't, anyway, and I didn't think anyone would buy me doing that. I wasn't sure what I wanted to do or even if I wanted to stay in the business. I didn't want to succumb to that. I had a lot of discussions with Darin about it. He was sincere about his attempts to adapt, and at least managed to pull it off to the extent that it didn't become a joke.

He was the most talented of the Sinatra wannabes, he certainly got Frank's attention. He had that kind of chutzpah and arrogance that kept him going on for a long time. He truly was a force of nature in pop music, along with Buddy Holly and Elvis Presley—those were the guys who would have ongoing careers, whatever happened.

Bobby Darin got very, very ill, at the end. One of his last shows was *The Midnight Special,* which he promised to come on and do with me. He should never have been there, because he was not well at all. I was very indebted to him because I knew he was not in good shape. We all knew it was just a matter of time. I went to see him shortly before he died, went out on his boat with him. He was always very fatalistic. He used to say, "I'm not going to live long." Toward the end of his life, he changed, became more mellow, humbler, more sensitive, and open.

—■—

I realized early on in my career, watching people come and go, that it was a very dangerous business to be in because the turnover was so rapid. One solution was to focus on writing, whether it was for movies, TV theme music, or writing songs for other singers.

I looked at it in terms of economics. I'd spent all of these years establishing myself, and by the early sixties I was making more money without hit records than I'd had with them, so on some level I was happy. I'd written the theme for *The Longest Day,* I'd come up with musical overture for the *Tonight Show* theme, so as a human being, as an artist, I was being rewarded, and even fulfilled. I had a strong foundation . . . but how to build on it?

By happenstance—and Irv's foresight—I'd had four years to prepare. I was the opening show for four weeks at the Empire Room in the Waldorf Astoria. Things were doing well on the global front, too. I put out my second Italian LP that year, *A Casa Nostra.* My record, "Ogni Volta" was number one in Italy, selling over a million copies soon after release. I sang it at the San Remo Festival that summer and it ultimately sold four million copies in Italy.

Then in July 1964, they typecast me. I played Sammy Glick in *What Makes Sammy Run?* temporarily replacing Steve Lawrence on Broadway. I'd been in all those teen exploitation movies but now I had to learn lines and try to *act*—as in acting. But then again it wasn't exactly *Hamlet,* it was a musical. I then put out my annual Merry Christmas ad in *Variety* to start the New Year, and I was off to Italy, where things were still going strong with my *Italiano* album from the previous year.

By now, with The Beatles dominating the charts and the airwaves, I figured I'd turn the tables and go to England from January 20 to 31. I'd basically sidestepped the tsunami of the British Invasion by going global and transforming my pop performance into main showrooms by '65; let's just say things were not going all that well for me. I went through a bit of a dip from 1965 through 1966, but managed to get through it. I was constantly recording, writing, and doing a lot of TV appearances thanks to my agent Sandy Gallen. Sandy has been a good friend all these years and has gone on to be successful in the personal management business, representing a lot of artists in entertainment. I only began to get seriously concerned in the mid-sixties, 1965 and 1966, when I stopped selling the number of records I was used to and began to question everything.

When The Beatles and the other British groups were invading the U.S., I was actually moving into their territory—Europe and Italy especially. I started learning Italian, writing songs in Italian, releasing albums there under my new label, RCA Records. Because my last name ended in "a," everyone in Italy assumed that I was Italian, and as a country, Italy embraced me.

I had hits on European labels. I had lived there, made friends there. So I never resented the British Invasion. In fact, I embraced it. It freed me.

I was already doing runs out to Vegas, and had an agent out there to handle all that: Jim Murray, who worked with Buddy Howe at GAC. In Vegas you figured out soon enough who the great artists were and their dilemmas, who had problems with their timing and who had problems period. The whole Vegas thing was a dream come true for me. I had to shake myself every day when I woke up: "Wow, here I am in the hottest spot in the whole damn country, and to go out there and see all these big names, some doing their act in the lounge, some in the main showroom, it was unbelievable. I had found a whole new forum, a whole new lifestyle that fit me just like a three-piece Italian suit.

Vegas to me was a place where you could go out and get as much as you wanted, go as far as you wanted to. In Vegas you could (a) check out what was going on in the heart of the glamorous beast; (b) see people you idolized close-up, get to know them; (c) find out where you were going to work and get a sense of showmanship—what you were going to take from all of that showmanship you saw and use it in your own act.

How I came to Vegas the second time was via the Copacabana. Playing the Copacabana led to a one-time shot at the Sands Hotel— and I knew from the first moment I was there that it was just where I wanted to be. I was still with Irv, of course, and still had my two or three engagements a year at the Copacabana in New York. Some strange stuff happened there.

I'll never forget the night of the disappearing table at the Copacabana. One night Sammy Davis Jr. was on stage, singing in what was basically a basement dolled up as an intimate nightclub. The stage was just a twenty-by-twenty floor with all kinds of chairs and nothing really phenomenal about it in a modern sense. It had none of the flair of clubs you'd find in Florida or Vegas in that era, in the Fontainebleau and what have you.

I was ringside sitting there at a table with Anne and a couple of guests and up on stage is one of my idols, Sammy Davis Jr. Sammy's singing the song that goes, "Sometimes I feel like a motherless child . . ." and about four tables over, little round tables, are two guys, and one guy says out loud, "And you look like one!"

Well, at the Copa the place was so small you could hear everything that was said in the room. You heard this big gasp go up from the crowd. Suddenly the lights went out, you heard the sound of fists, and then in the semi-darkness you see security carrying the two guys out with the tables and the two chairs and bringing in another table and two more chairs all in one minute. Then the lights went up and Sammy picks up the song right where he left off.

———■———

In 1966, I re-signed with RCA. My buddy Jimmy Bowen, who I used to tour with, produced "Strangers in the Night" for Frank Sinatra that year. Ernie Freeman, my old friend from the fifties—from the time I recorded the "Blau Wilde De Veest Fontaine" at Modern Records— was the arranger on that record. I remember seeing Bobby Darin that year and he was pissed because he had already recorded "Strangers in the Night," but it hadn't done anything. Frank, on the other hand, was thrilled with having that hit and that his daughter was doing well with her kinky hit, "These Boots Are Made for Walkin'."

In '66, I also did *The Dean Martin Show*, *The Hollywood Palace*, *Hullabaloo*—all those variety shows. My TV appearances were still on-going, my recordings were still making it into the charts. So, me and my mini orchestra, we're off to Paris, Italy, Germany, Sweden, and London, in nightclubs doing engagements. We're in Puerto Rico at the Caribe Hilton Hotel where I'd had a relationship for years. Then back to Sands in Vegas and the Copacabana in New York. A lot of great activity, a lot going on, but I knew there were problems in my career and I started looking for my next move in terms of music. Where to go from here on in?

How did I deal with the anxiety at the time, what with The Beatles and the British Invasion and the drug scene? Very simple: I had to grow up—fast. In November 1966, I released my *Strictly Nashville* album. I've always loved country music and for me it's always been adult music, as opposed to much of pop music, which is directed at teenagers.

I never did hit bottom. In fact, in parts of the world—some of them in the USA—I was still wildly popular. When I performed at the Coconut Grove in Los Angeles in 1966, Hedda Hopper called me "a one-man Texas oil gusher." After a concert in Vancouver a newspaper voted: "Anka for President." "I've seen very few standing ovations," the journalist reported, "and as far as I can remember, I've never seen one in a Vancouver nightclub, until Paul Anka came to the Cave. I have never seen anything like it. By the end of the first show, if they had called a snap election Anka would have been elected Prime Minister—or King—by acclamation."

My philosophy became: When you're earning a million a year, what's there to complain about? Are you gonna cry because you don't have a hit record?

Five

PAINTED WORDS

And then it occurred to me: Paul, what had been your original ambition? Writing!

The one thing I've learned is that great pop songs never go away. The influence of the '50s carries on even as far as Elvis Costello. Elvis Costello is Buddy Holly reinvented. He took the Buddy Holly look and adapted it to the '70s.

It was always my plan to focus on writing, really. Everything came from that. Your career becomes problematic when you don't write your own material. Writing was one way for me to separate from the pack.

One of my major concerns was, How do I write a hit again? It wasn't until 1967 when I wrote "My Way" that I started realizing what was at that time lacking in my life—hit records. I had to adjust.

The songs I wrote were typical of the era we came out of and as time went by and I got a little more sophisticated, the lyrics became a little bit more complicated. But I never wanted to write songs that I had to explain. My songs are very basic—they're all about love and life. I wrote about what I felt and what I knew. My songs tend to tell a story—an autobiography, or fragments of autobiography. All of my songs back then were composite. Part of it was things I really felt and part of it was indigenous adolescent songwriting. When the audience hears it, it identifies.

We all wrote to the same formula in the beginning. The structure of the music was also simpler, it was just the classic *AABA* format. A represented the verse (that is, the story of the song), the *B* being the bridge (the chorus). So it goes: first verse, second verse, bridge, third verse. That's the way God and BMI meant it to be. You were told by the record company and the radio stations to keep it under three minutes, so most of those records in the beginning were 2:56 or 2:50—otherwise they wouldn't get air play on the radio. Only years later did they start getting longer and longer. Part of the obfuscation of song lyrics has evolved from the kids versus the parents thing. It became a code that only kids understand.

People sometimes ask me what comes first, the music or the lyrics? Basically, I just want to nail the feel of the song, the vibe, and build on that. In most cases I start by using dummy words to get a melody structure. Once I get the structure of the melody down, I go back and finish it, refining the words and changing them until they work. That's essentially how I work—I say that, but really I have no idea how it happens.

You start out with a lyric like, "Isn't it a lovely night that we're having, holding you here so good." Right there you've got your melody and your structure, although things can easily change if you find a great hook. The hook to the song is everything, it's the engine—it's what grabs you. I use nonsense words until I get the right ones—the way Paul McCartney used "Scrambled Eggs" before he came up with "Yesterday." You scat, you go *da da da,* just keeping the basic idea in mind. The words are generally tweaked later. Like a house, you need that foundation to build on. You need the music. The words are only as good as the notes under it. That's where the magic comes in, when you have that real strong melody.

It's a craft, basically, songwriting. You're isolated, sitting there on your own and drawing on your imagination. On *A Body of Work* and *Walk a Fine Line,* I collaborated with a lot of good writers, and it really shook up my way of working. Suddenly you're driven by who you're writing for. But when there's no specific goal, you just put down random ideas.

"I Don't Like to Sleep Alone" was written when I was living in Sun Valley. It all started with "(You're) Having My Baby." My friend, Bill Harrah, owned a bunch of casinos and kind of set a new standard with the look of his resorts. A lot of the guys in Vegas took a page from these places he created in Lake Tahoe—they had a very modern, clean look. He was a character, a hell of a guy. I had access to a place he owned up in the mountains in Boise, Idaho. We used to fly in by airplane; it was a remote place right on the river that was aesthetically very inspiring. I wrote a lot of that up there, and at Lake Tahoe. "One Man Woman/ One Woman Man" I wrote on a guitar in a motel in Muscle Shoals, Alabama. The ideas were just flowing.

Some songs are really personal for me, but I have to admit that some others just felt like hits. "Having My Baby" obviously came out of my life. Whereas "I Don't Like to Sleep Alone" and "(I Believe) There's Nothing Stronger Than Our Love" just struck me as good ideas, not autobiographical in any sense. The latter so was basically a conceptual song. I was just checking out what was out there. The songs all tell stories, but I've rarely tried to decant autobiographical material directly into any particular song, the way someone like Al Green or Randy Newman might.

The Painter is the closest I ever came to a concept album. Usually it's just bits and pieces. But *The Painter* was a very special album for me, one of my favorites from that time and place, and I certainly approached it very differently from anything else I've done. Michel Colombier did an incredible job on the arrangements. I was collecting art on a grand scale at the time, thus the title. I was seeing everything through the eyes of an art lover. It's also why I used Michel Colombier— because he was a subtle French composer and writer and he brought some really incredible colors to *The Painter*. I loved working with him; he was just a brilliant musician who approached song content like an Impressionist canvas. Sadly he died a few years ago from cancer. He'd done some work with Herb Alpert, and I got Herb to work on the *Painter* album, too. Michel was a brilliant, brilliant arranger.

I've always written well on the road. The road is for writing! I'll lock myself in a motel room with a piano and once I get the basic idea—a few lines of a lyric, or a melody, I'm off and running. I can write anywhere. In the early days, I wrote a lot on the road because that's where I was most of the time. I got a lot of my ideas out there. "Puppy Love," "Lonely Boy," and "Put Your Head on My Shoulder" were all ideas I got from playing record hops.

I start out at the piano and begin getting into a groove, something that takes me away from what I've been doing all day. I'll work out a melody and, perhaps in the course of that process, a title will occur to me. A catchy title is always a great start. Outside of "Diana," which was a poem I had written for Diana Ayoub, I've never written a lyric first and then gone to the piano to put it to music.

There are professional writers who sit down and say, "Well, Tuesday morning . . . got to write a song." And they do it! I can't write that way. I've got to have a congenial environment to write in—and once I get a feel that glues the bits and pieces together that have been floating around in my head start to gel and then it begins to take shape at the piano.

For a while I tried to force-write. But I soon stopped. I stopped writing for a few years in the mid-sixties because I felt my songs were getting "commercial," that I was prostituting myself. Then I started again to say what I really felt. I no longer wanted to project the idea that Anka equals everything's perfect. I felt I could be honest about my situation in my songs. Nothing sweet, just the truth as I felt it.

Now I wait until I'm in the mood. It's mostly at night or early morning around six o'clock. About 90 percent of the pencil and score-sheet labor goes on between three and six in the morning. Now I know to just wait because I know my pattern. I won't write for a month and then I get a feeling and I'll just knock it out. I keep a typewriter beside the grand piano so I can work on lyrics and melody simultaneously. When I finish a song, I'll sing it into a tape recorder and send the cassette off to one of my arsenal of music arrangers so they can score it. The longest time it took me to write a song was "My Way." Sometimes songs have a quirky double life. "Diana," for instance, was given a new lease on life in Britain, due to the marriage—and breakup—of Lady Diana Spencer and Prince Charles.

I often wonder where songs come from and how I get to write them. It doesn't add up that this is what I ended up doing with my life, coming from where I did, born in a town that size, and from my background. Who ever thought of becoming a songwriter in Ottawa? Why wasn't I a hockey player? Lord knows I played enough hockey, but I wasn't any good—I was short and I was ducking all the time. Even now I can easily conceive of myself getting on skates and playing hockey—that doesn't seem remote at all. But who dreams of being a songwriter when you're sixteen? Elton John? Bob Dylan?

When you're writing a song, all of a sudden you know when you hit that area—your body reacts like a pinball machine that has just hit the jackpot. But as to how that happens, I don't have a clue. It's a weird thing, really. You're dealing with air. By and large, music is magic; when the pinball machine lights up, it's the best feeling in the world.

At first, as a songwriter for other people, I trapped myself. When I started out I wrote songs and sang them and some would become hits. But since I recorded all the songs I wrote up to a certain point, whenever I offered one of my songs to another singer, they'd say, "If it's not good enough for you to do, why should I do it? Am I just getting your rejects?" At that point I decided I would have to invent another Paul Anka, the one who is mostly a songwriter and is known for writing for others. That Anka had to come first. The most important thing was to get the part.

In the late '60s I began to observe how French songwriters like Charles Aznavour and Georges Brassens worked. Although it's not easy to translate what they were doing lyrically, it was through French songwriters that I learned how to use emotions. And I knew we were ready for that style of song here.

The message of my music is the romantic ideal—my songs are all about the strongest emotion in life: love. I'm a writer for lovers and their problems. I've never written for what was currently in vogue. There will always be enough people out there who deal in the tangled game of love and want to hear a lyric that reflects the state they're in. "Do I Love You" is a poetic love song. I write for women in that lost group of souls who still believe in one man. I could never come on like a Rolling Stone. "One Man Woman/One Woman Man," "I Don't Like to Sleep Alone," "(I Believe) There's Nothing Stronger than Our Love," "Anytime (I'll Be There)," "Make It Up to Me in Love," "Everybody Ought to Be in Love," "This Is Love," "As Long as We Keep Believing," "Think I'm in Love Again," "I've Been Waiting for You All of My Life," "Hold Me 'Til the Morning Comes." That's ten years of love songs—1974 to 1984.

I wrote "(You're) Having My Baby" for women who wanted children but didn't necessarily want to be involved in a relationship—because men are not as honest in relationships as women. I try to find a common theme and reach as many people as I can, not only through my lyrics but also the melody that carries it. I generally try to represent myself with signature-type songs, like Lionel Richie did. And every decade, I set out to make a statement that says, Anka is still relevant. I'll always have something to say.

I've always been a businessperson, always thinking of a way to last in this crazy, mixed-up industry. Collecting money owed you was a tricky business in the early days of pop music. There was a lot of looseness and monkey business in the accounting in the beginning—still is—regarding how the record companies dealt with royalty statements. We were all selling a lot of records, but not seeing anything like the money owed us. All of us performers knew we weren't getting the royalties and money from records due us. There was a lot of funny business going on and we were all aware of it, but there wasn't anything we could do about it. After I got screwed financially, I wanted to take care of my own business, which meant I had to be aware of what was out there myself.

I've never wanted to have teams of people around me kissing my ass and telling me how great I am. I never had an overkill of personnel in my entourage like pop stars do today, but still it's in the nature of the business to have a lot of people hanging around and their natural inclination was to pump you up. You've got road managers, publicity people, managers, people from the record company. Even though it was minimal it was still an entourage. But I didn't have a posse of fifteen people fawning around me, cocooning me like artists do today.

Generally, I tried to make myself aware of how the industry worked. I wanted to see how I fit it in. But then there's people who make it in pop music brilliantly by *not* fitting in. With Bob Dylan, I understood his talent. I saw he was very, very different from the rest of us. That voice! For one thing he was not a pop writer. At some point, as a writer, I realized he had made a radical shift in his lyrics. Many crooners and big band singers didn't like him at all, didn't get rock, period. Sinatra couldn't stand the sound of rock music, he never wanted to sing it, and he *hated* the sound of Dylan's voice. He never got any of that stuff. And yet, there Dylan was, at Sinatra's eightieth birthday celebration, singing "Restless Farewell," with Frank beaming. Go figure.

I don't know that it's necessarily totally true that romance is gone out of today's music altogether. Rap is a new and aggressive kind of music. Its frequently misogynistic lyrics certainly have turned the traditional romantic lyric on its head, but underneath all the bravado and braggadocio, it's all about relationships between men and women. I'm not crazy about rap, but I don't think I'd like to see the same kind of music wall-to-wall, year in and year out. The way music evolves and changes is essential to society—and inevitable.

I started out as a songwriter and that's primarily what I am today. The performer in me developed through the years. It's rougher to write for myself than for someone else, but it's a writer's world today. I'm glad I'm not just a performer. I'd be just as insecure and as batty as any of them.

I've written songs for The 5th Dimension, Sonny and Cher, Engelbert Humperdinck, Andy Williams, and The Partridge Family. Elvis Presley, Barbra Streisand, Linda Ronstadt, and Robbie Williams have recorded songs of mine.

Barbra Streisand did "Jubilation"—that was around the time Jon Peters was still her hairdresser. Next thing you know he's her producer, and he's producing mega motion pictures. Barbra can sing the phone book. She has no problem singing *anything*. She's got one of the great voices, like Celine Dion. When I did *Body of Work,* my duets album, I had Celine and Julio Iglesias on it. I did "It's Hard to Say Goodbye" with Celine, "She's a Lady" with Tom Jones, "Hold Me 'Til the Morning Comes" with Peter Cetera, and "Do I Love You" with my daughter Anthea (and Barry Gibb). I tried to choose the songs to suit each artist's personality. Your songs are like your children; you can't really compare them. You have that special feeling for all of them. But my favorite interpretations of my songs include Brook Benton's "My Way" and Buddy Holly's "It Doesn't Matter Anymore."

After you get to a certain age, it's not that easy to get airplay. But you can still write songs, and if you've been a performer yourself, you have a certain advantage. If it's "My Way" for Frank, I can do Frank as I'm writing, the way he phrased a lyric, the way he might say, "ate it up and spit it out"—with that swagger—but I can't carry that off onstage. You can only write well for others when you know their limitations. The song has to fit the image we have of them, but also their self image—you want to flatter them by letting them know you wrote it just for them—or, better still, let them think that they could have written it for themselves.

A composer writing a song—for someone else to sing—is no different than a screenwriter creating a movie for a big star. What's the actor like? What kind of situations would he be in? I thought of Johnny Carson when I was writing the *Tonight Show* theme. I thought: cool, late night, big band—and the rest was easy.

—◼—

My mad road map right up until 1965 consisted of constant touring, clubs, TV shows, traveling. I was reeling from the enormity of these changes in my career. I traveled and toured so much I rarely got time off to be with Anne. Vacations became important. I tried to fit in three or four of them a year just so we could be together. One evening when we were in New York together I invited Anne to go to dinner with Frank Sinatra at Jilly's bar—something I stupidly thought she'd be thrilled by. She hated the place. At one point she tells me she has to go to the ladies room but she's scared. It's dark in there, the characters were sinister looking and she was the best-looking girl in the room. Sinatra overhears this and says, "I'll take you, honey." He takes her by the hand and waits for her and brings her back to the table. Pure Sinatra gesture. He loved to play Sinatra.

Dinner with Teddy Kennedy wasn't quite so charming. We're at this French restaurant La Grenouille. Teddy gets plastered. He's a terrible drunk. He was notorious. His dialogue was getting filthier and more obnoxious with gutter talk "Cocksucker did this . . ." and "Cocksucker said that . . . Hell, a penis is a fucking penis, any cock looks alike." All this vile stuff. The way Al Pacino behaved when he got plastered in that restaurant in *Scarface*. Anne and I weren't sitting together. She was on the opposite side of the table. All of a sudden I saw this look on her face. I looked back at her as if to say, "What's wrong?" She simply said, "I would like to go." "Are you not feeling well?" I asked. No explanation, she just insisted. "We go now. Please!" Off we went and as we left I probably looked at her as if she was absolutely nuts. She just said, "I can't tell you now but I'll tell you later." She'd only say she'd been exposed to things that she'd never been exposed to in her life. It turned out that he'd put his hand on Anne's knee. And she freaked, naturally.

We were trying to be together as much as possible, but to her dismay that meant she ended up in Vegas with me quite a bit, a place she'd barely heard of—and hated with a passion: a vulgar, glitzy place full of mobsters, hookers, gamblers, and showgirls.

Sometimes it was just pure slapstick. One night in Vegas I'd made arrangements to meet singer Jerry Vale, who had a huge Italian following in the '60s and '70s. I had written a song for him and he was coming to hear it. But we didn't agree on where. Before I got in the shower, I told Anne, "The valet is coming to pick up my suit. Tell him to have it back in time for the show tonight and give him a dollar." What transpires instead is that Jerry Vale comes over to my bungalow and knocks on the door. Anne opens the door, hands him the suit, gives him a dollar, and shuts the door, telling him to have it back by seven o'clock. A flustered Jerry Vale called on the home phone in the lobby. It's all new to her—she had found herself in this upside-down world where night is day, the bad guys are the good guys, and there are no clocks anywhere.

Six

VEGAS

There's a gorgeous woman perching at the bar in a low-cut dress, sipping a dry martini. She's looking at you over the rim of her glass, knowing you're in with the in crowd, and she wants to be there, too. It's perfection. A song, a tinkling piano. The ice is clinking in the glass, the music is soft, the lights are low, the crooner up there on the stage knows how you feel about that girl, makes your dreams come true. All your problems evaporate. After a couple of mellow verses and melancholy choruses and a few shots of Johnnie Walker, even your heartbreak starts to get a golden glow. Frank—Frank Sinatra—tie loosened, he knows what you're going through, he's been there himself . . . many times. Just about every song he's ever sung, as a matter of fact. Just hang in there, kid, the worst is yet to come, "So make it one for my baby, And one more for the road." You're in good company, the best company in the world. Sinatra is the only guy I ever knew who, when you heard the first five seconds of a song, put you in the mood right away.

The very first time I walked into the Copa showroom in Vegas, I knew this was the kind of place you never want to leave. You want to live there forever. You settle in the big upholstered booth, a waitress in fishnet stockings and a tiny sequined skater's skirt is asking if you'd like another drink. "Oh! Omigod!" she says, "It's *you*! Aren't you the guy who does 'Put Your Head on My Shoulder'? I *love* that song! Can I get your autograph?"

Frank introduces me from the stage, hangs up the mic, and walks off to huge applause. Across the table some babe is giving you a wink. Frank is telling Dean Martin a joke, the table is a haze of smoke. A couple at the next table are requesting you sing a song, *their* song. He's telling you it's the song they played when they made love the first time. The wife is saying they named their first girl Diana. You're their idol, and if you'll just sing "You Are My Destiny" and dedicate it to their wife, they'd be *in heaven*. And all I got to do is what I love to do. Get up on that stage and sing. Gimme an A. . . .

From the time I first heard about the Rat Pack I wanted to be around these guys, and amazingly they took me in. You can learn a lot from people you idolize. You see the kind of impact they're making and you want to emulate that. Sammy became a close friend. He taught me a great deal in terms of style, energy, and pacing, and so forth. Frank, the same way. He had that incredible breath control, something he used to say he picked up from Tommy Dorsey. He hung around the musicians so much he had the rhythms down; they were second nature to him. He had it down to where he could take a long phrase and really stretch a lyric out like a rubber band.

There are all kinds of lessons you can pick up—and that would include *not* imitating everything they do, too. Not drinking too much, not smoking too much, not gambling every single cent you own. Sammy Davis Jr. was too much, and it was that too-muchness of everything that ultimately killed him.

As I began working Las Vegas, I got to know those guys better. They taught me. I said to myself, *I can do this, I can stay for a lot of years and do the casinos, I can make it. Here I know what I'm doing. I may not always have a hit record, but I can make my way.* And then, as soon as The

Beatles hit, all the old-school American teen idols were wiped out, wiped off the radio. I was the only one that wasn't obliterated by it—I still had hits, "Love Me Warm and Tender" and "A Steel Guitar and a Glass of Wine" and I was thrilled to find a new place to dwell. I still had a momentum going for me. I had the foundation that Irv had built for me. I still had the international ace in the hole working for me.

But, for the longest time, Vegas has had a bad rap. An entertainer too closely connected to Vegas tends to get pigeonholed, dismissed as a glorified cabaret crooner. This didn't apply to Sinatra, Dean Martin, and Sammy Davis Jr. because they *were* Vegas. For a generation prone to write me off as just another Vegas performer, I found this annoying, but I didn't take it too seriously and then after "My Way," everything changed for me again anyway. I've always known when to slide into the next groove. That's why I did covers of Nirvana, Oasis, Van Halen, and Bon Jovi on *Rock Swings* in 2005—to shake people up a bit, to remind them that after fifty years in the business I'm not only still around, I'm still stirring it up. I'm constantly thinking of what other songs I could interpret. Maybe I'll do Prince's "When Doves Cry" and Anka-size that.

———◾———

There are really only two enduring myths in American culture: the cowboy and the gangster. The cowboy got tired of sagebrush and beans, rode into town, tied up his horse, lost the chaps and spurs, bought himself a fancy suit from back East, and opened the Dry Gulch Saloon. After a few shots of white lightning and watching Lillie Langtry, the naughty petite Jersey nightingale, crooning at the player piano, he said, "Boys, I think I'll stay."

Around 1946, the mob arrived in Dodge and the Dry Gulch Saloon turned into the bar at the Flamingo Hotel. Actually this originally had been the dream of Billy Wilkerson, owner of the *Hollywood Reporter*—to turn the sawdust-on-the-floor joints on Fremont Street in a Euro-style resort, that would attract celebrities to come out to the desert, but he couldn't lure enough movie stars out there. The mob, however, saw an opportunity—a virtually tax-free cash cow in the gambling industry. That's where the first great American gangster Bugsy Siegel comes into the Vegas story, opening the Flamingo at a cost of six million bucks in 1946. And you needed entertainment, right? So no sooner had the first casino began rolling the bones that another great American type showed up: the boogie-woogie man, the crooner, the pop singer, the entertainer, the guy you go to hear who'll take you away from everything, put you in some kind of trance, and let your mind float downstream. That place was a state of mind: in the 1950s and 1960s it was Las Vegas.

Even though it wasn't a media-driven society back then, you still heard everything that was going on. We all knew what the wild and horny senator John Kennedy was doing; we knew what was going on behind closed doors, but nobody talked about it. People left you alone. It was controlled. They didn't run out with every piece of gossip, but it was out there.

When you hear the words, "the mob in Vegas," your average person gets an image of this bunch of violent guys in suits, black shirts, and pink ties. That's straight out of the movies; it was nothing like that. In the movies you've got mob guys cutting people up and planting them in cornfields, vicious fights, shootouts. You can't take these stereotyped guys from the movies literally, that's bullshit—well, maybe not the burying mobsters in cornfields part . . . and it wasn't even a cornfield, actually. Still, *Casino* is probably the closest to the facts with Joe Pesci as Nicky Santoro from the infamous Hole in the Wall Gang, and Robert De Niro as Sam "Ace" Rothstein, but even there, even when they retold actual stories, it was blown up out of proportion—naturally.

When the mob ruled Vegas, that's when all the serious skimming went on. All the money, whenever it came in they would send it around the country. If you went back to one of the counting rooms in those days, the private rooms in back, you'd see these wooden boxes. Everything except the hundred-dollar bills went in those boxes. They didn't bother with the twenties or the fifties. They'd divvy up C notes, $100 bills, to the various Outfit guys around the country. They'd go, "This one's for you, this one's for you, this one's for you." The mob guys never bothered with the small bills.

I knew Johnny Roselli from when he used to spend a lot of time at the Sands—he was a dapper, stylish guy. He was an essential character because of his looks and his knowledge about what went on at every level. The Mormons were clueless about casinos, gaming, or whatever else went on in the sin-filled dens of Vegas. As one of then said, "None of us knew snake eyes from box cars." So they relied on Roselli to guide them through the Vegas underworld.

Johnny Roselli was an even-tempered guy. He had the demeanor of a diplomat, and could deal at any level of society. He was a fixer and that is how he eventually landed in Vegas. He was connected to Chicago and to the Dragna mob family in L.A. The guys that I knew at the Sands—Carl Cohen, Charles "Tooley" Kandel, Jack Entratter, and Roselli—essentially corralled Howard Hughes via Bob Maheu into purchasing the Desert Inn, the Sands, and a group of other mob casinos— the mob naturally still running and robbing the places even after he had purchased them.

Roselli had been part of the Hollywood scene in California, and that's why the mob eventually moved him out to Vegas. He would sit at the bar and talk to me in the early '60s. He was very close to Moe Dalitz, a racketeer who ran the violent Cleveland Syndicate before moving to Vegas.

Moe was known as "the toughest Jewish mobster in Vegas," notorious for savage beatings, unsolved murders, and shakedowns. He'd once killed a Cleveland city councilman just because he'd thwarted one of his plans.

Moe Dalitz owned the Desert Inn, the hotel Howard Hughes eventually took over. When Hughes slipped into Vegas Thanksgiving of '66 they took him right to the Desert Inn; his right-hand guy Bob Maheu made all the deals, he was the guy behind the scenes. Hughes came in on a train, his own personal train. I'd met Hughes a couple of times at the Beverly Hills Hotel with Ben Silverstein, who owned it. I think Hughes was coaxed to come up to Vegas by Hank Greenspun who owned the *Las Vegas Sun,* and the idea appealed to Hughes on account of the tax situation. He arrived and settled into the Desert Inn Hotel. At some point Moe Dalitz sent word to the Hughes people that he wanted Hughes out of the penthouse because he needed it for gamblers, some high rollers were coming in. And that's when Hughes decided that rather than move, he'd buy the place. Dalitz was receptive because the government was looking into him for tax evasion even though he was in tight with a lot of local political people. Whatever transpired, Dalitz was later acquitted on those tax evasion charges but he could see which way the wind was blowing. Who knows what goes on? Hughes got his license to operate, no problem. The word went around that Hughes got taken but he either didn't know or care, and, in any case, he still needed the mob to operate the casinos.

Moe Dalitz, however much a vicious thug he was, was well liked around town and did a lot for the city. He built the hospital in Vegas. I'd see him driving around in his yellow Studebaker. He was dapper, tallish, soft spoken—in appearance, a gentleman. His real name was Morris but everybody called him Moe. Moe was a very important casino developer/operator, and had the endorsement of senators and governors, key to a guy like him is that they could never nail him for anything. He was connected to the mob in Chicago, but was a member of the Las Vegas country club, fitting right in with the Vegas gentry, if there is such a thing. It was not unusual to see him eating alone at his regular table. He spoke very softly, and loved to tell jokes. They tried to pin him to the Detroit mob, but he seemed to be a mild-mannered business guy. There was a very soft side to him—he didn't come on strong, like a movie mobster. He was responsible for a lot of the growth in Vegas from the 1960s right up into the '80s, and made a lot of people very wealthy through shopping centers, the development of supermarkets, and hotels. He made millionaires of a lot of people.

Everybody around town loved him. He was an important figure in the transition of the old to the new Vegas. He was close to Jimmy Hoffa and in that way was linked to the Teamsters, in connection with money coming into Vegas. As suave as he was, though, there was a real scary side to him as seen in the infamous confrontation between him and Sonny Liston at the Beverly Hills Hotel. Liston gets into an argument with Dalitz and threatens him. Dalitz tells him, "Whatever you do, you better kill me now because I'll make a few phone calls tonight and you're gonna die *very slowly*."

By 1960, the strip in Vegas with its flashing neon had become lit up like a pinball machine. From 1960 and on, when I was in my full stride there the who's who in show business converged on Vegas. But, if you look through the press archives of the 1950s through the 1970s you'll find that no other celebrity has been written about like Frank Sinatra. The public even loved him for his outbursts—his temper tantrums only illuminated his image and gave more sizzle to his celebrity. He took no shit from anyone. He was a people's star. We all wanted to emulate him but knew we couldn't. He was the boss.

When Sinatra heard Don Rickles had been rapping him on stage, saying rude things about him—which is Don's style, of course—he decided to play a trick on him. Now, Don was the guy of the hour, see; we all heard about this outrageous act where he insulted people and went to a midnight show in the lounge at the Sahara after one of the Rat Pack shows. Frank wanted to teach Don a lesson in a semifriendly way—but, nevertheless, send him a message. We all sat ringside in this lounge before Rickles came out. There were about twelve of us, including Sinatra, Dean Martin, Joey Bishop, Jilly Rizzo, his bodyguard, Sammy, and me. Frank sent Jilly to the newsstand to buy newspapers and we hid them under the table. Announcer comes out, "Ladies and gentlemen, Don Rickles." Don walks on; Frank says, "Now!" and we all picked up the newspapers and opened them and started reading them at the table ringside while he was trying to do his act. Don sweats a lot, but that night he really sweated. Imagine a tight room of three hundred people and here's Sinatra and all his pals down front reading newspapers. He had good reason to sweat. Sinatra had previously had some wannabe mobsters beat up two comedians who had made fun of him. Don's trying to be professional but the scene is unnerving him. Finally he makes a joke that hits home, we all laugh and everyone relaxes and we can enjoy the show. I've known and loved Don and his wife, Barbara, for years and, forget the stage persona, he's a loveable Teddy Bear.

Sinatra ruled supreme. Even with rock 'n' roll and with the British music scene just off shore, Frank was the most popular and controversial figure around. Whenever he was there, he submerged himself in Las Vegas like it was his own private hot tub. Keep in mind, he had been singing in Vegas as far back as 1951 at the Desert Inn when there were only four hotels on the strip at that time.

There was a certain kind of electricity that prevailed when Frank, the Rat Pack, and their famous celebrity audience were in town. The showgirls, the call girls, and all the hot women were put on hold, especially when they heard Jack Kennedy was coming. There was a pungent sexual frisson in a town that small in size when those guys hit Vegas, and they would hit town often, and all of us benefited from it in one way or another. And then just put all of those mob figures in the mix, especially Sam Giancana, who brought Judith Campbell Exner into the scene, a 10-out-of-10 beauty, who Sinatra got involved with. Ultimately Frank introduced her to Kennedy and that had a lot to do with JFK getting elected. Keep in mind that Giancana delivered the state of Illinois to Kennedy. Everybody knew the Mafia boss from Chicago was someone not to be messed with. He was a small, short guy, my height, was always smoking cigars in beautiful suits, and had a violent MO. He had interests all over town. He was seen around town with one of the MaGuire sisters, Phyllis, a beautiful all-American looker with a lot of hit records. I covered one of her records, "Sincerely," in the late '60s, a single originally covered by The Moonglows.

But the bottom line is, Sam was a murderer. Frank had worked for

him many times in his nightclubs. I guess he felt indebted to him because there was a time when he couldn't get work and Sam hired him.

The clan, the Rat Pack—call them what you will—were in full
stride. Oddly enough Sinatra constantly verbalized to all of us that he
was not happy with the way the media depicted him as the leader of the
so-called Rat Pack. Be that as it may, it was always a great fun event to
sit and watch all of them together on stage. There was nothing like it.
They all loved getting up on stage at night just to have a lot of fun. It
was as loose as a goose. But from the all-night drinking sessions to the
steam-room scenes, I realized how punishing it was on their bodies to
keep up such a routine. The drinking, the smoking, staying up till
three, four, or five in the morning. It wreaked havoc on their voices
and their lives.

The big moment of change for all of us in Vegas—and it tied into a
specific event actually—was when Howard Hughes came in Thanksgiving of 1966. It all changed. All the old mobster world courtesies
went out the window. Even though the mob guys out of Cleveland and
Chicago still ran the casinos on a day-to-day basis, you could see a big
change coming. For whatever reason, or whatever Hughes's alliances
were, overnight he made it into a corporate atmosphere. Bob Maheu,
who was Hughes's right-hand guy, came in and bought up everything
and that changed the atmosphere forever afterward.

Meanwhile Hughes is upstairs in the Desert Inn—or so we hear. We
never see the guy. He's the ghost in the penthouse controlling everything, the invisible man pulling all the strings and very soon we start
feeling the change in the town. We knew when Hughes was in town
because of the nutty TV programming. You'd get back to your room,
turn on the TV at two in the morning and *Ice Station Zebra* would be
playing. At 5:00 A.M. it would start showing all over again. There was
limited programming on TV anyway, but this was ridiculous. It was on
almost *every night*. In the beginning nobody could figure out what was
going on. People were asking, "What the hell is going on?" Eventually
we figured out what was going on. Howard Hughes had bought a local

TV station—it was just a fifty-by-fifty-foot clapboard shack run by a couple of guys—and any given week he was in Vegas, you'd see *Ice Station Zebra* showing continuously. Hughes loved that movie. What probably appealed to Hughes about the movie was the frantic search for a traitor out to sabotage the mission. He was very paranoid. For instance, the Silver Slipper burlesque theater had a fifteen-foot-tall woman's high-heel shoe as part of their sign and Hughes believed there was a photographer hidden in the toe, taking photographs of him in his bedroom from there.

Things got nutty pretty fast, not just because Hughes was so eccentric—and he was—but because he had some peculiar employees like Walter Kane, who refused to follow the old codes.

When a guy like Howard Hughes came in he operated strictly through intermediaries. Walter Kane was one of his right-hand men and took over the job of entertainment director from Jack Entratter and therefore had all this power. He not only worked for Hughes, word was he acted as a pimp for him, too; he got the women, he screened them. He was the perfect guy for this job because Walter was gay, so no threat to Hughes in the female department. Kane fancied himself as a kind of superagent who would dispense with all the other talent agents in town. He'd come in with a list of performers. "We wanna get this guy and that guy and bring what's-his-name in." He'd treat the agents funny because it was a new regime and Kane was changing the rules. Word soon got out around town that this guy Kane was looking to make direct deals, cutting out agents from the picture. What Walter tried to do was go around these agents and go directly to people like Debbie Reynolds or Wayne Newton, who became his buddy down the road. By making deals directly, he cut all these agencies out of their commissions and they weren't too happy about that. There were some loyal entertainers who wouldn't be a part of this because they'd had the same agents for years, and the agent had taken care of them.

My agent Jim Murray had a showdown with him. He was nervous that Kane was going to steal his clients, like Debbie Reynolds, and

Kane wasn't being truthful about it, although he was making deals behind his back. Back then Jim was a pretty heavy drinker. I think it was about two in the morning after a few double bourbons on the rocks that he showed up at Walter's door—Jack Entratter's old place—and said, "What are you trying to do, going around me and hustling my clients?" "What do you mean?" Kane said, stalling for time. Jim wasn't going to let him get away with that. Kane was wearing a nightgown with one of those Santa Claus type hats on his head. Jim got so mad he grabbed him by the throat and said, "You're lying to me, and you're lying to Debbie, you son of a bitch," and he got him up against the wall. And then out of the room next door came another Hughes employee, a guy named Perry Lieber, who must have been Walt's boyfriend, with the same hat and the same nightgown. And he starts yelling at Jim, "Don't worry, don't worry."

You know Walter was kind of a devious guy and that's when all this kind of shit started in Vegas—when you didn't have the mob guys with their code of behavior, a whole way of life in Vegas ended. It was the new bureaucratic regime where you had all these rules and lists, and functionaries were running around with clipboards, all obeying the great eye in the sky over there at the Desert Inn. A cold, new impersonal wind was blowing—the mood changed, the people changed, and an era was over. All that funny stuff began with that new regime—the Mormon clique. It wasn't only among Hughes's group—Parry Thomas, the banker who advanced loans to many of the casinos was also a Mormon. There was a weird connection to the influx of Mormons in Vegas and Washington—to this day they have a strong presence in Washington.

The mob guys didn't put up any resistance when Howard Hughes moved in—in fact, they welcomed it because there was a lot of heat on them and Hughes becoming a casino owner took the pressure off them. And in actuality, they still ran the place. They were still running the casinos, still ripping them off with all the games they played with the money. Blatant stuff, outrageous stuff. But it took the feds years to figure it out. There'd be two legitimate crap tables and one that was fixed, siphoning off the money but hiding behind the fact that Hughes owned it.

———◼———

I've seen all the transitions the Rat Pack went through in that environment, so many nuances. Back when I first went to Vegas, it was mob driven, totally. It was a whole different atmosphere than present-day. A handshake meant something. Loyalty was the code of the day—unlike today. It's a different world with these younger guys where you can shake their hand but you'd better have twenty white-shoe law firms read the fine print.

It's an era that is totally gone now. There never has been anything like it, and never will be again. It was a time of incredible buzz, of fashion, everyone on display, egos to the max. Frank ruled. He was feared from Hollywood to Vegas to New York, know what I'm saying?

Vegas was such an irresistible place and it all revolved around Frank. Everyone—movie stars, business moguls, and women, of course, were magnetically drawn to him. Even future presidents wanted to hang around with Frank because at that time—late '50s to early '60s—he was the hippest, coolest cat around. Frank was king of the hill. JFK and Frank got very tight, so tight that Sinatra started building guest quarters for JFK at his house in Palm Springs.

In 1961, Frank spent an enormous amount of time and money creating a compound specifically for JFK, building new cottages, putting in new phones, buying new furniture, and installing a fancy specially built bed above which hung Frank's little in joke: JOHN F. KENNEDY SLEPT HERE . . . from which he had diplomatically omitted WITH NUMEROUS WHORES. The walls were covered with photos of Frank, Jack, and Peter Lawford. Frank was therefore utterly humiliated when in the spring of 1962, JFK, on a visit to California, ignored Sinatra's invitations and never saw the sumptuous quarters Frank had built for him in

Palm Springs and had hoped would become the Western White House. Instead, JFK chose to stay at Bing Crosby's home, which threw Frank into a rage. He began smashing pictures of the Kennedys and took a sledgehammer to the heliport he'd had built for JFK to land on.

After JFK became president, he wanted to put some distance between himself and Frank because of Sinatra's connections to the mob, and the compound sat empty. That hurt. Frank felt it was a slap in the face, and went nuts. Whatever Sinatra's ties to JFK's father, Joe Kennedy, or what his obligations were to JFK as a friend, Kennedy had to sever the connection. JFK, of course, loved the ladies and the situation played right into the whole sexual circus. I saw the reality: Kennedy and the hookers, the women who hung around Frank, and the mob. It was a shop window. The media at that time was controlled, so they wouldn't write about it. But never doubt the intensity of it. The things that I saw and witnessed, it was all part of show business, but it was pretty wild. All the JFK escapades with showgirls happened in Vegas.

—■—

Back in the day, the airport was tiny, the size of a forty-by-forty-foot room. It was a wood shack, actually. You walk across the tarmac, come in the door—it was just like an old-fashioned railway station: wooden benches, lockers, a big old clock. Nothing fancy, nothing glamorous about it.

You didn't need a glitzy airport lounge, you went to Vegas to be entertained. You had the best of everything: best-looking women, the greatest artists in the world. You went back to meet them and there was no arrogance, self-importance—they were very touched at your compliments, and would introduce you to whoever was in the dressing room: politicians, movie stars, other singers. It was a town of tight little showrooms and was still very quaint when I first went out there. It was also intimate, as if you were right up there with them. You'd see Count

Basie and Sinatra performing twelve feet away from your table. It was the biggest thrill of my life meeting Martin, Sammy, and the whole Rat Pack—all there together, hanging out, telling jokes, spinning wild tales. There was something uniquely theatrical about Vegas—there were all these layers, all this stuff going on. There weren't really tourists in Vegas the way there are today, but the visitors in general were oblivious to what was really going on. The performers, on the other hand, were somewhat clued in, but the staff, the call girls, the pit bosses, the showgirls—all knew the real behind-the-scenes stuff. They saw what was going on in the showrooms on the floor and quite a bit about the murky world that controls them. And then there were the mob guys—that's a whole other underworld that no one but they knew.

Everybody who worked there knew what was going on. Couldn't keep secrets like that down. I think for a while they were running a coke factory out of the backroom of Caesars Palace. All kinds of deals went down there—everything from real estate to contract murder—all courtesy of the management.

With all that interconnectedness of the mob and the Vegas scene, how did I avoid not becoming involved with these people? Nobody ever threatened me; no, nothing like that. You can't threaten a nineteen-year-old kid, and who ever heard of a nineteen-year-old being killed? Especially one who had the number one record all over the world. Yeah, if you're Sinatra or you grew up with these people and you're asking them for favors and you want people to get beat up, sure, they're going to threaten you if you don't keep your word.

So, here's me—I'm young, I'm making money for the mob, my songs are on jukeboxes. When you're that young, you're, "Yessir, yessir!" These guys are taking me under their wing because I worked hard at being the little gentleman. I'm this young kid walking in their world and they're going, why the fuck not?

From all that I've told you about the crooked noses, as we called the mob guys, you might get the idea that it would be dangerous to your health to hang around guys like that—not exactly the kind of friends your mother would want you to make. But these guys didn't threaten anybody unless you crossed them. And even then, it was almost always between themselves. They really didn't need to threaten people, people were already very wary of them.

Not only did nobody ever threaten me, no one ever said to me, "Kid, I'm gonna take you over, you're our property, *capisce*? Their attitude was, leave the kid alone. "Whatta ya gonna talk to him about? Gonna go to the police? Naw, he's a kid!"

Sinatra was a different story. Sinatra was a guy who was fascinated with the Mafia. He liked hanging out with them and thus maybe he got the bad rap that he was owned—and there probably were some ties there because of favors they'd done him and what have you.

With me, they knew I was bringing in business and that was it. It's very simple; to the mob, business was business, and though their business was different from other people's, the same rules applied. It's somewhat of a fallacy to think of Vegas as this film-noir landscape with bodies in the alley, bodies thrown down elevator shafts. People along the periphery make assumptions and these perceptions become reality.

Nobody ever walked through the door and said, "You're making this and doing that and now we own you." Never. They kept their end of the deal and I kept mine. Anyway, I was never the kind of a guy who needed the mob to bail him out. I never got into the kind of trouble where you needed these guys—gambling debts, deep into drugs, abusiveness.

You start out in a mob-owned business in one part of the country— and the USA's not a homogenous nation, by any means—you're going to keep things separate. This isn't like Soviet Russia where at one point they'd break down your door and drag you out to the firing squad. I worked within a system where I had no choice as to the kind of the people I would be dealing with. They were gangsters, but they were American gangsters. They functioned in a system that followed the pecking order of American society. We were a country where the Irish, the Jews, and the Italians had a lower place in the pecking order, and they

all eventually figured out a way to overcome that. Some were connected, some weren't, but they all functioned within that system.

Sure, I heard about bodies in the desert, guys that cheated at the
tables, guys who disappeared, but I was never directly in the line of fire
or frightened of anything—never, ever. There were hundreds of artists
performing in Vegas, talent agents, managers, etc. who had no mob
connections whatsoever. By and large the mob guys were just worried
about their own.

But I loved being around these guys, I loved the security of it. If
they respected you, they protected you. I worked for them and there
were perks that went along with that. I've had them say, "If you ever
need anything, you want somebody taken care of, Paulie. . . ." But I
knew better than to take them up on any of that. You do that once and
you're in their pocket for life. With the mob in control, Vegas was the
safest place to be. Even walking around in the middle of the night you
didn't have to worry about being mugged. In fact there was a rule
among the families that no one was to be killed in Vegas. They didn't
want gang wars, bodies on the sidewalk—bad for business. A lot of
guys who had contracts on them would hang in Vegas because they
knew they were safe as long as they stayed there. But once you left
Vegas you were in trouble.

During this time, let's say during the '50s and the '60s, you soon
learn what's going on. The town was controlled by the boys. Back then
you had all these different fiefdoms in Vegas—the colorful larger-than-
life characters who ran the various casinos. I mean, you start out with
the Desert Inn, which was one of the cleaner ones of the bunch. That
was operated by Moe Dalitz. El Rancho was Beldon Katleman's place.
I believe that was the place where Presley played and didn't make it—
the first time he came to Vegas. He played the Venus Room at the New
Frontier from April 23 to May 6, 1956 as an "extra added attraction."
But, on the other hand, it was in Vegas that Elvis first heard Freddie
Bell and the Bellboys rehearsing a comedy burlesque version of Willie
Mae "Big Mama" Thornton's song "Hound Dog" that had the line in

it, "You ain't never caught a rabbit, and you ain't no friend of mine"—or at least that's what he thought he heard. Elvis started playing it on TV shows and in concert and by July it was a hit record, with "Don't Be Cruel" on the flipside. So even though it took him another dozen years to make it in Vegas, Vegas did him a solid.

The New Frontier was run by the Detroit guys, the Flamingo was owned by Al Parvin and Paul "Red" Dorfman, an Outfit guy from the Chicago mob (and stepfather of Allen Dorfman, who owned the Stardust Casino—featured in *Casino* as the Hotel Tangiers). The Dorfmans had a big furniture company back then. He worked for the boys at the Copa—started out there as a waiter actually. From there Eddie Torres eventually went down the line to end up running the Riviera.

The fans, the help, the mobsters, the entertainers, the pit bosses, the showgirls, the waiters, the call girls, the bartenders, the cocktail waitresses, the guys who ran the casinos, the tourists—were all part of the pageant.

There was this guy Jack Entratter, who'd been a waiter and bouncer at the Copacabana, moved out to Vegas where he became the entertainment director at the Sands. Tall, good-looking guy. We used to call him slue foot, because he couldn't walk normally—he wore these funny shoes because his feet were square. He had all kinds of problems, and they weren't all confined to shoe problems, believe me.

All the casino managers were more or less controlled by the boys. That was pretty much the landscape. The entertainment directors came and went, but the mob or "the boys," as they called them, stayed the same. People like Eddie Torres and Jerry Zarowitz.

B.H.H.—before Howard Hughes—was the golden era in Vegas, the early fifties through '66. It was like a family thing then; if you were performing at the hotel, they made you feel like you were part of the family. If you left and performed somewhere else, you stayed loyal to your casino, you did it the right way.

Vegas was a community, it was a family environment—not exactly the family on *Leave It to Beaver,* or today's family entertainment in

Vegas, but a family nevertheless. If anybody got sick we'd fill in for them. It was that kind of tight situation. In those days we had entertainers like Louis Prima, Harry James, The Mills Brothers—people of that caliber. That was when the lounge business was very big.

It was a time when nobody locked their doors. Who's going to steal anything when the mob's running the store? Back then, in its quaintness, in its feeling of control, there was this unilateral sense of dress and behavior and calmness. . . . Until, that is, somebody stepped out of line and got caught and murdered, and put in a car, and dumped in the desert. Who knows how many bodies are buried out there?

You'd have guys come in who you'd read about in the papers. They were wanted for this or that crime, and they were like, "Ahhh, fuggetabawtit! It's just an aggravation, I'll be okay, whaddya need, let me send you some cannolis." The next day the three guys would walk in with boxes of Italian pastries, cannolis or whatever you wanted. It's funny, you'd watch these guys gamble, and see how meaningless money can be to some people, to where they're losing half a million, a million, two million dollars. And the way some people played at those tables was just mind-boggling.

At the Sands there was Carl Cohen, the manager and mob's point man, and this one little guy whose name was Charlie Kandel. We used to call him Toolie. He was a mob guy, but the sweetest man imaginable. He was always so impressed that I wrote the theme song for *The Longest Day* because, aside from being a mobster, he was also a decorated war hero. Used to show me his little parade hats and occasionally give me one of his medals. He always slept with a baseball bat next to his bed in case somebody came in and threatened him.

He would look after me. He'd meet me in a coffee shop after the show and eat coffee ice cream and tell me little bits of mob protocol: "Just don't you ever do this or that, that's a no-no, stay away from that." He would always tell me, "Walk in the shadows." He'd sit in the back of the show every night, have a coffee ice cream, and a cup of hot lemon juice before he went to bed. Everything he did, he did very meticulously, methodically, all his little routines. Maybe he had OCD—like Howard Hughes. All these guys had their eccentricities. Every time he'd eat, he'd bring his own utensils, put them under boiling hot water, clean them as if he were sterilizing them for an operation. He wouldn't touch a knife or a fork unless he'd first cleaned them himself in boiling water.

It was at the Sands that I first met Marvin Davis, an oil guy, one of the richest in the world. One time or another he was the head of Davis Petroleum, bought Twentieth Century Fox (with his partner Marc Rich), and owned Fox Plaza, the site of the Nakatomi Plaza building in *Die Hard*. He would come in frequently to gamble at the Sands. That's where you began; everybody started at the Sands. I made so many friends at the Sands.

——◼——

The year 1967 wasn't very good for blue-eyed crooners—and things only got worse for Sinatra. It's true he'd had a number one song that year, even if it was that "Something Stupid," recorded with his daughter Nancy. He got named chairman of the Italian-American Anti-Defamation League, an institution he wryly referred to as the "Dago NAACP."

One of the things that bugged Sinatra was rock 'n' roll, especially the British Invasion. At first he thought it was just a fad, like hula hoops, but by the late '60s it was clear it wasn't going away anytime soon. The Beatles, he said, at least weren't as bad as Elvis. He developed an irrational loathing for Barbra Streisand and any number of other things.

During this period Sinatra seemed to be constantly angry and frequently flew into rages. The problem was that Sinatra was no longer the god he had once been. Rock 'n' roll had eclipsed his fame and notoriety, and worse, he was now considered schmaltzy and unhip by the new hip generation of the sixties. By the late 1960s Las Vegas itself had become uncool and tacky. Once the Mafia had sold Vegas to Howard

Hughes the sense of danger and decadence that made it luridly attractive was gone—it was just "a Disneyland, with slot machines."

But his big *bête noir* was the Howard Hughes organization. After Howard Hughes settled in in 1966, a new infrastructure got established. Things were becoming more and more uptight, more rules, more lists, more people running around checking on things. When Hughes took over, his people wouldn't work with him. The mob didn't own all the casinos anymore. When things began to change Sinatra got massively pissed off. The Hughes situation was getting intense and it impacted nobody more devastatingly than Frank. There was a new code in town.

In 1967, Sinatra was the headliner at the Sands. He ran up gambling debts at the casino and then disappeared over Labor Day weekend. A few days later Frank was back with his teenage bride, Mia Farrow. Showing off, Frank grabbed one of the golf carts used by the bellhops to transport luggage and began crashing around the casino with Farrow in the passenger seat, eventually smashing into the glass entrance to the casino. It wasn't, as has often been told, intentional, nor did he drive through it. But he'd been drinking and the golf cart got out of his control and the window shattered. Fortunately neither Frank nor Mia were injured in the crash. It was just one of those freaky things that can happen in Vegas where people and machines can spin out of control.

Then there's the big blowup. Frank's been performing at the Sands, say, for a week. It gets down to where they won't give him any more markers. Markers are chips. Frank would cash them in and keep the money and not pay off the markers he owed on. The casino bosses let Frank do that, let him have markers for, say, $50,000, and, let's say he'd make $75,000 (meaning $50,000 would actually belong to the casino), he'd keep it all. When Hughes came in, he said, "No more of this. Give us back our fifty grand, keep your twenty-five." That's what started the problem between Sinatra and Hughes. So the resentment starts building up.

I'm sitting at the bar of the Sands hotel, next to the casino with Jilly Rizzo, Sinatra's friend and bodyguard. He told me Frank was in a rotten mood. From what I understand, Sinatra's rage about the markers situation had started a night earlier. Frank got so pissed off he called Jimmy Blue Eyes in New York. Vincent "Jimmy Blue Eyes" Alo got his name from this game that they played in New York where they'd get on each other's shoulders and then you'd hit each other with their elbows. But because of his small size Jimmy got hit in the eyes so much they'd be black and blue. That's how he got the name Jimmy Blue Eyes.

Now Jimmy Blue Eyes was one of the guys that got things done in Vegas. Sinatra would call him whenever he got pissed off at anybody. He wanted Jimmy to fix it then and there, but Jimmy said, "Frank, go to Palm Springs and relax, we'll try and do something." But Frank didn't want to go to Palm Springs or cool off.

Frank was understandably upset. You don't insult Frank. He's a man's man. And when people didn't treat him with respect, he'd overreact. I knew that Frank had called someone "who could get things done." But despite what you've heard or read, I never saw any indication that Frank was ever a mob guy. The thing you have to remember is that in those days in Vegas we had to make choices that your average person wouldn't normally be confronted with. And let's be honest, like everybody else in America, we were fascinated by gangsters ourselves—they had their own dark glamour.

It's late at night, were all in the lounge bar, and Frank's still steaming about the night before. The next thing I know, he's standing up on the blackjack table in the middle of the casino. And of course everybody stops playing. People's mouths are wide open. Frank's buddies are rushing over: "What's up, Frank?" The pit bosses are trying to calm him down, figure out what's the matter. And Frank's going, "This place was sand when they built it, and it'll be sand when I'm fucking done with it." He's ranting on and on, cursing. The pit bosses are telling him, "Aw, Frank, c'mon down, man, forget it." Finally they get him off the table and into the operator's room at the Sands. He doesn't want them to call Carl Cohen, the manager of the Sands. This scene gets reported to Carl Cohen who is a salt-of-the-earth type of guy, always the greatest gentlemen, an individual who I never saw lose his temper. I loved the guy; he was my godfather. It's 1:30 in the morning, but Carl is going to try and sort it out, make Frank see reason. Carl was the front man for the mob bosses. He wasn't a made guy—and that was his value—he acted as an intermediary between the mob and the civilians.

They wake Carl up 'cause the management guys who worked at the casino all lived on the property, in these little villas in the back in an area called the Aqueduct. Carl comes over in the middle of the night, in his bathrobe, in a golf cart, parks behind the coffee shop adjacent to the casino. We are informed that Mr. Cohen has arrived; Jilly and I take Sinatra back to the coffee shop so that he can talk to Carl. There's a large security guard standing next to Carl. In his tantrum Frank throws a chair at the security guard.

There's a pot of coffee on the table. Carl is sitting there in his bathrobe, and he and Sinatra get into it. Frank is standing in front of Carl raging and Carl is reprimanding Frank about the chair incident, trying very reasonably to explain that things have changed. "It's not our joint anymore, Frank, can't you see that? There are rules. We can't give you the markers anymore, we just can't do it."

With that, Sinatra says, "You fat Jew motherfucker." And he pulls the tablecloth out from under the coffee and everything on the table falls onto Carl Cohen, scalding him with the boiling-hot coffee. That's it, Carl had enough. He gets up and punches Frank Sinatra right in the mouth and knocks his caps out, they're all over the floor. At least they were caps! They rush Sinatra out, Jilly says to me, "Paul, get him the hell outta here, the cops are going to show up." Which they do and make a report. Meanwhile, they get a Learjet to fly Sinatra out, back to L.A. to go get his teeth done, and see Dr. Stein. The entire town applauded Cohen for what he did—Frank's behavior had been getting more and more abusive. Frank threatened to have his legs broken, he wanted Jilly to go after him, but nobody was going after Carl. He was respected.

You have to understand, the mob still ran the place, and Carl was one of the boys from Cleveland. Frank was a singer, who may have all these mob connections but he wasn't a mob guy. He was an entertainer. A whole different category. However much esteem the mob had for Sinatra, no one, not even Frank, was going to interfere with their crew. And, besides, the mob had a strict code of behavior. Whoever you were you were expected to behave properly, and Frank had stepped over the line. If you get out of line, they put you in your place. They're not going to let him go bully these guys up like that.

Those guys killed each other for less than that! You see what I'm saying? Mob guy or not a mob guy has nothing to do with it. It's your *behavior,* how you conduct yourself. Like he sings in that great Johnny Mercer and Harold Arlen song, "I could tell you a lot, But you gotta be true to your code."

—◼—

In 2001 I had a small part in the movie *3000 Miles to Graceland,* playing a pit boss. I would take all the actors out gambling every night. What I tried to teach them was that ultimately you're going to lose, that's why those buildings are here, that's why there's a pyramid there now, a Statue of Liberty, so you need to count the cards, you need to use common sense, because luck is a very fickle lady at the tables. After all my years in Vegas I learned this stuff from the boys, the mob guys—they knew the odds were in their favor. And, if by chance, they weren't, well, they had ways of changing the odds. Unless you count or have a system or knew how to gamble, you are not going to win, period. So I would load the table up with whoever, directors, actors, friends. I would say "Okay, let's hit, it's plus," when it looked favorable. "There's paint coming," I'd tell them, meaning king, queen, jack. "With picture cards you're going to win." Guys you see in movies about the casinos like George Clooney wouldn't last the night in a real situation because they don't know the smell or the feel of the room.

I gambled much more in the '70s than I do now. Today I gamble very intelligently. You'll find me at baccarat and 21 tables, less at the craps table. I've sat down and gambled with guys who lost a million at the tables. On the other hand there were gamblers who laid extravagant tips. A wild media tycoon from Australia, Kerry Packer, one of the richest guys in the world asked a waitress if she had a mortgage on her house. She said yes, as a matter of fact she did. How much? $120,000. No problem. He paid it. I've seen him tip $100,000. His reckless gambling was legendary. In 1999, he lost $22 million at a series of London casinos. On one occasion he played $1 million at four roulette tables, lost every penny, and simply walked out without any qualms. He also won huge amounts, like the $33 million he won at the MGM Grand in Vegas. When gamblers start winning huge amounts of money, say, at blackjack, they'd bring in guys called mechanics, who would come in with a single deck and deal from the bottom or the top of a pack. Those days are gone, doesn't exist anymore.

In the old days with Frank I got pretty extravagant with my bets, but my gambling limit now is $100,000. We'd often tip the dealers three or four thousand because we knew they had families.

The odds for gambling for the whole country—whether it is sports, horse racing—were set by one guy. It used to be a guy called Roxy Roxborough, who sat in the condo behind the strip, who would set the odds for everything—one guy. He'd set every football game, he'd set the odds for basketball. He introduced mathematical formulas and computer models into the megabillion-dollar sports wagering. The point is, if you're going to be a serious gambler you need to know what you're doing, and how to analyze the line that has been put up, to favor both sides. Do you take the dog? Now if you're playing cards you've got to have a system for every game to win and that means money management, spreading to three hands, how many aces are out, how many face cards are out. If you're losing, you change the table because there are systems in play that you are not going to beat.

Meyer Lansky, the mob boss and financial brains, was out of Miami Beach. Miami was a great hang but there was no gambling. Except for the private card games, sports betting shenanigans that went on surreptitiously on the balcony. You had the weather, the food, the lavish hotels. Ben Novack ran the Fontainebleau for the mob when Miami was the place to be, and he was a royal pain in the ass. Ben was a nebbishy kind of guy but he was the boss of the hotel and he always wanted to hang around with us. The stars, the girls, the action that surrounded the stars. He was crazed to get in on the action but he was a drag and we never wanted him around. And he was a chiseler, to boot. He'd pay you $25,000 for performing there but then he'd charge you $15,000 for food and incidentals. Naturally you could get really pissed off at this guy.

One day I said, "We really have to do something to stick it to this pain in the ass." I'm a natural born prankster—it's in my DNA—and if ever anybody needed to be pranked it was Ben Novack. He always wanted one of the girls Frank or I had, so I got ahold of this audio porno tape, put the tape in the tape recorder in the adjoining bedroom, and turned up the sound. I called downstairs to Ben's office. "Ben," I said, "come on up, we got some great action going on, we've got a wild girl up here who'll do absolutely anything. I know you'll want to get in on it." Ben always wanted our women, because we always had the best. He was always crazed to get laid, but we'd always blow him off. I put my cousin Bob Skaff in there to make noises and act as if he's in the middle of this sex scene, so that Ben would think this was live action. Ben shows up with his Moroccan servant Boo and his Alsatian dog. I said, "Ben, get ready! Take your clothes off because when the guy in there is finished you're next." He sits down. He's got his clothes off.

He's holding his hearing aid. After hearing the commotion coming from the bedroom, with his dog next to him by the chair, even the dog is panting and sniffing around, reacting to the noise.

Ben's hearing screams from the next room, "*Oooooh,* baby! Oh, do it to me!" He's getting excited, my cousin Bob Skaff runs out of the room and says, "Ooh, man, that was *out-rageous!*" I say, "Ben you're up, go get 'em, sport!" He runs into the room, holding his hearing aid remote wired to his ear, with the dog running after him. He runs over to the bed and sees the tape machine. You should have seen his face. God I love pranks. Nothing like getting even.

The Rat Pack was a perpetual New Year's Eve party, but there was a darker side to the group, and although I saw it, I didn't feel obliged to follow it. I knew all their bad habits: the late nights, the drinking, the smoking, the womanizing. I decided to do what they did on stage and chose not to imitate the rest.

After Sinatra's scene with Carl Cohen, Frank never came back to the Sands. Caesars was the competition across the street and in solidarity with Frank we all moved over to Caesars to perform. I still had a contract at the Sands so I stayed there a bit longer until I'd fulfilled my commitment. But the truth is, after the Carl Cohen incident at the Sands, the thrill was gone.

Caesars was the new sizzle in town, until the next wave came with my buddy Steve Wynn. Caesars Palace turned into an incredible store; everything about it was just up up up, sizzle sizzle sizzle, from the showroom to the restaurants, and that became the new hang place.

Jay Sarno, Jerry Zarowitz, and Nate Jacobson were behind Caesars Palace. Nate had this wild idea: he wanted to create a high-rise casino. The mob guys laughed. "Dream on! You'll never see a high-rise in Vegas." Wrong!

I can remember when it all started. One night in the early '60s while I'm performing at the Sands, I met Nathan Jacobson. He was in the insurance business, and he tells me he wants to own a casino, a high-rise casino. I knew him through Irv Feld; we had some investments with him. Nate, who was never a mob guy, came out to Vegas with this dream. Jerry Zarowitz and Jay Sarno, the guys who'd built Circus Circus, were also involved in the casino and had ties to mob figures. Sarno in fact had borrowed $18 million from the Teamster's pension fund to build this hotel/casino they were planning. Caesars became the biggest real estate bang and return of money in the United States.

They didn't have a name yet, but Sarno figured the Roman general Julius Caesar had the right kind of monumental ring to it, so it was named Caesars. Nate used to sit with me at the Sands Hotel when I was there and show me the blueprints of this casino he was going to put up and I'd give him suggestions about how to design the showrooms, the vestibule, the look, and so on. Out of the blue he said, "We want you to come in with us to open the place, we'll give you 5 percent."

I huddled with my business team and Al Rettig to discuss the matter. They said, "Nah, you don't want to take it. It's trouble, the kind of trouble you don't wanna attract. If you apply for a gaming license, the government will look under your toenails. They're all over you, and you're so clean, Paul, you don't wanna invite that kinda scrutiny. When the feds start looking at you you're tainted whether you're innocent or not—you are guilty by association. People assume, understand?" But I was kind of torn. Because I loved the environment.

You are either on this side or on that side and I didn't want the government poking into my business—that's never a good idea. You don't want the association, the implication. Let's say you are hanging with the group of investors and half of them are connected guys; just being in that room with them you're compromised.

But still, Nate Jacobson kept after me with this crazy idea of his of a high-rise resort in the midst of all these flat, one-story and two-story casinos. He was laughed at in the beginning by Jack Entratter and Carl Cohen; all the Vegas old-timers were saying "You'll never see a high-rise; people don't want to come to Vegas and go up in elevators, for chrissake. They can get that back home." But Nate was convinced. He was totally focused on getting this place up. He and Jay Sarno wanted to pattern it after the Fontainebleau Hotel in Florida.

Like Nate, Jay saw the Fontainebleau and was completely taken by it. Jay lived in Atlanta and he thought that Morris Lapidus, the architect, was a genius, and the Fontainebleau was the ultimate dream palace. He went back to Atlanta and built a motel called the Cabana that in effect was a little mini Fontainebleau. The Fontainebleau was so famous it didn't even have a sign outside—it didn't need it, that's how distinctive it was. It was the most romantic, idyllic place. Like Steve Wynn says, "It was one of those places that was truly better than the real world."

Anyway, here's how the story continues. I'm in Italy recording, making records in Italian, making videos in Italian. Nate's still chasing me to get involved, to the point where he tracks me down over there. He's in a limousine with me and his decorator and we're driving around Rome, and you know Rome, aesthetically, it's bursting with statues, and the history and the ruins. . . . We're driving through the Piazza Navona, Nate sees a bunch of old Roman statues and he's going to his decorator, "Ah! Lookathat! I want eight of those—but with heads; I want six of those with legs; I want nine of those with arms." He wanted literally to copy all this history and take it home with him—all of Rome. Rome wasn't built in a day, but nobody told Nate that. Anyway, that's what you see at Caesars—as much of Rome's 1,000-year history that he could fit into a casino. All the statues that fit! That was Nate's motto.

When they finally opened Caesars in 1966, they only had $70,000 in the cage to pay money out to winners. This is a miniscule amount compared to today's casinos where millions and millions are brought in by trucks for their bank cages to pay off the gamblers. It was a huge success, but did it make Nate and Zarowitz happy? Of course not. They were a big hit, you'd think they'd be congratulating each other, breaking open magnums of champagne, but no, it was out and out war. Nate and Zarowitz fought tooth and nail. I mean it was a never-ending feud.

Caesars becomes the new happening place. Later on, due to Sarno and Zarowitz's mob connections, the gambling commission makes them sell it to Clifford Perlman, who owns the Lums chain of restaurants. Soon Nate gets himself into such a pickle, the typical Vegas scenario: legitimate guy, family man, moves out to Vegas, makes money, loses money, winds up in a little gambling joint on the north shore of Lake Tahoe, Nevada.

I'd go to visit him because he was always a good guy. One of the last times I saw him I find him at 2:00 A.M. He's got some cute little side dish with him. You can't gamble in your own place in Nevada, and by now it's two in the morning and Nate had had a few, so we go to this other joint across town. I'm just being courteous and going along, 'cause he was always decent to me. He starts throwing craps, and he's losing *huge* amounts, like $200,000.

I'll never forget this. He's playing and he keeps losing and losing— meanwhile there's this guitar player in the lounge, thirty yards away tops. The guy's playing "Raindrops Keep Fallin' on My Head." Nate's losing, the place is almost empty, not many people around, and Nate by this time has had a few more. *"Arrgghh!"* he says like some seersucker pirate, putting his glass down, saying, "You!" He looks at the guitar player. "Hey . . . Come over here!" He's shouting at the guy. The kid puts down his guitar and comes over. Then he says to the pit boss in this up-all-night voice, *"Aah wan him ta roll!"* The pit boss figures "Aright, he's in two hundred large, what the hell."

So the kid starts to roll the dice for Nate. It's snake eyes. He rolls again and, Jesus! It's a square pair. It's a hot table. The kid keeps winning and Nate walks out with a hundred-grand winner. Anyway that's the last time I saw Nate and probably the last time anybody saw the guitar player.

God, I remember the first time I played Caesars Palace. Management called and said, "Paul, Muhammad Ali is here. He loves your music, and wants to see the show." "Muhammad Ali? You gotta be kidding!" After the show he comes back. I got a bunch of pictures with him taken back there, he and I. He sat down on that couch with me and said, God, I love to sing that 'Lonely Boy' song." He's got that inimitable voice and he just sat there and sang it. There's Ali, King of the World, singing my song to me in the most sincere growly voice imaginable. Goddamn!

> *I'm just a lonely boy*
> *Lonely and blue*
> *I'm all alone*
> *With nothin' to do*

From there he went on to do "Puppy Love," "Diana," "You Are My Destiny." I was blown away by that. I got such a big kick out of that Muhammad Ali, man. The most recognized figure in the world at one time, very cool. A man I respected who was smart and funny.

—■—

Sammy Davis? Loveable character, very funny man. A very talented guy who had his ins and outs with Frank because, you know Frank could be pretty brutal on him. I'd watched Sammy perform up in Canada from a young age; then all of a sudden there he is sitting at a table in front of me. We had a lot of good times together. Amazing, hilarious impressionist, great singer, didn't really read music; it was all memorized. I did a few benefits for him, and wrote "I'm Not Anyone" for him.

> *I'm not anyone*
> *No, not just anyone*
> *I have the right to lead*
> *A life fulfilled with every need*
> *I'm not any man*
> *Designed to fit someone's plan*

I have my own desires
Of the things a man aspires
I'll not be used
Misled, deceived or abused
No sir not me
I am free

Sammy was different from Frank, but I think in his heart of hearts he wanted to *be* Frank. Sammy was all with the drinking and the cigarettes, he was the funny playful guy—loved his cameras. He was just out there. I tried to surprise him at the Sands one time, when it was his birthday. He did two shows that night. After his last show, he did another one at two in the morning. We all got into that habit. It was our way of meeting all of our other performers and workers who could not normally catch our show. This was "our way" of giving back. So it was the two in the morning show and they were going to bring the cake out, etc. The plan was I was going to hide under the room service table. We think we're ready to go and I get under the table. Sammy, like a lot of us, improvised his act, so it was unpredictable as to how long his act was going to go. He'd carry on, get caught up, somebody says something in the audience, and it would get him off on another riff, and he'd go on and on. By now it's 3:30 in the morning and I'm on my knees under this tablecloth, the table with the cake on top, and I'm waiting, I must have sat under there for twenty goddamn minutes. My crouched knees are *killing* me. I didn't know whether to get out or stick it out. Finally somebody wheels the table out onstage and I'm sitting there, hurting like a son of a bitch. I was waiting for a cue I was going to be given, but I got tired of waiting. I said, "Fuck this Happy Birthday shit. I can't move my legs!" and I climbed out onstage in the middle of whatever he was doing and started singing. I did a special lyric of "My Way" just for Sammy. Everybody got a kick out of it.

Sammy was a very cool cat. Could do anything, even impressions, and he was passionate about everything he did, even when the stuff he got into got very funky. He was the hippest, coolest cat that was. I watched him from the light booth at the Gatineau nightclub, across the river, in Quebec, where I used to go to do my amateur contests—like the time I took my mother's car.

—■—

As I said, my agent in New York was Buddy Howe at General Artists Corporation. Howe was a very conservative-type guy, a dancer prior to that, and was married to Jean Carroll, who became a popular comedienne on television and in clubs. Well dressed, a shirt-and-tie type of guy, glasses, grayish hair, very calm in the way that he spoke—in other words unlike the cigar-smoking agent stereotype. An honest face, a very trusting guy. He came into my life early, before Irv Feld became my manager. When my crooner career began it became necessary to adapt the kind of songs I'd been singing to more of a Vegas-type format. We also had to add other nightclub type material, knowing we needed to gear my act to a more sophisticated audience. This involved creating a new song set and a new way of performing those songs.

The guy who did all the bookings for Buddy Howe at GAC's Vegas office was Jim Murray, who only booked Vegas. What was unique about GAC was that they had representation out there in Vegas, whereas most of the other agencies didn't. They just did their business from New York or L.A. Jim Murray was an Italian-type guy: tall, good looking, he exuded a lot of confidence. A real fast talker, well-dressed: the suit, the shirt, the tie, and the casual look that went with Vegas when he had to. He'd started out as an office boy at MCA way back in '43, and then became an agent, the only agent that lived in Las Vegas, as a matter of fact. Did twenty years with MCA, which was the Lew Wasserman–Jules Stein setup, a very conservatively dressed bunch. Their mantra was "Dress British; speak Yiddish." Lew Wasserman and Jules Stein were the pillars of what Hollywood is today. They controlled everything in the industry. I hooked up with Jim Murray in the '60s, around that time Buddy Howe had been my main agent in New York.

Jim was assigned to Vegas, and he was what all the agents were supposed to be when they moved there: nongamblers. The talent agencies never wanted their agents to get into bad habits, so they chose guys who never went to race tracks or played cards. Jim was perfect for that.

They didn't choose these guys *because* they didn't gamble, they just "encouraged" them, shall we say, not to gamble. "You don't wanna gamble, I'll just say it like that, and you can take it any way you want. But if you do, *dah dah dah*." The reason they didn't want them to get involved with gambling was because that's where all the funny business went on with the mob.

Jim was that type of agent, loved to drink, a golfer. And the women! The biggest problem with Vegas, at that time, was that it was a very small community. And the crooked noses all knew each other; they were buddies, they talked with each other all the time. And they were honest—at least with each other. If they wanted to be dishonest or when they wanted to skim a little off the top, it was up to them, because they were very tight with each other.

For instance, if Jim was making a deal for Andy Williams or me and wanted a hotel, and if you tried to negotiate with another hotel, to make a move to another casino, to get more money for your client by the time you'd get to the next hotel, they already knew what you were up to, so they'd say what the fuck are you talking about? You already went to— whoever!—for the same price. They already knew everything.

Jim was aggressive and feisty, the way agents were back then. There was a guy who worked with him—we'll call him Larry—who was kind of a rogue agent; and was typical in the way of all the stories you heard about these guys. Very flashy, quick moving, five-sevenish—the typical show business type. Once you got into business you could easily get into a lot of trouble because there was temptation everywhere: women, gambling, booze, drugs. Hey, you were in Sin City.

Larry lived about five blocks from Jim. One day this Larry said to Jim, "I have no money and I need new tires." Jim was an open guy with a big heart, but he was careful with his money, so he said, "Well, I don't know what you're going to do. I can't lend you any money because I don't know yet what you're gonna do."

But Larry was the kind of guy who wouldn't take no for an answer. He went to the gas station where he knew the owner very well and got four new sets of tires for his car, and left the car parked in the lot where Jim parked his car.

Jim sees the tires. "Larry, where'd you get the tires?"

"Hope you don't mind I charged them to you, but don't worry I'll pay you back!"

So what does Jim do? He had the car brought back to the gas station and had the tires taken off!

Another time this kid Larry, who was representing everybody but being this flashy get-in-trouble type guy, he started up with a hooker at one of the big casino hotels. Remember, he's an agent representing talent. Larry screws the hooker and when she wants to get paid, he tells her to go fuck herself. The hooker called security and all the security guys got after him. There weren't any cell phones back then but they had these beepers, that's how they contacted each other. The hookers, everybody was in touch. It was about two o'clock in the morning when Larry told the hooker to beat it. She told security what had happened and where this guy was in the hotel, asking security to get over there. They stripped him down bare nude, Larry all the while spinning this story claiming that the hooker had stolen $100 from him, and that was why he called her a fucking whore. That shows you the alliance between the waiters, the owners, the hookers, and the security guys. They were all this little fraternity, and if you didn't play the game right or were hard to work with, you were in trouble.

Larry was the kind of guy who would walk in a dressing room and take over. He was the show. The opposite, in fact, of your average agent behavior. The agents all used to come backstage and grease you. They'd see the show, come back, and kiss your ass. Let's say Kenny Rogers was in his dressing room, he'd be watching, say, the news, Larry would walk right in and change the channel to *Wheel of Fortune* or whatever he wanted to. And Kenny would look up outraged and say who the fuck is this guy? *Chutzpah!*

———■———

Segregation went on well into the sixties in Vegas, and it was a time when a lot of my friends—whether it was Sammy, Lena Horne, or any of the other black acts—could work but couldn't stay in the same big hotels we did. The black attractions basically stayed at the Moulin Rouge.

I remember once when Jim Murray was handling the amazing torch singer Della Reese. She was performing at one of the hotels, I think the Flamingo, and she's sitting by the pool but because she was black they didn't want her there. And Morris Lansburg, who was the owner of the Flamingo, went to Jimmy and said: "What's purple gums doing there? Get her out of the pool. They're gonna empty the pool and the guests are gonna check out of the hotel."

Whenever the agents would try and get reservations for someone, like, say, Lionel Hampton, at any of the big hotels they wouldn't let him stay there. Whenever they tried it, the management just refused. Even Harry Belafonte, if you can believe it, wasn't allowed to play on the public golf courses.

Desegregation may have started in the fifties and become the law of the land in the sixties, but the change happened slowly in Vegas and other places around the country, too, believe me. Sinatra finally put his foot down somewhere in the early 1960s and that all changed.

———■———

Dean Martin. I have to tell you about what a good guy he was. He got up and played golf every day, did his show, went to his room. He wasn't a drunk the way everybody thinks—that was an act. He was a laid-back cat who played a loud, goofy lush.

He didn't really hang out and for that reason I knew Dean less well than I did Sammy and Frank. He was kind of a loner, even with Sinatra whom everybody worshipped. Dean followed his own drumbeat right down to the end. On their last tour together Frank tried to motivate Dean to stay up and carry on after the show, but Dean got on the plane and went home instead. He's the kind of guy who wanted his little bowl of pasta, watch a Western, go to bed, get up, and go play golf.

He was a naturally funny man, and the humor came out of him effortlessly, especially in the steam room when we were all in there together. He would do funny shtick, like when we'd all get our massages. Neil Lepo ran the health club, would pour oil on Dean and as they'd rub him from his waist up he had a way of sliding off onto the floor, as if they'd poured so much oil on him he just slipped off like an eel. That kind of physical shtick. Frank adored him. The drinking bit was really a prop item for Dean; he wasn't the lush, it was often just apple juice. Frank and Sammy were the bigger drinkers. With Dean it was mostly for show. He didn't even drink to calm himself down. He'd come off stage and sit in a little tent and watch cowboy movies on TV or go upstairs to his room and watch more TV. A truly great stylist, the loveable lush character he created was so seamless and flawless no one outside the inner circle ever guessed it was an act. As a singer, Dean emulated Donald Mills, the lead singer of The Mills Brothers. It may seem odd, but Frank and Dean at one point were doing the Bing Crosby thing along with the whole look, the hat and the pipe and all of that.

Bing was squeaky clean and wholesome, which these guys definitely weren't. But this was all before the Sinatra Rat Pack came into being. The Rat Pack was originally put together by Humphrey Bogart and Betty Bacall. They came up with the name when they all started hanging together. Sinatra, Dean, and Sammy idolized Humphrey Bogart. Prior to that they all took after Crosby.

Perry Como was different; he had his own thing going. Como was a barber originally, used to cut hair, and then he evolved into singing and had his own show but he was always a separate entity. Even Nat King Cole, whom we all admired, didn't partake of the Rat Pack shenanigans. He was unto himself, a very classy kind of a guy, always with the cigarette holder, and dressed to the Ts.

The lounges out there were big. There were shows every night, you saw all the great performers, all the comics, all the tall leggy blondes in fishnet stockings and feathers you'd ever want to see. You'd go see Shecky Greene, Louis Prima, and Keely Smith at the Sahara. Don Rickles, Vic Damone, great talents. It was fantastic. Some of the lounge shows were better than any of the shows in the main showrooms, or anywhere. You'd make the rounds, going from one show to another, and it was great fun.

I learned a lot from hanging around with songwriters Sammy Cahn and Jimmy Van Heusen—that experience really broadened my craft. Van Heusen and Sammy Cahn wrote *Ring-a-Ding-Ding!* Sinatra's 1961 album—no ballads, just up-tempo swing—specifically for (and about) Frank. A *ring-a-ding* was someone who has dazzle and sizzle—that was Frank all right, but it might just as well have been applied to Van Heusen who was a flashy dandyish type of person. He'd been born Edward Chester Babcock but had adopted the Van Heusen name from the famous shirt manufacturer. Jimmy Van Heusen and Sammy Cahn—they wrote many of the great Sinatra classics: "Come Fly with Me," "Call Me Irresponsible," "My Kind of Town," "The Look of Love," "Swinging on a Star." The Sands was the hot spot of the world at that point. Beginning in the '60s, that's where everybody met or wanted to be and not everybody could get in. When you're hanging out with that crowd you know you're sitting on top of the world. And being accepted into this exclusive club had always been my focus—they were my idols, the biggest influence on my life.

Sammy Cahn was a truly great lyricist; he was like my adopted brother, father—everything. I didn't know Van Heusen as well. Jimmy was the playboy type, a real party guy, always after the women. He lined up all the women for Frank. Jimmy lived large, he flew airplanes, and every night was party, party, drink, drink, drink. With Jimmy, it was just fun, fun, fun. He was the guy that Sinatra wanted to be. He traveled with Frank, and when Sinatra needed to get introduced to women, Jimmy was the guy that did it. Van Heusen was that singular animal and nighttime creature, piano player, an all-around wild guy.

I was tight with Sammy, Jimmy I'd more often see on the periphery. Chester, that was his nickname, was closer to Frank because he was very like Frank in a way: gregarious, more of a playboy type—the women, the drinking, the girls, and all that. The two of them wrote material for my 1962 album *Young, Alive and in Love!* on RCA Victor. And that's when I saw the full impact of that great songwriting team at work. Just the three of us in a room. Full impact. My songs weren't particularly sophisticated, and here I was with two of the most sophisticated songwriters in America. They were what I aspired to be. Sammy also wrote special material for me to use in my nightclub act. He'd adapt songs like, "I'm Getting Married in the Morning" with clever additional lyrics. He created a version of "One for My Baby," substituting the line, "one double malted and one more for the road," which always got a big laugh. Sammy became a friend and a father to me, a guy with great integrity.

You were around the best professionals in the business, and life was good. The real inner sanctum was the health club. Everything went on there. We all had our own robes with nicknames on them that Frank gave us. Sammy Davis was Smokey the Bear, I was the Kid, Dino was Dago, Vic Damone was the Voice.

After the shows we would all meet up there. That's where the kibitzing went on in the early hours of the morning, and the food was great, the girls were hot, tiptoeing into the steam room giggling. That's where the fun was. We'd be sitting around talking, bullshitting, and all of a sudden a couple of showgirls come in, and they're naked, too. Frank would have women of the night brought in now and then. They would come in, take their clothes off, these beautiful women, standing there stark naked. There were little rooms, massage rooms, and what have you, off the main steam room and that's where you'd go if you wanted to have sex with them. There were no gang bangs or any stuff like that going on with Frank around. He didn't go for any of that; he would just disappear into one of the little rooms. Jay Sebring would be giving us hair cuts at 3 A.M. Sadly, he later got killed at Sharon Tate's house the night of the murders by the Manson family.

Once you did the Vegas thing and got in with that crowd, you were surrounded night and day by these amazing people. What was Frank like? Hanging out with him was the hippest thing I've ever done in my life. He was not shy about expressing his likes and dislikes. There was a singer named John Gary on RCA Victor records. Frank hated him. Couldn't stand Johnny Mathis, either. There was a saying that you could walk through Johnny Mathis's vibrato it was so wide. Secretly, quietly, I loved Johnny Mathis's voice for years but would never voice that to Frank.

Everyone knew everyone in Vegas and for that one stretch Sinatra was the guy. He was king. Vegas was his own personal fiefdom. The scene revolved around him. It was Sinatra who gave Vegas its tone. He was its social atom, and gave the place its zing, its glamour. The buzz was always around Sinatra wherever he was.

There was a time when it was just all about Frank. Case in point: Johnny Carson was fascinated with Frank, obsessed with him, you might say, in the same way as many people were. Certain people can walk into a room and it'll light up. That was Sinatra for sure. Carson was a drummer and a magician, and the best comedian on television. But he was also a big drinker and a bad drunk. After his show, which was aired at a studio not far from Jilly's bar on West Fifty-second Street Carson would wander over there in the hope of running into Sinatra, get drunk, and cause scenes. The bar was owned by Jilly Rizzo. A sweetheart of a guy, but with a lethal punch—the secret of which was the police blackjack he concealed up his right sleeve. When he got into a fight he'd let it slide down into his fist and that punch would hit you like a ton of bricks. He looked like a big tough guy, a bruiser, but he was actually a pussycat—unless provoked—with that one little cockeyed eye. He opened his own restaurant and bar hangout. He had a wife named Honey, a houseboat down in Florida, and he'd travel with Frank. Everybody would go to Jilly's, especially when Sinatra was in town, and hang out at the restaurant because that's where you'd always find Frank. They would always have a little trio in the corner. Piano, bass, drums. It was a great place to go.

One night, Carson went to Jilly's, either thinking Sinatra was going to be there or because he wanted to be in that kind of buzz. Carson was fascinated by anything to do with Sinatra, but Sinatra never paid any attention to him at all. He went in there on occasion; he'd play drums or drink at the bar. When Carson got blitzed, he was a real bird dog with women. So there he is this one Friday; he'd been drinking heavily prior to going there, and he spotted some girls at the bar and started pinching them on the ass. Unbeknownst to him, these women, known in the parlance of the day as side dishes, were the girlfriends of mob guys—who, as it happened were in the back room of the club. When they caught wind of Carson hitting on their women they came out, yanked him off his bar stool, and threw him down a small flight of stairs and started kicking the living daylights out of him. They probably would have injured him really badly if Jilly hadn't run downstairs and called the guys off. Jilly probably saved Carson's life that night.

The crowd Sinatra hung with were a bunch of wild guys. They'd laugh and drink and throw cherry bombs under the table, they'd explode and the women would be screaming. Games, games, games.

Frank had a very interesting double side to him. When he was with people like Anne and me he was well behaved and really nice. When he was with his close and comfortable buddies, he was more rough and tough. You never knew which you were getting with him.

I was with Frank and a bunch of guys one night in Florida. We were hanging out and at some point decided to go up to his room. Frank was sitting there; a dark cloud came over him. Something pissed him off. I knew what it was. The FBI was bugging Frank's room. He'd go in his suite and there'd be holes all over the walls and the floorboards because the feds were bugging him. Frank would have a guy there to redo the phones. Soon there were holes all over the place from disconnecting phones and installing new ones, planting bugs, and so on. He said, in the spirit of having fun, "Jilly. Get rid of this shit." Jilly starts taking all the furniture from the penthouse and throwing it onto the beach. This is all happening in the middle of the night. The next day a couple of little old Jewish ladies are walking along and see all this stuff—tables, carpets, chairs, lamps all over the beach and they're asking, "What happened here, Sadie? There was a storm we slept through, maybe?"

There was a great old-time doctor named Max Som out of New York. He was the doctor's doctor for throats. He looked after me and Sinatra and everybody. A dear guy from New York. He always said to me, "Paul, whatever you do, *do not smoke*. It is the *worst thing* for the throat." All of the guys I knew that were singers who smoked ultimately got cancer.

I've never been a smoker, and after a couple of exposures to the anatomies of heavy smokers I'm glad I never developed the habit. My innate curiosity from time to time drove me to watch operations and autopsies on cadavers. Dr. Michael Hogan and his wife Margo were dear friends of Anne and mine. On one occasion he let me go to New York Hospital with him and gown up. Here I am, all five feet six inches of me, wrapped up in a gown that doesn't fit, watching a cancer operation. They're cutting someone open for lung cancer. When the bodies were cut open the smell was awful and I would see the black lungs of heavy smokers. I saw with my own eyes what smoking could do and, if nothing else, this stopped me from ever smoking.

Max Som also taught me to get as much steam as you can get on your vocal chords. That became a part of my regime from 1960 on.

Steam, steam, steam and no smoking. It puts moisture on them and shrinks them. If there's no steam room you used to boil some water in a steam kettle and put a towel over your head. You have to take care of those vocal chords. I used to say those two square inches on my neck—that's my business. I travel with steam kettles that don't turn off, throw a towel over my head, and suck in the steam, keeping my vocal chords moist.

The other thing about steam rooms is that they're great for detoxing, getting the poisons out. The Vegas Rat Pack were all jammed out of their brains with the booze and the cigarettes, and the steam oozed the booze out. I've been doing that since 1960—I'm as steamed as a Great Neck clam.

When I first got to Vegas, Sinatra used to tease me that I had too much hair. Little did he know how long pop singers' hair was going to get when the British Invasion came along. Frank was meticulous about his own clothing and the way he presented himself to the world. He was always very opinionated about your appearance; unruly hair and scruffy clothes and all of that would enrage him. He hated sloppiness. At his record label he demanded that everyone's shoes be polished to a high shine. Frank always projected a tough-guy image but he was actually very vulnerable. He was in a lot of pain after he broke up with Ava Gardner. Now, Frank could be very blunt. He would tell you straight out if he did not like something. For instance, he hated strong smells, especially perfume.

Case in point—he was in Europe filming the movie *The Pride and The Passion* with Sophia Loren and Cary Grant. There he was on a set pining for Ava, in a pair of tights pulling a cannon up a hill. He wanted off the film as quick as he could get out. Ava, in Spain, was madly in love with a bullfighter and Frank was not happy. One night at a bar with the group, he met a beautiful German girl, who was living with her mother. So it obviously became very difficult for him to get together with her. He got her phone number.

When he got back home to the U.S. after the film shoot, all of his buddies planned a trip to go to Hawaii. Frank remembered the girl from Germany, gave Jimmy Van Heusen the phone number and he arranged to fly the girl over to meet them in Honolulu at the Kahala Hilton. They flew her from Germany to New York. One of the guys took her shopping, bought her new luggage, jewelry, perfume and decked her out. After they got her trousseau together they flew her to Hawaii. Everyone is up in the suite playing gin—Frank is by the window waiting like a little boy. Sarge Weiss, who worked with Frank, is in charge of picking up the German girl and bringing her to the hotel. The bellman calls us to say that she has arrived; she is on her way to the room. There is a knock on the door and she walks in with her luggage. Frank looked at her and his eyes lit up. Keep in mind he hated strong smells. She came up to him, hugged him, said hello Mr. Sinatra, I am so glad to see you again. He looked at her and sniffed her like a dog. "What is that?" he said. Between the smell of her body odor from the long trip and the strong perfume she had on—it was wicked. "Get her the fuck out of here" he said—and that was that. My friend Jerry Weintraub was there, and said she was off the island in three hours.

Frank was as scrupulous as an airline pilot about being on time. If a show was due to start at 8:30 he'd begin whether the audience was seated or not. No disrespect to the audience—just his way. Frank was also an impulsive kind of guy. George Schlatter, my very funny and talented friend who produced *Laugh-In*—he amuses me to this day—used to say "If you go to dinner with Frank, bring your passport." I remember one night I met up with Frank in Philadelphia, flew back to New York on his Learjet, ended up on his boat and at his apartment, and didn't get home for two days.

There was a guy over at Warner Bros. Records, Stan Cornyn, who wrote great liner notes, almost poetic, and on one of Frank's albums he came up with the phrase, "Old Blue Eyes" and it stuck. That came later in his career, when he was a legend. But Frank went through bad periods. He was counted out more than once. During one of those bad spots he was suffering a serious bout and then, as I said, the Ava Gardner breakup wrecked him. That was a very turbulent time in his life. Then came the Mia Farrow period. He went very "flower power" during that phase. That was an interesting transformation for someone as cool as he was but it ended pretty quickly. He has had some major women, but at the end of the day he said he never understood them. And, to be honest, it is very hard understanding women. Frank never got it. But then again why would he? When Sigmund Freud was asked on his deathbed was there anything in his life of studying human nature he hadn't solved, he said "Yes, I could never figure out what women want."

Frank and his women—that was always a big mystery. There was a huge buzz when Sinatra got engaged to Juliet Prowse in 1962. Nobody could figure it out. They were at the opposite end of the pole and no one got the fit. Jilly would tell me he never understood it, especially since she was pretty ballsy and aggressive, not exactly Frank's type. In the '60s, I'd see her often and hear the stories and when I was performing at the same clubs as Frank, such as the Fontainebleau in Florida, another mob stop, I'd hear Sinatra's side.

In 1967, Frank was down in Florida filming *Lady in Cement* during the day and working at the Fontainebleau at night. He was uptight about breaking up with Mia Farrow. She was into all that yoga and Zen Buddhism and he wanted nothing to do with that. I remember one dinner we all attended at the Fontainebleau with Mia Farrow when it was obvious their marriage was coming to an end—you could tell they had been fighting from morning to night and you could feel the tension at the table. Then she just left town. They were divorced in August 1968, the year that Sam Giancana fled to Mexico.

Jilly Rizzo told me about the Jacqueline Onassis connection with Frank. In one of our hangs at the bar Frank told me he hated the way Onassis treated her. Frank always had a hot nut for Jackie O and apparently they started a dialogue in the summer of 1975. He invited her to his opening show in New York. Jilly, in his cute little way, told me he had to bring her to the Uris Theatre—what happened between Frank and Jackie we'll never know. Frank never would kiss and tell, but flying back with him to Philly on his Learjet I could see it was going nowhere with Jackie. I remember sitting around drinking at Patsy's or Jilly's with Frank, and it always came out how much he loved Ava Gardner.

He started dating Barbara Marx, who had been a showgirl at the Riviera and had married Zeppo, one of the Marx brothers. I believe it was in 1976 that he proposed to Barbara Marx, a match which we all celebrated because it brought some stability into his life. You could see a change in Frank at age sixty—not slowing down exactly, but wanting more of a peaceful existence. But his mother Dolly was not thrilled about her future daughter-in-law, and from what I understood, neither were his children. Later that same year they announced their wedding and got married in July 1976.

By the early '80s those of us around him realized his marriage to Barbara was strained. Frank's lawyer Mickey Rudin, one night at dinner, told me every time they would fight Frank would spend a lot of money on Barbara by giving her jewelry. He began to name his tours after the big jewelry houses. There was the Tiffany Tour, the Cartier Tour, the Van Cleef Tour, etc. Throughout the '80s, Frank kept on smoking, kept drinking. Moderation was not the way for Frank and Sammy.

You'd hang with Sinatra after the show at Steve Wynn's Golden Nugget, say, everybody sitting around the restaurant drinking, talking, congratulating Frank on his great performance. He was always very gracious, but he didn't really care for all that adulation. He didn't want to be treated like a god, although in that he had little choice. He'd be surrounded by dozens of beautiful women, all wanting to get close to him. I've seen Sinatra with the greatest women in the world and generally he wasn't happy the way you'd think he'd be. I soon came to realize that there was a lot about Frank's character nobody knew. All that praise and idolization couldn't dispel his demons. As he said about himself, "Being an 18-karat manic depressive, and having lived a life of violent emotional contradictions, I have an over-acute capacity for sadness as well as elation." As he became more and more famous, and then a living legend, he began to meet accomplished people from other walks of life. Everyone from politicians to movie stars wanted to get to know him and be his friend, and Frank wanted to be able to talk to them on their level. He didn't want to be treated as a mere performer. And this brings up another aspect of his character that *was* surprising given who he was and the way people saw him as the supreme swinger. Sinatra was sophisticated and educated in a way you wouldn't expect. He was a big reader, for one thing. And beneath all the swagger, he was insecure. He always felt inferior to all the socialites he went out with. He wanted to educate himself so he could keep up with people he knew, like Bennett Cerf, the publisher of Random House. Frank was very different from someone like Elvis. Elvis just read self-help and spiritualist books, and had no real curiosity about the world. But as I said, Frank was a big reader. He socialized. He wanted to better himself even though he felt inferior to those people. He read as much as he could so that he could participate and get involved. He wanted to learn. He was very conversant with whatever was in the air. He was a lot more social than Elvis; he liked to go out. Frank starved for an audience. He was a totally different creature from Elvis, although the ironies and the paradoxes of life prevailed, and Elvis was always fascinated by Frank—even by Frank's rejection of him.

In January 1977, I remember one night around five o'clock getting a call from Sid Gathrid, the head of entertainment at Caesars, saying Frank Sinatra's mother, Dolly, had been in a plane crash. She'd been flying in to see him. Dolly so hated Sinatra's new wife, Barbara, she had refused to fly in the same plane with her. Frank never blamed Barbara for this freak accident, but he tormented himself over it for the rest of his life.

The jet company that we all used picked up Dolly in Palm Springs, but that night they were using two rookie pilots and these guys lost their bearings—it was bad weather—and the plane crashed right into the mountains, and she and her companion were killed. Gathrid called me and said, "We've got problems. Frank thought you could help out, do the show?" I told Gathrid I would do anything for Frank and his family. The answer was yes. They sent a plane for me and I flew down that night and filled in for Sinatra. I'll never forget the somber feeling in the place. The next day Frank wrote me a lovely little note which closed with, "At the slightest provocation just call me and I'll be there. If anybody ever hurts you, just call me, kid."

Sinatra clung to his tough-guy image, but he was a soft man when you sat down and talked to him because many of his insecurities came out. It's hard, I know, to believe in such a thing as a soft Sinatra, but that's the way he was. At times.

Bobby Darin and I were lucky we got to hang with these guys. There was nothing else like it; that was the scene. The way Sinatra sang and what he represented was exhilarating and intimidating. Ever since he got up in front of a swing orchestra he made it difficult, everybody came second. He knew how to do that thing. It's true he abused his power, he could be downright nasty. When Frank started drinking, and if things didn't go his way he could be mean. The combustible mixture started with Jack Daniel's, then he'd move on to red wine, and when he got to the martinis—watch out! Get out of town. He could be difficult, but he was always honest about his mood swings and contrite in retrospect when he felt he'd been wrong. He was a man's man, and if he liked you, you put up with the bullshit. Frank stood up for civil rights, and all of that, too. We were all dead against any kind of racial prejudice from the early sixties on. We all fought to get the black performers equality.

Frank tried to be fair, but he also liked to teach people lessons: A famous French movie star checked into the Sands. He was a good-looking guy; I'd met him a number of times in Paris but he was very arrogant and obnoxious. He's bragging what a big cocksman he is. At one point, he had two showgirls from the Sands sent over to his villa to feed his ego and he started getting abusive. Word got out. Frank heard about it and something about this guy got in Sinatra's craw. "This cheap, lousy French actor and two of our beautiful broads!" The two showgirls were quite capable of taking care of themselves, however. In the Frenchman's villa they'd gotten so mad with the guy, they'd tied him up, tied his arms and his legs to the bed. Then they called down and told the manager what had happened. For good measure, Frank had the bellmen come up and take the Frenchman and the bed with the guy in it and throw it and him into the shallow end of the pool.

—■—

We lived in Vegas for eight and a half years and Anne mostly hated it. One of the few things she liked was Elvis. She had such a crush on Elvis, they got to be friends. She would put the kids to bed, get dressed up, go with her girlfriend, and see Elvis's show twenty-five times in a row or something. Elvis was sweet to her. He would always come up to her table and say, "Hello, there!" and smile and give her a hug and a kiss. Then we would go backstage and hang out with him, so that was fun for her. Other than that she hated it. The vulgarity, crassness. She felt she just didn't belong. Just very out of sync with the whole routine.

You wouldn't see Elvis in a public restaurant the way you'd see Frank almost any night of the week holding forth at a table full of friends. Ever. That kind of thing didn't interest him. Elvis was scared to death to do that. He thought he had to be Elvis all the time and he wasn't always sure who that was. You can't do that—you can't be Elvis twenty-four hours a day. If you are smart about it, you separate your persona from all the other stuff so that you can have some kind of a life.

There was one way in which Elvis and Frank were similar: they were both very generous. Frank never took a penny for his charity work; many other performers who say they do benefits actually get paid, some up to a million bucks, but not Frank. It's been estimated that over his career Sinatra helped raise more than $1 billion for charitable organizations around the world.

I only really got to know Elvis well near the end of his life. You only had to hang out with him for a few minutes to know he was out of control. It's like the theory of chaos; you can apply it to the atom or you can apply it to human behavior. When one link drops in the chain, the domino effect of chaos takes over. It's the same in life. You have to prevent any semblance of chaos in your life for too long because it just has an incredibly destructive impact. If it's out of control it's going to wreck everything. And I saw it happen so graphically right before my eyes after he came into Vegas. I'd met him prior to that because we were on RCA Victor together. He would show up, this incredible God-like figure. He had everything. And the voice—what a great voice he had!

In Vegas, we'd meet and we'd talk. We'd talk about everything: music and girls and movies. You'd sit there with him drinking and there'd be all these guys around him, so it was mainly small talk: bullshit, songs, music, *buh buh buh buh buh*. Slowly he started coming over to see my show; he'd sit up there and I'd come back after the show and we'd talk music. And then all of a sudden he started growing out of his skin. There seemed to be a different Elvis; you saw this guy gradually becoming disfigured. What I've discovered is that all of us have our natural face and when you go too far with weight, you stretch your skin to the point where you no longer have your real face anymore. If you're a little overweight it's livable—most of the world's overweight—but Elvis was way beyond that.

And his whole thing near the end with me was very disturbing, with all his graciousness and all he was going through. "My Way" meant so much to him as a song, he was going to do it. And I'd say, "Elvis, it's not really your kind of song." And he'd say, "Nooo, Paulie, but those words, they mean so much to me. Boy, I want to do that song one day." It was one of the last songs he recorded. In the end, that song and those words had resonance for him but not in the way I intended.

Basically, given Elvis's pathetic state at the end, it was in the opposite sense that the words had had for Sinatra. There was nothing defiant or heroic about Elvis at that point.

It was the same way he lived his life—he destroyed himself. Just went too far. He became another statistic. Life is about construction and destruction. It's all in that balance, everything we see when we can look far enough. When you lose track of that, you self-destruct. And that's what happened to my talented friend.

I was in Vegas, got up, turned on the news. Elvis Presley—gone. I cried that day. He was a cool guy, a nice man, but was too young to go. Really blew it.

I got to know Elvis pretty extensively when he first started coming to Vegas. He would come over to Caesars Palace, see the show, come over and visit, sit backstage. Through that whole evolution, from when he hit town to when things started going bad for him, and where he started losing control, I would sit with him and just try to tell him, "Man, you've got to get it together, you can't live this twilight half life. Get ahold of this situation or it's going to pull you under." But he couldn't—would usually only see me in his suite.

His social terror was extreme. I'd say, "Elvis why don't we just go out to dinner, go for a walk?" "Oh, no!" He was terrified of that. You'd go over to his hotel—we both worked the Hilton—and he'd have aluminum foil on the windows; he never wanted to see the daylight. He'd go up to Vail, Colorado, and I'd be up there with my family skiing—in the daylight. Elvis wouldn't get up until the sun went down, and only then would he go up on the mountain with the floodlights turned on, to snowmobile. He was that kind of creature. Nice guy, but so locked in that prison of celebrity, of who he was, and his image, the person inside shriveled up. Sometimes you sat and talked to him and it was as if he were already gone. You couldn't save him.

Elvis imprisoned himself, and lived in a perpetual night. And then there were the guns. He hated Robert Goulet, and every time he was on TV, Elvis would shoot the television. There were bullet holes all over the room. He was shooting at ghosts and in the end became one himself.

—■—

It must have been something about the air in those casinos that kept affecting Sinatra now and then that got him doing crazy stuff well into the '70s. He never learned. Frank was King Frank and he thought the rules simply didn't apply to him. I was there the night this casino boss Sandy Waterman pulled a gun on Sinatra in the casino. After the incident, in the Sands coffee shop with Carl Cohen, I thought I had seen it all.

A few weeks earlier Sinatra and his neighbor Danny Schwartz won $2 million at Caesars' baccarat table. This particular night Sinatra, gambling on his own, was playing $8,000 a hand and ended up in debt to the casino to the tune of $400,000. Although he still had a handful of white $500 chips, he demanded another $25,000 worth of markers, but was refused. Frank's sense of outrage had a very low flashpoint when he felt he hadn't been treated fairly.

The pit boss called Caesars executive vice president Sandy Waterman, who tried to reason with him: "C'mon, Frank, you and Dan just won two million a few weeks ago. You took it with you. Now you owe us. The boys want their money." Frank threw his white chips in Waterman's face and slapped him across the forehead. At that point the generally cool Waterman lost it. He went to his suite and returned with a loaded gun which he pointed at Sinatra's head. "Listen, you! If you ever lay a hand on me again, I'll put a bullet through your head." Frank dismissed it, saying that playing with guns went out with Humphrey Bogart movies. Sinatra's sidekick Jilly managed to knock Waterman's gun to the floor. Waterman, afraid for his life, ran to the cashier's room to escape from Sinatra's rage. Frank tried to push his way through the door, but Sinatra's left arm—in a sling from a recent vein surgery—got crushed in the door and blood started spurting everywhere. Sinatra was rushed to his third-floor suite, where a doctor was sent for.

———■———

I'd done the theme for *The Longest Day,* I'm doing Vegas, touring Europe, I've got "A Steel Guitar and a Glass of Wine" and "Love Me Warm and Tender" in the charts—I'm feeling good about myself. Okay, I have to figure out what I'm going to do next. I'm at a critical juncture here. Sure, I was working steadily, but I knew it could all go very wrong— because when hard rock hit, the venues all changed again. I still had my Vegas base, thank God, and I was still getting gigs out there. But a few years, 1962 to 1966, were hard. Everybody was waiting for that next something from me, and that only came with "My Way" in 1967. What I was writing wasn't all that different from all the other stuff I'd written and I knew it. I hadn't really crossed over that line into new territory. "My Way" changed everything, the whole feeling about me shifted. It gave me a new prestige and respectability. Everyone started saying, "Okay, there's some legs here, this is something entirely different, this is Anka Mach Two."

As I got to know Sinatra and hung out with him through the years, he'd always joke with me about writing him a song. I was always very intimidated by that because I didn't have the balls to give him "Lonely Boy" or whatever else I was writing at the time—what would he do with that stuff anyway? I'd heard him when we were hanging, ranting on about mindless rock 'n' roll and moronic rock 'n' rollers. How was I going to write something for him that he'd conceivably want to record?

———■———

The first time I met Sinatra was at Trader Vic's, it must have been 1958; he was sitting at the next table. Sinatra hated rock 'n' roll, and dismissed it as "written for the most part by cretinous goons" and went on to say that by means of its "almost imbecilic reiteration, and sly, lewd, in plain fact, dirty lyrics, it manages to be the martial music of every side-burned delinquent on the face of the earth. It is the most brutal, ugly, desperate, vicious form of expression it has been my misfortune to hear." But Frank liked me—and I wasn't exactly a hard rocker, either. Maybe my clergyman's answer to rock 'n' roll was less threatening to him than the guitar-driven rock 'n' roll of Elvis and Chuck Berry.

Now it's the sixties, I want to give him a song, but most of the stuff I'm writing is not really in Frank's genre—to put it mildly. "Lonely Boy"? I don't think so. "Puppy Love"? Not too likely. In the back of my head I want to write that song, but I'm scared shitless. I'd be competing with guys like Sammy Cahn and Jimmy Van Heusen. I don't have those kind of chops yet. It wasn't until 1965 or 1966 that Sinatra began putting out pop records, because by then he saw the writing on the wall. The long and winding road to writing a song for Frank began in 1967 when I had rented a house in Mougins, a quaint little town in the south of France near Cannes, and one day sitting by the pool with Anne and my daughters heard this song on the radio. It was a pop record, light rock 'n' roll: *"Comme d'habitude,"* which means, "as usual." It's a story about a couple breaking up, a very French lyric: le money, les eyelashes, le coffee, whatever. It was okay, it wasn't a huge hit. But I heard something in the melody that grabbed me.

It had been written in February of that year by Gilles Thibault and Jacque Revaux, recorded by Claude François, in September and October, and released by Barclay Records on November 3rd. On December 17, I negotiated to acquire the rights for my company, Spanka Music, with Eddie Barclay at the Plaza Hotel in Paris. I knew Eddie Barclay well, a larger-than-life guy who'd had seven wives—he was Mr. France. He was close to Quincy Jones, who, to this day, is one of my dearest friends. Eddie and I had become close, I'd done some business with him, published the James Brown catalog in Europe with him, so I called him up and told him what I wanted to do: take the melody, write new words to it. He said, "Yeah, take whatever you want. It's not doing so well, you want it?" It was a small industry back then, so he gave me the song—no money. It was just two pieces of paper. I mean, we weren't buying the pyramids here. He gave me the publishing, the right to re-create the song. I went back to New York and put it in a drawer. But I never forgot it was in that drawer—it was in there, palpitating, waiting for the moment I'd awaken it.

I knew there was something special to this song. I heard the melody as a foundation to something very interesting—but what? It just had such a solid base to it, I knew that the story was going to be very dra-matic and have a grand sweep to it. And I knew the kind of story I was going to lay over it would be very graphic. It was inspiring to me but I didn't quite know what to do with it yet. I began playing *"Comme d'habitude"* on piano again, and everything came together. Then it re-ally grew into itself. I transformed it on piano, got the right vibe to it, taking it away from the original Europop version. But I hadn't figured out the hook yet.

Sometime in 1967, I'm in Florida performing at the Fontainebleau Hotel. Sinatra was doing a film down there, one of those detective movies, *Tony Rome,* I think, and I get a call from Jilly Rizzo. He says, "Kid, come on over, the old man wants to have dinner with you." I go and have dinner with Frank at a restaurant. We're at dinner, and Frank tells me that he's going to retire from show business. He's had enough. The Rat Pack thing was starting to wane. It was splintering off, and other things were starting to bother him, certain harassments; he felt he had enough.

Frank was vulnerable. There were irritating kinds of things going on in his life all the time, to the point where he decided to do one last LP with Don Costa, who had always been my guy.

"Kid," he said, "I'm fed up, I'm going to do one more album, and I'm out of here." And after he'd finished bitching about his problems, he lightened up and said, "Hey, kid, you never wrote me that song."

"Frank, you got me there. I gotta think about that."

"Don't take too long!"

When I contemplated the idea of Sinatra retiring I got quite emotional. I went back to New York. It's one in the morning and I'm haunted by the idea that he's quitting. I couldn't quite accept it.

I was living in a midtown apartment in the 70's at the time. I would write songs on my Selectric typewriter. I was afraid to start, because he was into Gershwin and all those other jazz-tinged composers. He never liked pop music and had only dabbled in it at this point.

I'll never forget the night. It's about one in the morning, I know there's a storm moving in, the atmosphere is charged, there's a sense of drama in the air. I'm all alone, playing this melody on the piano, writing it as if Frank were writing it, in the person of Frank, tuning in Sinatra's vibe, a sense of foreboding and finality. I get that first line, "And now the end is near, and so I face the final curtain." The rain is getting heavier. The great legend is leaving the stage, the lights going out. It needed to be operatic, a big, swelling moment. I start typing like a madman—forget the craft, I told myself, just write it the way he talks: "Ate it up . . . spit it out." I finish it in about four hours, and edit it down to what I think it should be, give or take, a few optional lines. That's the way I do it, building it up, adding, rewriting, etc., and then cutting it back until only the essential emotional core is there.

Little did I know I was to write a song that would ultimately revitalize his career and change the direction of mine.

I had the first verse done and then—wow! I said, this is for Frank. I'm going to finish it for him. The title, "My Way," which came to me first, gave the story a particular feel, and I went along with it. Sometimes you write something very special that starts to write itself. I know that from the get-go. The song has to be treated as a person in a sense, the person who is evoking those feelings. It was a departure for me—I would never under normal circumstances write something so chauvinistic, narcissistic, in-your-face, and grandiose. The reason I pursued it was that I knew now that this was for Sinatra and that he could pull it off. One unexpected side effect of "My Way" was that it came out right on the eve of the Me Generation—it was all, me, me, me which is possibly why the song became so popular among a very diverse group of singers.

I finished typing my final draft of "My Way" at five A.M. in the morning. I know Frank is at Caesars, I know he's offstage, drinking at the bar and I know he's there with Don Costa, because I'm also working with Don, and I say, "Frank I've got something very interesting, I'm gonna bring it out." I then flew to Las Vegas in August 1968 and I played it for Sinatra. I knew Frank loved the song when I originally played it for him but he always wanted to be cool, so all he said was "That's kooky, kid. We're going in." Coming from him, you have to understand, that meant he was ecstatic.

They carefully planned to record it when Sinatra had a week off. Frank went to Palm Springs, rested, rehearsed the song, knew it well—doing what he liked to call woodshedding. Meanwhile I called Claude François, the French writer, on December 7, to tell him Frank planned to record it. Frank and his daughter, Nancy, went into the studio on December 30. He knew it so well he sang it in one take. All the musicians were there, this huge orchestra playing live. Everybody who'd worked with him through the years was there, they all stood up and gave him a standing ovation.

I get a phone call from the studio on Sunset Boulevard and Sinatra played it to me over the phone and I started crying. And that was it. That was the turning point. As a writer, it was like a miracle; it was hugely important for me to have Sinatra record a song I'd written finally come true. They decide to make "My Way" the single off the forthcoming album and I send Claude François a copy.

"My Way" is released on March 28, 1969—in May it gets to #27 on the charts. In January 1970, I receive a special citation from BMI for a million plays on American radio. In December 1970, I meet Claude François for the first time in Paris—unfortunately he never got to meet Sinatra, he was electrocuted in the shower with a hair dryer under bizarre circumstances. "My Way" goes on to be a megahit for Sinatra, the Coca-Cola theme song, and the most-played, most-covered song in the world. I wrote a second song for Frank, "Let Me Try Again," which was the follow-up, but nobody expected that lightning was going to strike twice.

Hanging out with Sinatra and knowing what he was about, the song came out of that. Everything in that song *is* him. I loved him. I could never have set it up as he did. It was written for Sinatra and it went to him first—no one else heard it.

I was with RCA at the time and when they caught wind that I'd given the song to Frank they were furious. "Why don't you keep it for yourself?" they asked me. "Hold it!" I told them. Forget the ego thing and forget the money and the guarantees, forget everything—none of that stuff means anything here. . . . The old rules don't apply. The song has to be treated as if it were a person in a sense, and that person was Sinatra.

There was never any question of singing it myself. I couldn't have pulled it off. The song wouldn't have had anywhere near the impact that Sinatra gave it.

"My Way" was Sinatra's way—and that was the right way, basically the only way. Although I do like the way Sid Vicious did it. At first I thought he was just goofing on the song. He starts out making fun of it, but then he gets into it, gets swept up in it. It's as if the song midway reaches out and grabs him by the foot.

I really questioned whether I was going to grant the license or not. But after I made some calls and realized his intent was sincere, I said, yeah, I'll let him do it. He's entitled. You know, I wasn't concerned about the copyright. Sid went in there, took primarily a jazz band in Paris, pulled some tubes out of the amps, and after his vision of it, and I think Jonesie—Steve Jones from the Sex Pistols—added some stuff later. It was believable and unique enough that when Scorsese called to use it at the end of *Goodfellas*, I was all for it. It had an anger to it, a voicing of his resentments.

Sid's version is not as extreme as what I did later on with *Rock*

Swings—although in my case in reverse—taking those songs and doing big band versions, but at that time it was shocking, when you first heard it. It was also very prescient. Prophetic for Sid, too. Sid Vicious's version isn't my favorite, and I can't say honestly that I would listen to it every week, but what he did worked as both a goof *and* a sincere take on it, which is a pretty amazing accomplishment in and of itself. Sid put himself into the song, and he really did do it his way. It's perfectly in sync with Sid Vicious going down that staircase in the video. An incredible visual, no doubt about that.

So when Vicious did it, I was pleased to hear that it touched him in some way, that he wanted to make that statement, and at the same time I was very amused by it. I was flattered that a punk like Sid wanted to do "My Way," someone who was into music totally different from mine.

I wasn't thinking in terms of the big picture, when I wrote "My Way," my only objective was to write something for Sinatra. I never really had any kind of premonition or design that it was going to be anything other than a song that Frank would want to sing. I wasn't thinking, *Oh, if I do this, it'll become a standard.* I had no idea.

"My Way" changed everything for me, for Frank, for our relationship. Even though I'd written outside the teen genre in the themes I'd composed for *The Longest Day* and *The Tonight Show,* it was with "My Way" that the second stage of my writing career began. And after the onslaught of The Beatles and Dylan, I now had the luxury of writing a new kind of lyric. I could stretch out. Everything had opened up. After that, I realized that I was going to be mature a whole lot longer than I was a teenager. Whenever Sinatra performed "My Way," he'd do a minute on how we met and how the song came about and how he felt about my writing, which was really nice.

In 1973, I hear from Don Costa whom I'm still working with, that Frank is going back into the studio so I wrote a song for him, "Let Me Try Again," as a follow-up to "My Way." Everyone was thrilled that he was getting back into the business. My good buddy Jerry Weintraub promoted Sinatra's famous comeback show at Madison Square Garden in New York in October, 1974. Who else but Jerry could have put that "main event" together? He's the best promoter in the world!

Frank kept going on and on touring as did Sammy and I, as you can see by the schedules we kept. We didn't care how old we got and as long as we were healthy, we were going to keep going. Despite the dispersal of the Rat Pack we kept crossing paths, hanging out, socializing through the '70s, '80s and '90s, Frank, Sammy, and I in Vegas, Florida, New York. From 1968 on Sinatra performed frequently at Caesars Palace as did I, as did Sammy. I'm there in February, September, and December of 1972, and January and March of '74. Sinatra is there again in June after his long absence in Vegas. I am there again in October and December of that year. In January, Sinatra follows me in, January 16th, I follow him, again on January 23rd. I am back in April with Freddie Prinze—who never finishes the engagement because of drugs. I am there in May and July. I am there again in December. In 1976, I am there in January, Frank follows me on January 15th. I'm back in June 1977, followed by Sammy Davis; I am there in August, followed by Sinatra August 25th, and so forth.

With each passing year Frank was visibly aging. And then word started coming out that Kitty Kelley was writing a book about him. He was not happy. Now, the Jack Daniel's had no limit. What freaked him out the most was how Kitty Kelley attacked his mother. He never got over the assault she leveled at Dolly. His mother had been his greatest supporter from the very beginning. Her belief in that skinny insecure kid from Hoboken had sustained him through the worst parts of his career.

Kitty Kelley also wrote a book about Nancy Reagan in which she implied that Frank and Nancy's three-hour lunches alone at the White House involved more than eating. But, as Sammy said, "At that age it probably took him that long to eat lunch." Barbara Sinatra's comment was, "If Frank and Nancy had sex during those three-hour lunches at the

White House, Nancy would still be smiling," alluding to the size of Sinatra's "pencil." As Ava Gardner said there was only 10 pounds of Sinatra but 100 pounds of cock.

Frank was upset about the Kitty Kelley book but tried to make light of it and encouraged the rest of us to mock it. So Sammy and I would think up jokes about it. I'd get up and say, "President Reagan's got a little suspicious of Frank and Nancy in the White House when he was passing the door and heard Nancy singing, 'All the Way' while Frank was singing, 'I Can't Get Started.'" Or Sammy would claim, "The book comes out in three editions: hardcover, softcover, and under the covers."

After "My Way," Frank and I became closer. We would hang a lot more and with the booze he would open up. If getting old is not for sissies, it was especially hard on the Rat Packers. He did not like the fact that he was aging—things were changing in his life. He used to joke about how his pencil wasn't working quite the way it did anymore. His image had always been almost as important to him as his singing. They were inseparable, really. When you listen to Sinatra, that image of the ultimate swinger instantly appears in your mind, and Frank hated to see that image begin to evaporate. The all-night booze sessions were starting to take their toll. You could hear it in his voice, which got wrecked by all those unfiltered Camel cigarettes he smoked. He had muscle problems with his right hand for which he had to have surgery in the 1970s.

He was very moved by his father's death, as he was about the death of Fred Astaire—he was very superstitious and found that an omen. One of the biggest blows for Frank and for me was the death of Don Costa. Don had recently recuperated from open heart surgery but unfortunately was a cocaine user, heavy smoker, and drinker—as well as being one of the sweetest guys on earth and a genius musician. Shortly before his death, he'd come to my home in Carmel. While working with him I saw he was not well and needed rest. I tried to convince him to stay with me at my guesthouse and take it easy, but he insisted he had to get to New York to finish an arrangement with "the Old Man" as he called Sinatra. He left me in Carmel and proceeded on to New York. The next afternoon he called me from the Warwick Hotel in Manhattan and informed me he had chest pains. I called Ben Dreyfus, my friend for many years, godfather to one of my children, and an incredibly stylish sophisticated and warm human being. I informed him of the situation and told him to get to Warwick with the ambulance immediately. He called me after they had put Don on a gurney. He told me that Costa wouldn't leave until they handed him the musical scores for the arrangement he was writing for Sinatra. They were in his arms in the gurney . . . while getting into the ambulance. I called Steve Ross, then the CEO of Time Warner, who had a similar heart condition and he did what he could for Don, but, by then it was all too late. Costa arrived at the hospital, they operated, but he did not make it. Later in the year I was in Vegas with Frank and we, along with Jilly and others, toasted him with tears—our friend Don Costa. I always think of him and miss him so much to this day.

When we would all meet for dinner, Frank would get bitter about the public's perception of him and the mob. We all knew it was just gossip but he was not happy with those innuendoes and blamed the press although it didn't stop him from being around the boys. We were all fascinated by them. By the summer of 1978, his mob affiliation was at its most evident. For example, we were all hired to work the Westchester Premier Theater in Tarrytown, New York. Word had it that the Mafia had financed the theater and that the Gambinos, the powerful crime family in New York, was involved. I was booked there along with Frank, Steve Lawrence, Eydie Gormé, and Diana Ross as well as many other performers. The trouble started when Frank took pictures with a host of these Outfit guys: Carlo Gambino, Paul Castellano, and Jimmy "the Weasel" Fratianno. Group shots backstage are something we all do every night after a show—but not usually with high-ranking mobsters. Unfortunately the Sinatra pictures got out and things only got worse for his reputation as a mobbed-up guy.

Because he was a larger-than-life figure, gossip grew around Frank like kudzu, but a lot of what's been said about him is pure hearsay. Incidents would get blown up out of all proportion. Everything had to be embellished and sensational. Unfortunately, Frank was a major target of all that. People would tell me unbelievable stuff that had happened with Frank—and I'd been there! But, as the philosopher Francis Bacon once wrote, "Fame is like a river that beareth up things light and swollen, and drowns things weighty and solid." Not unlike the rest of us, he was—aside from being a superstar and legend—also a fallible human being and therefore not always a paragon of good behavior. The guy who really helped keep Sinatra together was his valet, George Jacobs. A valet! I'd never heard of such a thing, but George was the guy who saw that the Old Blue Eyes airline stayed on schedule. I liked George a lot; he was civilized, a gentleman, and dedicated to Frank.

I started out in Vegas in 1960 with Sophie Tucker at the Sahara Hotel. Whenever Irv and I came to the West Coast on tour we'd always make a detour to Vegas, see all the acts because I was really sponging up all the information I could get so I could become the kind of nightclub performer I aspired to be. I'd see Johnnie Ray and Eddie Fisher at the Desert Inn. And it was at the Sands Health Club that I got my taste for steam rooms and that whole social scene. These weren't big fancy spas like today. They were modest, aesthetically speaking—to put it mildly. Just dressing areas, a few cubbyholes and a little, old television with rabbit ears that was on a gold stand on wheels that you could move around and watch when you were getting a massage. The guy that ran the steam room, his little fiefdom, was Neil Lepo. Later on a guy named Chick Stein started to work with him. Later, when Sinatra moved to Caesar's, Chick Stein and an ex-boxer started running it over there. But the key social scene in the '60s was the steam room at the Sands with these guys Neil Lepo and Chick Stein.

As he approached 60 the age factor became the predominant topic of his conversations. He obsessed about his age and his appearance. We all realized he'd had some plastic surgery done, and he hated wearing the toupee.

When I went to visit Frank toward the end I could see he wasn't well. He'd had some serious medical procedures—they had a bad effect on him and he wasn't happy. He was always stoic but I could see how upset he was about the damage the operation had done to him. The physical handicaps he faced depressed him immensely—they inhibited his ability to move around on stage the way he'd always done. For a man who always prided himself on his appearance, it also had a devastating psychological effect on him.

I would see him from time to time in the '80s at the Golden Nugget in Atlantic City. Time was marching on, and I could see that these three heroes of mine—Sammy, Dean, and Frank—were in the September of their years; they were physically and emotionally beat up. I would see Dean Martin at a restaurant in Beverly Hills after the death of his son in a jet crash. Dean was half alive after that. Whenever I would run into him at a little Italian restaurant in Beverly Hills called La Famiglia on Canon Drive, I would ask him, "How are you doing, Dino?" He would be sitting there with his false teeth in a glass of water, look up at me and say, "Just waiting to die, pally, just waiting to die."

Eliot Weisman from the Westchester Premier Theater became a friend and a great manager, booking Sinatra, Sammy, Liza Minnelli, Don Rickles, and others. We became pals and on occasion business partners. At dinner one night with Eliot, he informed me that Frank, Dean, and Sammy were reuniting—the optimistically named Together Again Tour. They indeed went out—these elder statesmen were forecasted to make a lot of money. Bottom line is, Dean never finished the tour. His manager and my agent, Mort Viner, were in Chicago when Dean just quit and went home. He didn't want to do the Rat Pack two-step anymore. He was old, he was tired, and he felt *finita la commedia!*

Toward the end of his life I stopped going to the shows, because it was so depressing to see Frank with the teleprompters, dropping lyrics.

Every once in a while, he'd lose the teleprompter and start looking for the words. It was very disturbing. One night he forgot to put on his toupee and went out onstage like that. He was forgetting the words he'd sung a million times and that anyone in the audience could have recited by heart. It was a tragic end to a brilliant career.

Frank had started losing his mental faculties. He would get confused as to where he was. You'd be with him in Vegas, and he'd think he was in New York. He'd say, "I got to call Barbara; she's out in L.A. and I'm not going to be seeing her for a while." We were in Nevada, only a couple of hours away from Los Angeles, and she was arriving the following day, but you couldn't tell him. It was very upsetting. It really broke my heart to be around him like that because I'd known him in his prime. Near the end you'd look in his eyes and he was a different guy, more vulnerable than I'd ever seen him, someone who had lost his bearings as to where he was, what he was doing—even *who* he was. It was scary to watch.

One of the last times I saw Frank was near the end, actually. I was having dinner with him. He became poignant and sensitive, going over and over old regrets in his mind. He suddenly became sad and said, "Paul, you know one of my big regrets was I wanted to play the Marlon Brando part in *The Godfather*. I don't know why they wouldn't give that to me. I called everybody, I mean *I'm him,* that part was me, I wanted to play that so badly." He became very emotional about it. Barbara would go, "Yeah, I know Frank, you're right, it should have gone to you, baby." She'd heard his lament a thousand times. Toward the end it became a litany, he repeated it over and over: "I should've been the one to play that, not Marlon Brando." It was because he was so fragile at that point in his life. It was unsettling to see him like that.

The last time I did see him was down at his house in Palm Springs. I was writing songs for him; he wanted to go back into the studio and sing again. I had one song called "Leave It All to Me." I think we were all set to go—Torrie Zito had done the arrangement and the band was booked and in the studio. We were all waiting for him to appear and he called and cancelled. I wasn't disappointed. I totally understood; knowing the circumstances, he could do no wrong in my book.

I knew all his sides—the macho side, the vulnerable side—and I think it all came out in his music. You will hear people say, *What a shame what happened to him at the end,* but I look at it differently. God bless him, he lived the life of three men. He lived life more fully than anyone I ever met. He was here, he was there, lighting up everywhere he appeared with that Sinatra magic whenever he walked in the room. He lived the equivalent life of a man who lived 150 years. It was the end of an era—you can close the book now. There was no one like him, nor will there ever be. He is sadly missed.

Seven

MICHAEL JACKSON, LIZ TAYLOR, A JEWEL HEIST, KINKY BRITS, TENNIS AT MIDNIGHT . . . AND THEN I GET PREGNANT

Things began to pick up for me recordwise when in 1971 I wrote "She's a Lady" for Tom Jones. The first meeting I had with Tom Jones, Engelbert Humperdinck, and Gordon Mills, their manager, they came to my home in New York and we tried to make a deal for my publishing company. It's late at night, and we were watching a movie at my house and they are all drinking champagne. The next day I woke up, looked in the living room, and my wife, being a significant decorator, and I were shocked to find all our bowls of potpourri empty. They had eaten all of it thinking it was potato chips.

I wrote "She's a Lady" on the back of a TWA menu, flying back from London after doing Tom Jones's TV show. Jones's manager wanted me to write him a song. If I have an idea and I don't have a pad of paper, I'll write on whatever is available. What's the difference? Paper is paper. And those blank pages on the back covers of menus are nice and hard. I like the look of them, and I can print on them without needing anything for support. When I'm writing, I generally toy with an idea until it manifests itself—meaning a phrase or a tune comes into my head and eventually begins to jell. When something hits me, I write it down immediately. I don't wait or it's gone. You just cherish those moments and write on anything—the stewardess's leg if need be.

My main problem in writing for Tom Jones was finding the right vibe for him. He's got a great voice, and he's a good friend. "She's a Lady" is not a song I would ever sing myself, but thinking of Tom it just came to me. It started with a verse.

> *Well she's all you'd ever want*
> *She's the kind they'd like to flaunt and take to dinner*
> *Well she always knows her place*
> *She's got style, she's got grace, she's a winner.*

Ouch! You get that first verse, and if you're lucky you've found your groove and the rest writes itself—theoretically anyway. I don't know where that stuff comes from, but believe me I'll take it. A germ of an idea in your head is all you need, but it does help to have an artist in mind. When I think about Tom Jones, I get a cocky, macho image—writing for other people is like playing a character and I thought, "What would this character say?"

What came out was pretty brash and arrogant, and sure, it was politically incorrect, but what the hell. I write like a Method actor, putting myself in his place. It's the shortest time it ever took me to write a song. I knocked off the lyric on that TWA flight from London back to New York. Later I went to my den and pulled the melody out in about an hour and a half. But I can tell you this, I dislike "She's a Lady" more than anything I've written. I'm not saying I don't have a chauvinistic side, but not like that. Still, I wanted to make it as realistic as possible, and Tom Jones is as swaggering and brash as a Welsh coal miner in a pub on a Saturday night.

Jones was all the rage at the time, he and a guy with the outrageous name of Engelbert Humperdinck. Well, when your real name is

Arnold George Dorsey, you've got to think of something that'll make you stick in people's minds. He took the goofy-sounding name of a German composer (who probably would have preferred to have been called Arnold George Dorsey)—and it made people pay attention.

Tom Jones's manager Gordon Mills was a larger-than-life character himself, a bigger star in his own way than either Tom or his other client Engelbert. Gordon pushed these kids around like puppets, ran an incredible company, and was kinky as hell—as only a Brit can be.

I'm in London doing the *This Is Tom Jones* show and one night Gordon says, "Let's go to dinner, have some drinks." He was shmoozing me, trying to buy my catalog. Tom was with us and after dinner he says to Tom, "Let's go over to you-know-where" (wink, wink), meaning some kinky place I didn't know about.

"Oh no, Gordon, what's that cost, then?" Tom asks. He was thrifty, real thrifty. We go to this house and when we get there I start getting nervous. The joint looks dodgy, and I haven't even put my head inside the door.

"What's going on here, Gordon?" I ask.

"Oh, don't worry," says he, "it's all lovely stuff." We go upstairs, and are ushered into a room with a curtain, which they ceremoniously open to reveal a two-way mirror and woman in there with a *sheep*. Wow! All kinds of sexual bullshit going on, and Tom and Gordon taking absolute delight in my reaction.

"What the hell are we doing here?" I'm asking Gordon.

"Bet you've never seen anything like that," he says. I had to confess I hadn't. So weird. Big, gypsy-looking woman in there with the sheep. When the British get kinky, they're kinkier than anybody.

This guy Gordon was the biggest egomaniac in the world; he just lived so huge, and made those kids big stars almost by extension of his oversize personality. He was married, but a big, big player. Always running around with a set of sexy little blond twins, and that was just for starters—just to get the conversation going. In the end I sold him my catalog, realizing I was in business with a maniac—but I understood his madness and his ego!

He was the kind of guy who would always challenge you, didn't trust anybody. He'd say stuff like, "Son of a bitch, I can't believe the flight is sold out from Las Vegas to New York. I betcha you can't get me on a flight. Tell ya what, I'll give you $10,000 if you get me on that flight."

"You're kidding?"

"Nope, $10,000 cash. Just get me on that goddamn TWA flight to New York, and I'll pitch you $10,000." I used to do favors for him because I knew he was a little crazy and I guess I like that (in case you hadn't noticed). He'd poke you so much about nonsense like that, to the point where you'd say, "I'm gonna get you on that flight and you're going to give me ten grand." I get him on the flight and, I kid you not, he gives me the ten grand.

Another time, Tom's in town with Engelbert Humperdinck. They're staying at the Riviera in Las Vegas, and Gordon, out of the blue, starts confronting me about my tennis playing.

"Anka, I can play tennis better than you. I can beat you any day of the week."

"Okay," I say, "try me."

"No," he says. "I can beat you, you son a of a bitch, and to let you know that I'm not kidding. I am going to bet you twenty-five thousand dollars that I can beat you."

"Okay, well when ya wanna play?"

"I'm going to call you up one night, and whenever I call, that's when I want to play."

"You're on, Gordon," I said. "Whatever you want." I'm already in that mode, thinking I know how to handle the guy.

Three or four weeks go by, they come back. He calls me up about 10:30 P.M. and says, "Meet me at eleven thirty. I've arranged with security in the hotel. They're going to open the tennis courts and turn on the court lights and we're going to play in one hour."

I stumble out of bed and get myself dressed. I pull up at the back of Caesars where we've agreed to meet and in he walks, dressed to the nines. He'd just come from a formal event at the Riviera with his wife and his assistant and his secretary. The wife is dressed in a full evening gown—he hadn't given her a chance to change—the assistant is in a tuxedo, and the female secretary is also in evening dress. He puts each of them in a chair at the boundary lines on the tennis court. One in the center, one on my line, one on his. It's now close to midnight, and it's clear there's been a lot of drinking going on—the poor wife, the last thing she wants is to be sitting there refereeing a fucking tennis match.

"Okay," he says, "now we're gonna start." We start playing, play till 2:30 in the morning. We play and we play, and finally he concedes that I've beaten him.

"All right you beat me, and I owe you," he says.

"You're gonna pay me right now, you son of a bitch," I say.

"What? You don't trust me?"

"You woke me up! We're going to the cage; I know you've got money." So we leave the tennis court, march through the casino in our tennis clothes—wife's in the nightgown, falling apart, wants to go to bed. We go up to the security boxes, he takes out $25,000 and gives it to me. Isn't that wild? Ah, what ego and power will do to people!

There was nobody that this guy Gordon wouldn't challenge including chance itself. He would bet on if a raindrop would land on your nose, if the odds were right. Or even if they weren't. He was a huge gambler—one time he lost a million dollars in that casino, when he was managing Tom and Engelbert. He lived large—reminded me of Colonel Tom Parker, a big roulette player. Tom was Elvis's manager, and he was always betting everything. Gambling was a big thing with the agency guys. Colonel Parker gambled so much at the Hilton that he sold Elvis for less than he was worth when he played the hotel. Ah, but then again he was just another victim of the Vegas virus! That's what all the fun was about. Madness!

All the performers kept an eye on what the others were doing, made the rounds, checked out each other's shows. Saw what we liked and took what we could. I lured Tom's conductor away from him in the end, a guy named Johnny Harris. He had one leg longer than the other, was very talented with a slight limp. Johnny had a lot of good years with Tom, then he came to work for me! It was fine with Tom, and there were no hard feelings.

I've always thought I was a pretty cool character, but my cool was seriously tested one night after doing Tom Jones's TV show. The studio was way out of London, some fifty minutes away from the city. We finished late. I get back to the hotel, and I'm up in my suite, one of the four suites upstairs at the Dorchester Hotel. This was in the '70s when the Dorchester was the place; they had butlers tending to you, real old English butlers straight out of the movies. I get back to the hotel around one in the morning. I call room service and I order some food. The butler says, "Most certainly Mr. Anka, but Liz Taylor's down the hall and she's not well. I need to serve her first, so I'll be a little while."

"Look," I said. "Please take care of her, I totally understand. Bring the food whenever you want; I'll jump in the shower." So I jump in the shower, thinking I have a little time and as I'm getting out, I just get the towel around me as the doorbell rings.

"Ahh, food," I think. I'm not dressed, but who cares? I open the door . . . and there's Elizabeth Taylor, standing in front of me in all her blazing glory, and with those eyes. She's actually holding two cats. I mean, I know she's a big animal lover, but seeing her standing there with cats in her arms is a surprise—and she's dressed in this sheer-looking nightgown. I'm just staring at her, going, *"Aaddadaadaadaaa . . .* How's your pussy . . . cats?" I finally manage to spit out. "Uh, I mean how's your . . ." God, what did I just say? Did I just ask her how her pussy was? Have I lost my mind? It was the most stupid, sputteringly stiff moment of my life. She was very sweet, very understanding; I guess she's used to it.

"Thank you very much for being so considerate about the food," she says. I'm not feeling well." I'm like *"wawellllwaawa!"* I couldn't put the words together—all that came out was this tongue-tied babble. All

I could think about was keeping the towel up. Standing there dripping like some wet seal and all that would come out of my mouth was, *Aahhhh.*

There are times when you feel you're so cool, but there are times in all our lives, no matter how sophisticated we think we are, we meet that one person we idolize and dream about and we just lose it. That has to go down as my supremely stupid moment . . . or at least somewhere in the top ten.

———■———

After Anne and I got married we didn't start having children right away, but eventually we had five girls. I was thrilled, I loved every minute with them, and yet for me there was always that wrenching dichotomy between my life on the road and my life with my family. The performer versus dad. Missing my wife and children, not seeing them often for months at a time. The family man with five daughters heading to the next gig, the entertainer returning home, trying to adjust to being just a dad. It's hard to explain what it was like, how hard that transition was from five-star hotels to changing diapers. The way I would float in and out of my girls' lives, trying to attend their school recitals, falling asleep in the middle of a performance and Anne nudging me. "Paul, wake up, you're going to miss the whole thing."

I'd pop up in their lives and then disappear again, like a funny irreverent phantom. Given my crazy schedule I can't imagine what it was like for my kids growing up. It was anything but normal. It doesn't matter to them how many hits you've had, to them you're just a dad. You don't get a pass for being a pop star when they're little—they don't even know what a pop star is. So, you're two completely different people. But at the end of the day I was still Dad. When I think of my kids, memories rush in. Traveling through Europe with five kids, driving through the hills of Mexico in a Jeep that kept backfiring while the kids laughed their heads off. The glorious chaos of it all.

I remember going into my children's rooms at night, the excitement of reading aloud to them from *Peter Pan* or *The Wind in the Willows,* sending them off to sleep with *Goodnight Moon,* or, more often than not, me falling asleep myself while telling them stories and snoring so loudly they couldn't go to sleep! Then the teenage years—with five daughters! Those were tough times for me coming off the road, exhausted and wired—the poignancy of missed birthdays, school plays, games, awards. It was a balancing act, trying to keep my equilibrium between these two worlds. In other words, it was hardly a traditional family arrangement.

When it came to parenting, I was doing the best that I could. And that includes my marriage, too, my relationship to my beloved Anne Anka. And then, as with my kids, I had to be away from her for long periods of time. Which made me feel vulnerable and disheartened at times. It wasn't an easy thing to do being a husband and father and a pop star over a thirty-seven-year marriage. But you can see we stayed close, Anne and I, over all those years, through all the ups and downs touring and being away caused and we've remained best friends to this day.

—■—

If you're in pop music you've got to deal with the changing of the guard.

Every few years, and by the time the '70s arrived I was well aware of the cyclical nature of the game. Pop music is a creature of the moment; it thrives on the mood of its time. Either you hook into that or you're not going to be part of it. What most people don't understand—and this goes for performers, too, the ones who most often suffer because of it—is that pop music is contemporary music, contemporary to a specific time, maybe three to five years tops. Another generation comes along with new attitudes, the culture shifts and the music changes. Pop music has to stay contemporary with the next group of teenagers—and in reality, the trend often reverses itself, which is a particularly painful situation.

We'd had the innocent, ecstatic joy of '50s rock 'n' roll, then came the early '60s, which were dominated by Brill Building songwriters and manufactured boy idols, followed by The Beatles and the Brit Invasion. But these changes were all more or less familiar—the music was based on melody—and the business itself remained more or less the same.

Aside from the cycles in the music biz, I believe an individual has a creative juice cycle and that it can get used up. Well, after thirteen years I was wondering if I could still find a new place for myself in the business. I knew I could survive performing my old hits—but what else was I going to do?

The melodic nature of pop music may not have changed all that much up through the mid-sixties, but, by the late sixties, musical trends were changing rapidly. You try to keep your integrity because the next wave, whatever it is, is going to be threatening—and I'd learned early on that, when it happens, you're no longer going to be a focal point anymore when it does.

Near the end of the '60s—the whole acid rock period of the Monterey International Pop Festival with the emergence of Jimi Hendrix and Janis Joplin—you had a truly convulsive revolution in pop music. It was the first time we'd experienced anything like that, the first time we ever saw anyone work an instrument the way Hendrix could with his teeth, behind his back. The first time we had ever heard anyone use their voice like Janis—someone who could somehow sing two notes at the same time. That was the next real kick in the head after the British Invasion. It's easy to talk about it in retrospect, but who in hell could have ever imagined this would happen? That out of Monterey would come two forces of nature like Hendrix and Janis?

Whoever knew there would be The Beatles and The Stones? Or that The Beatles could go from "I Want to Hold Your Hand" to "A Day in the Life." These weren't just cultural changes; we were looking at our own mortality as performers in terms of making a living in the industry. You were asking yourself, How can I compete with *that*? I felt totally intimidated. You are sitting there going, "What just happened?"

These new managers mirrored the change in the music as it evolved. When hard rock and flower power came in, the business and the infrastructure changed. Younger people began to take over the business. It got very interesting.

Then suddenly Janis and Hendrix were gone and everybody thought things would calm down a little. But a new crop of singer/songwriters emerged, such as James Taylor, Jackson Browne, and Carole King.

Along with the music, the music business changed. You went from General Artists Corporation, a company that had been around since the beginning to these younger guys like Albert Grossman, Andrew Oldham, Jon Landau, and David Geffen. Geffen wanted to be my manager in the sixties, and had I not been with Irv, it was something I would have done.

Jerry Weintraub was a classic case of the showmanlike promoter. He was married to Jane Morgan, who was also a client. I wrote a song for her called, "Kiss Tomorrow Goodbye" under the name of Dee Merrick. At that time I wanted to write under another name. I can't remember why.

Jerry was one of the guys around New York that I knew and liked. Very resourceful, smart, and ambitious. Creative. He went to Colonel Parker, offered him a million bucks to promote Elvis Presley. That got the Colonel's attention, and he started doing Elvis's tours.

I knew Jerry long before that, when he was still carrying hat boxes and gowns from gig to gig for his wife, but even then he was a smart guy and he knew the business. He evolved out of the motion picture business into his own big management firm. Jerry is the ultimate showbiz, spieler—which is why he called his autobiography *When I Stop Talking, You'll Know I'm Dead*. Somewhere in his book he says, "I knew Paul Anka before he was Paul Anka." And he did. I've known Jerry since the fifties and we're still very close friends. A lot of love and respect here.

Jerry Weintraub is Mr. Showbiz. He'd show up in Vegas, come backstage with, say, Neil Diamond, or another of his famous clients to say hello—always a big thrill. He's represented or promoted a boggling mix of artists: Charles Aznavour, Pat Boone, Jackson Browne, George

Burns, Eric Clapton, John Denver, Alice Cooper, Bob Dylan, Neil Diamond, Connie Francis, Jerry Garcia, Waylon Jennings, and Elton John.

I spoke to Jerry the first time I played at the Aladdin Vegas. How the hell he happened to pop up in my life at all these different events in my life I don't know. He's a kind of showbiz Zelig. He's a flamboyant, colorful character, easily the charismatic equal of any of his clients. Jerry's the classic showbiz entrepreneur who's been there throughout history. Aristophanes knew this character, Ben Jonson wrote plays about him, Billy Wilder immortalized him, and Woody Allen bottled him in *Broadway Danny Rose*. Woody and Jerry once worked in the same office building and Jerry speculates he may have based the Danny Rose character on himself from listening to his spiels in the elevator, yelling at his dumbstruck clients: "You're not just a *juggler*—but an artist! Do you hear me, an *artist!*"

In the '70s or '80s when I was living in Vegas and had my jet plane company, I got a call from Jerry and he asked me to fly in a newborn baby from Vegas to L.A. It was his adoptive daughter.

—■—

In 1969, in Monte Carlo I was actually crowned backstage by the Monte Carlo, Sporting Club ballet dancers at their performance of their ballet, *"Femmes."* That was the kind of coronation I could get into. The Nice *L'Espoir* reported that it was the first time *"la jeune grande vedette Américaine"* (big young American star—that would be me) had performed in Monte Carlo, a city I would get to know a whole lot better as time went on.

Hanging around the Rat Pack I had separated myself from my generation, but I wasn't their contemporary, either. I was some twenty-five years younger than Sinatra and Dean Martin, and sixteen years younger than Sammy Davis Jr. Generationally I was in a kind of limbo. I was apart from my generation, but I felt very much in tune with its dissatisfactions—with the war, the government, and outdated cultural attitudes.

On the morning of October 4, 1969, I was apparently feeling upset about a lot of things. "If you just work as a star, you're mad," I told *The Sydney Morning Herald*. "In spite of everything I've gotten out of life, I'm deeply worried. I feel like it's getting harder, more dangerous. Today, young people at least know where it's at. When I was young they didn't have the grim knowledge and power they have today. In our country, 65 percent of the country is under twenty-five. My generation were puppies in their teens. Not now. And every time the kids have gone out to make noise, they got what they wanted. They sat still through my early years and got nothing but promises. They live in fear of the bomb. I know, because I'm with them every hour, every day. And they live in hatred of the government we have. Religion is dead for them. I still believe in God, but at twenty-eight, I'm an older generation man, God means nothing to them. What they want is not in an afterlife. It's a chance to change this one. They want the vote. Why the hell, they say, can't we have one? We can serve in Vietnam, can't we? We want a vote at eighteen. I'm going to end someone's life, they say, well, why can't I decide what guy is going to send me to kill? Their parents have no answers."

—◼—

As we fell into the seventies and eighties, everything became disposable. We learned to live in a disposable society. It was always funny to see all those changes, what with the Neil Bogarts, the Jon Peters, and Peter Gubers. The movies—*Five Easy Pieces, Easy Rider*—reflected the new climate in Hollywood. The power started being taken away from the old guard.

It just wasn't my time. You sit there saying to yourself, "Maybe the older I get, things may revert, and maybe I could be 'in' again." That sort of thing happens a lot in pop music. It was getting to the point where I was old enough to become new again. You are constantly watching the demise of this or that person or style of music. That's what life is all about. Construction and destruction. Something else comes in and defuses something else. It has been an interesting trip, to say the least.

I began waiting to see what I could do next. I had a family I loved, I had kids to raise . . . but I also had this career that was not where I wanted it to be. The business as I knew it had been wiped out.

In the meantime I ran after a performing career. I thought if I could be a performer and have those kind of legs, I would always work. But as to what to write, that was my dilemma—I had to bide my time. I kept waiting for my chance, to see where my writing could lead me into that next thing. You're always waiting for that next window, but you can never really anticipate these changes until they arise.

I had tested this song a few years before it came out, and the disc jockeys told me they couldn't put a record out with a singer talking about his wife having a baby; it just wouldn't fly. Anne postponed having children for a couple of years after we got married but then they came one after another: Alexandra was born November 25, 1966. It was a natural birth and I went through it with Anne. "I now understand the word 'miracle,'" I told the *Philadelphia Daily News* a few days later. Right after she was born I had to leave for Philadelphia to do *The Mike Douglas Show*. Amanda was born in '68, Alicia in '70, Anthea in '71, and Amelia in '77. I had written "(You're) Having My Baby" as a tribute to Anne.

When I thought the time was right I began thinking how to approach "(You're) Having My Baby," so as to make a delicate subject like this sound as heartfelt as possible. I'd met Odia Coates when I was producing the Edwin Hawkins album for Buddah Records, and he introduced her to me. My cousin Bob Skaff, who at that point was a United Artists executive, suggested I make "(You're) Having My Baby" a duet. Odia had a great voice, she came out of gospel, and was the daughter of an evangelical minister. All the great black acts came out of gospel: James Brown, Otis Redding, Sam Cooke, Ray Charles. I've always been into gospel, and I had an idea: I would try to integrate gospel into my songs. Odia sang with me on "(You're) Having My Baby," one of the first black and white duets, and it went to number one in 1974. We went on to make more hits with "One Man Woman/One Woman Man" that same year, plus in 1975, "I Don't Like to Sleep Alone" and "(I Believe) There's Nothing Stronger than Our Love." Sadly we lost her to breast cancer in 1991—she was only forty-nine.

"(You're) Having My Baby" was a song I thought nobody would object to—who could possibly be against that? But it ended up stirring up quite a bit of controversy. We were growing up as a country, things were evolving, and obviously the situation of women was changing radically. A whole new wave was starting. Some women's magazines thought it was condescending and hipsters naturally found it corny. *Rolling Stone* hated it. The National Organization for Women gave me their "Keep Her in Her Place" award, and *Ms.* magazine called me "Male Chauvinist Pig of the Year." But there really is no such thing as bad publicity. It generally ends up doing something for you; controversy is always a plus. In the end I never needed to get up on a soap box to answer my critics because suddenly everybody was coming to my defense. Even *Time* magazine said, "What are you getting on this guy's case for? We're in a war. We've got a drug plague. We've got shit going on in our country. Give him a break, he's writing a song about his wife." Overnight, with all that heat, the record went to number one. Go figure.

———■———

Everyone has a dark side, but in those days no one guessed that there could be a dark side to Michael Jackson. However, I saw it early on and it wasn't pretty. I had a cool run of stuff in the early seventies, but at some point I decided to get back to writing with other people. I love collaboration and the diversity it brings to a song.

When I first met Michael Jackson I knew he was immensely

talented—this was before *Thriller* and his huge hits—and I began to think about collaborating with him. I'd known the Jackson family for a while. They used to bring their kids to Caesars to see my shows when they were young. They were a theatrically driven family. You could see that. I knew of Michael's talents, saw him growing up—everyone knew it was going to happen. Later on I met Michael again through a guy named David Gest, a real go-getter who eventually married Liza Minnelli.

I first sat down with Michael Jackson and talked about collaborating in 1980. We started working together at my house in Carmel. It was a fun place to be—he was using my guest house, playing with my girls in the Jacuzzi. He clearly had a real fondness for kids—he was very childlike himself and related to them on their own level. When Michael and I talked, we were rapping. Even then he had this fascination with plastic surgery, a major obsession, obviously.

Anyway, Michael and I start messing around with the songs we were working on. I was very impressed with the way he went about the writing process. He knew how to make his way around a song, not only because he had an incredible vocal quality, but he also had a capacity to make complicated singing licks from an initial one-finger tune played for him on the piano. He didn't seem at all like a disturbed character when he was working. He was just very tenacious, very focused on what he needed to do. But you could tell he was also wildly ambitious and capable of anything; I sensed an absolutely ruthless streak.

The concept of the album I was working on for Sony, *Walk a Fine Line,* was collaborations, with other artists: Kenny Loggins, Michael McDonald, David Foster, and Chicago, plus the two tracks I was doing with Michael. But the thing is, while we were doing *Walk a Fine Line,* Michael was also doing tracks for his album, *Thriller.* Well, *Thriller* comes out and is an absolute smash, and of course I can't get Michael in the studio to finish what we are doing. But I had tapes sitting in the studio in L.A., at Sunset Sound I think it was—all the tapes from when we were working together. It was right around then I started to see Michael's true colors. It happens.

I'm trying to finish my album, and suddenly I couldn't get him on the phone. Then he sent one of his people over to the studio and they actually stole the tapes we'd been working on.

When I heard about this, I went, "*What*? Michael went in and just took them? Holy shit!"

Then Michael disappears, and only after weeks of threatening, did I get the tapes back—finally. But I knew then that this kid was headed for trouble.

I just thought it was a terrible thing to do. How do people become ruthless? What mania takes over them is always a mystery. What happened? This boy was a child when I met first him. Who knew what went on in that family? I saw him a few years after the disappearing tape affair, at a law office, ironically.

I worked many years with my two loyal and smart lawyers—and close friends—Stu Silfen and Lee Phillips on this issue. They were involved all the way through in the negotiations regarding the posthumous release of Jackson's song, "This Is It." The song was originally titled, "I Never Heard," when it was written in 1981 for the album I was recording. In the end we prevailed—I got 50 percent of the credit and "They did the right thing," I said at the time. "There were only honorable people involved. I don't think that anybody tried to do the wrong thing. It was an honest mistake."

Some time after the stolen tape incident, Michael called and asked to meet me. I could tell he was disturbed and sorry, but I mean, what could you say? This was a major talent who got derailed too early in his life. It was never a good situation, and see where he winds up. You could almost sense it coming.

For example, between the Jacksons and the Osmonds, there was always a certain rivalry despite the fact that they were two family groups supposedly competing with each other in a friendly way. But Michael could be scathing about the Osmonds. He thought they were a kitsch exploitation group compared to the Jackson Five.

While we were working together he'd call the Osmonds and talk them up in a nice, chatty manner, and as soon as he'd hung up he'd rip them apart behind their backs. The Osmonds were not in good shape at that time. Donny is a nice guy, he and Marie both are. He has kind of kept it together the best that he can. It'll be interesting to see what he can make out of the next phase in his life.

Teen idols have a tough afterlife. I know because I was one—and so was Donny Osmond. His subsequent career, after the Osmonds initial hits, was checkered, to say the least. His trajectory as a performer is somewhat similar to many people that began very young. They start out as kids and then, like me, they have a big problem dealing with the next phase. In 1972, Don Costa had the bright idea of Donny recording two of the songs I'd had hits with as a teenager and they both became hits for him, too. "Puppy Love" was number one in the UK and number three in the U.S. and "Lonely Boy" got to number three in the UK and into the Top Twenty in the U.S.

Anyway, on this one occasion, Michael Jackson in his fashion floated to Vegas and was staying at a villa next door to us at the Mirage. I saw the parade of kids going in and out—scary. He was at the end of the stay but they were trying to get him out of there anyway. They swore never to let him return.

At first, Steve Wynn and Michael earlier had been all buddy-buddy. Steve even called one of his suites, the Michael Jackson Suite—but he didn't know then what was about to erupt. And when it did erupt, Michael was ensconced at the villa next door to me. The maids and other hotel staff would come to me and say, "We can't even go in that room; if we have room service we gotta leave it outside." When they finally get Michael out, after weeks of trying, they go in and there's broken glass, perfume bottles, food—the place is an unholy mess, the Jacuzzi has bubble bath pouring out of it, there's rotting food everywhere.

They finally had to renovate that villa for tens of thousands of dollars. Once they got him out, they never did let him back in that hotel.

While we were living in Vegas, I got a place in Sun Valley because the heat became insufferable. My daughter Alex went on to become a ski instructor and lived in Aspen for many years. It was a safe and healthy place to raise kids. In 1975, I got to work on a project that involved my family and expressed my love for them. That was the Kodak commercial, "The Times of Your Life." Even though I had previously licensed my songs to several companies, I'd never wanted to do commercials. I was always very careful what kind of product was linked with my songs. You associate Kodak with family snapshots, wedding pictures, photos of your children. Kodak came to me with the idea, with Jack Gilardi, my friend and agent at ICM. I loved the concept and together we put this piece together. I produced the record, which became a Top Twenty hit. The campaign was very successful and I was really happy to be a part of it. All of my kids were in it, and I think that's why it was such a hit—it connected.

Eight

VEGAS REDUX

In the early 1970s I moved my family west from New York to Vegas and that turned out to be quite a very different experience for all of us—what with bright lights, high rollers, mobsters, and movie stars.

But what I remember most about moving to Vegas, regardless of public opinion, was that you could have a wonderful family life there—and we did. The simple everyday joys of the girls coming home from school, making milkshakes and pizzas for them, helping them with their homework. They loved everything four-legged and furry and I loved to see the expression of pure joy on their faces when I'd bring home stray animals, dozens of cats and dogs. Then there was Mary Rizzo, who was my secretary for many years, very much part of the family—and a real character. Mary loved to wear very tight jeans and one day my kids came running to me and said, "Dad! Dad! Come look! Mary's got hair in her pants." I peeked at her jeans and I saw they'd split wide open in the crotch area and all her pubic hair was spilling out.

Vegas itself was growing and changing, and soon I found myself very much a part of the new scene. In 1978, I became one of the partners in a lavish discotheque called Jubilation (named after one of my songs) with Steve Lombardo and Marty Gutilla, two guys from Chicago who'd been in the restaurant business, and a third partner, Bob Marsico. None of them were mob guys, but it was from Lombardo and Gutilla that I heard some alarming stories about underworld types they'd got to know through their business dealings. My cousin Bob Skaff introduced me to these guys who owned restaurants and clubs in Chicago. We had a meeting at Sweetwater, one of their establishments. I liked them and trusted them and we became partners. My intuition was to put up the first freestanding disco in Vegas, the first freestanding nightclub. At that time, all these facilities were in-house at the hotels.

But given the Italian surnames of my three partners, even getting a license was a big hassle. As Marty Gutilla says, "We applied for a license to open a club in Vegas—it wasn't an easy road. Coming from Chicago and being Italian—this was a bit of a problem for us. They didn't like no I-talians in Vegas in those days. Tony Spilotro, the Chicago mob enforcer, had poisoned their minds so badly they didn't want to hear about any Italians. You could've brought Enrico Fermi there and they weren't going to like him. No Italians of any kind. Because three of us had Italian names—Steve Lombardo, Bob Marsico, and me, Marty Gutilla—we had to pay a fee and bring the investigators out to Chicago. They sent these two guys to investigate us who were like my old high school principal. Two Western shitkickers. We put them up at the Ambassador Hotel in Chicago. They had the greatest time. They were investigating everything and they came up with nothing.

"And that was just the beginning. It took three years to build and everybody was robbing us blind. I knew we were getting ripped off but I didn't know I was getting gunned down in broad daylight."

Marty would say to a cement contractor, "Maybe you could bid my job."

The guy comes back with, "I already did."

"Wait a minute, how could you do that? You haven't even seen the plans."

That's the way they operated. There were five or six cement contractors and they'd trade off the jobs. One week they would select one guy to get the contract, the next week another guy. It was all fixed. They'd make outrageous bids and the guy with the lowest bid would get the job that week—and his bid was still 30 percent higher than the price it should have been. It was all a big joke.

Marty and I often hung around the casinos to get away from this nonsense. Jubilation took from 1975 to 1978 to build. During that time I met some interesting underworld characters. These mobsters weren't my dear friends or anything like that. I just knew them from hanging around and you would see a lot of these things. Because of the new Howard Hughes era, with its corporate mentality, things got even more complicated. With the old mobster regime everybody knew where they stood—now it was all mixed up. The mob were still around but the corporate structure on top of the mob arrangements confused everybody; even the cops were conflicted. We—meaning me, Marty, Steve, and Bob—were right in the middle of the changing time in Las Vegas. They were great partners, and friends to this day.

I must say Jubilation was one beautiful building. It won all kinds of big-time awards. Jubilation was way edgy for Vegas. It was an oasis in the desert. In those days you walked two blocks off the strip and it would be all cowboys and guys in spurs and ten-gallon hats in any direction you looked. It was wide open. The International Hotel, for example, was in the middle of nowhere. That's where Elvis spent the last seven to eight years of his life. He rarely ever left.

We brought in three hundred trees we had chosen individually from all over California. We took silt from the bottom of Lake Mead, $100,000 worth of dirt, to put those trees up. People thought we were crazy bringing black dirt from San Bernadino for that amount of money. In 1970, $100,000 was an appreciable amount of dough. There were forty to fifty trees in the atrium that separated the restaurant from the nightclub—the rest we planted outside.

We built a retaining wall around the whole building so you could look out and see shrubs and trees with lights on them, but you wouldn't see the ugly side of Las Vegas. It was all glass on the outside. The architect was a student of Frank Lloyd Wright. You could see outside and look at the trees all lit up. Jubilation was the only place in Las Vegas that had anything green anywhere near it. Not a tree could be found anywhere else in Las Vegas at that time. There were glass windows in the bathrooms so you could look outside. There was a retaining wall and trees all lit up and shrubs in the foreground. You couldn't see in the bathroom unless a guy wanted to climb up the wall and of course they did do it, by the way. Whatever you think they could do, they did. In *Casino,* they showed booths covered in leopard-skin fabric. Marty was outraged at that; he found it so embarrassing. He would hate anyone to think that he'd ever have put leopard skin in an elegant place like Jubilation. That was such hokey Las Vegas crap. Jubilation was nothing like that.

Opening night of Jubilation in 1978 was a big splashy event with a lot of stars. It was huge. As Marty says, "Those cocktail waitresses we had; beautiful, five-foot-eleven college girls, were sensational—sparkling starlets. I would put them against the Dallas cheerleaders any day."

There were celebrities packed up there like sardines in the balcony. Joe Frazier was there, as were Tony Curtis and Jimmy Cagney. Bob Hope came. I'll never forget how he stiffed that beautiful tall blond waitress we had working there. She waited on Hope from ten at night to three in the morning; he had five or six people with him. It was a pretty big bill for something like four or five hundred bucks and that was just for drinks—nobody ate. In those days that was a big check. When the bill came, Bob gave her a napkin with his autograph. I don't know what he was thinking. She said, "Can you believe that sonofabitch stiffed me? Here is what he gave me, a fucking napkin!" I saw it and I will never forget it. "You're the greatest, you're the best. Love, Bob Hope." I guess he figured that was enough. Funny. But it wasn't so funny for her. I told my partner Marty Gutilla to go over and give her two hundred bucks to make it up to her.

Months later I met James Cagney there. Marty had met a lot of celebrities, but Cagney was his guy. In the restaurant part of Jubilation we were having dinner with Kirk Kerkorian, an old friend and stand-up guy. Kirk is one of the sweetest men that you will ever meet. I've known him since the fifties and he's never changed. He's still the same guy. You go to his house and everything is very humble. There would be two sports jackets and one suit hanging in the closet. With Kirk there was none of the Vegas flash and wretched excess. In casino-owner terms, he's totally the opposite of Steve Wynn. What I mean by that is he doesn't sit down with crayons and draw everything out in detail and run his business as fastidiously the way that Steve Wynn does. I don't know if he even goes to his properties that often. He's a bottom-line guy, not into décor or architecture or any of that.

It was around seven thirty as we were leaving—the nightclub didn't open until nine o'clock—and there in the entrance to the club was Jimmy Cagney. Kerkorian stopped to say hello to Cagney, whom he knew from before, and he introduced us. The music was just starting to roll inside the club but no one was in there yet. Cagney did a little dance step to the music—it was just amazing. He said, "Nice joint you got here." Or something like that. Marty Gutilla was just in heaven—for him Cagney was the number one guy. He used to come in and have dinner at Jubilation fairly often. A character from another age, he was an old man then; he died a few years later in 1986.

Atlantic City began happening as a rival gambling location in 1979 and knocked the shit out of Vegas, but Jubilation flourished despite it. You walk in there on a Saturday night and there'd be like three thousand people throwing their money around.

We had the Khashoggis there all the time, birthday parties for his kids and so on. The Osmonds used to come in on a Sunday, upstairs, the whole family. King Faisal of Saudi Arabia's son went to the University of Southern California. He would come to Jubilation on the weekends and hang there. There would be all these G-men around him, government guys, because he had diplomatic immunity—they wanted to make sure nothing bad happened to him.

The prince went to school somewhere in San Diego or L.A. He would come in every weekend. He only got like two hundred thousand a day allowance, poor kid, and when he ran out of his money gambling, he would come over to the joint. He had a Ferrari and a limo. The Ferrari was there in case he wanted to take a girl for a ride in his fancy Italian sports car.

One night I remember the prince was sitting at a table with ten or twelve women and drinking champagne. There was an empty table next to his with couple of seats, so Marty Gutilla went and sat down at the table. A guy comes over and says, "Excuse me, you can't sit there." This guy had a button, I swear to God that had a "G" on it—to say he was a G-man, a government agent. And Marty looked up at him with his you-talking-to-me expression and said, "Excuse me?"

The G-man tells Marty, "The prince doesn't want anyone sitting behind him."

"What the hell!?" says Marty. "Tell the fucking prince that him and his whole outfit they can go fuck themselves, *blah-blah-blah*."

Now Mike Weber, the maître d', sees Marty going into his act, and comes over to me. "Paul, we got a situation here. What should I do?"

I go over to Marty and plead with him. "Marty, please don't screw with this guy, he's a Saudi prince and it could get ugly." Marty calms down. This G-man wanted to throw him out. He wasn't one of the prince's bodyguards, he was a secret service guy, and apparently Marty was sitting at his stakeout table.

Jubilation was open from 1978 to 1984. It did big business, it was the hot club in Vegas—twenty-five-thousand square feet of wall-to-wall Vegas swank. I'm going to guess it brought in on average $250,000 a week—we did close to $180,000 in two days at the party for HBO alone. In other words, Jubilation brought in roughly 4 to 5 million a year.

Meanwhile we needed a guy to sit there until seven in the morning and watch that these people who worked for us didn't rob us blind. There wasn't anybody there to do that. I wasn't going to do it. My dad wasn't going to do it. My dad was ready to retire and get out of it by then. Anyway, at his age he couldn't stay there till five in the morning. I'm sure the people who worked at Jubilation were robbing us every which way you could imagine. From three to five in the morning they were on their own. We had some managers and we had some good guys, but people in Vegas will take your eyes out if given a chance. You had to keep tabs on these guys. It would require a guy that did nothing but watch these people. We did a lot of business there, and I used to say, where is the money?

As to the staff ripping us off, one night Marty said to me, "C'mon, Paul, watch this." He goes over to the bar and orders a drink. "The guy doesn't know me," he says, "so let's see what happens." Marty puts down a twenty-dollar bill, the bartender takes it, gives us the change but doesn't ring up the tab on the cash register. In other words, he just pocketed it. At this point, Marty tells the guy, "I'm one of the owners. Don't let me ever catch you doing that again."

We could have made a fortune in that joint if we'd paid more attention and watched it, but nobody really did. That's what happens when you don't keep your eye on the ball. Anyway, nobody got hurt, and everybody turned out okay.

There was a lot going on at Jubilation. I'll never forget the night the bookie "Fat Herbie" Blitzstein's kid got married at Jubilation; Herbie got remarried there, too. Tony Spilotro, the mob enforcer, was sitting there. I knew only too well who he was. I'd been in Vegas since the early sixties. I knew the whole scene—who the players were and what part they played in Vegas's underworld. But I also knew not to get involved with these types and to keep my mouth shut. But you can't help bumping into these characters when you own a joint in Vegas and it becomes the hot place to hang out. Here I had been this young kid just out of Canada who had made it, working their joints, selling their rec-

Me *(second from right)* with Irvin Feld *(far left)*; Bob York, president of RCA Victor; and producers Hugo and Luigi; 1963.

Freedomland, August 13, 1963.

Performing in Times Square.

On my arrival in New York City!

Burt Bacharach *(far left)* and me at a recording session.

I led the opening day parade of bullfighting season, on the horse El Cid from Charlton Heston's movie of the same name.

Performing my hit "Ogni Volta" in Italy. It was the first million-dollar seller in Italian history, and sold 4 million copies.

Having some fun on *The Mike Douglas Show*.

Frank Sinatra's birthday party, 1970. I brought an orangutan as a gift.

Anne and me with our daughters in 1977. Anne is pregnant with our youngest, Amelia, here.

Muhammad Ali and me, backstage at Caesar's Palace, Las Vegas.

Alan King, Barbara Walters, me, and Anne.

My father and me in March 1986.

Don Costa and me.

Michael Jackson and me.

Me and Michael
Bublé in Las Vegas
when we first met.

Paying tribute to my friend, Frank Sinatra.

With the great Peggy Lee.

At the White
House with
Ronald and
Nancy Reagan,
1986.

On the links with my good
friend Steve Wynn.

Eddie DeBartolo,
his lovely wife
Candy, and me,
many years ago
after a Super Bowl
win.

At home composing a song, 1997.

My son Ethan, my girlfriend Lisa, and me.

My grandchildren *(left to right)*: Allegra, Lucian (in Allegra's lap), Anessa, Alessio, Milo (in Alessio's lap), Andrew, Francesca

Ethan and me going on vacation.

My beautiful daughters *(left to right)* Anthea, Alexandra, Alicia, Amanda, Amelia.

In the recording studio, 2013.

ords on the jukeboxes, keeping my nose clean, and now here I was again with my own club, running into these guys again.

The kid's wedding was supposed to be over at midnight, but everybody was still going strong. They turned all the lights up in the joint, but nobody was going anywhere. Some of the guests were drinking that Cordon Bleu cognac like there was no tomorrow, everybody was having a good time—Tony Spilotro and his crowd, too.

Spilotro and Lefty Rosenthal, the mob's point man in Vegas, were at Jubilation three or four nights a week. They were there almost every day that meant anything, Tuesday on through Saturday. When he was there Tony was always a perfect gentleman. He was a professional killer, a vicious guy, but he knew how to behave. He was a lot more articulate when he wanted to be than he made out when he was with his lowlife friends. He and Lefty Rosenthal would bring all those showgirls with them. The feds were always there watching them. They weren't supposed to talk to each other—the mobsters and the Feds. They never socialized, but they hung out in the same places, often at adjoining tables.

The G-men and the Outfit guys all knew each other—mobsters and FBI guys. They loved it. They got to ogle the girls from the Lido de Paris and all that. Tony and Lefty would arrive with ten or twelve showgirls from the Lido, all five-ten, gorgeous girls, with their theatrical makeup and identical beautifully toned bodies—they all looked exactly alike, the ultimate blond pleasure model. Lefty and Tony would be drinking champagne and eating like everybody else and Lefty would be picking up the tab. The FBI would be at the next table. This one FBI agent, William Roemer, was assigned almost permanently to the Vegas mob detail—that was his job, observe Tony. "That was the best detail I ever had," he joked. He wrote a famous book, *Roemer: Man Against the Mob*. Roemer was the government's guy in Vegas, let's put it like that. The whole country knew Roemer's name from this gig, the only visible G-guy that everybody knew. He became famous on the basis of his detail in Vegas.

The relationship between the feds and the local police was a peculiar one. It was a very weird dance. Ralph Lamb, the Vegas chief of police, hated Tony Spilotro so badly! Lamb was after him like white on rice. But the FBI had that town wired—they had precedence, and they didn't want the local police messing up their investigation. Tony would walk out of Jubilation about 5:30 in the morning. His car would arrive, and then an FBI car would pull right in behind him. If, say, he invited you to go somewhere with him you'd be nervous to get in the car, not only because of who he was, but also because the feds were right on his tail.

"No, no, don't worry about them," Spilotro would say. "The only reason I'm alive is because of them. If it was not for them, I would be dead in five seconds. These fuckin' local cops would have killed me a long time ago. They whacked Frank Blue, Frank Blustein. Shot him outside his car—twenty-three times they shot him. They said he ran a red light or something. You shoot someone twenty-three times for running a red light?" Some say Frank Blustein happened to be eating one of those big sandwiches on a roll—like a Subway sandwich wrapped in tinfoil—just sitting in his car at a stoplight and the cops thought it was a gun. Others—including the detectives and mobsters who saw him that night—said he did have a gun, that he was paranoid, and thought he was being robbed. There are a lot of different accounts of the Frank Blue story, but when you drove around Vegas in those days with Illinois plates—meaning you're from Chicago and probably a connected guy—he wasn't—it obviously wasn't all that good for your health.

You couldn't have a better bodyguard than the FBI. They didn't want Spilotro killed, either—that was the big joke. This was in 1975. At six the next morning the FBI would still be there outside his house. That was one thing they left out of the movie *Casino*.

The FBI had the town bugged: hotel rooms, home phones, etc. One evening I called my dad up and in a mock mobster's voice said to him, "Hey, Andrew, Tony Spilotro here. Last night I was in your place. What's with the warm champagne, eh? What kind of joint you runnin' there?" He actually thought it was Tony! My dad answered very courteously and cautiously, saying if there were any complaints he had he should take it up with Bobby or Marty. Something like this would totally throw my dad; he'd never been around people like that. I'd called him from my home and the next thing I know I get a call from two FBI agents and next thing I know they turn up at my door. They come in, show their badges. "We monitored a call Tony Spilotro made from your house." "You got to be kidding," I said. "Spilotro was never in my house. That was me, it was a practical joke." I did my impersonation for them and they were satisfied with my explanation, but warned me about the dangers of impersonating mobsters—they didn't have too much of a sense of humor about that. But it shows you the extent of the surveillance they had everywhere in Vegas. I thought that was amazing. I called back my dad who wasn't all that amused, either. He said, "Son, one thing you never want to be is in the wrong place at the wrong time."

If you saw the movie *Casino,* the way the Mafia was portrayed in that swanky club with the showgirls, the high rollers, the flashy dressers—that was Jubilation. The town needed a place like that and we did very well with it. It was very modern—had a lot of glass, a very high ceiling, two restaurants, one upstairs, one downstairs, and a huge dance floor. We had great sound and great lighting. Ahead of its time for the city. Eventually we sold it in '84 and they renamed it the Shark Club. It was named the Shark after Jerry Tarkanian the famous basketball coach (that was his nickname). It became a sex, drugs, and rock 'n' roll kind of place. And then they sold it again in 2003 to a time-sharing company.

My father began having trouble at the end of our time at Jubilation. The stress got to be unbearable for him. Behind my back he was still smoking, which he knew I was not pleased with. He had had a couple of strokes and after that he retired and then had open heart surgery. If my mother was the instigator of my dreams, it was my father's steady sweet and reasonable nature that kept me from running off the rails many times in my life. Whenever I felt I was getting too out of control or too full of myself, I could always feel his benign hand on my shoulder, reminding me how lucky I'd been and that it was my duty to honor that good fortune by not throwing it away carelessly. My mom was very solid and steady but my dad was tough when he had to be—in his own way.

I can't tell you how important my father's influence on me has been. Mom was strong but my dad was uncompromising in his own way, too. He became such a hero in my hometown because he stood up for the things he believed in. He was a born diplomat, but he'd never back down from the things he believed were right. That's why in Ottawa it wasn't Paul who was the famous Anka, it was Andy. He ran all these different organizations. He was head of the school patrol, he was president of the Humane Society, and on and on. He was a hero—and he was *my* hero. He was the rock in my life and when he died on April 6, 1993, it was a crushing blow to me. I also have his wedding ring, which I keep in a box along with my mother's.

—■—

It's a myth that mobsters ran the casinos day to day in Vegas. These guys couldn't get licenses from the gaming board to save their lives. No, their strategy was to hire Jewish bookmakers to run their casinos. They'd bring in a bookmaker from Dallas, a bookmaker from Seattle, a bookmaker from New York or Chicago. Two reasons: (a) the bookmakers were thrilled to be legitimate at last and not be doing stuff they could get arrested for, and (b), these bookmakers would become a natural merchandising network because they would know every player in every city. The mob would put up the money and they'd let a bookmaker buy 1 percent or 2 percent of the casino. The guy would move his family to Las Vegas, they'd hand him a phone, and have him dial up his old contacts and invite guys he knew from his old city to come and stay at their hotels to gamble. It was a very successful formula pioneered by the Sands and the Riviera. So when you look at the original ownership in the 1950s of these old casinos it's a combination of Jewish bookmakers and savvy connected Jews, the kind of guys who ran speakeasies during prohibition, guys who were tired of being pinched by the DA on his latest reform movement. By this time these guys were in their fifties and sixties, and here was a chance to immigrate to Las Vegas and be legitimate members of the community. It was an arrangement that suited both sides: promote Las Vegas and no longer be an illegal person. When you look at the Riviera, the Dunes, the Sands, and the Flamingo, that was the story. Forget Bugsy Siegel and the 1940's—that was an aberration, it was some crazy scheme to sell the Flamingo and the place closed the second night. His friends killed him—for whatever reason.

But after that, whether it was Meyer Lansky or confederates of Meyer Lansky's, the Flamingo, like the rest of these places, was run by guys who'd been on the fringe of gambling illegality in other cities and who wanted to make a better life out there in Vegas. Very few Italians ever came on the property. There was never any violence. "We don't want no blood there," said Chicago mob boss Tony Accardo. "It's bad for tourist business." This idea that the Mafia ran the casinos is bullshit—they could be partners, but they couldn't come to Las Vegas. The mob guys stayed home in Chicago and Kansas City. They'd tell these old bookmakers, "You're gonna own this casino. We can put up a little money but we expect to get 20 percent out of it. You take the money in cash and give it to us when you see us." And it was small money back then.

Steve Wynn is one of the most polished guys in the world and he got to where he is today without any mob connections. But, naturally, if you work in Vegas you get to know connected guys. One time Steve was at a charity event with my friend Carl Cohen, who ran the Sands. Steve was running the Golden Nugget at the time and asked Carl, "How much money did the Sands make in the era of the Rat Pack?" And Carl told him one of the funniest stories about the perception and reality of the amounts of money that actually got skimmed.

The casino bosses used to play gin at the Desert Inn Country Club.

They had a card room there and they would go over in the afternoon and play gin. And Hank Greenspun from the *Las Vegas Sun* would be there. They'd have the TV on in case some sports event came on—they would bet on everything. One time during the Senate hearings on organized crime (they were investigating mob rule in Vegas), Senator Estes Kefauver comes on the TV and he's grilling one of the honchos from the Dunes—we'll call him Harry Gold. "Mr. Gold, isn't it true that you and your associates at the Dunes and the Sands Hotel and Riviera have skimmed hundreds of thousands and millions of dollars from your casinos in Las Vegas and this money in fact is supporting the spread of organized crime in the USA?" Ridiculous setup question. Gold knows he isn't going to have to testify, and he says, "On advice of my attorney I'm going to take advantage of the protection of the fifth amendment. . . ." But the senator's grandstanding, so he ignores this; it's his chance to graze on his ass with these rhetorical questions. "Mr. Gold, is it not true . . . now is it not true, Mr. Gold, that instead of turning the money collected from the money owed in markers that you all keep that money and don't report it?" He's going on and on, mentioning these millions Harry Gold is supposedly skimming. Suddenly these three guys playing gin jump up and shout at the TV, "You dirty son of a bitch, we never got that kind of money! Hell, we only skimmed like ten grand a day."

That figure was about right. In the old days, it was around ten grand a day. About 3.6 million a year. They showed about $600,000 to $700,000 in profit and they would make a few $100,000s extra with the holidays and special events. That gave the owners somewhere between 5K and 15K a month to play with—it was money for girls, and money to go to other joints and shoot craps and then the next day a runner would take money from that guy's box to pay off his markers so Major Riddle's money would go to the Sands, Harry Gold's money would go to the Dunes, Aaron Weisberg's money would go to the Flamingo, Jake Freedman's money would go over to the Dunes, and so on.

Vegas and the mob and all that money they were skimming became legendary. It was obviously serious enough money for the Chicago and Kansas City Outfits to keep their hands in the till but how much money was actually in the cage back in those days? In the old days the casinos made, say, five million a year. Not a lot of money. Still, they were all raking off personal fortunes—it was all in cash, no taxes.

There had always been high rollers, but sometime in the late 1970s to early 1980s, the really monster players came along. When this trend started, all these Asian gamblers came in. They had the highest betting limit in the world at the time. The old betting limits were miniscule in comparison to the standard bets you see going on in those days with these guys from Beijing and mainland China at the Wynn, Steve Wynn's resort and casino in Vegas. These guys were betting twenty-five to a hundred thousand a shot. Who had ever heard of a limit like that? That was off-the-street cold.

The standard bet today is *huge*. The last time I was there two guys won a million each. Every single day these guys are betting 150K to 250K a card in seven- to eight-hour sessions. Mr. Wong from Taiwan and Mr. Mawar from Malaysia in Salon 2. The highest roller that hit the city was from Japan: a Ken Mizuno, who has become something of a legend, having accumulated gambling debts in excess of $60 million. Steve pays a ton of money in taxes on the winnings. There are more tourists in Vegas now, visitors just checking out the games, what they call lookie-loos. Back in the old days at Caesars there weren't that many lookie-loos simply because there weren't that many rooms in Las Vegas. The guys who came were serious gamblers, they were all betting $500 and $1,000, which was serious money back then. By 1966 you'd see $20, $50, $100 chips everywhere; $500 chips were unusual to see.

—◼—

When Steve Wynn and I became neighbors in Las Vegas, I realized what a true genius he was—and still is. An entrepreneur and a supreme perfectionist right down to every tiny detail. Plus he's very charismatic. He took the gaming industry to a whole new level. Howard Hughes brought the first change to Vegas but could never have taken Vegas— and the worldwide impact of gaming—to the point where Steve Wynn has taken it.

I've seen how he treats his employees, always in a superb manner on every level. He knows how to motivate them, and how they, in turn, treat the hotel customers. Where the employees eat—the esthetics of the place, etc. To work for him is a challenge on the executive level. But you better know what you're doing to stay ahead of the game. And if you do, financially to work for Steve Wynn is the best in the business. We know each other very well. And how to deal with each other. That is why we are such very good friends.

Steve Wynn has created some of the great casinos in Vegas—the Mirage, the Bellagio, and now the Wynn—and he realized from the very beginning his success would be based on style and atmosphere. The model for all the swanky resorts Steve built was the old Fontainebleau Hotel in Miami. Aside from all the facilities and luxury accommodations and restaurants, what makes a great hotel—or a great casino—is fantasy, magic. That was the secret of the Fontainebleau. Steve also knew that gambling brought in the money, but what attracted the high rollers—aside from the tables—was atmosphere and Sinatra personified that in spades. He had that hip, suave style down cold. He was his own planet and wherever Frank hung he brought his own gravity, which magnetized gamblers and tourists alike. No entertainer has embodied that solid-gold charisma like Frank Sinatra.

At the time Frank was getting paid 100K a show at Resorts International in Atlantic City and at Caesars in Vegas, but Steve had a plan: one way or another he would get him to move to his casino. The problem was at the Golden Nugget they had only minimal seating—a few hundred people—and a small ballroom, so how was he going to be able to afford Frank? Well, Steve had this fierce belief that somehow he'd figure a way to convince him. His logic was: "I can afford Frank because he will bring his aura when he's here and when he's not here I can get him to do TV commercials. Either way Sinatra's charisma—which in Vegas is king—is going to attach itself to my place. Frank is the guy, the swinger—he represents the good life, the guy all the other guys want to be."

Mickey Rudin was Frank's lawyer and longtime business partner. He took care of his whole life as manager, agent, producer. If you wanted Sinatra to do anything you went through Mickey. He'd graduated from Harvard Law School, a wonderful guy and very traditional. Frank called him the Judge.

Steve proposes his idea to Mickey Rudin, that Frank would agree to work sixteen shows a year: four shows a weekend, four weekends a year. He'd do a show Friday night, two on Saturday, and one on Sunday. Occasionally he'd do an additional show on Thursday. He also proposed that Frank do customer parties three or four times a year with high rollers and prestigious customers—by invitation only in the showroom. And that's how he made it worthwhile. The idea was that Steve would make money but Frank would be the boss—and get shares in the casino. Rudin says he would take it up with Frank.

Rudin calls Sinatra. Frank's unhappy. He's going on about the money. "It's just not enough bread, man." Rudin keeps going back to Sinatra, trying to convince him. "Look, Frank," Rudin tells him, "if the stock goes to eleven it'll be worth over two million," but Frank's still saying, "No, that's not enough." Finally on the fourth phone call, Rudin says, "But, Frank, if it goes to thirty-three it'll be worth eight million." And at that point, Frank said, "Take it."

As it happened Sinatra did not like Resorts International, where he was currently working—it was not a classy place. Steve's place was. Also, Steve has always been a very savvy operator and Sinatra respected him. What really appealed to Frank was that in this arrangement he wasn't just relegated to being another entertainer, another act—he was the centerpiece, the overriding presence at the place. Plus he had an ownership role. Rudin called Steve back and told him, "Sinatra says he'll work the first two weekends—no contract, no nothing; you don't have to pay him a nickel. You can have him try it out a couple of times, and you be the judge at the end of that. If it works the way you think, you pay 50K a show back pay and you give Frank stock in the Golden Nugget."

Mickey asks Steve when he'd like Frank to play. Steve suggests Sinatra's birthday, December 12, which traditionally just happens to be the worst week of the year. Besides which, Frank has never worked on his birthday before. But he agrees! They hold a birthday party for him on Thursday night, he does two more shows Friday and Saturday. They turn the hotel over twice. One group of New Yorkers and shooters was invited on Friday, another group came on Saturday. It was a huge success and Frank loved it. They blew the roof off. Danny Schwartz, a friend of Sinatra's, and high-end player for Steve, dropped $4.8 million at the tables that weekend.

The second time Frank played was on Steve's birthday, January 27th. Another big hit. This time around Sinatra made his first commercial. They started playing it in New York, it was huge—and, better yet, Frank liked it. Everything was going great, the third trial was coming up in April, but at this point Steve called Mickey Rudin to tell him, "It works like a dream, just the way I'd hoped." Sinatra got the stock options and he made another four maybe five million out of it, something like that.

———■———

The smartest guys in the entertainment business long ago figured out that you have to check out everything yourself. When you make a contract with someone you have to make sure it's going to stick, that both parties are going to live up to their obligations. You've got to do it like Buddy Hackett's mother. She went to the dentist, and just as he was about to put the needle in her jaw she reached over and grabbed the guy's testicles, and said, "Now, I know we're not going to hurt each other."

I get a call from my buddy, saying, "Paul, I have a great club, a fantastic lineup, Sinatra's going to make it his base, come join us!" But, it's another thing altogether making a deal with a friend. I negotiated my own contract with Steve Wynn. Steve came to see me about performing at the Golden Nugget, his casino in downtown Las Vegas. Because I knew him, and he was my neighbor and a friend, it made things more complicated. Steve tells me, "Listen, I can't pay the $50,000 a week you're used to getting. But I will make it up to you with stock options."

We've grown up together albeit in different parts of the business. Meanwhile as I'm negotiating with him I'm thinking to myself, "Here I am negotiating with my buddy Steve Wynn about my slot in the same club as Sinatra." Back in Ottawa when I was still fantasizing about this stuff, the idea that I would be the anchor at the club that was Sinatra's home base would have blown my mind. Steve wanted me to work twelve to fourteen weeks a year—which is a lot. The idea was that while Sinatra was going to perform there four to five times a year and be the centerpiece, I would be the anchor, which was flattering. Eventually my contract comes to an end and we're renegotiating.

Two years go by, contract negotiations would get bogged down for any number of reasons. This happened to me in the mid-1980s when I negotiated a renewal on my contract to appear at the Golden Nugget. I said, "Steve, listen I love you, we spend our time together, we take trips with our families together, but this 20K, 30K, 18K a show, the money isn't making it. You've got to understand that by the time I get done paying taxes and working fifteen weeks a year I'm having a hard time getting to five million a year and that's what I need to maintain my lifestyle." Steve is a friend and he's sympathetic but he's a hard-nosed business guy, too, so he says he'll think about it. This goes on for a couple of weeks and finally I'm fed up.

I'm in Carmel on the telephone for about four hours, trying to hammer out a deal. It got to the point that Steve is going ballistic and we're at a stalemate. But I know my friend Steve very well and what he's about. As I've always said, humor is the final refuge of sanity and with that philosophy I had a plan.

Knowing the deal was in jeopardy and Steve wouldn't budge, it was my turn to get the situation back on track. I arrived in Vegas around midafternoon. I called the Vegas ambulance service and asked them to send over an ambulance with a gurney and two male attendants. I tell them I want to pull a joke on Steve Wynn over at the Golden Nugget. When the ambulance arrives, I tell the attendants to bandage me up to look like I'm beat up and to tape an intravenous drip in my arm.

I get driven by ambulance downtown to the Golden Nugget Hotel. I give the guys $500 for going along with the stunt. So now it's late afternoon and I'm laying on a gurney in an ambulance going along the freeway to the Golden Nugget. We arrive at the hotel and I instruct them to carry me through the front entrance of the hotel, through the casino, and into the elevator up to the second-floor executive offices from where Steve runs his casino empire.

I am on the gurney as we enter Steve's office. We pass by Joyce Luman, Steve's secretary at the time, one of the most perceptive women and a great asset to Steve. We proceed through two glass doors, which are bulletproof and electronically controlled. They put the gurney down on wheels. Steve is sitting at his desk, going over some paperwork. You have to keep in mind that he suffers from retinitis pigmentosa, which affects his peripheral vision.

I say, "Good afternoon, Steve." He looks up and says, "Who's that?" I say, "Don't you recognize me? It's Mr. Bellini!" (The nickname he gave me on our trip to Italy.) Steve says, "Okay, I give up, let's sign the deal, you win!" He starts laughing out loud. He says to me, "Don't get out of the gurney, I want to get a camera and take a picture of you." He takes the picture and by the way, he still has that photo. Guess what, he agreed to all my terms. He said, "You know you're absolutely right." We hugged and kissed and it was done.

My first call when I got off the gurney was to my attorney and business manager, Al Rettig, to draw up the papers. Al was there in the middle of all the action and, to this day, is one of my dearest friends.

Whoever is lucky enough to have him, has himself a great attorney and loyal associate, more important, a friend for life.

——■——

In 1971 Tony Spilotro came from Chicago to become the mob enforcer in Vegas, and very soon he had a tight grip on the town. He was working middle class, from a nice neighborhood, but he was a vicious little runt from the get-go. He grew up a tough, ruthless kid in high school, the kind of kid who's in the alley with a brick. One of those guys. He just kept on going from there. He would go into assignments. He was a mob kid.

Everybody in the town was petrified of Tony Spilotro. He had big arms, too. The mob were thick as thieves with the Teamsters and the unions—the Teamsters had a lot of pull. If anyone from the casinos messed with the mob they wouldn't get any deliveries. If you were at Caesars and you wanted to give someone a hard time, fine, but there won't be any liquor in your bar. Your steaks aren't going to get delivered. They would stop the Teamsters from bringing the goods. They had full control. They built Vegas, and still owned it until the corporations came along in the '80s. The guys who wrote the book, *The Green Felt Jungle,* said it best: "The town was built for degenerates by criminals." That's about the best way to put it. And Tony was the archcriminal. Mob money came out of the Teamsters pension funds—that's where they were getting all that dough.

The mob put up the fifty-million-dollar loan to buy the Stardust Casino. A big development deal. They were just stealing money out of the pension funds left and right. Fortunately for them, someone had enough brains to start building a few hotels with the money instead of simply stealing it and spending it. Tony had total control of all that all of the time. Tony and Lefty, Frank "Lefty" Rosenthal.

How tight did Tony Spilotro run the town? In the 1970s and early '80s, he was the boss. I'll give you an example: The bookmaker "Fat

Herbie" Blitzstein's wedding was at Jubilation—the guy whose kid had gotten married there earlier. Now, there were some twenty guys lined up to talk to Tony, and Tony is sitting at the head of the table. Each of these guys is kneeling down to talk to him. The music was so loud and he was talking so low you had no clue what they were talking about— and didn't want to know. Twenty of them lined up—he was that powerful because, in an underworld sense, he ran that town.

Tony Spilotro was a blight on the town—he was a curse, a really bad guy from the bad old mob days, who was still around creating mayhem. Until the big corporations started coming in in the mid-eighties, he was a sinister presence. Those corporations would eventually take over—which they did. Tony would have been taken care of by his own crew, but he didn't live long enough to get out of it in one piece. Caesars was controlled—I don't know how but believe me, they fell in line just like everybody else did. I don't know what that really meant. I just know that nobody wanted to mess with Tony. He was a horrible fucking scary guy. It went to his head eventually. If he'd stayed low he would have been okay, but he started doing the shit, and that's what brought him down.

Strictly speaking the Italian mobsters weren't allowed to come to Vegas period, but naturally they did. When these guys would sneak into town and come to Rat Pack shows in the late 1950s and 1960s, if the spotlight accidentally strayed into the audience, you'd see six guys jumping under the table.

As much power as Tony and Lefty Rosenthal wielded, management wouldn't let Lefty or Tony in any of the hotels or casinos. They had this black book that 86'ed certain people from entering the casinos. Tony was one and Lefty was another. Lefty was a boyhood pal of Tony's, a sports bookmaker, a casino owner, and, in FBI lingo, "organized crime associate." The character Sam "Ace" Rothstein played by Robert De Niro in *Casino* was based on him, just as Joe Pesci played the Tony Spilotro character as a Mafioso loose cannon.

Lefty, the cool partner in the deadly Tony Spilotro–Lefty Rosenthal duo, had a highly popular prediction show. In the movie, *Casino,* they have Lefty starting his show at the Stardust (which they call the Tangiers Hotel in the movie), but actually the first year he did it from Jubilation. Every week they had different guests. Lefty would come out and give his picks on the games—that went on for quite a while. Was it a year? I would say at least six months, some version of that. He was a sharp guy and still is, there was no one sharper, an incredible oddsmaker. These new guys, they couldn't carry Lefty's underwear. He, too, worked as a technical adviser on *Casino.*

Lefty handicapped the football line. At some point we realized we didn't want him in the club. It was too scary having Lefty and his buddy Spilotro in there, but no one knew how to approach Lefty or Spilotro. How exactly do you put the bell on these cats? I remember the night the management objected to Tony and Lefty being at Jubilation and they asked Marty Gutilla to eject them. "Are you seriously asking me to go tell these guys they gotta leave?" He didn't want to go personally to tell Tony and Lefty they had to get out of there. That wasn't going to fly. Marty just told management, "I don't think that's in the cards right now." Fortunately, the situation resolved itself in the end for technical reasons. They needed more production equipment and decided to move the show to the Stardust.

Doing Lefty Rosenthal's wife wasn't a smart move on Tony's part. Lefty was making a lot of money for him. Especially at the Stardust. Every bookmaker in the country used Lefty's line, the line being Lefty's inside line on the bets. Lefty always gave the guys at the Stardust the line first. Nobody got it before they got it at the Stardust—not anybody. The bookmakers were cleaning house. Those were the days before computers, but take all the computers you want, it's still tough to overcome the eleven-to-ten odds. It goes like this: If you make a $100 bet on a football game and you lose, you have to pay $110. If you win, you win $100. That doesn't sound like a lot, but extrapolate that over hundreds of thousands of bets and that's serious money. Let's say one bookie had 20 grand on team A and another bookie has 20 grand on team B. If team A wins, you collect $17,000 plus $1,700. That's $18,700. If team B wins you pay 20 grand so you lose $300. Now you collect $2,200 from the losers and 817 from the winners so you now have $5,000 on an even proposition. Think about it: if you lose, you lose $1,300; if you win, you win $5,000. A 3.5 increase on your money. What is it you wouldn't have to do if you were making that kind of money? It's that innocent $110 that does people in. People don't realize how strong that is until they begin gambling and consequently start paying up. It'll gobble you up. It's like interest on a credit card—pretty soon you see what's happening. Did you ever know a bookie that didn't drive a Cadillac and smoke a cigar? Sometimes a bettor will win 15 million. That's what keeps people coming back—that once-in-a-blue-moon win. With luck, you got a razor's edge on your bets. Lefty was making an absolute fortune for Tony.

It was an odd relationship between Tony and Lefty. Tony would always bark at Lefty, and Lefty would kind of take it but the truth is Lefty knew that if he went to somebody and said this guy is out of line or he is this or that or he's fucking my wife, that would be all he would have to say. Tony's involvement with dope dealers is what in the end brought the heat on the bosses in Kansas City. That was what absolutely did him in. That was the icing on the cake. They might have even been able to deal with the fact that he had his arm in the dope dealers. They might have been able to straighten out the Lefty and his old lady deal. But they could not straighten out that they were all going to jail because Tony had gotten so crazy. These old mob bosses were so ancient, they came to trial with oxygen tanks. They were really old men. Do you think these guys want to go to jail at eighty years old because some guy is doing wild little shit and is up to ten or eleven in the morning betting all over the country with their bookmakers?

Tony was using "Fat Herbie" Blitzstein's account, betting all over the country for him. He owed this guy three hundred, another guy six hundred, another guy two grand—all on Herbie's account. People didn't know it wasn't Herbie Blitzstein's money he was betting with.

"Fat Herbie" was Tony's buddy. Tony was stiffing the bookmakers, stiffing them, and blaming Herbie. These guys would come from New York to Vegas, and ask him, "Tony, how do we get our money from Herbie?" Tony would say, "I can't get my own fucking money from him. How do you want me to get yours?" But, in the end, everybody knew it was Tony. He was becoming pretty blatant about it. But who would challenge him? Eventually, though, he brought heat on himself. Herbie himself came to a bad end in the early nineties—the mob wanted his auto repair service (Herbie's front) and so they just killed him.

Tony becoming a coke head was bad enough, but messing with Lefty's wife was his first big fuck-up. Even in the movie, his character says, "This is a big mistake. I don't know how I got involved with this." Tony could handle any situation, but now he knew he was fucked. He was messing with other guys' wives. Lefty was making him a lot of money . . . well, what they thought was a lot of money. To be a millionaire in those days was considered really big bucks.

Since under normal conditions you couldn't meet Tony in the casinos you had to hook up with him in these joints on the strip. You had to go to a place called Rube's, a dive owned by this guy named Rubenstein from Chicago. A bar in one of those little shopping centers. Marty remembers seeing see him there and saying to him, "Tone, what are you doing?"

Marty tells me, "It's ten in the morning and there'd be Tony, he hadn't gone to bed yet—probably been up for days—going full blast. I am going, 'Why is this guy still up at ten o'clock?' I started figuring. Unless you are gambling, or messing around with hookers or tarts until ten in the morning, you're doing the shit. Then I started hearing some rumors about him hanging with dope dealers in Vegas."

That really pissed everybody off, especially the bosses in Chicago, Kansas City, and Cleveland—the Midwest mob scene. Their beef with him was all about the drugs. The drugs were warping Tony and he was getting out of control and that was bringing heat on them. He was now way over the line—whatever line there was, he was past it.

Tony Accardo, the big mob kahuna in Chicago, didn't like what Tony was doing with the dope. Accardo was one of those guys who was totally antidrug. You couldn't even mention the word "drug" in front of him, any level of it—weed, coke—I don't care what level you were on. Whereas in New York that is all they did, the five big families. They spread out into the drug business in the forties. Remember *The Godfather*? They didn't want dope around the schools, they all agreed, but otherwise it was wide open. That would never have happened in Vegas because of Tony Accardo—he was the big boss in Vegas. There would not have been a discussion. That was the end of it.

I don't remember exactly how Tony's fall began, but an accountant got caught with all the names in a book nobody was meant to see. It was some action Tony had taken to get the guy heated up to get him caught. Needless to say they killed the guy—Allen Dorfman. They all liked him, but after that he was fucked. In *Casino,* one of the characters says of Dorfman's character, "Oh, he is a good, stand-up guy." The next mobster agrees with him, "Yeah, a stand-up guy. And his old man was really a stand-up guy, too." And he was. Al Dorfman was a good guy. The last guy goes, "Ah, yeah, but why worry about it." Then they rubbed him out. In reality, Tony did the hit on Dorfman in Chicago, at the Hyatt in Lincolnwood where he was staying. He was walking to breakfast, and Tony walks up behind him and hit him in the back of the head. You know how they do it. That was the end of it.

Tony hung out with these two small—and deadly—guys: They were both shorter than Tony, and Tony was short—he was called Tony "the Ant" Spilotro because that's what William Roemer had named him, "that little pissant." When someone said "The little guys are looking for you," you'd see men messing their pants. Tony was a master of torture. He fed a guy salt pork for two or three days until the shit started coming out of his nose and out of his ears and eyes. He'd boast about this stuff. He was supposed to be the guy who in 1961 had hung William "Action" Jackson, a loan shark enforcer, on a meat hook and then tortured him for three days with a cattle prod. He was a real monster.

It was probably around 1980 to 1982, some version of that, when Tony had all these problems. Lefty, they tried to rub him out, too. Fortunately for him General Motors had installed a steel plate in his Eldorado (to correct the car's balance)—and that's what saved him in 1982 when his car was bombed.

Tony was getting the mob nervous. And when they get nervous you don't want to be in that spot. Tony got these Outfit guys jumpy, then he got them all indicted. Then *he* was gone. It wasn't even a close call. It was a 200-to-1 favorite that Tony would be eliminated. His brother Michael opened his mouth. That's how they got the brother, too. He said, "Anybody fucks with my brother Tony has to deal with me." They said, "Well, okay, we will deal with you, too, then." You can't make those kind of statements to guys in the Outfit—they don't like that, you know.

Even though his old buddies were informing on him, Tony was never going to get to court because all those Outfit guys in Chicago, Kansas City, and Cleveland had already decided his fate. They lured him and his brother to a basement, beat the shit out of them, and then buried him in Indiana, right over the border. The hit men were too lazy to dig too deep so they dug a real shallow grave and threw some sand on them. Sand was found in their lungs in the autopsy so it looked as if they'd been buried alive. Some farmer found them, Tony and his brother. It was said to be in the middle of a cornfield, but it wasn't even a cornfield.

Tony's gone, but no one wants to tell too many tales about him. He has brothers and he has people who still like him—the kind of people that you do not want to piss off.

—■—

In Vegas, you'd mix with all kinds of people, high rollers, movie stars, CEOs, Arabian princes—and mobsters. They'd come backstage, I'd see them in Jubilation. You'd hang out with these people, and the next thing you know, their story begins to unravel. "Hey, Paulie, ya know the guy that was just in here? This was the guy who dissolved his victims in acid and served their finger bones up in soup for his guests."

Instead of people being horrified by this stuff, they're enamored with it. Let's face it, everybody is.

When I worked in Vegas, from time to time the casino heads like Billy Weinberger or Sid Gathrid—who was in charge of the entertainment at Caesars Palace—would bring people backstage to meet me. I just assumed they were high rollers. Even if they happened to be unsavory characters, they don't introduce these guys to you with their full histories including their rap sheets, mug shots, warrants for their arrests, etc. When you meet and greet, they don't say, "Hey Paul, I want you to meet Tony 'Rat Face' Solano, a big, big fan of yours and, incidentally, a mob enforcer out of Detroit." No, these guys would be standing there smiling, handing me some gift they'd got for me, champagne, flowers, chocolates, tickets to a game. When people come backstage they're very nice and complimentary to me, so I don't always get to see the dark side of their personalities. The other thing was that in Vegas there were all these layers of stuff going on. Gangsters, hustlers, business guys wanting to bask in show-biz glamour (and, of course meet showgirls), guys with some deal they want to lay on you, maybe, and plenty of out-and-out gangsters on the periphery of the last Vegas casinos. But the stone-cold killers were as gentlemanly and polite as the garment district guy and his wife from Westchester—they all behaved in the same way. On one occasion they brought back these two brothers to meet me. Very complimentary, well-mannered, very gracious to my band and Odia Coates, who was performing with me. Later on I read in the paper one of these guys was a notorious drug smuggler who'd tried to buy a judge with a $10 million bribe, and when that didn't work had had the judge *and* the DA killed—a kind of hit man's two-for-one deal, and you think, "Jeez, two nights ago I was telling jokes and drinking champagne with this guy!"

In Vegas we worked within this infrastructure that had been made by mobsters and run by Jewish bookies. This was the hand we were dealt. But it was colorful all right, and exciting and edgy. Everybody is enamored by the mob story in Vegas. Right now, they have two museums in Vegas, dedicated to the mob. The mobsters, even the really pathological hitmen like Tony, were civil in the clubs. You still had remnants of the mob popping up in Vegas into the mid-eighties. I've been around mobsters much of my life. I feel like I'm in the play but I'm not a part of it.

Now that the underworld characters are gone it's a little poignant, because this was the end of the old Vegas. However down and dirty and criminal that was, it was a flashy hot spot. This is about the evolution of where Vegas was going in the '70s. It was the end of the era of Lefty Rosenthal, Tony Spilotro, and that group of mobsters.

Vegas had all levels of clubs, casinos, and joints—from the swanky to the skanky. At Jubilation we would start to slow down about four or five in the morning. Most of the workforce on the swing shift got off around four in the morning. And then they'd head over to the Brewery. It was like a saloon in the old Wild West. It *was* the Wild West. The guys who ran the Brewery were old-timers. They were well-connected good old boys, all related and inbred to the old Vegas families. They all had names like Rex and Tex. Good old boys.

At nine on a Tuesday morning it was like New Year's Eve in Times Square over there. Everybody all whizzed up, doing the shit, wild-eyed and crazy at 5 A.M. There were ten or fifteen doormen dribbling guys out the door one after the other. One morning Marty and I drive over there from Jubilation. We pull into the parking lot and we're just getting out of the car, when a guy comes screeching around the corner and crashes into three cars. He hits them with such force that one guy flies out of the window of his car—he's all torn to pieces. It was a horror story, really unpleasant thing to watch. There's blood all over the place and people screaming. The ambulance arrives and the paramedics are trying to save the guy. Now, I swear to God, twenty minutes went by and another car comes tearing into the parking lot. (This was the '70s when fancy cars were a lot faster.) The guy slams into the ambulance so hard he kills the ambulance driver and the guy he was attending to, who, I'm assuming, was fatally injured as it was.

Casino is as true to what it was like as you could possibly imagine. Joe Pesci hit it right on the head. Imagine a guy like that on the loose. If you want to go see something that's the most realistic thing you'll ever watch about the mob in Vegas, that's *Casino*. They changed a few names around is all. In the movie, they called the Stardust the Tangiers, little stuff like that. Mob guys got hired as technical advisers—they were paid peanuts, but the dopes thought it was a lot of money.

You know who were technical advisers on *Casino*? Joey Cusumano, Tony's bodyguard, and Frankie Cullotta, he has a credit at the end of *Casino* as technical adviser. Not only was Cullotta a technical adviser on the movie, you can actually see him in the scene where they're burying Tony and his brother. That was a real interesting moment, a shock, really, because he was always hanging around Tony at Jubilation.

Frankie Cullotta was a guy who grew up with Tony Spilotro and he ratted Tony out in the end. He turned out to be a beefer. In those days there was no such thing. With the mob nobody talked. It was *omertà,* a conspiracy of silence. Today, everybody talks. They rat on anybody. In those days it was an outrage when this Frankie Cullotta came out and ratted on Tony. They killed together. They did whatever they had to do. What Frankie Cullotta knew about Tony was devastating. So it was really like a horror story when this guy turned on him. Maybe he saw the handwriting on the wall and wanted to get out. Who knows why? He turned on Tony and became a government informant. Cullotta got out of it all by turning Tony over.

Cullotta walks around town now, and nobody bothers him. He walks around like you and I do, strolls into a bar, has a drink, and walks out. He isn't concerned about anyone coming after him anymore. Who is going to bother him? This guy is old. One of those other old mob guys that are still around, you think they're going to run the risk of doing a hit because they want to take care of some guy that beefed on Tony?

When you're around that ballpark you hear stories. They told me what happened to Jimmy Hoffa. You know what they did with his body? Somebody in his family fingered him. They picked him up and put him in one of those wood choppers. That used to be one of their favorite disposal methods. We are talking about cutting their victims up into tiny little pieces and spreading them around. It was a specialty of this guy, Frank "the German" Schweihs.

The feds would basically focus on the big fish. They would create some ruckus about a guy they would figure was a headline-type mobster—that was their MO. These U.S. attorneys were indicting guys that they thought could get their names on the front page. That's mostly what they were doing it for—for the publicity. They didn't give a shit about justice. You tell them some black guy killed twelve people and they don't want to hear about it. That's when they tell you, "Call your local police department." Yeah, right.

There was another interesting character, we'll call him "Snake Eyes," a guy that I knew who was a genius handicapper. Snake Eyes would have three TVs on at the same time on which he used to watch the games. That was when you couldn't switch between channels with a remote, so you had to have different televisions with three different channels on. He was so good and so many people got in his line it created problems for the insiders. He got too hot. Once the word got out, the bookmakers on the inside got crucified and I mean across the whole country. Snake Eyes would give out his information and that guy would tell another guy and before you knew it two thousand guys had the number and then there'd be another two thousand in. Multiply that by ten and you have two million guys betting the same game. The insiders didn't like that. When he was good, he was right on.

Snake Eyes had a very interesting premise of odds-making. This is the way he explained it to me: "Forget about all these sportswriters, locker-room bullshit. See, when you're dealing with the odds you don't have the time to weigh the merits of this quarterback, that running back." Snake Eyes would embellish but he wouldn't talk about one player or another, it didn't make any difference to him. He didn't want to overplay it. You could tell him, "Snake Eyes, I hear there's a great quarterback out from South Carolina, what do you think?" You hear these stories. He would say, "So?" I said, "Well, we've got the dope on this guy, isn't that useful information?" To which he'd say, "I will tell you one thing: all the times you go back and change, half of the time you will win and half of the time you will lose and it isn't worth it; just let it go." Thinking about quarterbacks wasn't in these guys' playbook. He was right. Half of the time, it meant shit. In the end, in the big bookmaker's lexicon, the Super Bowl is just another game.

Snake Eyes had a stroke, but recovered and to this day is still betting twenty dollars a race. He's still with that big girl he hooked up with after the two stripper sisters passed on. Those sisters loved Snake Eyes once they married him. One of the sisters died and he married the other one. I met Snake Eyes when he was with sister number two, the first sister had died of lung cancer. It was like one sister—the one who was dying—told the other one, "Snake Eyes is going to be really upset when I go, so you gotta marry him." They were strippers and they'd found their sugar daddy after seven bad marriages between the two of them. Both smoked like chimneys. A couple of strippers and a high-profile bookie. Classic Vegas tableau.

The second sister took care of Snake Eyes like her sister asked her to, and worshiped the ground he walked on. And then when she died, he found this girl and he's been in Vegas with her twenty years. Some version of twenty years. They pulled him back from the dead, literally. Snake Eyes is still alive. He's got to be in his eighties by now. He's old but believe me, he is still as sharp as ever.

—■—

There was a lot of shady stuff going on at those Vegas poker games, too. Scams were ongoing. Even Marty, who had seen a lot of crazy stuff, was surprised at the extent the hustles that went on. One night, Marty suggests we walk over to the Dunes. "I want you to see this hustle that's going on over there." We get there, the chips were this high. The big chips. There were five guys in the game. Sal Romano was there—he was an Outfit guy from New York. He, too, incidentally, ended up ratting his friends out.

We walk in, watch this poker game going on with huge bets. Marty says, "Sal, I know those two guys in that game are partners—they're in cahoots." Sal Romano, and this I remember, he looked at us and smiled and said, "You know something, you're getting better. What about *all four of them* are partners? The only live guy in the game is the big fat guy next to the dealer. They bid him out of four hundred thousand or something. Why should they fight with each other? It was *all* set up. You don't have to worry about who's gonna win and who isn't. Better that they each go home with a hundred thousand bucks. The fat guy wants to play big poker? Let him. He's a restaurant owner; he says he owns a restaurant in Alabama." Marty says, "Really? Where did he get that four hundred thousand bucks from? I've owned restaurants. You don't make that kind of money in the restaurant business." Anyway, this guy wanted to play big-time poker and he got his wish.

They used to bring Major Riddle in. He owned the Dunes, and when he showed up it was like they rang a bell and players would pop up from nowhere and wake up from their sleep because the major wasn't a very good player. They'd deal in this partner a big Jewish guy, Sid Wyman. These games are stacked and these guys are fucking with the guy. Stay out of these games.

One afternoon Marty Gutilla said to me, "Hey, let's go over and check out this kid who's beating everybody up at gin, poker, and what have you." "A kid?" I say. "Ya know, that kid Stuey Ungar." Then I remembered the story. Sal Romano had brought this kid Stuey Ungar back with him from New York. And so it was through Marty that I got to meet the wunderkind. In the movie, *High Roller: The Stu Ungar Story,* they kind of fudged it—it was based on the book, *One of a Kind,* which he told to Nolan Dalla. Michael Imperioli, the guy from *The Sopranos* played him in the film.

Stuey would be sitting in the Dunes and when he wasn't playing, he'd be reading a book. Sixteen years old with the glasses. A little

Jewish kid from out of New York. He hadn't gotten into the drugs yet and Vegas was alien to him. He was so young he couldn't go into the casinos so he would read a book or sit around until they had a game. It just killed everybody how good he was. He was a sharp kid. He had it all figured out. He'd started when he was ten. Genius. A sixteen-year-old kid playing gin *this fast*. That's how he played—at warp speed—I couldn't believe my eyes.

This kid had played anyone and everyone in the world of gin—and nobody could beat him. After a while nobody would play him anymore. Then he played poker and he won the poker world series—twice. He was the best kid there ever was, but he had to stop playing, because no one would play him anymore. They brought these guys in from L.A. They brought them in from New York. Nobody could touch this kid. They put him in Vegas. At forty-two, Stuey died of an overdose—he'd gotten into cocaine to stay awake in all-night poker games and then moved on to crack.

Bobby Martin was another infamous character. He was the guy in the backroom who used to skim the money at Churchill Downs. Like almost everything else in Vegas the line was a setup, too. The bookies would all be sitting around—all drinkers, all Jewish and they all drank Canadian Club and water. Don't ask me why they drank that stuff, but they all did. It would be like six in the morning and Bobby Martin would be sitting there. Someone would say, "Bobby, it's nine thirty in New York. You've got to get a line out." There were these five bookmakers; they would consult with each other over the phone and set the odds. I don't think they even knew each other. They were just five guys that he respected and he used them as a barometer. It worked for an awful lot of fucking money. That is how they made all of their money—by laying off their bets.

How respected was this guy? When Bobby Martin died in 2001 they had a moment of silence for him. JFK, Bobby Kennedy, and Bobby Martin are the only people these guys in Vegas stopped gambling for as a tribute. John F. Kennedy, when they buried him, they stopped gaming for one minute. Otherwise Vegas never stops. Their caddy-up is to keep going.

Lester "Benny" Binion was another larger-than-life criminal type at the time. He was the owner of the Horseshoe, among other casinos, a self-styled cowboy, a mobster, a killer, who always kept a sawed-off shotgun handy. He's the guy who founded the World Series of Poker. Benny Binion testified at Vegas police chief Ralph Lamb's trial. Lamb was making thirty or forty grand a year as a cop but he was living large on a big ranch with the Cadillacs with the steer horns on them.

In 1977, Lamb was indicted for tax evasion. The government claimed that he earned money from illegal activities, which enabled him to build a home complete with a guesthouse and horsemanship facilities, and had evaded paying taxes on it. They tried to show that certain loans including one for $30,000 from Benny Binion were never meant to be repaid. But the U.S. district judge Roger D. Foley acquitted Lamb. Marty Gutilla, who was in the courtroom that day, tells a more dramatic version of what happened:

"When they asked Binion if he had bank statements showing these loans, he said, 'Nah, it was in cash.' And then he added, 'As a matter of fact, if he needs more, I brought more with me.' He opened his coat and he had like a half a million dollars in cash taped to the inside of his jacket and on his body. The whole courtroom busted out laughing. Here is a guy who brought a half a million or million to court and didn't turn a hair. So, what could they do?" Marty may have exaggerated his numbers, but the story accurately captures these larger-than-life characters.

My sister Mariam has another view of Ralph Lamb. She says he kept an incredibly corrupt and dirty-dealing town under some kind of restraint. He came down hard on mobsters and cleaned up the rampant prostitution in the city. Many people felt he was a kind of local hero. As a kind of cowboy sheriff straight out of a Western, Lamb is now about to be the subject of a CBS-TV series starring Dennis Quaid called *Vegas*, to be written by Nicholas Pileggi (*Goodfellas, Casino*). And the eighty-five-year-old galoot can talk that sagebrush talk like Pat Garrett must've done down at the Dodge saloon: "Why, he got so darned excited," Lamb said of Pileggi's reaction to his goldarned tall tales. "He said it was the gawd-darndest thing he ever heard. He said this is the greatest thing he ever wrote."

Vegas was full of shady characters of every stripe from mob guys to hustlers, scammers to cheaters, down to the doctors who wrote scripts—drug prescriptions—for big stars. They'd write anything—any pill, any shot, in any amount. There was a Dr. Elias Ghanem, a Palestinian from Haifa. He was the fight doctor, he'd be at all the big fights in Vegas. Real debonair, good-looking guy. He was the guy who was so helpful in writing scripts for Presley, Elvis gave him a Cadillac. This Dr. Ghanem was at Jubilation just about every night. Elaine Newton would come over to my house to see Anne, and to complain about her marriage to Wayne Newton, which was not good. I often saw her in Jubilation with Elias Ghanem, who gave Presley all those pills, Presley and Ann-Margret. Ghanem was the "scriptwriter to the stars." He was a nice guy in a highly dangerous situation. He never got pinched, never even got indicted. See, in those days it was different. What with what happened to Michael Jackson and everybody else, today you'd be indicted in two months. This guy who gave the same pills and shots to Presley and Michael Jackson never got pinched. Different times.

Jake Freedman was a classic character from the old wild and wooly days of Vegas. He was from Dallas, an immigrant from Russia or Poland. He came to the U.S., settled in Texas, and learned how to speak English with a Texan accent, a little Jew with a Texas drawl on top of a Yiddish accent. He was five-foot-four and he would stand on a box to shoot craps. He would dress up in cowboy suits like Roy Rogers did, all costumed in Nudie glitter getups. He'd say, "Howdy pardner! Ya doin' ok, ya ol' galoot? Good luck to ya!" This is almost straight out of Yiddish vaudeville, but it was taking place daily in Las Vegas in the

'50s. I wish I'd been old enough to witness it. What a scream that must have been!

—■—

Sammy Davis Jr. was an inspiration to me from a very young age, from when I started collecting records. When I heard his Decca recordings in the mid '50s, where he did imitations, it motivated me to do the same thing. I saw Sammy when I was a teenager and he came to Canada with the Will Mastin Trio. I would see him perform at the Gatineau nightclub on the Quebec side and I was always mesmerized by him.

When I hit Vegas and started working the Sands Hotel, I was obviously very overwhelmed that I was actually in his company. Through the subsequent thirty years that I knew him, I would see the change in the man as I did with Sinatra—less so with Dean Martin—who never liked to hang out that much into the late hours of the evening. Keep in mind I was younger than all of the Rat Pack members and slowly got included into their crowd. I toed the line, acknowledging their seniority and being wary of their partnership with the mob. As Sammy explained to me later on in our relationship, very early in his career he had asked for money from the mob, which he needed not only back then, but actually all through his life. So he was under control of the boys. Frank liked him and protected him as best as he could even though they had two major breakups in their friendship. The second one was the most severe. Frank was aware, as we all were, that Sammy was into cocaine and ongoing sexcapades that had gone to a new level. As Sammy would later graphically explain to some of us that he was close to, including Sinatra and the rest of the group, he became absolutely obsessed with the world of porno. All of us knew it and saw it because we all worked at Caesars. Whenever he performed there, there were always a bunch of porn stars in attendance in the audience and backstage.

I remember around 1972 a group of us were in England. I was doing

274 · PAUL ANKA

some shows there, and Sammy was there, too. They really embraced
Sammy, the English—that was a special place for him. At dinner Sammy
said, "After the show tonight, I want to run a movie at this private movie
house," something he had done many times before at home and on the
road. Everyone said, "Let's go!" We went down some stairs to a screen-
ing room. There were about thirty or forty of us, and no one knew
what we were going to see. We get in there, sit down with our bags of
popcorn—we had the whole place to ourselves—and the lights go
down, and on comes . . . *Deep Throat!*

Everybody was sitting there in shock. You have to understand that
our mutual friends, Gary and Maxine Smith, whom I have known for
years and who are very dear friends of mine and my wife's were watching this hard-core porno movie with their jaws dropping—as were
Anne and I. Gary was one of the top television producers, and at the
time produced Sammy's television shows. Anne and I and Sammy's
wife, Altovise, all socialized together, but we hadn't actually seen this
raw side of his secret life. Sammy really got into porno stuff with a
vengeance later on, by having sex parties with porn stars like Marilyn
Chambers and Linda Lovelace and her husband. They would have
foursomes with Sammy and Altovise.

But at a certain point we sensed that his marriage to Altovise had
taken a different more sordid turn. He had met Altovise a few years
earlier, when she'd been one of the dancers in his previous shows in
England. They dated for a while and then got married. He was also
seeing another dancer, Lola Falana, but it was his infatuation with porn
star Linda Lovelace, the star of *Deep Throat,* which was beyond belief.
Linda Lovelace had spectacular sexual prowess. She was able to perform fellatio on a man to the point where his penis would totally disappear inside her mouth and down her throat without causing her to gag.
At the time it caused a huge public sensation. Sammy became obsessed
with her. She shared his bed, with Altovise's consent, and Altovise
eventually joined them.

Frank knew what he was up to; we all knew. We were a tight group of people—you just can't keep those things quiet. I would just go hang out with Sammy after his show; keep in mind I lived two blocks from Caesars. Over drinks he became very open about his sexual life. He invited me to go to strip shows with him. I declined, not that I was a prude . . . far from it. It just wasn't my scene, and my kids and Anne were at home. Frank was hardly a prude himself but he found Sammy's new porno fixation disgusting and didn't forgive him for years. Sammy would tell me in his droll delivery that fellatio was as far as he went with Linda Lovelace. "Eatin' ain't cheatin'," as he put it.

He'd tell me about all this weird stuff he was into. He had another life eventually, beginning at the end of the sixties and on through the seventies, where Sammy, at a certain hour, would gravitate to that porn crowd. It was the drugs and sex and all of that. His whole thing was, "Shit, I'm only living once; I want to do what I want." It was a very, very strange situation and Sammy was just off the wall with that.

As time went on, Sammy's kinky sex habits got kinkier. He became obsessed with Linda Lovelace and got very close to her, and also her husband, Chuck Traynor, who had a sadistic relationship with her. (She later claimed he beat her and forced her into porn movies at gunpoint.) He got into threesomes with them. They'd come over to his house. Sammy's wife got involved with Traynor.

After the midnight shows, Sammy had a whole other life from the rest of us. He got seriously into drugs. Frank and he didn't talk for a long time because Sammy got heavily into coke and Frank didn't approve. They didn't make up until years later. The wives got them back together, got Sammy off the blow, and got him back to his old self.

He just enjoyed life. Curiosity about *everything*. Explored everything. He was completely open about his sexuality, and got into his bisexuality. He loved England, went over there a lot, and was very open with an eclectic group of people he hung out with. He would confide these things to me, how cool it was to be involved with two women, with guys. He'd say, "Hell, man, I'm living my life the way I want to. No restraints, no hang-ups. It's my time and I'm gonna do it the way I want to."

Through the years I would see him change—more booze more drugs—but I must tell you he was probably the most talented guy I have ever seen. Loveable, socially easy to be with, and the best friend you would ever want. He loved to cook. I would see him not only at Caesars Palace but in other cities, where he carried suitcases of utensils with him. We'd eat and hang and talk shop as men will do. He would tell me how much fun he was having and the escapades of his sex life.

One thing that massively upset him was the famous photograph of him hugging Richard Nixon. The backlash that caused was huge. On one occasion in Vegas, I sang with him at a charity concert for sickle cell anemia, and after the concert we sat in the coffee shop at the Sands Hotel and talked about all the things that bothered him. He was very down. He had been very hurt that his own people, his black brothers and sisters, now perceived him as being white, as an Uncle Tom, and as Frank Sinatra's court jester.

Furthermore, he always had money problems with loans from the mob but by the '80s he was in more trouble than ever with the IRS. "I don't give a shit about the IRS," he'd say. "I don't have a head for numbers—just broads and booze." And physically he was in bad shape. He would complain about his hip, which he later had to have operated on. I heard much of this from my physician, Dr. Ed Kantor, who became my doctor when I came to the West Coast, but beyond that, he's one of my best friends and one of the most respected, renowned throat specialists worldwide. He was my throat doctor, as well as Sinatra's and Sammy Davis's. A truly loved human being. He and Dr. Robert Koblin, my cardiologist, have kept me in check as to the lifestyle I live. Koblin himself has been a friend for years, again another one of the greatest guys I have ever known.

Anyway, at dinner one night, I told Dr. Kantor that I had heard rumors about Sammy's condition. He told me what he could: that Sammy was having throat trouble, which was something that Sammy had already confided in me in Vegas. We all saw it getting worse and eventually he was diagnosed with throat cancer. From that point on, it all got very sad. He began to miss shows. Everyone tried to keep quiet about it, but then the inevitable happened: unable to work he was sent home. Sammy died in May 1990. It was a very sad ending for someone who brought so much joy to so many.

I kept in touch with Altovise and saw her a few times when I was performing on the road. I started doing a piece about Sammy built around the song I wrote for him, "I Am Not Anyone." I'd recorded it with him for Michael Curb for Curb Records. Curb was a very astute record executive. After Sammy's failure at Motown, he took Sammy under his wing and gave him the song "The Candy Man," which became a huge hit for Sammy in 1972.

Sammy's passing was devastating for me. My love and admiration for him went back to the first glimmers I had of becoming a performer. He motivated me do my first nightclub act at the Copa. As a tribute to him, I used "Mr. Wonderful" (written by Jules Stein from the Broadway show that Sammy was in) as my opening song.

Nine

IF DONALD TRUMPS
WHO WYNNS?

Sometime in the mid-sixties, I'd gotten into the art scene through my wife Anne who'd introduced me to a gallery owner named Paula Cooper in New York. I soon got very curious about contemporary art and started buying early, a full menu of the contemporary painters: Ellsworth Kelly, Donald Judd, Mark di Suvero, Andy Warhol, Frank Stella—it ran the gamut. I had those three huge color panels of Ellsworth Kelly—they were walls in themselves.

And then one night in the late '70s I was gambling at Caesars Palace and I was on a real lucky streak. In those days, I will admit I was betting more than I should have on cards, playing blackjack. I would even play five hands at a time. Not having any other bad habits, that was one I caught from Sinatra. I mean when we played, we played. Took over a table. You know when you're at those places, you're just captured. It starts out as a social thing and suddenly you're deep into it—it's hard to explain. I loved it at that time; I'm certainly not doing that anymore, I'm not hanging like I used to, nor do I have any desire to. Yeah, just keep telling yourself that, Paul. But anyway, that particular night I'm playing and playing and . . . I'm winning.

I'm up most of the night till about six or seven in the morning and we're having a good time. I knew the dealers. I got to know them so well they actually gave me a plaque! An award from all the dealers, as one of the top tippers ever. I figure these guys have families, they're nice people, and I tip them well. Especially when Atlantic City started up, Vegas became somewhat of a ghost town for a minute.

So I'm playing with one of the dealers I know. I would play with Sinatra and we had our favorite dealers. Anyway, one night I'm winning like crazy. I finish the next morning with about $100,000. I take the money home. I was drinking margaritas all night, I needed to sleep. I normally sleep all day and then I call this doctor friend of mine, John DiFiori, who always checked me and Sinatra and all the singers out whenever we had throat problems. He comes over and he's laughing as he comes in, about five o'clock at night, hours before my show.

"Before I check your throat," he says. "I'm going to tell you a funny story."

I said, "What?"

He proceeds to tell me that one of his patients came into his office a few hours ago. "The guy is bitching and complaining that he was up on a catwalk, watching this guy win money all night." This was in the days before they had electronic monitoring systems, technology they have today. Back then they had catwalks, platforms in the ceiling above the tables—guys walking around in these dusty attics, looking down on the players through *holes* so they can watch the players and see if there's any hanky-panky going on. We called it the eye in the sky.

"The guy complains, 'And I'm watching this guy all night long and we can't figure out how he's winning, *rah rah rah,* and I got dust in my eyes, my nose is stuffed up, it's running from watching this guy and look how red my eyes are. I'm coughing, sneezing—and I already got allergies. I'm a mess.'"

Doc says, "Oh, okay," and he fixes him up, sprays his nose, and then asks him, "Did you ever find out who the guy was who was winning?" And he says, "Oh, yeah, it was Paul Anka!" Of course the doctor doesn't tell him he's coming to see me. So John comes in, tells me this story, and we get a big kick out of it.

Anyway, I take the money home and I'm saying, "Man, what am I going to do with this?" Now, Anne and I had always wanted to own something by Robert Rauschenberg. I said, "You know what, I'm not going to go back and lose it, I am not going to gamble it. I call my wife Anne and I say, let's get the best Rauschenberg that's out there right now. And there was one called *Sleep for Yvonne Rainer,* beautiful thing.

I have to give Anne all the credit for my getting into the art world; that was her scene and it was because of her love of contemporary painting that we eventually developed a joint love of art. It was Anne who first introduced me to this exotic world. We went to cocktail parties with the art set, attended openings at New York's Leo Castelli Gallery and Mary Boone Gallery. We met James Rosenquist, John Chamberlain, Andy Warhol, Roy Lichtenstein, Frank Stella, and Robert Rauschenberg. This was in an era when artists were still genuine bohemian characters.

I call up Paula Cooper, I tell her my intention, and she tells me it's selling for such-and-such a price and we start negotiating. End of the story, I buy the painting.

I had a lot of big canvases, really large-size paintings: Ellsworth Kellys, Frank Stellas, the bird series, the Rauschenberg, huge, huge pieces, and *Jasper's Dilemma*—a very important black-and-white and color Stella.

We had come west to Vegas, then Sun Valley, and then I took my family up to Carmel. Sister Carlotta's nuns ran a girls' school up in Santa Catalina. I was so into the art I built a house in Pebble Beach designed by two great architects, Buff & Hensman. I built the house around the art collection, with plenty of wall space and forty- to fifty-foot ceilings to accommodate all the pieces.

After all my kids were in college—the only one left was Amelia, and she wanted to live in L.A.—we left and moved down to Los Angeles. The Pebble Beach house sold for a record amount of money—and a woman moved in with thirty cats. Obviously we couldn't accommodate all these huge paintings in a smaller house and we started selling it all off. By that time, the value of my Rauschenberg had gone through the roof. Everybody had started ruining the market. It escalated to a point where it was prohibitive to buy an art work. One of my last pieces, was a beautiful Rosenquist piece, his 1977 painting, *Terrarium.*

When I lived in Sun Valley, Idaho, I started *The Painter,* one of my favorite albums. I finished it up in Carmel, and I said, okay, it's going to be called *The Painter,* and I'm going to commission Andy Warhol to do the cover. I flew Andy out to Vegas and met with him and we had some preliminary discussions—such as they were. Andy did eight portraits, I paid him forty, fifty thousand, and I used a couple of the portraits on the cover of the album. I donated four to the museum in San Francisco and gave the rest to Anne.

———■———

I've known Steve Wynn since the late '50s when we were teenagers together in Florida. I was performing at the Fontainebleau Hotel. Steve and his parents came to see my show and the following afternoon he was out by the pool and his father who was involved with the hotel in some way came over and introduced us. I was maybe twenty, Steve was nineteen, in his second year of college—we're almost exactly six months apart in age. He was home for Christmas vacation and wanted to meet me, not so much because he was a big fan of my records but he envied all the girls that would hover around me.

The Fontainebleau opened in 1954, and, in the fifties, it was *the* place. When you walked into the Fontainebleau you went, "Oh shit!" It was the spectacular glitzy palace of Golden Era glamour invented out of the scene itself, the swanky vision of legendary architect Morris Lapidus, with a luxurious stage on which everyone could play out their fantasies. When you walked in you entered a perfect rose-colored and gilt world of your ritziest dreams. It was the ideal architecture to go with the mock-gangster allure of Sinatra, Sammy Davis Jr., and Dean

Martin, and sultry high-heeled women. It was an architecture spun out of torch songs.

There was a seven-foot-wide staircase that winds counterclockwise out of the center of the lobby, like those stairways to heaven in movies—it looks like it doesn't go anywhere, but actually went to the card room, a choice, if shady, location where under-the-table gambling went on. It had a balcony that came out of the lobby in an arc but the balcony wasn't actually cantilevered—there was a curved wall that ran about forty feet underneath it with a mural in brown paint on it that looked like a Roman wall painting of a canal and columns. Behind the curved wall was the pool bar, which was the hooker bar. That's where the call girls were. Steve and I were too young to go into the bar but Steve was always going up those stairs—his dad played gin and pinochle with a mobbed-up guy named "Sonny" and other gamblers there.

The card room was not run by the hotel per se. There was always a heavy presence there of a guy with the name of Max Raymond. Maxie Raymond and some dark skinned Sicilian guy were always in evidence, watching over their shady business interests. Raymond was hooked up with the unions, which was code for being an Outfit guy and that card room at the Fontainebleau must have had a rake at the tables, some kind of fee. It must have also been the kind of place where you could bet on sports. I think the bookmakers worked out of the card room and paid a fee to this guy Raymond, who had been put there by whoever it was that got the Fontainebleau's owner, Ben Novack, his loan from the bank. The owners of the hotel were Novack and his brother for about 30 percent of the building. A major chunk of the equity was put up by a guy named John Frumkis from New York, a connected real estate guy and Abe Rosenberg who owned J & B Scotch. Abe took this obscure British brand and made a fortune, made millions— but that's a whole other crazy story from this crowd.

The Fontainebleau was the only place to play in Miami. The *only* place. Belafonte worked at the Fontainebleau, Mathis, Sinatra, everyone. Meyer Lansky used to sit in the lobby in the morning—that's where he dictated his letters and contracts.

It impressed me and left a lasting impression on Steve, too. Steve has always been in love with the idea of trying to create out-of-this-world resorts. The two of us were just that right age to see what the future could be.

My dear friend and fellow prankster Steve Wynn is the boy wonder of Vegas. He's the guy who single-handedly changed the face of the place. Vegas has always been my second home. Whatever I did, wherever I went I'd always touch base with Vegas. I'd go off to Europe, make some records over there, play all around the world but always come back. I never gave up on the place. I was there when Vegas was seedy and mobbed up, I was there when it was swinging with Frank, and I'm still there now that it's family-oriented, thanks in a large part to Steve Wynn. Steve is mainly responsible for helping clean up Las Vegas's image. But, as he once pointed out to a convention of casino owners, "We don't want to make Vegas *too* squeaky clean—it's got to be a little edgy, a little naughty; otherwise why would anyone want to go there? How would it be different from Omaha?" Which I guess is how they came up with the phrase, "What happens in Las Vegas, stays in Las Vegas."

Steve created a new era and style in Vegas. He had a vision that changed an entire city. He and his wife moved there in 1967 and invested in the Frontier Hotel. He'd hardly been in Vegas the year, when the state authorities, concerned about Vegas's reputation, persuaded billionaire Howard Hughes to buy the Frontier, believing that his corporate security people would clean up the town. Through most of its history as a resort, illegal gambling, hidden ownership, and skimming schemes had been winked at, but now the federal government was focusing on corruption and criminal activity in Vegas.

Steve's first big coup was essentially a parking-lot ploy. Hughes had neglected to buy a small strip of land adjacent to the Frontier, which Steve and banker Parry Thomas happened to own. Steve called Hughes's bluff by announcing that he was going to build the world's narrowest casino on that strip of land, forcing Hughes to buy it for $2.5 million. With his profits Steve began investing in the Golden Nugget, borrowing funds from Parry Thomas's bank, and by 1973 had become the major shareholder. When he took over the Golden Nugget he became the youngest casino owner in the history of Vegas. The hotel rooms at the Golden Nugget were appointed impeccably glamorous beyond belief.

The next wave in swanky Vegas casinos came with Steve Wynn in 1989 when he built the Mirage. The Mirage took it away from Caesars and everybody else in town—sixty days and it was over. Steve's always been in search of his casino dream palace. With the Mirage, the motif was nothing like Vegas had seen before. A hotel with great art, shops like you'd find in any great metropolitan area, as well as restaurants that could match those of any city in the world.

I saw how Steve changed the town with the Mirage Hotel, where the consumer received a lot more that they had ever received before in Vegas. He could multitask. He is so multifaceted. I have seen all sides of him, from his lovable side to his volcanic temper—which he has never directed at me. I have great memories of Shadow Creek—the golf course he built in 1999. He bought me a set of clubs, and he and I would go alone to play the course. Of course it was immaculate and esthetically beautiful. I had my own locker down from Steve, near Michael Jordan.

Steve's genius in the late 1970s had been to reeducate Wall Street money managers and pension fund people about gaming. He took them up on the catwalks so they could look down on the tables and see the inner workings of the gambling industry. Once these people had been disabused of all these stereotypes about casinos being a seedy enterprise and saw it was just a business like any other—and firmly based on statistics—their attitudes changed.

And this is where Michael Milken, the wizard of Wall Street—and to some the black prince of finance, who unleashed the plague of junk bonds on the world—enters the picture. Milken said that the gaming industry needed a white knight, and in Steve Wynn he found him. Steven stood for integrity and the Wall Street people needed somebody they could believe in. When someone like Steve brought that kind of business logic into the marketplace, they were willing to give him everything he wanted.

I'd known Michael Milken ever since I met him and his wonderful wife Lori with Steve Wynn in Hawaii, and we have remained close friends ever since. I'm very fond of him and his wife. We played tennis and I sat around the pool with him as he talked to Steve about using junk bonds to finance his new casino hotel, the Mirage. I realized then and there that the guy was brilliant—he was a financial genius, one of the smartest human beings I have ever met.

I flew home with Steve who was still feeling his way with Milken. Long story short, Milken raises the money for Steve's new hotel casino, the Mirage. Among other things, it featured an artificial volcano. The Mirage opened on November 22, 1989—a bold move since this was at a time when Vegas was in decline. It was the most expensive hotel casino in history, costing an estimated $630 million, built with Wall Street money, principally junk bonds. These were risky investments that however paid high interest rates—essentially it amounted to betting on risk.

—◼—

Then you've got the battle of the giants. I believe the feud between Donald Trump and Steve Wynn began in the early 1980s when Steve took Dennis Gomes, a key executive, from Trump and brought him to Vegas to work at the Mirage. He got sued by Donald for millions. It was settled out of court.

They were both huge personalities then. Steve had Nevada wrapped up, Donald had the East Coast. They hated each other with a passion. I knew them both; I worked for them both. There I was in the middle, juggling these two, with ferocious name-calling on both sides—and I do mean major language. The insults and allegations went on and on.

Donald was famous for his oversize personality, Steve for his clever TV commercials, like the ones he did with Frank Sinatra for Atlantic City. I wound up doing three of them myself. It was a brilliant promotional tool. On the other hand there was Trump branding his own name, and we know the power of personality; on the other was the meticulous Steve, planning beautiful, aesthetic resorts.

I was with Steve when he made the transition to Atlantic City. I worked for him in Atlantic City. When they legalized casino gambling he built an incredible hotel, also named the Golden Nugget. It was smaller than a lot of the other casinos there but the most profitable. Everyone loved working for him there. I was there with him when they opened in 1980. In the city where there were many poor people, the casinos had not done much to improve that environment. There you had over-the-top hotels with all of their riches, etc. surrounded by all that poverty.

Meanwhile there was Donald Trump. He came into Atlantic City with all the power of the New York real estate development that he had taken from his father and built into a mega real estate company. He had a tall imposing figure to go with it and all that hair and the personality backed by a lot of confidence. He opened the Trump Plaza in 1984, where I worked And the Taj Mahal in 1990. Where Steve flourished and made money, though, unfortunately Donald struggled. My impression of Atlantic City after working the steel pier in my teens to what it became when gaming arrived was totally different than my impression of Vegas and its allure. Vegas had it all: great hotels, etc. Atlantic City was not a destination stop. Vegas was. The exteriors and interiors in Atlantic City could not match the styles of Vegas. I loved working in Atlantic City, at Steve's place, the Golden Nugget, where my old friend Charlie Meyerson, one of the most special caring human beings in our business, was head of casino marketing.

In Atlantic City, where Steve was trying to make his next move,

Donald Trump and his associate and fellow casino owner Arthur Gold-berg had it in for Steve from the start. It was a huge rivalry and they were out for Steve.

Goldberg was a tough and nasty executive from New Jersey, who'd been in the trucking business. But he had neither the celebrity of Trump's name-branding nor Steve's savoir faire. But behind the scenes he was lethal. We all knew he was jealous of Steve and did not want him in Atlantic City.

I met Trump originally through Roy Cohn. Here's how it came about. ABC Records, my first record company, was owned by Leonard H. Goldenson who started the ABC television network. His children had cerebral palsy as did the children of another successful New York businessman named Jack Hausman. So Goldenson and his wife, Isa-belle, hooked up with Hausman and his wife, Ethel, to find ways to improve the quality of life for their children and for other children like them with cerebral palsy. And through Leonard Goldenson I got to be friends with Jack Hausman. From the day I met Jack Hausman, I com-mitted to be a part of his and Goldenson's charity, which was a yearly televised telethon to benefit cerebral palsy. I was proud to be a part of it from the beginning in New York City in 1963, and did it every year with Steve Lawrence. In 1979, I was awarded the Cerebral Palsy Char-ity Honor.

One day Hausman said Roy Cohn wanted to meet me and intro-duce me to a guy named Donald Trump, who wanted to be in the ca-sino business and would I meet with him and just give him all my wisdom about casinos, *blah-blah-blah-blah.*

We go into Roy Cohn's living room. I'm talking to Roy and Jack Hausman and in walks this guy, very sure of himself, making a grand entrance—you expected to see papers flying about the room in his wake—Donald Trump. He was very much a prototype of what he is today, thinner, but with the same kind of confidence—and the same hair. We sat down and I talked to him about the gaming industry, everything that I knew, marketing, etc. So that's the Cohn-Trump connection. Trump wanted to get into the casino business in the worst way—and wanted to know *everything* about gambling. Eventually Trump and Steve got together and they, too, sat down and talked. Steve, of course, had far more experience than I did in the gaming business. And you know the rest: in went Trump head-first, into the gaming industry.

Later on I wound up working for Trump at two of his resorts— Atlantic City and Mar-a-Lago in Palm Beach, Florida—and this was while he and Steve Wynn were still fighting tooth and nail. Trump would come on with such animosity about Steve. And Steve would say similar things about Trump: "Look at that guy! He's like a cartoon of himself." I mean, they were at each other like you wouldn't believe. They were just cursing each other out. It was wartime. Big, big wartime. *Geronimo!*

In January 1990, Donald called me. He had a serious problem on his hands. He had a big fund-raising gala at his casino in Atlantic City, and his star attraction, Barry Manilow, had backed out at the last minute. Apparently Manilow was offended by side-by-side photographs of himself and Christine Whitman on the cover of a local magazine, which jokingly pointed out a passing resemblance between the two, and suggested they might have been siblings in a past life. Manilow, a lifelong Democrat, was also apparently irritated that this charity event promoted a Republican governor elect. I got a chance to be a hero, came in on a moment's notice, did the charity concert, and saved the day, for which Donald—and all involved—were extremely grateful.

I got a very appreciative letter of thanks from Donald:

Dear Paul,

You have my everlasting and heartfelt thanks for coming to our rescue on Saturday night . . . What could have been a disaster became a giant success for you and all of us. I am very grateful to you, Paul, and hope you know there will always be a place for you in one of my casinos— and my heart.

Some $300,000 was raised for the Children's Hospital of New Jersey, National Pediatric AIDS Foundation in Newark, and Respond Inc. of Camden that night, and I was glad to be able to help out those good causes and get Donald out of a tricky situation.

——■——

Steve Wynn and Donald Trump are two utterly different types of people—opposites, basically. Later on—much later on—Steve told me an outrageous story. He said the Trump organization had enlisted a spy who was trying to get a hold of Steve's best casino customers, high rollers. All these allegations wound up in court papers in a lawsuit Steve filed against the Trump group. Steve had two high powered guys on his security team, they were serious crime busters. As Steve tells it the security guys turned the spy and convinced him to gather information for Steve's organization. They had the spy meet with his Trump contacts where the spy would tape everything the Trump guys had to say. The idea was to gather proof that the Trump organization was stealing Steve's trade secrets.

Trump's lawyers denied all of those charges. But then, Steve explains, Trump filed a countersuit in federal court accusing Steve's people of using illegal recording equipment. "Under New York law you can't use this kind of device in single party situations." Steve was devastated. I had never seen him so distraught over anything. "So incomprehensible was that moment," Steve told me, recollecting that afternoon, "that sitting in that big room in the Bellagio and hearing this news was the single worst day in my business career. Never had a moment like that since my father died."

It turns out that the government is not subject to the taping prohibitions that apply to laymen because everything they do as government employees has to have judicial approval in front. His security guys said they didn't know this, but how could they not know?

According to Steve, "It was a pure filthy stalemate. Filthy and ugly and uglier. I'm feeling I'd like to kill someone. . . . The whole thing is so mean but Donald thought that was okay in those days. Business is war—that mentality. Thank God everybody's outgrown those kind of things."

A few months after that I was hiking at a spa in St. George, Utah, with Steve. It was one of many hiking trips that Steve and I would take together throughout our friendship. We were standing on top of that little mountain and just looking at the beautiful vista lying before us and he turned to me and said, "You know, I really have a great time doing what I'm doing and I've accomplished a lot, but I'm really tired of this new crop of people that are there, like Goldberg and all these other people coming in, who from my point of view have no class and are trying to do anything they can to get their way. I'm sick of that fucking town. And what's happened to it. I'm done with this, with guys like that."

It was really Arthur Goldberg who had become a real thorn in his side. Trump's friend and Bally Entertainment CEO, Goldberg was a ruthless greenmail raider, a guy who'd been in the trucking business before getting into the gaming business. Steve had dealt with some tough customers in his day, some very unsavory characters, but this was just hell.

Richard "Skip" Bronson, who worked for several years for Steve Wynn, is from Connecticut, and like me, he is a former paperboy and a college dropout. I met him when he started working for Steve on Steve's Atlantic City project—the Atlantic City Nugget hotel and casino—and that's when he became one of my closest friends. I was working for Steve Wynn downtown at the Nugget at the time. Steve Wynn hired him at a board meeting at the Nugget. Skip worked as an executive at the time, putting Atlantic City together for Steve and has written a great book about the whole mess called *The War at the Shore,* detailing his adventures with Arthur Goldberg and Donald Trump and all the things that happened in Atlantic City. It got really ugly.

In Steve's mind, Donald Trump isn't an out-and-out prick like

Goldberg—he isn't a vicious guy. A little crazy at times, marching to the tune of God knows what—we didn't know; we'd never heard that music before. But once you figure him out, Donald is the wrong guy to fight with; you don't want him as an enemy because he'll do *anything*. He's the wrong guy to have saying the wrong thing about you. I don't think he's a mean-spirited guy, just a loose cannon. Arthur Goldberg, though, was another matter altogether—a mean, cruel guy, a pull-wings-off-a-butterfly type of guy. He would verbalize in a very vicious manner if he got into a confrontation with you.

Trump knew I was a close friend of Steve's and would never rap Steve to me. He knew not to tread there with me, because I was very tight with Steve. When I worked for Trump I treated him as a separate entity without getting in the middle of it. But whether I liked it or not I was involved in nitty-gritties. The Trump-Wynn feud became a problem for me because I worked for Trump and was a friend of Steve's, and worked at Steve's and I knew Trump, so I was smack in the middle of that. I knew what was going on, and without getting directly involved I wanted to help get them back together.

Then one night I was performing at a special gala at Mar-a-Lago for Donald, at Trump's resort on Marjorie Merriweather Post's former estate in Palm Beach, Florida, and I decided I could end the feud. While there I had a few talks with Donald and could read between the lines that he didn't want this feud to continue—and, by this time, neither did Steve. One night, I decided to see if I could end it. I called Steve from Mar-a-Lago and said, "You know, Steve, this guy doesn't want to go to war with you. He doesn't want to sue. Get rid of this lawsuit. At least talk. He will talk to you. Donald would really like to settle this and end the feud." So I get them on the phone together and they mended their beef. Trump had cost Steve three million in legal expenses by that point but Steve dropped the lawsuit anyway. And they started talking and then they never shut up! Because they're both big talkers. With Steve Wynn, you take a breath in a conversation and you lose your turn, but you don't mind because he's such a colorful storyteller—and one of the toughest guys I know. You knew you were among two great businessmen when you were with them. I am happy to report that as of this writing after all of the insulting barbs that were thrown at each other between Donald and Steve, it has been long put behind them. I was so happy to have made that phone call that brought them back together.

As Steve says about Donald, there are two very different Trumps: "If he likes you, he can be so sweet and caring. I went down to Mar-a-Lago for a birthday party that Oprah Winfrey threw for Maya Angelou on her seventy-fifth birthday. I called Trump, I said I'm coming. 'I'll take care of everything,' he said, 'you'll be my guest.' I land, a car picks me up when I get to Mar-a-Lago, he's waiting at the door in a pink tie, and a suit. It's ninety degrees but he's all dressed up! He can be a honeybunch."

The great thing about Steve's character is his resilience. And he's one of the smartest and toughest guys I know. He found a healing way to think about this monstrous thing Trump had done to him. "After the Trump-taping fiasco," Steve tells me, "that was the point in my life I didn't want any extended beefs with anybody. I chose to take a page from the Dalai Lama's playbook. Just ask yourself one question and the rage will subside: 'What in the world happened to that person, what unhappiness or insecurity or terrible wrong has this person suffered to make him do something like that?' It's their karma. Force yourself to say that and the rage drains right out of you."

Donald Trump is in ecstasy when he's the subject of public focus. No matter what he said, or what's said about him, it's a beautiful fucking day. He's truly a man who believes, "Say anything about me, good or bad. Just keep talking about me." When he gets ignored he dies. That TV show of his didn't exactly help reduce his ego, but at that point he was not in good shape financially, and that show was the right thing at the right time for him. And whatever you say about him, he did a great job with his children. His daughter is a wonderfully poised woman. In the end you have to say Trump is a remarkable but remarkably odd character, sometimes totally bizarre. He's behaved in a manner most of us are told not to behave, but my pal Donald does it his way and I like him a lot. We have always had a good relationship.

—■—

In 1987, when Steve Wynn sold the Golden Nugget Atlantic City, I worked for Trump in various other casinos. I also worked for Arthur Goldberg when he had the Hilton. He is from New Jersey, was a tough and nasty executive, and was a huge rival and was out for Steve. He did not have the notoriety or celebrity of Trump or Steve, but behind the scenes Goldberg was lethal. We all knew he did not want him in Atlantic City. He was a tough-and-rough businessman who started out in the trucking business. He's no longer with us—he died of bone marrow failure in October 2000.

I would spend many hours alone with Steve in his office. He and I and his German shepherds. The feelings he would expose to me regarding the Goldberg and Trump situation were harrowing. It is public knowledge how Trump and Goldberg launched an offensive on Steve. I told you of the time down near the end when Trump was having problems with his hotel and how I made the call for Kirk Kerkorian and Terry Lanni who worked for him at the time. Lanni was another intelligent and classy no-nonsense type of guy who headed MGM resorts.

I shared the triumphs from what was a rough journey for my buddy Steve and Skip right down to the ground-breaking in November 1998 of the Atlantic City–Brigantine Connector, the tunnel over which Trump, Wynn, and Goldberg had had such acrimonious feuds, due to disputes over which casino would have direct access. But even after the ground-breaking, I shared more of the skirmishes that went on between Trump and Steve in 1999 about trade secrets being stolen regarding high-roller lists. It ultimately took a different direction when Kirk Kerkorian came into the picture. Kirk is an old friend of mine since 1959.

He is ninety-five years old today. His approach to business and life is quite different from that of Steve and Donald. And what a success story he is in his own right.

Kirk began as an amateur boxer, became interested in flying, and is something of a daredevil: as a member of the Royal Air Force in the 1940s, he transported de Havilland Mosquitoes to Scotland via the treacherous "Iceland Wave" current. In 1947, he bought Trans International Airlines for $60,000 and sold it in 1968 for $104 million. He began investing in real estate in Las Vegas and owned a number of hotel casinos and megaresorts, most notably the MGM Grand, which at the time was the biggest hotel in the world. He's reportedly worth $15 billion.

While Steve and Trump were active in Atlantic City, Kirk and MGM Grand were looking at the possibility of building there. Steve was still trying to design Atlantic City. The Bellagio was doing incredible business in Vegas but the Beau Rivage, which was the Bellagio's original name was now in Biloxi, Mississippi. I made many trips down there with Steve because it was not doing as well as expected. Steve had a small percentage of the company. In March 2000, it was at half the price that it was at the previous year.

One thing led to another, and Steve ended up having a conversation with Kerkorian regarding building on his land in Atlantic City. Kirk came back with other things in mind. The bottom line was he wanted to be involved with the whole ball of wax. In other words, he wanted to be the buyer of Steve's Mirage Corporation. I was with Steve in his office the week he got the letter from Kerkorian and told me his company was in play. I lived through that whole scenario till the company was bought, from A to Z. I witnessed it from Steve's initial reaction, to where he realized it was an opportunity for him.

Steve is an honest dude and a very tough one. He always cared about his shareholders. I also had a number of conversations with Kerkorian during that period. He was a friend of mine, too, after all. I remember the final key conversation, at a Christmas party at our mutual friend

Kenny Roberts's house. Kirk and I peeled off from the crowd to a quiet corner. He asked me what I thought it would take to buy the Mirage Corporation, informing me that Wall Street would not let him go over seventeen dollars a share. I knew from Steve's side that this was not going to cut it. I simply told Kirk that I believed if he put a two in front he would have a great chance—and he did, he made it twenty-one dollars and he got it. At the end of the day Kirk bought the Mirage resorts for over six billion dollars. And everyone walked away happy. It was an emotional moment for all of us. In Steve's case, he now had no place to hang. At the completion of the deal, Kirk thanked me and asked me what I wanted. I said nothing at all—Steve was a friend and Kirk was a friend, and that was that. "But," I said, "I do love the Mirage and the MGM." We sat down with Terry Lanni, who I worked for at Caesars, and they gave me a five-year deal. The smartest thing Kirk did—and he verbalized it to me—is that there was not a "no competition clause." Steve Wynn could do what he wanted. Kirk understood that having him down the street, creating a new hotel casino was good business.

In the 1990s, when I was preparing my new act for my appearances in Vegas and Atlantic City, I teamed up with a couple of writers, two of the most creative people I've had the pleasure of working with over the years: Buz Kohan and Kathy Stone. And here I've also got to mention Marc Shorr. While working with Steve Wynn, Marc was Steve's right-hand operational manager and always saw that things in that big complicated machine that is a casino hotel, ran smoothly and efficiently.

I have since worked the newest and best spot in town—the Borgata Hotel in Atlantic City, run by Boyd Gaming Corporation. It opened in July 2002 and cost one billion dollars. I might add it was the first hotel to have the glamour and appeal that a Vegas hotel had. It became the highest grossing hotel in the history of Atlantic City and I was happy to be a part of it. And in a strange way if it were not for my buddies Skip Bronson and Steve, that hotel would not be standing.

—■—

One summer in the late '90s Steve and I and our wives Anne and Elaine, went to Italy together while he was building his new casino hotel, which at that point he was going to call the Beau Rivage. Steve wanted the four of us to go over to start looking at the terrain up at Lake Como. When we got up there we started tooling around the lake on a friend of ours boat, Gil Nickel, owner of the Far Niente Winery. Steve wanted his new casino to have an Italian look so we're looking at the aesthetics of the canopies, we were walking around taking pictures of interesting architecture, picking out details—ornamentation, how they framed their Renaissance doorways, medallions, crests, pillars and all that kind of stuff . . . you know what a detail freak Steve is.

I said, "Steve, we're checking out all this Italian ornament and 'Beau Rivage,' well, it's French, it's just not indigenous to Italy, you know, it just doesn't fit. It means 'beautiful beach,' which creates a charming image, *in French* it sounds even better. It may have been the name of the chateau Picasso painted in in the South of France, but you're building an Italian-style hotel and Beau Rivage is not Italian."

"No, no, no! It's got to be called 'Beau Rivage.' Beau Rivage." He was adamant.

It started to rain one day when we were on the lake as we were looking at the vistas and looking at all of the shrubbery and trees for ideas because he wanted to have a lot of flowers and greenery in the entry to the hotel, and we pulled into this little island for lunch to get out of the rain, and we were sitting there at the restaurant and there was a little sign that I could see from where we were sitting and it said BELLAGIO. It was the name of this island, this little, tiny town. It means "place of rest, home of rest," something like that. And I looked at Steve and I said, "Bellagio! That's the name of the hotel! It's a great fucking name."

He looked at me like, O my god! "Shit, Bellini . . . that's it!" So he renamed the hotel right there, and that's how the Bellagio got its name. Eventually Steve used Beau Rivage as the name of the casino he built down in Biloxi, Mississippi.

The Bellagio opened on October 15, 1998 on the site of the demolished Dunes Hotel. It was the most expensive resort ever built at that time. It had fountains outside dancing in sync to music, and contained Steve's famous art collection—he'd become a serious art maven—which included paintings by Claude Monet, Alfred Sisley, Alex Katz, Helen Frankenthaler, and Roy Lichtenstein.

How Steve became an art connoisseur is a very Steve tale. Well, he'd seen my modern art collection for years and other collections and had never taken any interest. Didn't get it, didn't like it, until . . . later on. So when he finally flipped and got into it, he did it with ultimate Steve style, because there's no one like Steve when he gets on a kick. He does his homework, absorbs it, and gets it—just amazing.

I went with him on his first art discovery trip. Steve hired the gallery owner Bill Acquavella to accompany him to Japan—because that's where a lot of the great art on the market was at the time. On this first art discovery trip to Tokyo, he called and said, "Bellini, you *are* coming with me." We would walk through these bank corridors, climbing over piles of platinum and gold bars to look at the art. Eventually it became so tedious for Steve because of his eyesight that we went back to the hotel and had them bring the art to us. And that's when Steve got the art bug, that's when it really kicked in. Before that he couldn't have cared less. But anything Steve puts his mind to he becomes an expert in. He started reading and studying and developed a brilliant understanding of buying art and the art world.

When you hang out with high-powered guys like Donald Trump, Michael Milken, Skippy Bronson, and Steve Wynn you can find yourself involved in some pretty extreme situations. In the late '80s with two friends of mine, Steve Wynn and Michael Milken, and an acquaintance, Ivan Boesky, I found myself somewhat in the middle of a huge financial scandal.

I knew Ivan Boesky before he became a corporate raider and *über* arbitrageur. He was the son-in-law of Ben Silverstein who owned the Beverly Hills Hotel, and that's where I used to stay when I came out to California as a young kid. It was there that I first saw Howard Hughes—he had a suite there. Since Boesky was married to Ben's daughter Seema, I frequently saw him socially so when I came to New York to perform in the late '80s he suggested we have lunch together it seemed a perfectly normal thing to do.

But the morning before I was going to meet with Boesky, a guy I knew in Washington who used to do investigative work for me called me up and said, "I know you see Ivan Boesky socially from time to time, but I want to warn you about what's going down with him. It's a dangerous situation and you should be very careful."

"What do you mean?"

"Boesky's cooperating with the feds; he's going to be a government witness. There's a big financial scandal coming and it's going to spread. Like this guy Dennis Levine, he's the managing director at Drexel Burnham Lambert."

"What's up with him?"

"Well, what we know is that he's going to talk to the feds; he's cutting a deal. He's already involved Boesky, and Boesky's cooperating, too."

"Wait a minute. What's this all about?"

"Rudy Giuliani is going after the big insider traders on Wall Street; he's going to nail Levine and Boesky and we think he's going after Michael Milken next. Milken would be a big trophy for him."

"Why are you telling me this?"

"Well, you're going to have lunch with him, right? And I thought you might want to know he's going to be wearing a wire."

"He's doing *what*? Jesus."

I go to meet with Boesky as if nothing had happened, just two old acquaintances having lunch at a fancy New York restaurant, where the biggest question generally is, "Is the fish fresh?" But I'm getting very nervous. My concern was whether my friend Steve might mistakenly get brought into this because Milken had helped finance his resorts.

I'm sitting there making small talk with Boesky and wondering whether the guy's wearing a wire! I don't know what his agenda was but I was extremely careful how I phrased my answers. It was a very disturbing situation to find myself in. Was he trying to pump me? Was he trying to get me to tell him something about Steve Wynn?

How Milken got ensnared in this is a long story I don't know, but I figure he can take care of himself. He was so smart that you had a better chance getting a sunrise past a rooster than outsmarting Mike. Boesky was something else again. He was just a corporate trader and unrepentant financial predator. They based the character of Gordon Gekko in the movie *Wall Street* on him. That famous speech he gives in the movie? That's really him. In 1985, at the School of Business Administration at the University of California at Berkeley, he gave a speech in which he said. "I think greed is healthy. You can be greedy, and still feel good about yourself." But in the end it turned into poison—and prison—for him and Milken.

I go back to Vegas where I was living at the time. I take Steve to dinner at a Chinese restaurant. I tell him, "Steve, I've got to talk to you about something that could be potentially explosive. I've been informed by someone in Washington that Milken is in Rudy Giuliani's crosshairs. He's going to try and bring him down any way he can. As you know, Boesky's been indicted and the whole situation is going to blow up. Dennis Levine is down in the islands with the money—and he's going to talk." I said, "Steve, you better call Michael right away and tell what you know."

I liked Milken and his wife Lori a lot. Around that time, I said, "Michael, don't kill the messenger, but . . ." And I told him about my lunch with Boesky, how Giuliani was gunning for him and so on. Milken didn't seem that concerned. "Paul, thank you for calling me about this. I'm only too aware of what's happening. The truth is I have nothing to do with it. It's not going to touch me." Well, you know the rest of the story.

Insider trading was illegal, but had not been strictly enforced until

Giuliani prosecuted Boesky for it. Boesky cooperated with the Securities and Exchange Commission and informed on Michael—and that was a devastating blow to Milken. Once the feds had Boesky as a witness, it was just a matter of time until Milken would also get prosecuted because Boesky could directly implicate Milken in insider trading transactions.

In April 1990, Milken cut his deal with the government. He pled guilty to six felonies. Milken paid $1.1 billion in fines and ended up spending less than two years in what's called Club Fed. You have got to hand it to the guy—he does the time. He comes out of prison the same day he finds out he has prostate cancer. He focuses on it—and beats it. Boesky himself was convicted of insider trading, got three and a half years and was fined $100 million. He and his wife are still friends, unlike many who prospered because of him and are no longer loyal to him.

———■———

Sometime in 2001, Steve Wynn and I were hiking in Sun Valley, Utah, which we love to do together, and during our climb he was on the phone with Barry Sternlicht, the head of Starwood Corporation about buying the land at the Desert Inn. They quickly closed the deal. The next thing I know I was riding around in a golf cart in 2002–2003 as his new hotel casino began to be built. Ultimately it opened in 2005 but he had shared with me for years as to the kind of new masterpiece he was creating. I cherish the days and nights I would sit with him, where the fellow perfectionist would sit with the plans and show them to me with such enthusiasm for what he was doing. My buddy Steve Wynn is still the eminent name in the gaming business.

Steve and his dream palace came up again in 2005 when he began to think about what to call his current hotel-casino. He'd originally wanted to call "La Rêve," which means "the dream" in French. It's the name of the famous Picasso painting in Steve's office, which Steve equally famously put his elbow through due to his eye condition. "La Rêve" is a beautiful lyrical name but there was a problem with it. In order to use La Rêve as the name of his hotel-casino he'd have to add a lot of other information as well. For one thing, people don't know how to pronounce it or what it means, plus it has a circumflex accent, which strikes terror in a country like the USA. In addition, in his promotional materials Steve would have to include his name and mention all the other hotel-casinos he'd previously created in Las Vegas.

To figure out what he should name his new place Steve hired David Arnell, a famous marketing guy who had done DKNY for Donna Karan. Arnell persuaded Steve not to call it La Rêve. "You want to promote yourself and your other successful ventures," Arnell told him. "You want people to know you're the guy who created the Mirage and the Bellagio, so how about you use 'Wynn' somewhere in the title, like, say, the 'Wynn.'" Which Steve did, although he was well aware of the pitfall of using your own name on a building. Donald Trump had done that in Atlantic City with disastrous consequences. Trump's success has always been with apartment buildings. Gaming was an unhappy, frustrating experience for Donald, plus he was in the unfortunate position of having his name on the building that failed. This is a double misery when things don't work out.

———■———

On April 26, 1981, I celebrated my twenty-fifth year in show business. As the eighties dawned, I found myself in the unusual position of having to reinvent myself all over again in a business where I'd already made it at least twice. My association with Las Vegas as a performer didn't help—in fact it was a curse at one time for a contemporary artist to even play there. But, true to my code, I continued to perform in Vegas no matter whatever anybody said. I was still playing internationally, but I'd always go back there. The hypocrisy is that all of a sudden everybody showed up there later on—Celine Dion, and eventually Elton John and all the rest. But back then the recording industry had decided Vegas was a dirty word. They developed a very negative image of Las Vegas. Vegas became a bad word; it was a put-down. "Going

Vegas" meant selling out. They didn't want to get behind any singer who had any connection with it.

I saw it coming. As far back as the early seventies I was told that no Las Vegas act could expect to have a hit song on the charts. Then I wrote "(You're) Having My Baby" and it went to the top of the charts. Critics cut me some slack after that, but to this day I'm sure they consider my Las Vegas appearances as a mistake.

In 1980 I had a top five AC hit on the charts for Sony records with "Hold Me 'Til the Morning Comes." By the '80s I figured it was time to try out other media. In 1980, I wrote a song for Louis Malle's *Atlantic City*—the movie tied for first place at the Venice Film Festival.

I've done a bit of acting, too. I'd been in all those teen movies and, of course, *The Longest Day*. I wasn't too enamored of the movie business but started doing a few cameo parts in the '70s and '80s. I played a yacht broker in *Captain Ron,* a pit boss in *3000 Miles To Graceland*. On TV I was on *That '70s Show* and *Gilmore Girls* (where Lorelai named her dog Paul Anka) and in the "Treehouse of Horror VI" episode on *The Simpsons*—now that's *almost* as good as a Grammy.

Yes, in the '80s, there was a lot of activity—especially foreign travel. I began touring a lot more in Asia, a part of the world that is fascinating and has my respect. It's been the most stimulating part of the world to tour and experience. I have sustained a long working relationship with two people who were my first promoters in the Hong Kong region, Florence and David Chan. To this day I hold them very close to my heart for their loyalty and friendship, Florence Chan especially. She is a very special and rare human being. Another couple dear to my heart are Dr. Albert Yeung and his wife Semon. Albert is one of the most successful and brightest men in Hong Kong. They are both giving and incredible hosts. I cherish the moments when I am in their company.

Ten

THE BELLINI EPISODES

I've always been a practical joker, ever since I was a kid, but my serious capers started in the late sixties and early seventies and onward. Steve Wynn and I became very close when we were neighbors in Vegas. Steve had never been to Europe so we took a trip there with our wives and families. As soon as we got to Venice we started drinking Bellinis, which is champagne and peach nectar. I loved bellinis so much Steve started calling me Bellini, and that became my nickname. And whenever I'd do a practical joke, he would call it "doing a Bellini."

On one occasion, we went to Monte Carlo with Skip Bronson, who at the time worked with Steve at Mirage Resorts. We went over to look at the Grand Prix race route because Steve wanted to bring it to Vegas. The idea was, shut down the strip, and try and re-create the Grand Prix in the center of the city. He's a great visionary and we have a lot of fun together when we get away.

The Grand Prix race lasts two or three days and on that opening night we get invited to the Palace to meet Prince Rainier, the ruler of the glamorous gambling kingdom on the Mediterranean—Monaco is one of the most beautiful spots in the world. We land, we go to the Hôtel de Paris, one of the most well-appointed and stylish hotels in Europe. After attending the second day of the Grand Prix, I feel it is the right moment to pull a Bellini. I pick up the phone and call Skip Bronson. We're all staying on the same floor, and I say, "Meester Bronson, this is Fridrici Baglatini over at the Palace with Prince Rainier." I'm doing my corniest Italien functionary's accent.

"Yes?" says Bronson.

"We are so happy to 'ave a Mr. Wynn over here as our guest for the Grand Prix and tonight you know we're 'aving the big celebration at the Palace. Mr. Bronson, Mr. Wynn we're very happy to have 'im 'ere, 'e's incredible business for the casino, and the prince would like to 'ave private audience with Mr. Wynn, to discuss casino business."

"Oh, wonderful, I'll put that together," Bronson tells me.

"'Ave 'im up 'ere at six o'clock. And make sure 'e wears a tuxedo, cause 'e's going to see the prince by 'imself."

"Oh, tuxedo? Okay."

"We'll send a car. You put him in the car; we will get him out. We got a department for people with any kind of a health problem"

"Well, but there's something you should know, Mr. Wynn has a problem with the eyesight. He has retinitis pigmentosa, so he can't see clearly when it gets dark."

"Don't vorry," I say. "You put 'em in the car, and we got a department for people with any kind of health problems. And vill take care of 'em." Then I add, "This is official visit, you cannot come with him, *capisce*?"

He says, "Oh, okay."

I say, "'Ere's my phone number, if anything *bup-bup-bup*." And I give him a phone number and he takes the phone number—but of course it's bogus.

I go down to Steve's room; he's been informed by Skip over the phone that the prince wants to see him alone. I walk into Steve's room, and he's on the phone with his wife, Elaine.

"I haven't got long," he says. "Turns out the prince wants to see me.

I gotta get this tuxedo ready. I go over to the Palace at six, just the two of us. We're going to discuss . . ."

And I'm going, "Steve . . ."

"Honey," Steve's telling his wife, "I gotta hang up, Bellini's here, I'm going up to see the prince. I gotta be there in half an hour."

So he hangs up and he says, "Bellini, come on, help me, what should I wear? The black, the blue?" He's showing me different outfits, because he can't tell the difference between the colors on account of his eye problem and I'm helping him through all of this. He's getting more and more revved up for the meeting.

I realize at this point I've gone too far and have to stop it. I say, "Steven, there is no meeting."

He says, "What do you mean, Bellini?" I tell him I just did a Bellini on Skippy. "That was me; I called Bronson. I just put him on. Just to get him. He had never experienced my humor before, and needed a "Bellini" pulled on him.

He says, "Oh fuck, Bellini, that's funny. You didn't!" As we're talking about it, there's a knock at the door and in walks Skip Bronson. He's got a pad in his hand and a pencil and he looks at us and says, "Oh man, these people are something over here."

So Steve says, "What do you mean?"

He says, "You know, I tried to call this guy back, who set this meeting up with you and the prince. I call over there; I can't get through. I must have taken down the wrong number and I could not reach him. So I called the main number through the hotel operator here and when they answer they said they did not know anything about the guy. So I said, 'Get me the emissary to the prince.' I get this guy on the phone, this real snobby French cat; he's telling me he doesn't know anything about the meeting. And I said to him, 'Well, you know what, you're out of the loop. I'm gonna have Mr. Wynn there at six.' They're trying to give me an argument, but I *handled* it, Steve! Told this Frenchman off, *da uh da*."

Steve says, "You told the Palace that you're coming with me, and you told the prince's emissary that he's out of the loop? And you're bringing me, hell or high water?"

Skip says, "Yeah, why?"

So finally Wynn says, "There ain't no fucking meeting. That was Bellini on the phone. Not some guy at the Palace."

Skip goes white, and he says, "You mean I just bawled out the entire staff over there—for nothing?"

He gets over it, and we're laughing and laughing about the thing. We go to the Palace at 8:00, stand in line with a hundred people in the Palace courtyard until they're ready for us, all still cracking up. Steve thinks it's the funniest thing he's ever heard, that Skip has told off the entire Palace. So now we get inside and Steve says, "I can't fucking believe this." And as we're talking, the guy who Skip called up and told, "You're out of the loop," comes walking by and is introduced to us. He goes white when he hears Skip's and Steve's names and storms off.

Now Steve says, "I gotta tell the prince what you did." So we flag down one of the emissaries and we say, "Mr. Wynn wants to talk to Prince Rainier." And she takes us over. At this point in his life the prince is not a late nighter. His health is failing, poor guy. He has been sick and what have you. The prince is over in the corner; I and the emissary take Steve over to the corner to meet the prince. It's dark, so he's not really catching the expressions on the prince's face. The prince is a pleasant old aristocrat and Steve is wildly enthusiastic. He starts to tell the prince the *whole* story and you could see that the prince was not that thrilled to be courteous. Steve shouts, "So we left him out of the loop" and the prince is going "Eh? *Heh heh heh.*" He's not following the story; he's just going along with it, not knowing what the fuck Steve's saying.

Now Steve is very articulate and he's a guy who can tell a story, he's one of the great talkers of all time and very intelligent. However, enough is enough. The emissary comes over to me, this big hefty woman, and says, "Mr. Anka, he's taking too much of the prince's time. You've got to tell him to come away." I say, "No, *you* tell him." I have never been able to stop Steve mid-story. Eventually, the emissary, out of exasperation, asks Princess Caroline to go over and see if she can do something. She walks up to him, taps Steve on the shoulder, and this of course gets his attention; she takes him by the arm and leads him away. Meanwhile the prince is sitting there like a dumbfounded character in a comic strip with question marks sprouting out of his head as if to say, "*Whaaa* just happened?"

———

We all go to Venice, Steve Wynn, me, plus wives and kids. I used to take my family to Cipriani; it's on a separate island and the only hotel in Venice that has a pool. It's beautiful, private, doesn't have a lot of rooms, a great hang for the family. We must have taken up fifteen rooms between all the families. Day before last, we're checking out the next morning at eleven o'clock. I call Wynn up.

"Meester Wynn, how are you. It's Piero Cariacci downstairs, such an honor to 'ave such great celebrity staying with us." Pause. "You know, of course, you're checking out tomorrow and we're a small hotel and the summer season, very busy time. All kinds of people, reservations, and so on, and they're going to come and get here early. Do you mind if you maybe check out tomorrow morning at six thirty instead of eleven? We give you free breakfast, compliments of the hotel, because we got the Arabs coming and we gotta give them the room."

Steve explodes. "This is outrageous. I have a hotel, and I would never do this to *anyone*. What do you mean six thirty? I have the Ankas and we have all these women with us, and there's seven daughters, and I would never—"

"But, Meester Wynn we got the Arabs a-coming for the room. We have got to clean and prepare the rooms so we are ready for their arrival. You already been here four, five, six days. We give you a free breakfast, how about it?"

"I don't want a free breakfast. I'm staying in my room till eleven A.M., understand? I'm sleeping in tomorrow."

I say, "Mr. Wynna, thatsa unfortunate. In that case, fucka you," and I hang up.

He couldn't believe his ears; he could not believe what he'd just heard the manager say to him. His wife, Elaine, one of the great ladies—gracious, stylish, caring—was trying to calm him down. He thinks it's the hotel management. I get to Steve's room as quick as I can so he doesn't get to the front desk.

He was tearing out the door when I got there. I said, "Where you going?"

"Those goddamn sonsofbitches, I'll tear them a new asshole . . ."

I said, "Oh, you mean that phone call?"

"Yeah, how'd you know about it?

"Steve, I know about it because it was *me*!"

Well, he fell down when he heard that; he loved it.

Now comes the classic Bellini: Ed McMahon. We're in Europe, Steve, me, the families—it was that same trip. We were staying at a fancy hotel in Antibes, France. It's tough to get a reservation there in the summer. Potential guests were picked by the hotel manager on a quota basis. He selected them like this: "We'll take two blacks, we'll take three Jews, we'll have two Italians, we'll have one of . . ." He does it like a dart board to make sure he gets whatever mix of guests he wants. And in the meantime, because of this arbitrary system, his elbow is permanently crooked from all the tipping that goes on, because tipping him big is the only way you can get in. You grease him up big-time to get a room. People from all parts of the world rush to get there cause it's the cool hang, but at the same time it's sort of a pain in the ass because you run into everybody you know from back home.

We're there hanging for a couple of days, Steve and I, looking forward to going on to Italy, and who should show up at the hotel but Ed McMahon with his new girlfriend Vicki—Victoria Valentine—whom he'd met as a National Airlines VIP hostess. Steve and I run into Ed and Vicki at the pool. Ed says, "I want to show Vicki Europe. Paul, I know you know Paris, you've lived over here, and I love the way you dress. I want to go to your tailor and get a white suit made, I heard he's the best."

"No problem," I say, "I'd be happy to introduce you to M. Cifonelli."

"Now, Paul, tell me, you're a friend of Regine's, aren't you?"

"Well, yes," I say, "she's a close friend."

Regine had sung with me at Caesars Palace—I'd known her since she was a hatcheck girl in Paris. Regine's was the famous discotheque that she'd created. It was all the rage then, but hard to get into and Ed wanted to be given the VIP treatment to impress Vicki. "No problem," I say. "Whatever you want, Ed. I'll arrange it for you. You'll get a call; somebody will fill you in on the details."

We all leave. Ed goes to Paris, Steve and I go to Italy. We're sitting around the pool at the Hotel Cipriani in Venice.

Now Steve and I haven't done a Bellini in a while so I say, "Let's get McMahon."

"Whaddaya suggest?'

"A phone call," I say. "We can tell him anything. Also, he's very tight with money, so we'll play on that." I pick up the phone and call the hotel where he's staying in Paris.

"Ed McMahon," I say. They ring through. Steve is sitting on the toilet, listening in on the other phone.

"Meester McMahona?" I say (using my German accent this time because the hotel managers over there, they're all Germans). "This is Helmut Schweitzer downstairs at the front desk there. Thank you very much for coming to the hotel, such an honor to have such an important American personality. We got a call from some fellows, two people, that Mr. Anka arranged an appointment for you at Cifonelli, the tailor. That's not going to be the problem, because you vant the white suit, okay."

"Thank you," says McMahon.

"But vee have a problem Mr. McMahon; they're doing some construction here at the hotel. And you know for the fall they're getting ready and we gotta do some sand-blasting. Unfortunately it's right now on your floor."

"Oh, okay." He was an accommodating kind of guy.

"We're gonna sandblast de floors, de valls, and de ceilings. For ten hours a day it's goin' on. It's gonna make a mess and, o, boy, ze dust!"

"Oh," he said.

"But don't vorry," I say. "Ve gonna make dis offer for you. We can move you down to the second floor, we give it to you half price, but the view it not so nice—the wall of the American Embassy. Or . . . You can stay where you are for nothing, no charge, and we give you zee sound proof ear muffs."

Now he goes, "One moment. Victoria! They're gonna sandblast *blah blah*. We can go downstairs for half the price but if we stay here for nothing we've got the soundproof ear muffs." She says, "Take the ear muffs; we can spend the money on something else." So he says, "We'll take the ear muffs." They thought, hell, we're out all day, they're not going to be sandblasting at night, why not settle for the free breakfast, we'll wear ear muffs and that'll be that.

"Fine decision. That's vonderful," I say as the German hotel manager. "Oh, Mr. McMahon, about Regine's. You want to go to the discotheque? Everything is taken care of."

"Great!"

"But zay are very busy in the summer and you called a little late. Because we got the people from all over: zee Arabs, Scandinavians, Germans, zhey all come here. But don'ta worry—we gotta you a good slot.

"A slot?"

"This is a small discotheque, Mr. McMahona, we can't put all the people in the same hour. But you got your own slot with the wife at five in the morning."

Now Ed's fucking going crazy. "Are you kidding me?" he shouts.

"So sorry, but dat's all that's available."

"Victoria! It's busy but we got our own slot, five till six in the morning?"

"Well, whatever you wanna do, Ed," she says.

"Okay, we'll take the slot."

This is all getting too much for Steve. He is choking with laughter and trying to stay quiet at the same time. He is waving at me from the toilet seat with his hand cupped over the phone. In a loud whisper he is saying, "Paul you have gone too far—I don't want to be a part of this. Just tell him it is you. I can't do this anymore, I can't take it."

So I tell him, "Ed, this is Anka and Wynn . . . and we were just having a bit of fun." He laughed in a stricken kind of way.

Eleven

MOVING ON

Adnan Khashoggi is one of the most interesting personalities I've ever come across. If ever there was someone who could be called larger than life, he was it. Adnan was flamboyant as they come, a character and a half. He was a billionaire, and that's just for starters. He was a Saudi arms dealer and businessman and was involved in the 1987 Iran-Contra deal in which several senior members of Ronald Reagan's administration had secretly sold arms to Iran.

Khashoggi loved Las Vegas and that's how I got to know him. He would come and just wrap the town up. Everybody was dazzled by him, especially the casino owners, including Kirk Kerkorian who had a special affection for him. He was just a likable guy—and a big spender.

Khashoggi would throw lavish parties and invite everyone in town. He would come with his family to see my show and bring forty or fifty people, and have a party afterward to boot. It would be the most opulent, wonderful bash you could imagine. He would throw it at the Sands Hotel, and there'd be over-the-top food, booze, entertainment, and just good, good times.

I got to know him pretty well over the years and would see him whenever I played Vegas, went to Europe, to New York, or to Paris. I did little favors for him as he had done for me. On one occasion he invited me to his New York apartment where he introduced me to a gorgeous young girl who wanted to be a singer. Unfortunately, she was a singer who couldn't sing. I advised her to get into acting and maybe take some voice lessons, trying to be as kind as I could. On that occasion I stayed for a few hours, which he thought reason enough to give me a few extravagant pieces of jewelry. I really didn't want to take them, but I knew he would be insulted if I didn't. Let's just say it's an Arab tradition: you accept a gift when offered to you.

A few years later, I was doing some shows in the Philippines, where I often went to perform. After my concert I was invited to the Palace by Imelda and Ferdinand Marcos. Imelda was very outgoing, gregarious, personable. Marcos himself was a quiet fellow. But every time I'd go there to do a concert, I'd have to go to the Palace after the show, around eleven at night, and socialize with ambassadors and VIPs. We had the usual outlandish dinner and after midnight Imelda got up to sing. Well, she would start to sing, and then she sang and sang well into the night—truth be told, it felt like an eternity. She'd sing till two in the morning. She didn't have a great voice but she had some tonality—it was bearable. She had a lot of desire and a big heart and was always a very gracious hostess. She'd be singing "Moooon Riii-Ber" and Marcos would be sitting there next to you—the poor guy got so tired after a while he'd be falling over. He needed his sleep. One night he fell asleep on my shoulder (he'd obviously been through this many times before). That particular night she finished around three-thirty in the morning, and that's when she got it into her head that she had to give me a tour of the Palace to show me her famous shoe closet. I think I got to bed around five that morning.

(On a one-to-one basis Imelda was a very gracious hostess and fun to be around. But she played the whole royalty thing to the hilt. There was a lot of money there. *Lots* of money.)

The next thing I know, I'm in Paris at Khashoggi's apartment. He asked me if I would help him sell three properties he owned in New York City (the Crown Building on Fifth Avenue, the Herald Shopping Mall, and the 40 Wall Street Tower).

He said if I could sell the properties for him he would give me a commission. We agreed and I proceeded to look for a buyer, but as I did so, I became more and more suspicious. Everybody I talked to was telling me Khashoggi didn't really own the buildings—they were the property of the Marcos family. People were warning me to be careful: "Watch out, Paul, it's a powder keg." I called Donald Trump to see if he was interested and he confirmed to me that Khashoggi was fronting for Imelda Marcos and that he had never owned the buildings.

I called Khashoggi and asked him why he hadn't told me Marcos was the owner. Turns out the properties were bought secretly in the late 1970s and 1980s and were the subject of a heated dispute between the Philippine government, New York Land Company, Canadian Land (run by Ralph and Joseph Bernstein and attorney Philip Carter), and Khashoggi, who was a friend of Ferdinand Marcos.

At that point I had to go to Khashoggi and say, "Don't put me in this awkward position. You know these buildings aren't yours, they're hers." I told him I didn't want to be involved in this stuff and that I was out of the deal. About a month later, he gets in trouble with the government and ends up in jail. Khashoggi was also the head of the Triad Holding Company, which built many properties in the United States and abroad. But he is mostly known as an arms dealer. He brokered deals between the U.S. and the Saudi government in the 1960s and 1970s. His luck ran out in 1988 when he was arrested in Switzerland and accused of concealing funds. He was held for three months, then extradited to the United States, where he was released on bail and subsequently acquitted. Well, *he* may have been acquitted, but let's face it, I felt I was obviously in over my head.

So in 1990, a U.S. federal jury in Manhattan acquitted Khashoggi and Imelda Marcos, now a widow, of racketeering and fraud. Justice?

Go figure. But through it all, I have a fondness for Adnan, a good man, with an incredible lady by his side, his wife Lamia.

Through Adnan I came to know Khashoggi's brother, Essam and his lovely wife Layla, also gracious hearts and good people. Visiting them, I almost didn't get out with my life. In Europe, my wife Anne and I were at Essam's house outside of London, being royally treated by Khashoggi, an incredibly lavish host—that's what billionaires do best. On the last day there, we were waiting to be taken to Heathrow Airport to board his private airplane, a 737, for the trip home.

Well, I happened to look out of the window of our bedroom, which was on the second floor overlooking the driveway below and saw a big van pull up along with two Rolls-Royces. I see what appears to be a jewelry box, a foot and a half by a foot and a half in size being loaded all by itself in the back of their car while all the luggage was placed in the back of the van. Essam and Layla Khashoggi had a large staff. When it came time to leave Anne and I went downstairs to get in the car. The van and Essam's limo proceeded out of the grounds ahead of the car that Anne and I were in.

As our car approached the gate to the property, it suddenly closed in front of us. I found it unusual but paid it no mind. Why had the gate closed so quickly? This delay in waiting for the gate to reopen caused us to fall behind by a few minutes from the other vehicles.

The neighborhood that Essam lived in was out in the woods, very secluded. As we headed to the airport we passed several industrial parks. We're driving along and all of a sudden an orange car passed us and pulled in between us and the other two cars, which had driven on and were about a quarter of a mile ahead.

We reached the top of a hill, giving us a view of the road below. As we descended to the highway, Essam's two cars approached another industrial park on the right-hand side of the road. I was looking ahead and I saw two other cars come from behind a building and cut off

Essam's car, while another car from another building bolted out and parks behind them.

Now they had Essam's vehicle boxed in. Then these guys got out with their masks and Uzis and they were running toward the car that has the jewelry box. I was looking at this and not believing what the hell I was seeing. It was frightening and chaotic and it suddenly hit me what was really going down. It was definitely a heist and maybe even a kidnapping and we were right in the middle of it. I told my wife Anne to get down on the floor of the car.

"Stop!" I said to the driver. "Turn around and get out of here. Look what's going on."

I saw Essam's car; his driver had been taught evasive action. He pushed one car out of the way, got over this ditch, turned into a field, and started off in another direction. My driver now stopped the car as I instructed him to do and made a U-turn on the highway. I saw that all the cars were also starting to head back. Anne was still frightened but things were settling down as we drove back to the compound.

We got back to the estate, and when Scotland Yard shows up to interview everybody, I took one of the detectives aside and said, "Hey, I've been around stuff like this most of my life, and I can tell you I smell an inside job." I told them over the weekend I'd seen some members of his staff exchanging looks and whispered asides. I mentioned the incident at the gate. I explained that I had told my driver to get out of there as fast as possible.

They said they would do a full investigation of the heist. We composed ourselves and were just thankful to be alive.

They drove us to the Khashoggis' plane under police escort. We couldn't get out of there fast enough. A couple of months go by and Essam calls me to say, "I'm sending you an article from the *London Times,* which lays out what happened. You were right. It was an inside job." Some of his staff ended up in prison in England. It was all about the jewelry—which was worth millions. I have to admit it was all pretty

wild and exciting—but only in retrospect—and the scariest by-product
of fame that I've ever been involved in.

———■———

In my life I've been introduced to many different people. When I meet
people either through friends, business associates, or showbiz colleagues
I take them at face value, but over the years I've learned to be cautious
and rely on the advice of my close advisors.

Critical to my financial health has been my business manager,
Mickey Segal. I've known Mickey and his wife Lee for over thirty
years. He's not only my business manager, but also a great friend.

Mickey's astute scrutiny and careful research saved me from a disastrous situation in the mid-1990s. I was performing at the Mirage Hotel
when I was introduced to a woman in Las Vegas who was a broker at
Merrill Lynch. She came recommended by my Las Vegas throat doctor,
who always took care of me and who I've known for many years.

Her name was Janie Thomas. She was known at the time as a broker
to "an elite clientele in the business and entertainment industries." I
decided to act on my friend's recommendation and use her services as a
broker. I told Mickey to give Thomas some money to invest in the
stock market. The market at that time was not doing so hot and was
relatively flat. Nobody was making money from the market.

He was a little nervous about using Thomas despite the fact she had
been recommended by my friend. I invested some money with her and
to everyone's surprise, the early returns on the investment were en-
couraging. I was very pleased, although Mickey remained skeptical and
decided to check out her credentials. Mickey called Merrill Lynch and
confirmed that she was employed there. He told me that she was a broker, she had business cards, and apparently she was legitimate. But
Mickey told me he wanted to take it one step further. He said the best
way to tell if Thomas was legitimate was to ask her for some money
back from my investment. He came up with a story about me having to

pay taxes to the government and needing some money in a hurry. But she came through with the money and even he was surprised by the kind of return she was able to make on my initial investment.

A few months later I'm performing in Las Vegas and I arrange a meeting with Mickey and Janie Thomas at my suite at the Mirage Hotel. The meeting is to go over the performance results of the money that I had invested. Thomas lays out these Excel schedules that summarize all the assets I own, the returns on my investment, and where the money is being invested, which is mostly in foreign currencies and foreign bonds.

The statements show my investments are doing great and I've made hundreds of thousands of dollars over a short period of time. To me everything seems perfectly legitimate, but it doesn't make sense to Mickey. He says the markets are doing lousy and here's this broker who is producing returns of about 40 percent. He's becoming more wary about Thomas, especially since she's not providing any official Merrill Lynch statements of my assets.

But I am getting excited and suggest to Mickey that maybe I should invest more money with Thomas. But he's still suspicious even though he was proven wrong in the past when I asked her for some money back and ended up with a good return. I tell Mickey I want to move some of my kids' money over to Thomas for her to invest. I could see now that he is starting to panic a bit. He decides to do further checking on the broker.

He has friends at Merrill Lynch who handle private clients in Los Angeles. He tells them about this broker. They tell Mickey the kind of returns Thomas is getting in the market are unheard of because it isn't a boom market. Mickey's friends at Merrill Lynch suggest he contact security officials at the company and have them check her out. By this time I'm due to make another tax payment to the government. Mickey suggests I again ask Thomas for more money. Merrill Lynch says if there's going to be an exchange of money they want to be part of the transaction. I ask Thomas for the money and she balks at first. She says she needs more time to get the money because they're not "liquid assets." That's an odd answer because usually if you're investing in currencies or anything else like that, they are normally liquid.

A few days after asking her she comes through with the money, about several hundred thousand dollars. But this triggers a series of events that begins to unravel the ingenious scheme this woman had devised. Mickey gets a call from the security division at Merrill Lynch. They say there's a major problem, which they can't disclose right away, but that I have to return the money. They say they'll explain in a few days and to just sit tight. The following day Merrill Lynch's security division and the police do a search of Thomas's home and office in Las Vegas. They are ready to arrest her. Thomas calls Segal at his office and says the whole thing is a big mistake and that it's all going to be cleared up. She says it was a bookkeeping error at Merrill Lynch and other transactions that were done out of Denver.

We find out her husband, Bobbie Thomas Jr., was also involved in the scheme and he worked out of the Merrill Lynch office in Denver. Mickey tells me all this. I can't believe it, there must be some kind of mistake. After all, my doctor friend recommended her and he earned a lot of money through the investments Thomas made for him.

The police go to arrest her but she disappears. They find her car days later in Los Angeles, near the airport. She disappears without a trace. A search warrant for Janie Thomas and her husband, Bobbie Thomas Jr. was issued in 1994 after they fled Las Vegas. The police and Merrill Lynch officials believed the couple fled to Mexico. In 2004, after being a fugitive for nearly a decade, Bobbie, a former financial consultant with Merrill Lynch, turned himself in. Authorities said they were trading customer accounts without authorization through false account statements they created to deceive their clients.

It turns out because of our investigation their elaborate financial shell game was finally exposed. Janie Thomas allegedly embezzled about $20 million from dozens of clients, including many schoolteachers in Las Vegas. Instead of giving out monthly statements they were mailed to

Thomas and then she prepared Excel spreadsheets, which were doctored to show what a client had or didn't have. If a client asked for money from their investment Thomas would take the money from somebody's else's account in order to pay them. It was the perfect scheme because referrals were always coming from friends who had invested with her.

It was a pretty successful scheme that continued for some time. Janie Thomas was a very persuasive person who knew the investment business. She knew what she was selling, she was professional, was sharp in our meetings together and was always well dressed. It took Merrill Lynch several months to figure the scheme out and even then they didn't want it to become a big story. I'm glad I didn't get burned for any money, and that I had poked around because we saved many people from losing a lot of money. After the couple disappeared, Merrill Lynch disclosed the scheme, the amount of money embezzled, and made restitution to the clients who were affected. Merrill Lynch voluntarily repaid about $17 million to clients. I got a settlement of about $250,000.

— ■ —

I'm a singer of love songs. I sing songs of everlasting love, how you're the only one—and I believe in it. But sometimes these things don't work out in your private life. I was married to Anne for thirty-seven years and I love her still. She's the mother of my five daughters who have all brought terrific sons-in-law into our family, and we had a great life together. I love this woman. I always will. Getting divorced from Anne was just something I had to do for myself. Our kids were gone, our lives changed, our relationship changed. I can't remain in something—even a long, loving marriage—when I'm no longer experiencing things honestly. I didn't want to be dishonest to someone I love, even if that meant separating, and so in 2001, Anne and I were divorced. There was no animosity, no big fight—I just wanted out of the box. We still talk almost every day.

We worked out the terms of the divorce in the same offices where

Tom Cruise was going through his divorce from Nicole Kidman at the same time. That was a war. I saw it going on and I said, "That isn't going to happen to us." We had one lawyer between us, Craig Leeds, a stand-up guy and good friend. I gave Anne everything that was legally hers, and I threw in our art collection (that is worth millions) because I know how much she loved it, and other considerations. But I said, "None of this down the middle stuff."

I can't say enough about my attorney Craig Leeds, and how diplomatically he handled my divorce from Anne, how friendly he made what could otherwise have been a trying situation. We all just sat down and talked.

——■——

The new musical environment has been somewhat of a dilemma for me and the Neil Diamonds and Burt Bacharachs of this world. There really aren't that many outlets for our music anymore, what with the rise of rap and the urban radio format (hip hop, reggae, rhythm & blues, electronica). It's been very difficult for a cross section of old-school songwriters. The market has diminished drastically. The infrastructure has changed and the opportunities are just not out there the way they were. I tell my friends, if I ever try to invest or bet into the Record Biz again they can shoot me.

Now it's all rap, which was the first pop music to come along without a melody. What bothers me is this: if you don't have melody, you don't have memory. For instance, if you took over a big banquet hall and put a whole bunch of people in it, and you played the songs of the '50s, '60s, and '70s and said, "EV-rybody sing!" most people could sing along with a pop song of the day. But if you did the same thing with the rap records of today and said, "EV-rybody sing," I don't know how many would be able to do that. There would be dead silence. Or am I just being an old fogey?

In the beginning, all of us who started in rock 'n' roll—even today— you lived and breathed the music. You get up in the morning, you play the piano, strum a guitar, and carry on like a rock 'n' roller right through the day until you fall down.

I may be old-school but I try not to be an old fart as well. Like rap music, for instance. Some of us don't get it, but there's a place in society for what it represents and anyway, it's like a freight train and once it's coming down that track, get out of the way because you ain't gonna stop it, it's coming through. Every generation wants its own music.

I don't know that it's necessarily true that romance is gone out of today's music. I think that with rap we're into a new genre of music— the same way we were in the late fifties when rock 'n' roll came along. It certainly has defused it a little, but I think there is some romance left. I don't think I'd like to see wall-to-wall of the same kind of music anyway.

When I started, people looked at the early rock stars and disliked them intensely. Mothers were against *all of us,* from the way Elvis wiggled to the way I cooed my love songs to teenage girls.

I got into the survival mode years ago. I'm a people's writer so I figure what I write about is always going to be relevant. I just had to figure out how to go about it. What do you do when you find you're no longer creating the flavor of the month, especially when music has gone viral—it's now all downloading and file sharing?

—■—

Well, I've had a decades-long romance with Spanish-speaking audiences. I've performed all over in Latin America for over fifty years, and those audiences have been extremely supportive of me so I thought it was time to give them something more than just twelve tracks in English.

In 1996, I made *Amigos,* a platinum-selling album of Spanish duets with well-known Latin musicians. I recorded such golden oldies as "Tu Eres Mi Destino" ("You Are My Destiny"), which I sing with Lucero; "Pon Tu Cabeza En Mi Hombro" ("Put Your Head on My Shoulder") with Myriam Hernández; and, of course, "A Mi Manera" ("My Way") with Julio Iglesias. There's also a duet with Celine Dion (an honorary

Latin American) on "Mejor Decir Adios" ("It's Hard to Say Good-bye"), which became one of the album's more popular singles. Kenny G is on there, too ("Do I Love You"); as is Ricky Martin who duets on "Diana" with me; and the biggest kick of the whole project is my daughter Anthea singing "Do I Love You" in Spanish ("Yo Te Amo").

Latin audiences got me early on. They loved "Diana," "You Are My Destiny," "Lonely Boy," and "Puppy Love." With Juan Gabriel I recorded "Mi Pueblo" ("My Hometown"), which quickly became a much-requested single at WCMQ-FM radio in Miami and all over Florida. The very fact that an American singer was willing to sing in Spanish with a Latin star seduced radio program directors such as WCMQ's Betty Pino.

The *Amigos* album was a labor of love. I was proud to be able to give back to the Latin community, who have been so supportive for so many years. Especially pleasing a friend of mine from Mexico named Carlos Slim, one of the smartest most gracious and supportive friends anyone could want. Being in his company has always been heartwarming. Forget about his billions, his incredible success, he is one of the most down-to-earth and warmest human beings you would ever want to meet. He does things his way. "My Way" is his favorite song and I will never forget the evening at the Plaza Hotel recently where my dear friend Carlos was honored and given the prestigious Eisenhower Award. I had changed the lyrics to "My Way," tailor made for him about his life. And as the tears swelled in his eyes my heart was full at that moment.

I got my old friend David Foster, one of the top producers in the world, to produce it (he produced Whitney Houston's hit "I Will Always Love You" and Natalie Cole's comeback album, *Unforgettable*). David Foster has been a close friend of mine since 1972. I brought him and his wife down from Canada in the early 70s. I recognized him immediately as a phenomenal talent. In his book he says I once tried to buy him out—his future producing, writing, etc. for $2 million. I have always believed he's that talented. One of the best projects and times I have ever spent with my buddy David was when we shared our enthusiasm and commitment and talents to record our fellow Canadian, Michael Bublé, who, of course, turned into this incredible phenomenon. Foster is a songwriter, talent spotter, artist, and God knows what else. In his autobiography, *Hit Man,* he credits me with teaching him what fork to use, and for getting him hooked on traveling in private planes. He says I turned him into a jet whore. He's got his eccentricities, like his fear of elevators—he will take only stairs. He stays on the low floors of hotels and will not be caught dead in an elevator. I once kidded him about his phobia by saying, "I'll tell why you don't want to go into elevators—you're afraid you're going to have to listen to your music." He says that when he started out he coveted my lifestyle, but I tell you he has nothing to complain about now—he has more than arrived.

■

The idea of duets worked so well on the Spanish album, I thought, what the hell, let's do it in the mother tongue . . . and I don't mean Lebanese. So two years later in 1998, I made *A Body of Work,* on which I redid some of my best-known songs with Celine Dion, Tom Jones, and Frank Sinatra. More about that last one in a minute.

Other duets were with Tevin Campbell, Patti LaBelle, and Peter Cetera. I ended up singing "Do I Love You" with my daughter Anthea—in English—one of my favorite tracks on the album. It's funny because when she came out of college a straight-A student, I asked her, "What are you going to do"? She turned around and said, "I want to be in show business and write." I said, "Oh my God."

I wrote some of the new ballads including "She's My Woman, She's My Friend" and "No Goodbyes" while I was recovering from a broken foot. I think being laid up for a month provided me with a weird creative opportunity. I was like, "Wow. I've got nothing to do here but write." So I wrote.

I got David again, who also produced some tracks on *Amigos,* to produce tracks for *A Body of Work,* and was also thrilled to be able to work with Walter Afanasieff, someone whose talents I much admired who has had many hits to his credit, and is in the same league as David Foster.

Frank Sinatra had wanted to sing "My Way" as a duet with me but he was in no shape at that time to do it. He was just too sick—he died shortly thereafter, in May of 1998. I sure didn't want to try and compete with Frank's original so I did my best to stay out of the way of his version. I checked out the bombastic Don Costa arrangement that Sinatra used for more than two decades on record and in concert. Thank God the Sinatra family lent me the original Sinatra eight-track tape. I went into Capitol Records with Johnny Mandel and the greatest engineer, Al Schmidtt, an old friend and great guy who I have known for years, as far back as RCA Victor. I told Johnny to create a very romantic and nostalgic arrangement for the song—he essentially rewrote the track on tape. Mandel had worked with me back in '59 and '60—he's one of the last of those great guys who can effortlessly create beautiful arrangements out of thin air.

I didn't want that aggressive, macho tone that everybody who sings "My Way" invariably brings to the song. I took out a verse and some self-aggrandizing lyrics like "I ate it up and spit it out," and instead put an instrumental in the middle.

When creating the illusion of a duet with Sinatra on tape, the last thing I wanted to do was to get in front of Frank's phrasing. Mostly I'm singing behind him because obviously it's a testament to him. The technology allowed me to take his voice right out of his track and isolate it totally and block it into a studio, with the track digitally stored. The orchestra and I were able to sing and play along with Sinatra's voice, creating the impression of an original duet. Frank's death shortly before the album was released gave a haunting, eerie side to the duet.

While I was finishing *A Body of Work* I got to get away and stay with Phyllis and Dennis Washington from Montana, who have a house in Palm Springs. They and their two sons have been my friends for over thirty years. In September of 2006, Dennis and I took a trip on his boat over to Victoria, British Columbia, to have some time alone, which I really needed after the intensity of the *Body of Work* sessions.

When Sinatra had his comeback with "My Way," he was the age I am now. It ignited a resurgence in Sinatra's popularity. At his last Chicago performance in the United States in 1994, he thanked "a little guy named Paul Anka who gave me a song that did a great deal for my career, 'My Way.'" So I always figure, "Who knows?"

When you're on the inside of the music business looking out, you see that many of the guys that you came up with for one reason or another didn't last. I thank God every evening around seven o'clock that there's still an audience out there for me. It's great to know that people still want to hear you and you hope your best work is in front of you. You need to keep telling yourself that because performing is almost like a drug. How could you possibly walk away from it? Also, it's an absolute necessity these days to put asses on seats. CDs are now, for all intents and purposes, just calling cards.

———■———

One of the hardest things for me was witnessing Sinatra's long decline. By the time Frank played Lee Iacocca's birthday party in 1997, he was having problems. He was sweet and happy, but he wasn't himself.

Steve Wynn recalls the last time he saw him. "At dinner with the Iacoccas and my wife and I, he was sweet and charming. Toward the end of Frank's life he had very few good days—they were mainly bad, but there was one moving thing he said to me over the phone that always touched me. 'How's your mom?' He asked that and quickly added an affectionate, 'I wish you good luck, kid.' He paused and said, 'You know, I have good days and bad days.' And then put down the phone. On my birthday January 27, 1997, my secretary Joyce handed me the phone. 'Hey kid!' I knew that voice, it's what Francis called me. 'It's your birthday huh? Thank you for helping me out.'

"It was on Sunday night after the show, and he was sitting in the front dining room, drinking Jack Daniel's. I asked him a question: 'Frank, of all the women you've known, who was the best in bed?' Dean Martin was sitting there with him, the two of them, sitting side by side. 'Easy question!' they said, like they were one guy. 'Angie!' Angie Dickinson. I would have thought Frank would say Ava Gardner, but she was tough. A beautiful, remarkable creature, drank in the Hall of Fame category— she was too ornery for Frank. No, it was Angie he loved the best."

He died a year later in 1998 in May. We all went to Frank's funeral, which took place in a Catholic Church called the Good Shepherd. His son spoke, and at the end of the service they played his theme song, "Put Your Dreams Away"—it was incredibly moving. What a moment that was. He was one of a kind.

Angie Dickinson was there. In front of the church at Frank's funeral she became nostalgic. I asked if Frank had ever proposed to her. "We were coming home one night," she told me, "and he asked me to marry him. We'd had the most fun relationship, we had such great times, and I thought to myself, if I become Mrs. Sinatra it's all going to change. I didn't want to rein it in, so I turned him down."

One of the stories going around about Angie Dickinson was that she'd given someone a blow job while driving along Mulholland Drive. And somehow that came up once, somebody asked her about it. Angie didn't even blink. "Yes," she said, "that was me. I was in the car with my husband Burt Bacharach; we were married at the time, we were driving home in the car, and I gave him oral sex." Angie was so cool, she didn't skip a beat. She let the guy think about it a minute, then she said, "And I, by the way, was driving."

—■—

In my time I've been involved in a lot of aspects of the music business other than singing and songwriting. Over the years I've tried to help other performers, tried to make a difference. I brought David Clayton Thomas down from Canada and signed him to Atlantic Records. I also remember early in our relationship that rainy night in San Francisco, when I brought David Foster down from Canada on my Learjet. We are at the San Francisco airport, and I arranged for him to get his green card. I also brought John Prine from Chicago and introduced him to

Ahmet Ertegun, president of Atlantic Records, and got him signed to the label. I've also helped John, Steve Goodman, and Odia Coates at various points in their careers. Then along came the incredible Michael Bublé. I was taken with his talent immediately.

At first nobody was interested in him but eventually I got a friend of mine from Australia to put up half a million to record him. Only after that we got him signed to Warner's, much to the chagrin of my Australian friend who otherwise would have made a small fortune.

When I did the Michael Bublé album, I saw a window for a revival of The American Songbook of swing music in Vegas (even though from my point of view it never really disappeared). He could re-present the Sinatra catalog. People have always been fascinated with the Vegas vibe and the Sinatra stuff, when it started to emerge again through Robbie Williams and all other artists who were into that. Michael's voice is a great transmitter for that music. He would come to Vegas, get up on stage with me, watch me work, and throw himself into the process. To underline what he was trying to do I gave him some of Sinatra's arrangements that Frank had given me. After all Frank had given me, I felt so good to be giving back to Michael. I am so happy for his success and how he is handling himself. He is a good guy in a business full of traps. And none of this would have been possible without the astute handling of Bruce Allen, Michael Bublé's manager, who's one of the best in the world, for my money.

Later on, a label in Germany, Centaurus, wanted me to do a swing album. A group of German investors—mostly doctors and lawyers—looking to lose some money! The German government offers an attractive tax credit for film and recording projects.

Initially they asked me to record an album of standards in the Sinatra style. But I said that I wanted no part of it—too obvious, too predictable. I was all for doing a big band album but I didn't want to duplicate Bublé's bag of standards and all the obvious songs. Those had worked for him because of his youth and his demographic appeal. I wanted to take hard rock songs, put them in the swing vibe, and let them have another life. The idea was let's try it and if it doesn't work we'll throw it out. So, that's how *Rock Swings* came about. *Rock Swings'* success started in Germany. It was thanks to the buzz emanating from Germany that Lucine Grange, the head of Universal Records in London, called me and asked me to come to London to make a deal for worldwide distribution. We did—that started the ball rolling. Lucine Grange is one of the smartest record men around in the business. I must give thanks to my German buddies and team who helped bring the project home: Alex Christensen, Juergen Hohmann, Gotz Kiso, all of them stand-up citizens.

I decided to concentrate on songs from the '70s, '80s, and '90s. I said, "I'll only do it if you allow me to find an original approach. For instance, there are songs from the '70s and '80s that are as important to that generation as 'I've Got You Under My Skin' was to an earlier one." I had *Billboard* send over a box filled with the charts covering those decades and made a list of my favorites, then set about making them swing. I turned "Eye of the Tiger" from *Rocky III* into a quasi Mack-the-knife tough-guy thing, complete with a growl at the end. I added the sexiness and romance of the bossa nova to "It's a Sin" by the Pet Shop Boys.

I was pretty familiar with the material because I had five daughters and that stuff was always playing in my house. "Daddy, you gotta listen to this." "Daddy, you have to hear these guys, they're so cool!" They played all kinds of stuff and that made it very easy for me to get to know these singers, these songs. I *was* apprehensive in a sense, but I'm a music person. I've been making records since 1957. I'm not someone who's going to go to do rap or go urban—I see the musicality in Dr. Dre and Eminem but that was a little too much of a stretch for me.

Anyway, as we developed the concept, and it morphed into its own orbit, we saw that this idea might actually work. My focus was now to get it past the critics because, if they took to it, the word would get out and listeners would have an easier time accepting it. I knew there was going to be an initial knee-jerk reaction to me doing this stuff—Anka does Nirvana, what a travesty! I knew some people were going to nail me for it. But I wanted them to at least listen to it. I hoped anyone open-minded enough and musically astute would look at it and go, "You know what, God damn it, I didn't want to like it, but the integrity, the quality is there. These are great songs; let's not pigeonhole them as rock songs."

It did very well. Surprisingly I found I was attracting a younger crowd and it opened my music up to a broader audience. It's cool (after fifty years of doing this) to still be around, period. It's been an incredible journey, and when you finally settle down and look back on everything, you realize how quickly it could have disappeared. The album might seem kitschy to some, but it's not a joke. It's not Pat Boone doing heavy metal—it's no novelty record.

Why court the derision that Pat Boone, a friend and a gentleman, suffered with his album of heavy metal cover songs? On Pat Boone's *In a Metal Mood,* he did a whole sendup. It was camp. He wore the leather. From the get-go, it was funny, and he naturally came in for a lot of flack for it. But this was a totally serious project. The message was: Let these songs find a life in another genre.

I got to use my favorite, Studio A at Capitol Studios in L.A., where Sinatra cut his sides, and where I had worked for years. I hired the best musicians and the best arrangers—Randy Kerber, Patrick Williams, John Clayton—and topped off with Al Schmitt engineering, his assistant Steve Genewick, and a talented producer from Germany, Alex Christensen. There was nothing humorous about this project.

On "Black Hole Sun," I decided to start out doing it as a ballad and then swing it, because with that song, both treatments work. Backed by a seventeen-piece band I tore into "It's My Life," turning Bon Jovi's hit into a brassy swinging song that would not have been out of place at a Sinatra show.

Every decade has its own form of poetry. I saw the grunge thing happening, I dug it, but I thought to myself, *now how do I pull this off? Where do I tie into this?* "Smells Like Teen Spirit" is an anthem, but I figured if I could keep the integrity, do it my way, and still keep it believable, maybe it'll work. I love the melody, the swing style, and the shout chorus. I think what I brought to it mirrors the angst of the original record. Hey, it works for me. "Smells Like Teen Spirit" works with a swing arrangement because it's poetry and it has a real cool melody to swing to—we did a romping chart on that one. I wanted to take unusual songs and do them a different way. The standards, those I can do in my sleep, they're easy. But this stuff was challenging.

David Grohl, Kurt Cobain's former drummer, saw me performing "Smells Like Teen Spirit" on TV and said, "It wasn't until halfway through the first verse that I thought, holy shit, that's 'Teen Spirit'! And I thought it was fucking amazing," he told *Rolling Stone*. "I thought it was so great." Well, al-*right*!

There was no doubt I was sticking my neck out on this album—and I did get a few whacks for it. The *Hamilton Spectator* said, "Chihuahuas should not be crossed with great Danes. And Paul Anka should not be allowed to sing 'Smells Like Teen Spirit.'"

When people ask me why I'm still so hungry for a hit, all I can say is: "I think I know what I'm doing at this point in my life. I can handle it. Could I have done it twenty years ago? Would I have had the balls? Probably not." If the guys who reviewed *Rock Swings,* or played it on the radio, thought it was a giggle, all the better. People have chuckled at me all throughout my career, so I'm used to it. I take it as a compliment, actually.

Back in 2005 and 2006 when I was recording *Rock Swings* and getting ready to release it, I had a chance to go with Sony Records but after meeting Randy Lennox, who runs Universal Records in Canada, I realized what a great CEO he was. Going with him was one of the best decisions I ever made. I was proud to be associated with Randy, Shawn Marino, Tyson Parker, and the whole Universal group. For introducing me to Randy Lennox I have to thank Peter Soumalias, who founded Canada's Walk of Fame in 1996 and inducted me in 2005. After meeting his new wife Barbara, who Lisa and I cherish as friends, we arranged for them to be married at the home of my dear friends Bob and Audrey Byers in California. My neighbor, Frank Visco, helped to arrange that special event, which meant so much to Randy and Barbara and his family. *Rock Swings* brought me together with a group who are brothers forever, and then business associates. Shawn Marino is as close to perfect as you will find, no business bullshit, right to the point. He has great passion for his work. Tyson Parker totally focused on getting the PR job done. Yes, that entire Universal Music Group. *Rock Swings*, swung, because of those guys' efforts and my go-to guy and great agent, Jeff Craib. Because of their efforts, indeed, success had many fathers.

Performers have glamour and that has enormous appeal to business-people, and to the world at large. We walk in this separate kind of world, and people who are successful in business—these CEOs of big companies—they have everything, but there's one thing they don't have, and that every self-respecting performer has to have: charisma. They crave it like mad, because that's the magic magnet. That's the reason that guys with the power and the ego all want to sit next to actresses and they all want to get laid. They love the glow of celebrity, they love being around it, so we always have to be careful about who wants us and for what and deal with it accordingly. I've found that businesspeople tend to gravitate to me for favors, maybe make a phone call to someone they want to meet. Or else it has to do with some business deal, someone they want an "in" with. One of the things I've learned about billionaires is that their "yes" is usually a "maybe."

The people who come to Vegas are a very transient group: there are the high rollers and there are the tourists who come there like they would to Disneyland. Vegas is Disneyland for adults anyway, and you never know night to night who the hell is going to show up. I was working down at the Golden Nugget for Steve Wynn in the mid-eighties, and I get a call from the maître d' Johnny Joseph, one of the best in town, who was always on top of his game.

"There's this Saudi guy who's been to a few shows, Prince something-or-other, and he wants to meet you."

"Well, why, do you think?" I ask.

"Don't know, but Steve would like you to say hello to him."

We finish the show, and this guy comes back, he's dressed in Western clothing, but he carries himself with that whole Saudi royalty demeanor. A Saudi princeling. He has his banker with him and he proceeds to explain the meeting. Likes my music, says, "I know that you know Adnan Khashoggi, who used to be the representative for the Saudis, but I do the deals for them now, for the arms and the planes." He's impressing me with who he is. Meanwhile I'm waiting for the other shoe to drop.

"But I want you to do me a favor," he says.

"Okay, what is it?"

"I know you know Brooke Shields. 'Cause she used to be at Khashoggi's parties, and I know that you know the mother, and also the father."

"Yeah?"

"So I want to meet her."

I'm thinking, *Great, another Arab who wants to get laid.* God gave us a penis and a brain, but not enough blood for both.

So I say, "Do you mind me asking to what purpose? I just can't call her mother out of the blue, because as you know this is a young girl with a mother who's all over her and I don't want to be put in any precarious or awkward position."

"Well, let me tell you . . ."—so *thick* Middle Eastern accent—"I hear she wants to do a Brenda Starr detective movie and I hear she can't get the financing. And I would like to give her the money."

And I'm going, "O-kay. But why?"

"Well, the truth is, I just want to just meet her. If you just get her the message, tell her she's got the money, then we can all meet wherever you say. I will send my airplane to wherever she is and we can all meet somewhere on the West Coast."

"Hmm . . . Let me think about it overnight and I'll let you know."

"Well, I'll come back to the show tomorrow night," he says.

The next day I call Brooke's mother. She puts Brooke on the phone. I tell her, "Look, don't kill the messenger, but here's what it is. There's a guy, a Saudi prince, and he wants to give you backing if you're still looking to do this Brenda Starr movie."

"*Yes!* I've been trying to get financing for ages and no one will put up the money. I can't get it financed to save my life."

"Well, look, don't hold me responsible for any of the left or right kicks, any of the dynamics that may go down—you're on your own with that, you're a big girl. But in the meantime I'm going to arrange a meeting with this guy at my house in Carmel."

So I call the prince. "Great," he says, "I'll see you tonight, yes?" He comes down to the club with all his people, and says, "Follow me." We go out after the show and I see about fifty people outside of the Golden Nugget, all of whom are murmuring about something they're eyeing on the pavement. The crowd separates and I see this *huge* custom-made car called a Zimmer, it's a neo-classic car, sort of like a Stutz Bearcat, an outrageous over-the-top retro vehicle, just short of a pimp car. It's got wood paneling and leather seats—all decked out. An incredible car—huge and long as a ship. He hands me the keys to the car and says, "It's yours."

I say, "Well, I don't . . . uh . . . you don't have to. . . ." The truth is I don't really want the car, it's a bit of a monstrosity.

"No, please!" he insists.

He gets in with me and we drive down the strip, and people are looking and honking. I don't want to make him feel bad because I know from meeting other Arabs, they don't take kindly to someone saying no.

We talk about our business *blah blah blah,* and I take the Zimmer home. I can't even get it in the driveway; my wife's ready to kill me. "Aw, don't worry, we'll keep it a while and then sell the thing," I tell her. "I can't seriously keep a car like this, I just don't want to offend this guy."

The following week he sends his 737 plane to Princeton, where

Brooke is in school. The mother and secretary also come out to be with her. The prince drives up to my house with thirty people. I had a guitarist playing nice mellow tunes under the stairs of my huge living room. I put tables and chairs out. They're cooking their special food and they're all over my house—my kids think I'm totally nuts. I drive down to the airport and I get Brooke off the plane and I tell her and her mother, "Now look, this is what it is, don't be nervous, I'll guide you through this, make sure everybody's happy, nothing gets out of hand *buh buh buh.*"

We're all at dinner, the prince is there, he's drinking and leaning toward Brooke and I'm propping him up, trying to avoid an awkward situation. I can obviously see what his intentions are but we're not going to let it get into anything like that. After dinner we go dancing and clubbing, and I'm just crossing my fingers. It's all to culminate the next day when they're going to throw a big lunch at a local hotel owned by my closest friend when I lived in Carmel, Ted Balestreri, he and his wife Velma. I have adored them both for years and cherish their friendship. Anyway, there we are in the midst of mounds of rice and lamb and more Middle Eastern delicacies. We sit down and we're getting through the lunch and Brooke says she wants to get back to school and the mother wants the check and you know what the prince wants—he wants *her.* He's way down on the end of the bench by now. So we finish and I say, "Okay, let's go out and talk the talk." There's me and the prince and the banker and the mother and Brooke. And we start talking.

In the end, Brooke gets the sixteen million dollars to make the movie. They give the mother the money, everybody disperses, she gets off the plane in Princeton, and there's a brand-new Mercedes waiting for her. Meanwhile, I've still got the Zimmer that I don't want sitting in my driveway like the *Queen Mary* in dry dock. So the kid gets her Mercedes, I get the Zimmer, Mom gets the money, and they start to make the movie. At this point I bow out of the picture for other reasons entirely. He wants to do other business with me but I discover there are some other characters involved that I don't want to be in business with. I've learned my lesson from my dealings with Khashoggi.

A few months later I'm performing at the Sporting Club in beautiful Monte Carlo. Brooke's off doing her movie. In the interim I hear they ran short of money, so the prince gives her a few more million. Meanwhile, on the nightly news I'm seeing a certain Clark Clifford and his attorney, Robert Altman, who was married to TV's Wonder Woman, Lynda Carter. Clark Clifford was a banker and Wonder Woman had moved to Washington to marry Altman, Clark Clifford's partner. There's some big bank scandal that is becoming the big news topic on the nightly news.

Bottom line, I get a call from the investigative department of the *L.A. Times*. I'll never forget it, I'm sitting on my terrace at the Hôtel de Paris overlooking the harbor in Monte Carlo and the reporter says, "Can I ask you a few questions?"

"Yeah, sure, what about?"

"Uh, I just want to ask you. About a Saudi prince. And the money that he gave to Brooke Shields, is all that true?"

And I said, "Well, wait a minute, what's 'all that'?"

He says, "Well, what's the link?"

"Look, first of all I don't know what you're going after and I'm going to tell you just what I need to tell you because it's none of your business. I arranged for the financing for the Brenda Starr film and that's about it. What's *your* interest?"

"You know what's going on with Clark Clifford and Robert Altman and the bank scandal?" he says. "Well, they were all tied in together with that bank."

"That's goddamn news to me," I say. "I didn't know anything about who they were tied into, and, yes, I arranged for the money. And, yes, she got the movie, but other than that I have no idea who they were involved with, so I can't help you."

I hung up and couldn't believe it. Who woulda thunk it? The press was all over this bank scandal. The prince was never accused of any wrongdoing, and Altman was eventually acquitted of all charges. What a scene!

No wonder the guy spent money like water. This prince—you knew if he came to see a show and hung out, he was good for three or four million a night. So a big spender like that, you needed to say hello to him. Whatever scandals he was or wasn't involved in, I didn't know any more about him than the man in the moon. At the time the reporter called I was still thinking, what the hell am I gonna do with that big tank of a car?

—■—

One night while I am working at the Riviera Hotel in Vegas, I get a call from a charming gentlemen, who I knew worked for Adnan Khashoggi. His name was Victor Danenza. He said, "Paul, Adnan Khashoggi wants you to do us a favor." He says, "I am in town with royalty from an island in Asia. They don't know him here at the hotel and they will not give him credit." The fact that I was working there, they knew I had contacts that could help them. He went on to say, "So, you see, they just won't give him the money, and I was wondering if you could meet him and his family, give him some CDs, autograph some photos, and take them to the movies, make them happy 'cause we need to arrange some cash for him. They're nice people." Okay, I go over. Pleasant family, bunch of kids. We go to the movies, kill time, come back to the casino, and they get it worked out—barely. Gave him $50,000, which is nothing in that world!

We're talking casually and I ask, "By the way, who is he?" And the guy says, "The Prince of Brunei." One of the richest men in the world! And they only gave him $50,000. It's a casino, but they don't know anything at these places outside the city limits. In Vegas they don't know from Prince the dog to Prince Ali Baba.

Then there's another Middle Eastern crisis: the fraught relationship between Adnan Khashoggi and Mohamed Al-Fayed—the guy who bought Harrods and whose son Dodi was dating Princess Diana.

The connection between Fayed and Adnan is an interesting and tangled one, Khashoggi claiming Fayed was a Singer sewing machine salesman when he hired him and Fayed saying Khashoggi worked for *him* and that he'd had to fire Khashoggi because of his gambling habits. Whatever the story was, the two families were intimately connected when Adnan Khashoggi's sister, Samira, married Fayed and became the mother of Dodi Fayed.

As I stated earlier, Khashoggi's empire fell in 1988 when he was arrested in Switzerland for concealing funds, but was ultimately acquitted. Fayed comes into power, buys Harrods, etc. and suddenly there's this young kid called Dodi Fayed running around, his son. I'd known him as a kid; now he'd grown up, and every now and then I'd bump into him. Sweet enough guy, kind of wants to get into show business, winds up over here because he's into the Hollywood thing—he's trying to make movies. He's Daddy's boy, and you know a father is a father and doing the best that he can to help him. Dodi looks up to me in a father-figure kind of way, but I know he's heavy with the cocaine and he's getting into skirmishes about his rent and so on. News travels fast in this town. I'm hearing all this stuff, but I don't judge him for it. I try and give him advice, tell him he's with the wrong women, but young and wild kids will do what they will do. Ultimately he gets a winner movie, *Chariots of Fire*.

I'm not running with his crowd, because they're young and with a group like that with no brakes it's always a bad ending. One day Dodi comes to see me, and says, "I gotta talk to you." He meets me at the Ivy, a superhip local watering hole. He begins with a big long ramble, which already makes me nervous.

"Paul, as you know we go way back, our two families, *blah, blah, blah.* I've known you all these years, and your family stayed at the Ritz, And we were all tight with Adnan. . . ."

"Yes, yes, of course."

"But I got a big problem."

"What is it?"

"Well, I was coming through customs from Europe and I didn't declare some money and they took $150,000 from me and I can't tell my dad."

"Okay. What do you want me to do?"

"Could you just loan it to me for a week?"

Now, I don't like loaning money. There came a point in my life where I realized, I don't want to make a liar out of anybody. You loan someone money, you're making a liar out of them from that day on because you never get the money back. I mean, I could make a long list of the people to whom I've loaned money, and then never heard from again.

I said, "Dodi, look, I don't loan money; don't put me in that position because—"

He pleaded; he was afraid to tell his father. "I beg of you, Paul. Please, just loan it to me. One week."

Well, I knew his dad, I'd stayed at the Ritz, the Fayeds were always very courteous. I don't know what got me to agree, but I did. I said, "Go to this address; go to Merrill Lynch, *buh buh buh,* and pick up the money."

He picks up the money. End of the week I try to reach him. He's in Australia chasing the actress Tawny Kitaen.

I think, *Okay, let me call Australia.* "Dodi, I thought you were supposed to—"

"Well, I came down here, I'm starting a movie thing, and *duh duh duh.*"

"But Dodi, you promised."

"No no. Don't worry. As soon as I come home this week I'll get you the money."

He comes home, gives me a check, Bank of America. I go to cash it and it's bouncing all over the room. Wall to wall, *boom boom boom.* I can't believe it. I call him.

"Dodi, I told you I didn't want to loan you this money. What are you thinking? And how dare you? What are you up to?"

"Oh no, I'm so sorry. It should have been in there. There's a Bank of Scotland in London, I'm transferring the funds tomorrow."

I know now that I'm smack in the middle of a bullshit story. And I'm livid. Checking around I realize that he hasn't even paid his rent for months, he owes people money for jewelry, and he's living way beyond his means.

Dodi gives me the name of a bank in London that I'm getting the money from, and I wait till about 12:30 at night—I'm living in L.A. and I call the bank, just out of the blue. I take a shot, I got nothing to lose, I'm already losing, and I ask for the bank manager. He turns out to be a fan. I give him a number to call me back, so he can check that it's me.

He says, "Mr. Anka, you know I'm not supposed to give out bank information, but I feel that you're telling me the truth, as to what the situation is. Let me be frank with you—this guy's been a problem. There is not enough money in that account to cover your check."

I go, "Oh, Jesus!"

I wake Dodi up, it's one in the morning by now, and I'm shouting, my voice is in the 120 decibel range. I'm so loud my wife comes down, thinking I'm being attacked by some intruder.

"You be here tomorrow," I tell Dodi. "Or you're going to jail." He comes over and in the afternoon pleads his case—the why and the what and the wherefore.

"You know what?" I tell him. "You need to be taught a lesson. You just can't do this to people. And it's not just me; I found out you've been doing this all over town.

"You are behind with your rent with that prominent lawyer in Los Angeles whose house you have been living in—way behind in your rent. There's a host of people you owe money: these girls, the jewelry, the doctors. How can you do this? I'm going to save you; you need help. I'm going to call your father."

"Don't call my father," he says. "Don't call Daddy."

He leaves. I call his father. "Fayed? How are you *blah blah blah*. I'm a parent, you're a parent. I think I'm doing the right thing here for you. I'm going to help you with your son; he's in big trouble over here with this one and that one. And now me, and I am right on the verge of calling the police."

"Please don't do that," he says. "Don't do a thing, don't call the police. I'm sending my brother in, and someone from our law firm; he'll be in your office tomorrow."

They show up, and a checkbook is put in front of me. "How much do you want? Name any amount."

"Only what you owe me, of course. I just want my $150,000 back." They give me the check, shut down Dodi's house, pay off all his bills, put him on a plane, and take him back to England.

Two weeks later I get a call from the doctor who treated Fayed's son Dodi. She talks in this very regal manner. "Mr. Anka, first of all, you know, I went to school with your wife in Egypt; please give her my best. Second of all, I want to thank you for what you've done for this family in sending this boy back. He needed the help badly."

Next thing I know I'm laying in bed at the Mirage Hotel in Vegas, where I was performing. It was months later and I'm watching the news on television. They interrupt the program with a news bulletin. It was about Princess Di and the car crash in the tunnel. You know when you just get up, like I did today, and there's not even a transition from sleep to being awake? I haven't even gotten kissed on the mouth yet and something like this hits you. It's like *WOOOWACK!* I see the car in the tunnel and I think I'm dreaming. My brain can't even take it in.

I've just gotten over the business of the loan to Dodi, just put the money in the bank, and now this. Suddenly I remember that Dodi was always very security conscious. He was paranoid. Frightened all the time about kidnapping, holdups, vendettas. And when he got involved with Princess Di all that anxiety must have increased exponentially because the paparazzi were on them day and night. Always living with the fear that somebody might want to kill him—or her.

The tragedy that took their lives was a sad and devastating end to a fairy story Dodi and Diana were beginning to write for themselves. It was so unexpected and unnecessary and such a terrible waste. I was very fond of Dodi. We lost him too soon.

———■———

They say you should never go home again, and after the way I'd been treated in Ottawa in the past I just stopped going back. That started a twenty-some-year personal Cold War with me. When I get ticked off, I get ticked off.

I'd gotten a scathing concert review in the local paper, the *Ottawa Citizen,* and in a 1962 cover story in *Maclean's* (Canada's answer to *Life* magazine), they called me "the world's reigning juvenile" and went on to say, "Although most Canadians can be excused for shuddering at the thought, our best-known countryman abroad is indisputably a squat, bowlegged rock'n' roll singer named Paul Anka."

But in April 27, 2002, I returned for a fund-raising at the Ottawa Congress Centre for the Canadian Liver Foundation. Basically I came back in memory of my mother, Camy, who was thirty-seven years old when she died of complications from diabetes in 1961.

My mother had witnessed my early success, but her untimely death meant she didn't live to see me really make it. My father, Andy, worked with me regularly and helped run Jubilation, my Las Vegas disco. When my dad died in 1993, at the age of seventy-four, I began reflecting on my feelings about not having my parents at the upcoming gala. Not having them there meant a piece was missing. My mother's death was from complications brought on by diabetes, so it was symbolic for me to come back to raise money for another desperately needy cause, pediatric liver research.

I know they thought it was a long shot, trying to entice me home to perform, especially after I had refused previous overtures by concert promoters to get me to return to Ottawa. I hadn't played there publicly since August 1981. But this time, they were ready to acknowledge me.

April 26, 2002, was named Paul Anka Day. The concert raised $250,000, so I was happy to be back, and to give back.

I'm sorry my mom never got to see it; she was my ally. She made the difference. My father was a straight-shooter, a practical person who was initially skeptical about my chances in a singing career. He wanted me in a legitimate business and back then show business to him wasn't legitimate. But he would have been thrilled to see me welcomed back by Ottawa's mayor and the prime minister.

—■—

I do believe there is a master plan. I believe that we are all given a gift. I also believe in luck and guardian angels. I believe there's an angel on my shoulder guiding me—or how else would I have made it this far?

One of my problems—careerwise—is that I haven't messed up enough. Seriously. Stories of success are always most interesting (and marketable!) when there are tragedies, when they're entwined with setbacks (well, I *have* had those), outrageous behavior, controversy, drug addiction, and despair. This has not been my lot (or ambition!) in life, and a career without them can seem as monotonous as a love story without a breakup.

In today's society it would probably do me good if I could get a little discoloration to my reputation. People love that. If I were to go out and tell all, or get a little funkier, there'd be an even bigger audience out there to eat it up. There are even a few popular national magazines that have offered to put me on the cover if I'd—shall we say—"open up a bit." It doesn't even have to be true, they tell me.

Well, come to think of it, there has been a frightening lack of boredom in my life in recent years. Around 2008, not only did I have the good luck to become the father of another great kid, but I had a second marriage, and a really scary divorce.

—■—

I was married for thirty-seven years. Despite our ups and downs, my ex and I are still friends. We can proudly say that we learned from one another, built a lifetime of memories, and have proudly raised five beautiful daughters all of whom I am, of course, very proud of. My second marriage ended in eighteen months. Need I say more?

So, I suppose, it will suffice to say the following: Anna Aberg and I met when she was my fitness trainer. Our courtship was quick, she was tall and blonde, I was a man in my sixties who, well, appreciated that she was tall and blonde. I am a man who can admit my weaknesses. At the time, she was in the middle of an ugly, messy divorce.

In the beginning everything between us seemed fine and that's the way we appeared in public. But you have to remember that we were only married a year and an inch by the time you heard us on *The Howard Stern Show*, telling this beautiful sexy fairy-story romance about our life together. On the inside things were quite different.

The problem is, in this age of reality TV, tabloid obsession, where society is bred to put their lives on display, whilst being a voyeur into the lives of others—not saying more is often an application of something far more sinister. So you find yourself at a crossroads. Do I answer the questions? Do I tell the tales about my ex-wife? Do I go through the details of what occurred and landed me in family court? Trust me, I have gone back and forth over this very question. And—I am still not 100 percent convinced of my answer. The problem is, this marriage in question produced a son, Ethan Paul. He, along with my daughters, is one of the profound joys of my life. To put this marriage under a microscope, while titillating to some—would put him in the position where one day, when he is surfing the Internet or sitting in a bookstore, he will have to confront every word that I have written here.

We live in a day and age when the world at large doesn't care, people have become accustomed to outrageous behavior. Even amongst presidents. I've gone through fifty-five years of being in the public eye with never a drug or a sex scandal. I've never been in the tabloids for any reason. The big problem today is the need to fill time on television, the twenty-four-hour newscasts.

I've had it so good in my life that ten years ago you could have danced on my grave. The wonderful thing about a child, especially at my age, is that you're no longer thinking of yourself, it's all about him—Ethan. I find myself doing things for him that I don't do for anybody else. It's all about my boy, it's all about Ethan. It's not about me anymore. When I see Ethan and how much he adores my girlfriend Lisa Pemberton it makes it all worth while. She is a very giving and good person.

My advice, for what it's worth, is to take precautions, keep your eyes open. There's a lot of men out there who have really suffered at the hands of women like Anna because of the inane divorce and custody laws and the way the legal system works. That's why I think I have to talk about it. I think the story has to get out there. I had lengthy discussions about the dilemma with my attorney Craig Leeds, a really good guy and a great lawyer, as to what can be done in the legislature about this horrible state of affairs in child custody and divorce and so on in California.

Craig Leeds was also intrinsically involved in my custodial divorce settlements with Anna. Eddie de Bartolo Jr. has been one of my dearest friends for years and is one of the greatest pals you could ever have. He's a big shopping mall developer—huge—and onetime owner of the 49ers. Heart of gold, helps his fellow man, and loves his friends and charities, one of the most giving people you will ever meet, a man's man to boot and just an all-around fun guy. I adore him as a brother. So, after all the disturbing business of my divorce from Anna, who better to go and hang out with than Eddie, his wife Candy, and his wonderful family. So, in July of 2011, Ethan, Lisa, and I went for a much needed getaway to his ranch in Montana where he held this great three-day Fourth of July event. Ethan loved the fireworks, the food, the show, and the spectacular environment. It was a joyful and healing experience that allowed us to put the past behind us and begin a happier, more loving phase of our lives together.

Twelve

AND NOW
FOR MY ENCORE

Showbiz is unpredictable but sometimes you get lucky in the timing. As hard as I worked, as focused as I kept myself, with as much discipline as I could muster, I still question, Was I supposed to last this long? I took my fifteen minutes of fame and worked it into a lifetime. This little guy about two feet taller than a fire hydrant—incredible.

Coming from a small town in Canada and not having a lot to begin with, I learned at a young age that I had been given this incredible chance. I knew if I blew this, it was a big shame on me.

Coming from a modest background, it's mind-bending to be thrust out in front of people and money and all that glamour. There's some kind of curse that goes with it. And if you don't realize that much, it could be over very quickly.

My father always said, "Things are going to change" and they always have. My philosophy is: Every day is a brand-new day. You don't have any expectations in life, you will be fine. I live in the moment and forget everything else. That's the way I've been all my life because while you're down here planning, God is up there laughing. I learned from my mistakes very early. In life, you make choices and every choice has a consequence. I took the blows.

Success in this business is not all about talent. There are so many variables. We're kind of pressured into marketing ourselves, creating an image. Art has no time.

People aren't aware of the business I run. You have to be aware. You gotta be sharp. I keep my eyes wide open. I sign every check myself, every contract. My focus all my life has been a decision to keep my eye on the ball and to continue doing what I'm doing to feed that hunger, that desire, that ongoing gut sense that I've always had, never to resign myself, to get complacent. I haven't put my flag on the mountaintop yet.

One of the secrets to having a long-running career is living a preventative lifestyle. I eat well. I drink a little wine, maybe a glass of brandy. I exercise regularly, mostly cardiovascular workouts, weights, and the occasional yoga routine. I consume huge amounts of an eclectic array of vegetables and fruit that have antioxidant value and serve me well in this preventative lifestyle. I drink a lot of tea (especially green tea), water, and certain juices. I saw my friend Sammy Davis Jr. slowly kill himself from abuse and I wasn't going to follow him down that path.

You have to be fit to go onstage, because in a sense you're like an athlete. You take the average player in a football game—it's fourteen minutes of action out of a three-hour game. I'm up there for two hours with high intensity. I've been around guys that shot up heroin. I hung around with the Rat Pack and saw what too much drink does to you and too much coke. I saw Sammy Davis die. Even around Sinatra and those guys, I never went over the line in terms of that line we all walk in life. I never went too far left or too far right from the center line we all walk in life.

But no matter who you are and what you've done, I've seen it, I've done it. Curiosity has always been a driving force in my life. I've been on drug raids with New York cops and other crazy adventures just because I wanted to find out what it was. Like trying out my nerves on the flying trapeze. My manager Irv Feld became the owner of the

Ringling Bros. and Barnum & Bailey Circus after we parted—he was always mad about the circus and so was I. I would say, "One day Irv, I want to go up on that high wire. I want to do that and fly around up there like those guys." He always discouraged me, but then one day I talked him into it. He took me down there with one of those acrobat families, the Flying Wallendas. They dressed me up in the gear and I went up the ladder—up, up, up until I was way up there at the top of Madison Square Garden. Way below me is the net. They walked me through the whole thing. I was up there flying and catching and swinging and dropping. I don't have a fear of heights—but still! Let me tell you, that was a pretty scary dive falling into a little net, forty feet below, but I was curious and wanted that first hand experience.

I have made 123 albums in English, Spanish, German, Italian. Every time I walk into the audience—when I am performing—is truly when I feel feedback of how I have affected people's lives. It is there that I feel what they sincerely give back to me. I am one lucky guy. You become a different person when you are onstage, because you are in an altered state. All the stuff that swirls around you during the day that can get aggravating—the phones, contracts, the business—vanishes. The moment you get up on stage that's what it's all about. There are no more phones, no more intrusion. It's all about that moment you're in—this love fest with these people in front of you. You can't flinch. You can't miss a step because they will sense it. It's like animals with meat. It's all so intense you can only focus on that. You're totally *there*. You've forgotten everything else; you can't *think* of anything else. You're only dealing in this incredible state of being.

The orchestra is motivating you into another dimension, you're now into the mathematical structure of every beat per bar, and every word that needs to go into that beat, every thought process is tuned in to act out what you're singing about. You're locked in there. There is nothing like it. It's almost like landing that aircraft. You're getting down to 120 miles per hour as you hit the runway. Your whole focus is in that instant. You've turned into another person, really. You're an actor—

singers are actors and as such you have to control everything around you. That band is feeding off of you. You're dressed differently. You're thinking differently, you're acting differently, you're feeling differently. What you're feeling is unlike anything you've done all day. You're dealing with the *unknown*—every minute you have to be improvising in response to whatever might happen. You're dealing with a look on the face of someone in the audience, a fan who rushes on stage and grabs you. There is nothing else that you do in your life that compares to that because of the nature of what it is. It's art and drama fused—with the music, the swelling rhythms of the band and the intimate lyrics, it's as if you have actually injected yourself into the audience's head.

I feel I have to capture the audience in the first ten minutes of each concert. The second I walk out onstage and all my vibes are open to getting a sense of what's happening in this particular space with these particular people on this particular evening. I always go out and perform like it's my first time. I've never thrown a show—I couldn't if I tried. I'm hooked, working the only way I know. If you do enough bad shows, you're out of business. Some nights you wonder how you're to go on, but the magic of what that is and the music and all of that turns you right on. It's the strangest thing. It's the next best thing to sex, maybe because whatever all those buttons are that get pushed that make it good, are the same. When I get up there, I don't want to just be good, I want to be *great*. It's a very odd occupation if you even want to call it that, because it isn't even work.

If you bomb, you have to learn from that. You have to make a decision and a choice to say, "I am still going to get them. I am going to do the best that I can here and get through this without blowing my cool or letting it get to me." I got through it.

Performing has never been traumatic for me. I never ran away or tried to escape or do anything to cover up my fright. I didn't need to be juiced out. I've tried marijuana, coke—I've tried everything, just tried, but I never went onstage in any kind of out-of-it condition. Performing was never a problem for me. I rather enjoyed it; even in the very beginning, I looked forward to it actually, from childhood on. I get a pulse the second I walk out on stage and all my vibes are open. I get so excited I can feel my nipples—and I didn't even know I had nipples!

As casual as Dean Martin appeared, I guarantee you there were nights that he would go onstage and he was scared. Annette Funicello was afraid of going onstage. On the other extreme, some people get a little *too* relaxed. When I was at Caesars Palace, I gave the Pointer Sisters and Freddie Prinze both a chance to open for me. They were so whacked out on coke and everything else, they couldn't finish the second night. The entertainment director Sid Gathrid at Caesars Palace, had to fire them and remove them from my show. They wanted them out of town and out of the building. A very sad commentary when you see such young talent with great potential.

I went whenever I could to watch Sinatra and the others. I saw that loose, carefree style of showmanship and that stuck with me. I realized it's one thing to just go out and sing and another to really entertain people.

Men and women are different. If a relationship is going to work, you have to first be friends, and as long as you have a friendship and an understanding along with the love you're going to be okay. When that goes you are just rolling the dice. In Austria back in the 1700s, somebody made disparaging remarks about the mistress of the king and there was an eighteen-year war over it! So you look at the power of that little piece of real estate—it's amazing—whether it's Eliott Spitzer to Tiger Woods or Jesse James, Sandra Bullock's ex-husband. That was a sweet trick with the king of Austria. That one has always *amazed* me. And you know what, it's never gonna change. It ultimately becomes an ego thing: guys get to a certain age and they want to keep up with the pack and make sure they're still vital, and their ego comes into play and they want to make sure they can still do it, and then they find out after the first honeymoon this isn't the ultimate sexual trip they thought it would be. Which leads us to the crude philosophy that's out there. Successful guys in today's world who've got all the money, all the position, they've got all the toys, they've got this and that—now what's really left? Women. A lot of guys I knew in the business, right down to Bob Hope, used to have women stashed all over the place, got a massage every day, and visited a girlfriend whenever he could. Ahhhh, life! It's amazing, isn't it? Wonderful. *Wonderful.* Just hang on tight! It's going to be a hell of a ride.

Sometimes a fan will get *too* excited and do crazy stuff. This happened to me once up at Grossinger's in the Catskills when it was Ladies Night Only. I was walking through the tables, doing "Put Your Head on My Shoulder," and looking for someone to act out the little scene with me. The tables were tightly packed together and as I squeezed past a woman at a crowded table she suddenly grabbed me by my cock— and wouldn't let go. I swear my voice was getting higher, and I am eyeing her as fiercely as I can, and trying to keep it going—but for her this is not a catch-and-release situation apparently. Then I figure, what if I pretend to go with it? I open my arms as if to embrace her, she loosens her grip, and I move away.

I'm very fond of older women, meaning women of a certain age— mine. I'll tell you how I once did a bunch of old girls a really good deed. It is always a great feeling when you can help someone. Make a difference and give something back and put your celebrity to use.

When I moved to Vegas in the early '70s, it was way off the strip and at the end of town. So here was this huge golf course and one hotel across the street, the Tropicana. Steve Wynn was my neighbor three doors down when I first moved there. There were only eight homes on this private driveway that paralleled Tropicana Avenue. There wasn't really that much action up at our end of town, which was fine with me. I had my recording studio, I was enjoying being there; it was quiet and peaceful. A few years go by, then one day I get a call from a Chinese real estate developer. "Hi, Mr. Anka, are you interested in selling your house?" I said, "What? No, I'm not interested, my house and property are not for sale." He kept persisting. Every two or three weeks he'd call and I'd say, "It's still not for sale, go somewhere else."

One day I am speaking to my friend and then-agent Mort Viner, Dean Martin's agent at ICM, and for some reason we started talking about Kirk Kerkorian. We marveled at the fact that he played tennis at least four days a week at his age and how he kept Mort running around the tennis court. He went on to say what a smart guy Kirk was. I said, "Yeah, I love Kirk, I go way back to the fifties with him." Then he says, "Ya know, he's quietly buying up the properties surrounding the Tropicana Golf Course. He's got this Chinese guy buying all that real estate over there for him and they're going to put up this huge MGM Hotel right on the strip there." A little bell goes off in my head. Kirk buys the golf course for about thirty-some million but they also need these homes, specifically mine because there's no access unless they have my property and the rest of the houses. Steve had moved by then but the rest of the houses were owned by elderly widowers.

They start coming at us to buy our properties and they go after the women but, of course, they lowball them, trying to get everybody out for like $120,000 a shot. I got all these women together and I said, "Now look, you all be careful, because they are trying to lowball this away from you, 'cause if you sell and after taxes and everything else, where are you going to move to? Just contact me every time you get a call, because we got to fight this out."

In the early '90s, I get into a tug-of-war battle with the MGM Corporation about this land, and all of the sudden I start hearing from Kirk. He comes to my shows at the Desert Inn—which coincidently, he owned. He came backstage—"How have you been?"

After we get past the small talk, I said, "Kirk, where are these women going to go? Why are you trying to lowball these homes—our properties—from us? We are not trying to hold you up; we just want what is fair." He replies, "Oh, well, you know . . ."

Anyway, it starts to get real wild. It is all over television, newspapers, etc. Nothing is getting resolved. It gets down to where we are going to court and let a judge decide. What they did was get the properties classified as eminent domain. Our properties are now classified as commercial properties but the eminent domain card is suspect because there was no substance for the property's usage—other than maybe a bus stop. I informed them that since our properties are now put in a commercial category, that I could have In-N-Out Burger putting up a sign on my property, and Steve Wynn, who I called, was prepared to put up a Siegfried and Roy sign. The MGM executives were not pleased.

The irony of the story is that when my children were growing up in Vegas and going to school, Anne and I would take them, when they needed shoes, to the Becker family shoe store. Our children knew the Becker children, as they went to school with them. We had a very warm and ongoing relationship with the Becker family. In the ensuing years, the father passed away and we, of course, embraced them in their loss and continued to frequent their establishment. Time goes by, as it does, and as we reach a stalemate with the MGM Corporation, we have no choice but to go to court. Lo and behold we go before the judge. Guess what? Mr. Becker's little daughter, whom we knew well, has now grown up to become one of the most prominent judges in the Las Vegas County.

She looks at the case and says to the MGM lawyers, "I know what you guys are up to and you are not going to do this. I know Mr. Anka, his reputation, and the type of man that he is. More importantly, I want resolution to this case." She shuts them down. We all received a fair amount of money, especially what I asked for the women, who after taxes, were now able to move and live in the style they were accustomed to—for what little life they all had left. Everything turned out fair, as opposed to the big corporation screwing everyone. Subsequently, Kirk and I have remained friends and live to chuckle about it.

———■———

At this juncture in my life I look at the industry that I grew up in, still participate in, and love so much, and see all the new dynamics that are coming into play—the good, but mostly the bad. Most of all I am very grateful that my fans still get that collective joy from seeing me perform live, because we live in a time when the public is not going to shows the way they used to. I'm as curious as ever as to what is happening to this industry, the huge, rapid changes that have taken place, thinking about the fate of radio, broadcast TV, newspapers—at this point the future of all media is precarious.

As was ever the case, rust and greed never sleep, and we're in a time where greed is as rampant and rapacious as it ever was. It's the music business, but first and foremost it has always got to be about the music, otherwise there will be no longevity to your career. There's a whole new crowd out there. All they want to do is line their pockets—the feeding frenzy is way beyond old-fashioned greed, and yet they are constantly whining about not having enough money; meanwhile they care less and less about the music, and too much about their bank accounts. Money is the root of all evil. I'm amused by the spectacle of artists who have the ability to sell out at concerts and move impressive amounts of product, but who induce such trepidation in so many people in my business that they are afraid to criticize them. Who would want to stifle criticism? Criticism keeps the music business healthy. If all you want in this industry is to make a fast buck, I don't want you in my sandbox.

Ah yes, the agents, the promoters, executives, and unfortunately some of the artists. Some of the people who represent these artists know nothing about the business. I've observed how frantically they embrace disposable music and make it momentarily popular. But the fact that it's hyped doesn't make it good. Just because someone is selling a new flavor of the month doesn't mean it doesn't suck. You have all this over-the-top PR coming at you every day about acts where you couldn't name one of their songs if your life depended on it. Don't for a minute think that what is so-called successful in the music of today is better than that of yesterday, because it is not.

The way we hear our music and get our information are not going to be around in a few years time. I've lived through the era of the 78, the 45, the vinyl LP, all the way to CDs and MP3s. Change is inevitable, whatever business you're in; we are certain to evolve into something else. Like a freight train it keeps on moving along down the track. Something new is coming at you. Just get out of the way. How many creative people today take the time to educate themselves about what came before them? Have they ever really sat down and studied the craft of writing and all the different elements that go into it?

There's a reason some of that early music is timeless. Study its ingredients and foundations and maybe you will reach new heights. As we have always said from day one, the power of that music is in the grooves, and no matter how it was recorded or on what device you listen to it on, it's going to give you goose bumps. It's that close encounter with an as yet unexpressed emotion that excites us and inspires us. As human beings we have always wanted to reach out and touch each other. People will always love that rush of emotion that comes from the communication of feeling from one person to another through music. A song is an emotion set to music, so any great, memorable song will take your breath away because it's not only an original expression of that feeling, but what it has to tell you is borne along on the direct current of the music. You can't substitute technology for feelings, and only the most talented performers and greatest songwriters ever reach that height of emotion that you will never forget. Something I always tell myself when I sit down to write a song is: if you are trying to scale those heights you can never settle. I live by the credo that good is the enemy of great.

So here I am, in the September of my years, where I look at life and count the summers I have left, realizing you can never replace experience. Being fortunate enough, due to discipline, I have been around for a while and am still doing what I love. The survivor from those infamous Rat Pack days. I have lived my whole life with passion, that tenacity of wanting to do it—there is still a part of me that still confounds me. When I look back at my upbringing, my Canadian education, my great parents—really great parents—and the time I was brought up in, I am always amazed. What was that seed in my brain that kept driving me? There has got to be some higher power that is driving us on.

As I got into the industry, at a very young age, everybody began catering to me. People were there pulling on you from all different directions, there for your every whim. Sometimes even pissing you off. I began saying to myself, *How do you keep from being an asshole?* That is what you have to worry about. Holy Jesus! How do you not become an asshole? Because you are always lit up. But the moment that happens, people are kissing your ass, telling you that you are the biggest thing ever—that is when you have to start counting blessings.

And then you reach that juncture in your life where it is not a question of the money. It's a question of what do you do with yourself if you don't work? I just would not know what to do with myself. I always believed, if you stand still, they will throw dirt on you. It would really scare me to do nothing. Especially when I find that I am still writing songs, producing, performing—and at this age—still having too much fun to stop. You can't walk away from it because it is something you are addicted to. It keeps you young, keeps your brain sharp. Life is not only short, it is getting shorter. Time is your greatest asset. Granted, with Ethan in my life, as well as grandchildren and family, my time has to be very well utilized.

Given my intense schedule—I still do almost a hundred performances a year—I need to get away from time to time. Over the years I became close friends with Bob Manoukian and his wife Tamar. I always enjoy their company—he and Tamar are incredible human beings and very gracious hosts. From 2001 to 2003, they invited me to travel with them on their superyacht the *Siran*. We spent great vacations in Sardinia and Capri together, frequently joined by our mutual friends, Dr. Ray Irani, chairman of Occidental Oil and his wife Ghada, who have been dear friends to me for many years. A more quality couple, you couldn't find.

Occasionally on my trips abroad I (gladly) sang for my supper. I went to Italy with Tom Girardi along with his wife Erika, both close friends of mine, and performed on his boat in October 2005, for a group of judges, friends, and lawyers. Tom is one of the nation's top defense lawyers with billions in settlements for his clients.

When I went to perform in Tel Aviv in 2009, I traveled through Europe and Israel with Jason Stone, who works for Live Nation and is one of my closest friends and my confidant. I work for him whenever I perform in New York or Westbury, Long Island, but, more important, he and his wife, Lisa, have always been very close to Ethan, Lisa, and me—which was a great comfort during some of the trying times we've been through.

Sammy Aroutiounian, president of Creative Talent Management arranged my first trip to St. Petersburg, Russia, in 2010, to perform for Vladimir Putin. When I landed in St. Petersburg there was a very bad snowstorm. Sharon Stone, Kurt Russell, Mickey Rourke and I and others were virtually stranded. It was below zero. Snow tractors eventually cleared the landing strip for us to take off. Sammy's a great guy, he's taken me to Russia many times since then. He's my rep when I do anything in Russia, but more importantly a close friend and brother! He deserves all his success.

When you work in the entertainment business, you've got to give back, as do many casino owners and other CEOs who frequently contribute to worthy causes, one of which is the Keep Memory Alive Foundation, and the Lou Ruvo Center for Brain Health in Las Vegas, which his son Larry created in memory of his father Lou, who had Alzheimer's.

Larry Ruvo has been my friend for years and is a salt-of-the-earth guy, someone you'd want to be in the trenches with. He lives in Las Vegas and is the head of Southern Wines, a liquor distributorship. In the 1990s, he held a huge charity event for his father. In February 2012, there was a Power of Love gala, an auction, and a performance benefiting the Lou Ruvo Center, featuring the cuisine of chefs Todd English and Wolfgang Puck. One of the auction items was the "My Way" lead sheet that I wrote for Sinatra. Sheldon Adelson, who owns the Venetian paid $30,000 for it. Larry and I were especially touched by that and his generosity to this troubling cause.

—■—

People often ask me if I get bored doing the same show over and over, eighty to ninety times a year. No, because whenever I perform the audience is reacting to what I am giving them and it stimulates me every night—just as if it were the first time. The Chinese say, *If you find something you love to do, you will never work a day in your life.* I am always reminded of this by my loyal and faithful executive assistant, Julie Zhu, who is from Beijing. Julie is like a treasured member of our family and has been for many years. She is Ethan's godmother. Ethan adores Julie and her husband Tom. Tom and Julie introduced Ethan and me to Nancy Callihan and her twin sons (Danny and Joey). They have become very close to us in our office and socially. When you talk about loyalty and work ethic and pureness of heart, you're talking about Julie Zhu. When people ask, "When are you going to retire?" I look at them and say, "Never; as long as I am living and doing what I do." In fact, I remind them if someone says to me that they are thinking of retiring, I reply, you already have. . . .

In the circles I walk in, there are guys who have made millions, billions; they have quit, and thinking that now they'll just relax and enjoy themselves. But, within months, their life goes downhill, they are out of time, and they die sooner than they should have. On closer to the home front, when Sinatra retired, I don't know which time it was, but on one of those occasions, I went to visit him in Palm Springs. He was playing with his electric trains. He loved painting, but you could see he still missed the action. He missed the smell of the grease paint and the roar of the crowd, and yes, all the action. Back he came—on the stage boards again. When you perform your old songs, you instinctively mix the past and the present, which I do purposely—to make that connection and feel the response of the audience, highlighting that fact that these are the songs that we *both* grew up to.

Whenever I meet any of these new kids on the block, they look at me and I know exactly what they are thinking: *Shit, I hope I can last that long.* When I am confronted with one of them, and their ego is in full stride, and they start telling me how great they are and what they are accomplishing, I tell them, "Don't tell me how hot you are, tell me how long you have been around!" You have to think about your longevity in this business. That has nothing to do with age. It's a potpourri of dynamics that go into the mix. And I think luck.

I have always existed in this business, believing that there is someone else out there that is better than you, but who has never had the opportunity. We are all living a life lottery. I believe any one of us, who are fortunate, could have been born in Afghanistan. But here we are. Be grateful for what you have in life.

The only time when I have any sense of what age is, is when I get sick. I am in my seventh decade and my childhood in Ottawa feels just like it was just yesterday. I swear I can't feel the journey being that long. In today's world, with the life expectancy much higher than it has ever been, where the mean age is around eighty-two, I throw my hands in the air with humility, laughter, and frustration. Why? I feel and act with my life and work onstage like I am a forty-year-old. I don't know what it feels like to be seventy! Of course, living that preventative lifestyle, and seeing others who are younger than I am who can barely walk, function, etc., you have to count your blessings. Of course, I take in the genetic factor, but I have to believe, and I share with you, that by doing all the right things, in terms of your body and your health, you have the opportunity to feel the way I do.

So my concerns are not of myself, as long as I keep to my program, but to the world at large. It would take another book to convey my feelings and my opinions of the world we live in today, a world that concerns me for the future of my children, and my grandchildren, who have to live in it. There are so many moving parts and dynamics, internationally, that will affect the survival and state of our country, so that everyone will benefit and have the opportunity to enjoy the American dream.

For all those earlier years that I grew up, the American-Canadian dream was to own your own home, your own car, and be able to support your family. Today, with my travels, not only here but abroad, that hope is gone and that dream is somewhat out of sight for millions of people. Love your country, but don't trust those that run it. What kind of world is my son, Ethan, going to grow up in? The state of our educational system? The fact that China and Germany, who we cannot compete with, make a cheaper and better product?

What will the opportunities be in the technology field and other sectors of the American infrastructure? How will we educate and create the incentive for all of our young boys and girls to become entrepreneurs? Entrepreneurial enterprise—this was the very backbone of what our country was made of. Will it be corporate America and all of those brilliant minds that run those companies? What if they all got together and told Washington to step aside once so that they could move forward and make a difference in getting us back on the right track? A tall order indeed.

I still continue to travel all over the world from Asia to the Middle East and Russia. They are laughing at this democracy of ours that is the most perfected democracy in the world. Because we're not a homogeneous nation, like many others are, the hurdles are higher for us in this modern world.

I fully realize that, as I share my views and opinions, there are people who are far smarter than I am, people who are in political positions of power, who are saying these same things and more. All of these concerns of mine at this stage of my life have led me to ask myself, "What really matters in the end?" It's not all that stuff, it's not the homes, the cars, the awards that are hanging on my wall, but those that I will leave behind, people I have loved, and who will think about me in a warm and loving way when this journey has ended.

Index

"Throughout the history of music, there have been all kinds of songs; to me, the classics still reign supreme. This endeavor, these songs, will be easy on your ears; they are the stuff that love and life is all about."
Paul
PAUL ANKA DUETS
Featuring collaborations with superstar artists
GEORGE BENSON
CHRIS BOTTI
MICHAEL BUBLÉ
PETER CETERA
CELINE DION
GLORIA ESTEFAN
MICHAEL JACKSON
TOM JONES
PATTI LABELLE
MICHAEL MCDONALD
WILLIE NELSON
DOLLY PARTON
LEON RUSSELL
FRANK SINATRA
For more information:
www.Facebook.com/PaulAnkaOfficial
www.PaulAnka.com
www.LegacyRecordings.com
LEGACY
"Legacy" and L Reg. U.S. Pat. & Tm. Off. Marca Registrada.